[d i g i t a l]
VISUAL EFFECTS
& COMPOSITING

New Riders

JON GRESS

[digital] Visual Effects and Compositing

Jon Gress

New Riders

www.newriders.com

To report errors, please send a note to: errata@peachpit.com

New Riders is an imprint of Peachpit, a division of Pearson Education.

Acquisitions Editor: Karyn Johnson
Project Editor: Nancy Peterson
Development Editor: Corbin Collins
Copyeditor: Rebecca Rider
Proofreader: Darren Meiss
Technical Reviewer: William Vaughan
Indexer: Jack Lewis
Production Editor: Tracey Croom
Compositor: Kim Scott, Bumpy Design
Cover Designer: Charlene Will
Interior Designer: Maureen Forys, Happenstance Type-O-Rama
Cover Image: Jon Gress

ISBN 13: 978-0-321-98438-8
ISBN 10: 0-321-98438-2

9 8 7 6 5 4 3 2 1

Printed and bound in the United States of America

To my three angels…
Brittany, Nastasia, and Sofia
with all my love.

Acknowledgments

I would like to begin by giving special thanks to my good friend William Vaughan. William is, by far, the most talented artist I've ever met. We share a common kinship—a love and passion for teaching the arts we ourselves love. William was kind enough to recommend to Pearson that I write this book, make the introduction, and then even come on board to handle the technical editing. I am always delighted by how insightful he is and by the straightforward, pull-no-punches honesty that we have with one another. I will always look forward to an opportunity to work alongside Will. This book would not have been possible without him.

I would also like to thank Karyn Johnson, Nancy Peterson, and the rest of the wonderful team at Pearson who allowed me the opportunity to create this book for you. Special thanks to Corbin Collins for his amazing attention to detail and for putting up with me whenever I bucked convention. I have, no doubt, become a better writer as a result of his guidance and patience.

No show of thanks would be complete without thanking the many outstanding creative people I've worked with, taught with, bounced ideas off of, or learned a trick or two from over the years, and who have helped inspire and shape what this book is, including Ron Thornton, Glenn Campbell, Bill Holshevnikoff, Scott Billups, Andrew Kramer, John Knoll, Ron Brinkman, Mike Seymour, John Montgomery, Ryan Pribyl and Debby Furnival at FXPHD, Jeff and Ann Scheetz, Saham Ali, Dave West, Mike Young, Craig Nesbit, Jason Pichon, Dan Smith, Michael Keith, Ed Ruiz, Matt Jolly, Anthony Marigliano, Amy Putrynski, Emma Webb, Errol Hanse, Pavel Hristov, Les Foor, Andrey Kasatsky, Justin Wildhorn, Matthew Wuenschel, Dylen Valesquez, Anthony Sollitario, Steve Porter, Beth Lockhard, the Digital Animation & Visual Effects School, Amir Rubin, Anna Vittone, Christian von Kleist and everyone at Paracosm, Enoc Burgos and the crew at Reallusion, every cast and crew member I've had the pleasure of working with over the years, all my students (whom I've always regarded as future colleagues who I just needed to quickly bring up to speed), and Kenny Pederson (for recording a year's worth of my classes, which allowed me to look back, reference, and recall subtle nuances that were important to students over the years).

I would also like to thank my dad and Jinny for all of their love and support and no words could ever express my thanks to my three angels, my daughters, Brittany, Nastasia, and Sofia for being my inspiration, the lights of my life and for being so amazingly understanding of their dad being "not-really-there-even-when-he-was-there" sometimes during the writing of this book. I love you girls more than words can ever say!

And last but not at all least, I dedicate this book to my mom who has always been my biggest supporter and champion. I love you, Mom!

Contents

Foreword

Since ancient times, magic has been a common source of entertainment. *Magic* is the act of entertaining an audience using tricks to create illusions of the impossible using natural means. An artist who performs magic is often called a magician or an illusionist, which has led me to think of visual effects artists as digital illusionists.

Visual effects artists have taken illusions to previously unimaginable places over the years and have carried on the legacy of the many illusionists who went before them. One attribute that separates a traditional illusionist from his digital counterpart is secrecy. Whereas traditional magicians kept secrets to preserve the mystery of their tricks, the best visual effects artists I know are quick to break down their digital illusions and share them not only with other VFX artists, but the audiences as well.

My career has afforded me the opportunity to work with many of these talented VFX artists over the years, both in productions and in the classroom. To produce digital illusions, VFX artists' primary skill is problem solving. Visual effects instructors must attain high levels of problem-solving ability, but they must also acquire the ability to pass their knowledge onto others. Finding a VFX instructor is easy. Finding a great instructor with the ability to inspire and create production-ready artists with the needed skills often feels like a magic trick of its own.

Jon Gress is among the rare breed of VFX artists who can move seamlessly between problem solving on a production and imparting his experience in the classroom. To truly appreciate Jon as a VFX artist, you have to see him in action during a production. I first met him ten years ago while he was directing the award-winning, live-action, visual effects-heavy student short film *NASA Seals*. I walked into the studio during the last few weeks of production and witnessed what looked to be chaos and a production that was out of control. It turns out, it was orchestrated chaos.

At the time, Jon was filming a few greenscreen pick-up shots of an actor floating off into space, directing artists working on several digital destruction shots, and fine-tuning the edit, among other things. It was fun watching how trivial he made the whole process look and how he effortlessly motivated the team of artists, even at the 11th hour of production, when most teams would be discouraged. It's no real surprise that some of those artists went on to work at studios like Digital Domain, WETA Digital, Zoic, Pixomondo, The Asylum, Cinesite, Prime Focus, and Walt Disney Animation Studios.

A couple years later, I recommended that the Digital Animation and Visual Effects School at Universal Studios hire Jon as the VFX instructor. The school was in the process of retooling its curriculum and needed someone with Jon's experience to come in and help enhance the training the school was providing. Shortly after Jon came on board, the quality of the work being produced by the students increased exponentially. More importantly, the students had a newfound love of the art of visual effects.

Jon brings a contagious energy to anything he is involved with, and he is passionate about the craft of filmmaking. Couple that with his hands-on experience with and knowledge of VFX and his ability to problem-solve and you have the skillset needed to train the next generation of digital artists.

Over the years, Jon has helped to keep movie magic alive and thriving by training hundreds of artists who have gone on to work on everything from summer blockbuster feature films to award-winning television series, and more.

When I heard that Jon was going to be writing a book on visual effects, I was excited that his knowledge would finally be bottled and find its way into the hands of more artists.

Throughout the pages of this book, Jon introduces you to the magic of visual effects and imparts his knowledge so that you can create your own digital illusions. Your audience will walk away knowing that what they saw couldn't have been real—but they will still believe.

—William Vaughan, Academic Director,
Digital Animation and Visual Effects School

Introduction

Over the past 20 plus years, I've done just about every job imaginable in the worlds of movies, TV, radio, and music—from writing, producing, directing, and visual effects supervising to cinematography, recording, and even performing. I'm one of those fortunate people who has always just known what they wanted to do… make movies.

I made my first "film" at four years old (see Figure 1) by hijacking my father's 8mm film camera and sneaking outside to surreptitiously film the gardener. It was by no means an epic, but even at that young age, I was already fascinated with movies. I had been bitten by the bug that early filmmakers called *silver addiction* (so named because of the filmmaking obsession that required expensive silver halide-based film stocks and processing the love and need to make movies. I knew, even from early childhood, that I wanted to be on the cutting edge of any new technology that could bring any vision imaginable onto the silver screen and into reality.

[Figure 1] My first movie (age 4) of the gardener; definitely no epic, but I was hooked!

By the time I was writing, producing, and directing my own productions, I found that I needed to constantly, and quickly, be able to bring the people working with me up to speed using these advanced technologies in order for them to be able to effectively help me work on these quests (and they were truly quests). It wasn't long, after repeating these little training sessions over and over, before I began formalizing this "film/VFX crash course" into a complete, concrete, teachable curriculum that I then refined, again and again, over the next decade or so. Eventually, I was formally teaching hundreds of visual effects (VFX) artists who, as a result of this material, are now successfully working at virtually every major visual effects company around the world. This curriculum had evolved into perhaps the fastest and most complete curriculum for becoming a competent and professional visual effects artist.

So that is what this book is: decades of production experience and more than ten years of refined teaching (training real-world visual effects artists—some with absolutely no experience at all), distilled into one book you can use to go after your dream of creating VFX and the movies *you* want to work on.

My Promise to You

I despise fluff, especially when it comes to training materials. Anyone who has read a training book, watched a video training tutorial, or sat through a seminar knows what I am talking about. That moment you heard the ninth regurgitation of a simple example or concept… after you've lost count of the never-ending *ummms* and *uhhhs*… the point after you've contemplated methods of escape from a presenter's incessant slurping, nervous coughing, monotone blathering, or pointless passage… that moment you realize, "Why am I sitting here for this?!! This could have been explained in one simple sentence! Hours ago!" Why is [the presenter] still endlessly drudging on about the same thing?!" Well, I agree with you. In fact, that is the entire premise and reason I am writing this book. I'm just like you. I can't tell you how many times I've exclaimed, "Get on with it already!" while reading training materials or watching a training lecture or video.

My promise to you, as one who can empathize, is that I will present to you, in as streamlined and concise a manner as possible, everything I can to make you an excellent VFX artist with *no fluff*.

What to Expect from This Book

If I do present something that might *seem* like fluff, be assured, it isn't. Any example or information I include related to film, video, art, history, and so on, or something that might seem to be extraneous, has been carefully selected and is included for a very precise and practical purpose. Usually, it is because the example is one of the earliest, and thus easiest to understand, and can form the basis for a very complex concept I cover later in the book.

I have taken a lot of artistic license with some of the scientific and technical information I will reveal and present to you in this book. Years of teaching these concepts and techniques have allowed me to refine them into very distilled forms that are easy to understand, relate to, and remember. I've even distilled some technical information into a "not so perfectly scientifically accurate" form, but one that makes sense to those of us with less-than-alien-sized heads who aspire to be excellent VFX artists, not engineers.

It is my opinion that what is crucial to being a good VFX artist is that you have a solid comprehension of the concepts and techniques of film and visual effects, and that you *do not* necessarily have to know every bit of science behind it or software button to be pushed. I would guess that you probably have no clue as to what the precise spark plug gap measurements are in your car or how to set them, yet you are able to drive perfectly fine. That is why I take a software-agnostic approach wherever possible, unless I am teaching a particular application or making comparisons between applications.

By the time you finish carefully reading this book, you will know most of what you need to know to accomplish virtually any visual effect you can think of. At the very least, you'll know how to proceed to accomplish any effect. Understand, *knowing* is only half of the equation. Actual *doing* must take place as well. With practice and perseverance, I have no doubt you will become the visual effects artist you aspire to be.

Special Features of This Book

But that's not all. This is not your ordinary book. Oh, not at all. Read on to find out about some of its hidden gems.

Downloading Files to Use as You Follow Along

I created numerous VFX and other image/movie files to use as examples in this book. I've made many of them available to you for download from the Peachpit website. This way, you can work alongside me, using many of the same files you see in the book's figures.

All you have to do is go to www.peachpit.com/register and follow the instructions for registering this book. After that, a download link will appear, and you can follow that link to retrieve your files.

Aurasma Augmented Reality–Enabled Features

Download the Aurasma augmented-reality (AR) app for your iPhone or Android device, do a search for *visual effects*, and then "follow" the channel that has the picture of the cover of this book.

Open the Aurasma AR viewer, point it at the cover of this book (whether the physical book on your bookshelf or even an image of it that you may come across online), and watch the cover image come to life with a dazzling preview of what's inside the book.

One of the amazing benefits of all of these great new technologies I work with is that I am able to continue to extend the features of this book far past the print version. From time to time, I will post augmented-reality updates to this book to add new tips, tricks, examples, and other amazing new content. I will list these on my website at: http://jongress.com/vfxbook/AR. To use these new updates, just open the book to the page and image listed in the AR Update, open the Aurasma app, and point your device's camera at the image to see the amazing new AR features.

Stereoscopic 3D Features

Chapter 14 is an entire crash course in stereoscopic 3D creation. To best experience the examples, you will need a common pair of 3D red/cyan glasses. If you don't have a pair of these handy, you can easily find them for around a dollar online by doing a simple web search for *paper 3D glasses*. These cheap paper ones work just fine, but if you plan on doing more extensive stereoscopic 3D work, I recommend that you invest in a pair of more durable plastic ones. If you have trouble finding them, head on over to my website at http:// jongress.com/vfxbook/3dglasses and I'll be happy to send you a pair for free (if you just cover the shipping).

But if you're so excited to get started that you just can't wait and you need a pair right now, Chapter 14 includes a make-your-own, guerrilla-style DIY method for creating a pair of 3D glasses in a pinch, using commonly found items; you can use these until your real pair arrives.

Extended and Bonus Features

Since I am constantly developing new concepts, techniques, and technologies, in addition to the AR and 3D content, from time to time I will also add new tips, tricks, techniques, and info about breaking technologies and more to the book. Check in now and then at the book's website at www.peachpit.com/store/digital-visual-effects-and-compositing-9780321984388 and my website at http://jongress.com/vfxbook.

How to Use This Book

This book (and accompanying materials) has been refined over my many years of teaching hundreds of Hollywood visual effects artists (Figure 2), to be a complete VFX course and reference. It is designed to take you from your current level of knowledge (whether you are a total VFX novice or have some knowledge already), to a professional level of understanding all the principles, skills, and techniques, from foundations and basics to the cutting edge of working as a professional VFX artist, in the fastest time possible.

[Figure 2] Teaching VFX artists live on-set

Each chapter builds upon the previous chapter, so your best bet is to read the chapters in order to gain the maximum benefit and then use the book as your go-to reference thereafter.

You may be tempted to skim through Chapter 1, which, in the lecture series I do, is affectionately called "Hell Week" by those I train, owing to the overwhelming and intense amount of technical information that I like to get out of the way as quickly as possible—typically in a week. Nevertheless, I highly recommend reading Chapter 1 in full. It's not critical that you fully comprehend, memorize, or even retain all the information in Chapter 1, but you should try to assimilate as much as you can. By simply being exposed to the information, you will undoubtedly retain much of it by osmosis.

I present much of my material in what I like to refer to as "Miyagi-style" (referring to the character in the movie *Karate Kid*). Mr. Miyagi teaches his student very effective skills, without the student even realizing he's being taught, through a series of simple, seemingly irrelevant lessons. So many important jewels of knowledge are hidden in the form of analogies, short, true-life production stories, and even simple or seemingly not-so-important skills. Remember my promise… *everything* in this book is relevant. Like Neo in *The Matrix*, you will catch yourself realizing, "Whoa! I know Kung Fu!" (In Chinese, the term *kung fu* (功夫) refers to any skill that is acquired through learning or practice.)

So without further ado… plug yourself in to the matrix… let's roll!

PART ONE

Concepts of Visual Effects and Compositing

CHAPTER ONE

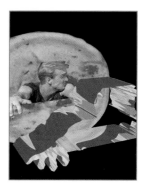

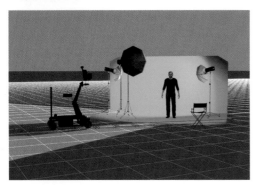 

Film and Video Primer Boot Camp for VFX

"Welcome to Hell Week!"

That is the way I start the first day of my live lecture series. Although many instructors opt for dallying in the shallow end of the pool and then easing into the icy cold water of more informative material little by little, anyone born and raised in Miami knows that just doesn't work. By the time you've eased your way to a depth that matters, the whistle has blown and swim time is over. I prefer the "jump in at the deep end" approach. The stimulation of cold water, like information, may take the wind out of you for a moment and make you gasp, but you'll acclimate almost instantaneously, and then you're off and swimming while the less adventurous are still tip-toeing around the steps.

The amount of information presented in this boot camp chapter can seem, well, overwhelming. The idea here is not for you to completely assimilate or memorize everything in this chapter, but to try to comprehend as much as you can without getting stuck and to just familiarize yourself with the material and concepts.

It's much more important to have that "Oh wait, I remember something about that!" moment and go back to refresh your memory than it is to memorize a bunch of facts and figures. It was Albert Einstein who said, "[I do not] carry such information in my mind since it is readily available in books.... The value of a college education is not the learning of many facts but the training of the mind to think." (This was in response to his not knowing the speed of sound, from the book *Einstein: His Life and Universe*, by Walter Isaacson (Simon & Schuster, 2007).)

It is important to note that each technique shown in this book is just one possible example of the many ways in which each technique can be created or applied. Think of each of these techniques as a building block that can be placed, added, and/or combined with others to form an endless variety, formation, and complexity of visual effects (VFX).

My fundamental approach to this book is in taking sometimes very complex concepts and techniques and distilling them down to very simple, easily understandable, retainable, and repeatable concepts and techniques. Therefore, I have taken some (and in some cases, many) artistic liberties with the exact translation of some of the scientific explanations in order to distill and translate them into their essence. This makes them instantly understandable. Many resources and technical papers giving exact technical specifics are available online for any of the topics you would like to delve in to.

Film school graduates who have taken this course have frequently commented that they learned more technical information in this one week than in all four years of film school. To me this isn't at all surprising because that is, in essence, what this is: a career's worth of film and VFX knowledge, distilled into one book.

So, take a deep breath and don't even think about it—jump right in!

Intro to the Motion Picture/VFX Pipeline

In the world of VFX, a *pipeline* is all the people and processes, in their order or flow, in a production. To understand VFX and be able to communicate with other artists in the VFX pipeline, you have to first grasp that VFX is only one small piece of a much larger picture. Many VFX artists quickly wind up in hot water when they fail to realize their role in the grand scheme of a production.

What Are Moviemaking and VFX?

The way to VFX excellence is by understanding what movies are and how they are made. Understanding this big picture allows you to fully comprehend what you, as a VFX artist, need to do and how to best go about doing it.

The Idea

A movie starts with an idea. This idea may be just a short concept, such as "An OCD neat-freak puts an ad in the Wanted section and finds a roommate. Trouble arises when the two fall in love, but the roommate is a completely free-spirited slob" pitched by a producer, or a fully completed script finely crafted by a writer.

Writing

Once the concept is decided on, the idea is set to paper by a writer. The key concept to understand here is that the writer is essentially painting a big *visual* picture of the story in words. The writer's, or writers', goal is to create the most compelling visual story possible. This may, or may not (depending upon the limits placed on the production by the producers) have anything to do with what is real or even feasible. The goal is to create a great visual story... period.

Pitch-viz

Pre-viz stands for *pre-visualizations* (created by visual effects artists to show producers the viability of a VFX sequence for the production, cost, and approval processes). More recently, this practice has extended to the creation of pre-visualizations before the production is even set into motion. These *pitch-viz* are created to help sell the idea of the production to prospective producers in order to help obtain financing, approvals, and ultimately, *green-lighting* (or approval) of a movie production.

Pre-production

Once the movie is green-lit for production, pre-production begins. *Pre-production* is the process of breaking a movie, or production, into its respective pieces or components, and then arranging those components into a shooting schedule.

Everything done in a movie production is examined under the lens and scrutiny of cost. Ultimately, at some point, every facet of a production boils down to cost: locations, sets, props, actors, stunts, insurance, animal and children wranglers, the vehicles for transportation, even the food the cast and crew eat... and yes, the VFX. In fact, in most cases, the entire reason for using VFX is to save a production money for otherwise more costly scenes. Because everything is examined and organized for the utmost efficiency of cost, it is only natural that this includes the order in which scenes are shot (or created, in the case of VFX).

Imagine a scene that takes place during the day in which a man walks into a hotel lobby, signs in, and goes to his room. The next scene shows him out to lunch with friends. He then leaves the restaurant and returns to the hotel.

The next day, we see him at a meeting, after which he again returns to the hotel. So far, in this short sequence, the man has been in the hotel lobby in three scenes. Would it really make financial sense to have the production crew all travel to the location of the hotel, take hours to set everything up to shoot the first segment of the man walking into the hotel, take hours to break everything down, travel to the restaurant, take hours to set everything up there, shoot a small fragment, break everything down, travel back to the hotel, and so on? Of course not. While the crew is at the hotel, they would shoot all of the daytime hotel scenes at the same time (saving the production an enormous amount of time and money). It is therefore customary to shoot a movie out of script order with all groupable shots being filmed together at the same time (in *shooting order* following a *shooting schedule*). Pre-production, then, is the stage of production where actors and crew are auditioned and hired, the script is torn apart and assembled into shooting order, and shoots are planned to optimize efficiency.

Pre-viz

It is during the pre-production phase that pre-viz is usually done. You can think of the analogy of pre-viz (short for pre-visualization) to a movie as being like a sketch is to a painter or a mock-up is to a designer. By creating rough visualization versions of VFX, production efficiency can be optimized in the planning and workflow stages, and potential problems, identified and solved before production even begins. Pre-viz can also be used as potential marketing materials as well.

Production

When all the cast and crew are hired and all production components are budgeted and scheduled, shooting (production) begins. *Production* is actually the re-creating of each scene of the written movie or story piece-by-piece, shot-by-shot, out of order. Great care must be taken to ensure continuity (that everything filmed out of order will match up and appear continuous when it is put back together in story-order).

Post-viz

As you can imagine, when hundreds of people are involved in a shoot and hundreds or thousands of pieces of a story are being shot out of order, things rarely go as perfectly as planned. A new production optimization step called post-viz has recently taken foothold. *Post-viz* is the process of doing pre-viz, but with footage that has already been shot. This extra optimization step helps fine-tune the VFX process by ensuring all approvals are done using the footage that was actually shot and not the footage that was hoped for.

Post-production

Finally, once all shooting is completed (or *wrapped* or *in the can*), it's time for *post-production*—arranging and assembling all the pieces back together into the new visual version of the picture. Since every shot, scene, performance, and so on has uncontrollable variables that will change—from the written scripted words, to the actual location found or built, to the actual performance given by an actor, to the VFX actually possible—the post-production phase means editing and adding to a "new" (hopefully better) version of the story from the material that has actually been filmed.

The challenge of a movie, or VFX, is the *suspension of disbelief*—that is, you need to keep the viewer's attention so emotionally involved with and wrapped up in the interest of the story that they forget they are watching a movie altogether. The moment something looks out of place or a VFX is noticeable as an effect, the illusion is broken, and the viewer's interest is lost. Movies change and evolve over the course of the production pipeline, but this is why it takes true skill to make a movie; you need to be continuously problem solving, rolling with the changes, and keeping the story great, however it evolves. A movie truly has a life of its own.

Principles of Motion Pictures and VFX: Film School Crash Course

For you to be able to create VFX to integrate into a live action movie, your VFX have to be photo-real. Creating photorealism first requires that you learn to see—see the differences between 3D and the real world. To learn to truly see, you must study reality. And that is precisely what this chapter is all about, learning how to see and how to study reality so that you can re-create it and integrate your creations with real images. You want to be able to add separately filmed elements, *computer generated imagery* (CGI), into real *background* (BG) footage, to remove elements from existing footage, or to perform a combination of both.

When creating your VFX, it is critical that you keep in mind the context of the whole or what part your VFX plays not only in the VFX shot, but in the relationship to shots before, after, and around it. Always keep an eye on intra-scene (within the scene) and inter-scene (between adjacent scenes) continuity. This can mean making sure the motion or direction of elements remains constant, that the scene does not draw the viewer's eye away from the intended subject, and that the timing of the VFX shot plays appropriately in the context of the sequence.

Persistence of Vision

When doing special effects, or any kind of motion graphics for that matter, it's important that you understand and keep in mind some of the fundamental principles that motion pictures are based upon. An excellent example of two of these principles, persistence of vision and Eisenstein's Law, helps establish the very foundations motion pictures are created upon. Moving pictures are, of course, not really moving. They are sequences of (slightly varied) still images, one quickly replacing the next, in rapid succession. The illusion of motion is possible due to the small fraction of time it takes the photochemical processes in your eyes to adapt to changes in light. If you stare at Figure 1.1 for a minute or so and then look quickly at Figure 1.2, it will appear as if a glowing ghosted version of the bird is in the cage. To even more closely simulate the effect of persistence of vision in motion pictures, if you photocopy or print the bird and cage images and paste them back to back over a pencil, pen, or skewer (as shown in Figure 1.3) and then twirl the images quickly, a seamless bird-in-cage illusion is created (Figure 1.4).

In 1824, Peter Mark Roget wrote a paper entitled "The Persistence of Vision with Regard to Moving Objects," which stated that the human eye, or really, the brain, retains an image for a fraction of a second after it has actually disappeared from view. This simple discovery led to the development of many techniques for creating "moving" pictures. Basically, if the brain retains an

[Figure 1.1] Black and white silhouette of bird

[Figure 1.2] Black and white silhouette of birdcage

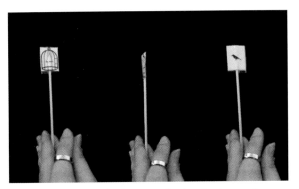

[**Figure 1.4**]
Quickly rotating between the images creates the illusion of one seamless image due to the phenomenon of persistence of vision.

[**Figure 1.3**] Placing both images back to back on a skewer allows for rotation between the two images.

image for a fraction of a second after it has actually disappeared, as long as that image is replaced with another image within that short fraction of time, the viewer's perception is of continuous motion and not of the two or more separate images being presented. So a movie (or motion picture) is really just a continuous series of still images replacing each other quickly enough so that the viewer's brain cannot see the substitutions (or flickering, as they usually appear).

Eisenstein's Law

Eisenstein's Law—named after Sergei Eisenstein, the great Soviet Russian filmmaker, not Albert Einstein—has been mathematically abbreviated to this: 1 + 1 = 3. Now, I know what you're thinking: "Duh, yeah, real genius, Jon." But this equation is actually just a mnemonic device that makes a lot of sense. What it means is that if you place one scene next to another scene, the viewers' mind will fill in the third scene between them. The viewer's mind creates the psychologically missing pieces, and even inserts additional (entirely new) scenes or meanings in their own head that never really existed on film—the third scene. For instance, if you see a scene of a girl falling from the roof of a high-rise (Figure 1.5) and the next scene is of a girl crying (Figure 1.6), you might easily deduce that the girl is crying because her friend has fallen to her demise (Figure 1.7). If the scenes are reversed, you might easily assume the crying girl in the first scene is the poor depressed soul who jumps in the next scene (Figure 1.8). In these scenarios, you never saw that the girl crying knew the girl who was falling, or, alternatively, that she was the same girl as the one falling or was even in the same place as the girl falling. In both cases, your brain has drawn its own conclusion or actually added its own scene, which never actually existed. Letting viewers come up with their own

[**Figure 1.5**] Shot 1 of girl falling from high-rise

[**Figure 1.6**] Shot 2 of girl crying

[**Figure 1.7**] If viewed in the order 1 then 2, the viewer might assume that the girl crying is reacting to the girl falling

[**Figure 1.8**] Viewed in the opposite order (2 then 1), the viewer might assume the girl crying is the one falling, and that she must have jumped.

conclusion can sometimes be even more powerful and effective than actually showing them the outcome or scene (this technique is often used effectively in horror and thriller movies).

Shots

Shots are individual filmed scenes. Although there are no exact dimensions for shots, they are commonly referred to by generalized proportion framings, depending on the subject. This means a wide shot of a person might be from ten feet away, whereas a wide shot of a building might well be from thousands of feet away.

Wide: A wide shot (or WS) typically encompasses the entire subject "in frame" from top to bottom. For a person, this means from head to toe. For a building this means from top to bottom (as shown in Figure 1.9).

Extreme wide: An extreme wide shot (or EWS) generally shows the subject small in frame. This can be used to establish location or, as we will see shortly, for emotional effect (Figure 1.10).

Medium: A medium shot (or MS) of a person will usually show from just above the waist to the top of the head, or about half a person or subject.

Close-up: A close-up (or CU) can be anything closer than a MS but usually refers to a head shot or chest-to-head framing (Figure 1.12).

Extreme close-up: An extreme close-up (or ECU) can be anything very close and closer than a typical CU, from the shot of an eye's pupil to water droplets hitting the surface of water (Figure 1.13).

One shot, two shot: The terms *one shot*, *two shot*, and so on refer to how many subjects are in a shot. One actor in frame would be a one shot, two actors a two shot, and so on.

[note]

The term *one shot* can also be used to describe a very particular shot in which an entire scene is filmed continuously, all in one long take (or shot) with no breaks or changes in setup.

[Figure 1.9] Wide shot (WS)

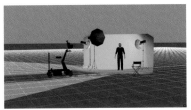

[Figure 1.10] Extreme wide shot (EWS)

[Figure 1.11] Medium shot (MS)

[Figure 1.12] Close-up (CU)

[Figure 1.13] Extreme close-up (ECU)

[tip]

A good visual photographic rule of thumb is never to cut people off in frame at a joint—ankles, knees, waist, neck, and so on—because it looks odd and tends to be distracting. Always try to cut off the framing of a shot between joints—that is, the shin, thigh, chest, and so on (Figure 1.11).

Establishing shot: An establishing shot is not as much about framing as it is about the subject. The purpose of an establishing shot is to establish or set the location and tone of the scene. You use an establishing shot to place the viewer in the mood and surroundings of a scene. An establishing shot might not even be in the same location as the scene. For example, if the scene takes place at a summer beach home, an establishing shot might be waves, or a seagull, or kids digging in the sand. Anything that helps the viewer see, hear, and feel the scene can be used as an establishing shot.

Master shot: Because a production's concern is always cost and efficiency, the greatest emphasis and care always has to be taken to assure that if "all goes wrong" while shooting, you still have a fallback. This is why it is common protocol to shoot an overall wide (or master) shot first and then move in to get closer, more detailed coverage shots only afterward. This both helps set up the scene in the mind of the viewer and provides a little insurance, just in case all goes wrong.

Coverage: After the master shot is secured, you can go in for *coverage* (or detailed shots). These are all of the MSs, CUs, and so on that bring the viewer into the scene to become more emotionally involved.

Over-the-shoulder: An over-the-shoulder (or OTS) shot is typically a way to make viewers feel comfortable, and emotionally participatory, when they are viewing a dialogue scene between multiple subjects. The scene is typically

[note]

A master shot sets up the scene, whereas coverage brings the viewer emotionally into the scene. Imagine a fight scene viewed from across the street. This might show you all of the components of the fight, but it wouldn't be very emotionally charged viewed from so far away. If, however, you were right in the middle of the brawl with punches wildly flying around you, you might not see very much of the scene, but your heart would be pounding—this is what coverage provides.

[**Figure 1.14**] Over-the-shoulder shot

[**Figure 1.15**] Over-the-hip shot

shot over one subject's shoulder from the foreground (FG) toward the other subject in the background (BG) and is then reversed (Figure 1.14).

Over-the-hip: An over-the-hip or (OTH) shot is just like the OTS but is shot from around waist height (Figure 1.15).

Insert: An insert shot is usually used to cut to, or look away at, some detail item that helps set the scene (such as a quick look at a statue when a person enters a building). This isn't always the case, however, and this type of shot can be of virtually anything. Insert shots are used frequently, from selected random interesting extra shots picked up on location, to cover up editing or performance errors. For example, in a courtroom scene, the power might have been lost for a split second, which resulted in a flickering light. In editorial, to cover the lighting error, the editor might paste a shot of a state seal on the wall that the director of photography (or DP) found interesting while they were on set.

Transition: Transitions in motion pictures are mainly *cuts* (where one scene changes immediately to another) or *dissolves* (where one scene fades into another).

Background, foreground, and midground: Background (BG) refers to the viewable area in a shot that is the farthest away from the camera. Foreground (FG) refers to the viewable area in a shot that is closest to the camera (and many times very close and blurred to provide atmosphere and depth), and midground (MG) is the area in between (see Figure 1.16).

[**Figure 1.16**]
The use of foreground, midground, and background

Foreground   Midground   Background

Camera Movement

You also need to know the terminology referring to a camera's movement and the types of motion (and their characteristics) you will try to emulate in VFX.

Still, locked off, on sticks: These terms all refer to a camera that remains motionless on a tripod (also known as a stick).

Pan: Panning is rotating the camera around its vertical axis (or its heading rotation). In a pan, the camera looks from side to side as you would if you were turning your head to look from left to right and vice versa.

Tilt: Tilting is rotating the camera around its horizontal axis (or its pitch rotation). When a camera tilts, it looks up and down the same way you would with your head, looking chin up and chin down.

Dolly: To dolly is to translate or move the camera forward and backward in the Z axis. This is usually accomplished on a wheeled dolly (yes, the device is called a dolly, and the motion forward and back is also called dollying; one is a noun, and the other a verb).

Zoom: Although zooming isn't a camera motion, I include it here because it is so widely confused/misused and this is the best place to explain it and make the comparison. Many people try to use a zoom (or change the focal length of the camera's lens) to make a subject larger in frame. And although a zoom does accomplish this, what it does not do is to bring the viewer into the scene the way a dolly does. There is no change in 3D space or parallax (which I cover shortly).

Truck: To truck a camera is to translate or move it sideways or in the X axis. This is commonly done to follow an actor or vehicle.

Crane: Craning is translating or moving the camera up or down. Where tilting is rotating it to "look" up or down, craning is actually moving the camera in the vertical direction (tilting is frequently also done while craning to maintain the subject in frame).

Jib: A jib is a constructed, counterweighted, extending arm that lifts and lowers a camera to accomplish crane movements.

Steadicam: A steadicam is a gyroscopically stabilized harness device worn by an operator that allows for smooth, fluid camera movement even when the operator performs erratic motions. A smooth camera shot that follows actors running up stairs is a great example of how steadicams are used.

Motion control: When you require precisely repeatable motions, motion control rigs are the answer. These programmable robotic camera platforms allow for the recording and playback of extremely precise, repeatable camera motions.

Flying cameras: Cable-guided cablecams, helicopter- and airplane-mounted gyroscopes, and drone-carrying flying cams are very popular in large scale sporting events, aerial sequences, action movies, and dangerous or hard-to-access locations.

UW cameras: Like their aerial counterparts, UW (underwater) housing for cameras like the GoPro Hero has made underwater filming accessible to just about everyone.

Shot Emotion

The lighting and camera placement (and movement) not only provide framing for the scene but also deeply impact and manipulate the psychology of the viewer. The inherent emotional instincts we are all born with can be effectively manipulated to elicit any desired audience reaction and emotion. Whether making movies or VFX, you always want to create some form of visual metaphor to create emotion in your viewers and hook them into the story. Let's look at lighting and camera placement, in relation to the viewer's eyeline (the height of the eyes), to see how it affects our emotional responses. To discuss lighting, you must first understand a few basic lighting concepts and some terminology.

The amateur photographer or videographer might choose to use the light that conveniently comes with the camera and usually resides right above the camera's lens. Although this front light might be a handy solution, the results will more likely resemble a mug shot (Figure 1.17) than anything cinematic.

The more educated photographer might have heard of a common lighting setup referred to as *three point lighting*. The importance of three point lighting is more in identifying this setup's components (and using these components as the basis for creating lighting) than the real-world use of three point lighting itself. I traditionally use a 3D head model William Vaughan created of himself (thanks, Will!) to demonstrate.

The first component of three point lighting is the main, or *key*, light source (Figure 1.18). The key light both provides the main source of light and defines the three-dimensional characteristics of a subject by *modeling* (or emphasizing by casting shadows).

[Figure 1.17] Using a camera's front light results in flat mug-shot looking images.

[Figure 1.18] Key light

[Figure 1.19] Fill light added

[Figure 1.20] Rim light added

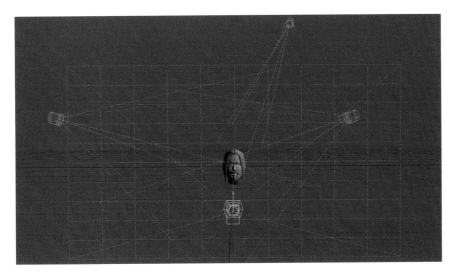

[Figure 1.21] Common three point lighting setup configuration

Using only a key light tends to create very harsh, dark, and unflattering shadows. A fill light (usually a softer, less intense light) is therefore used to "fill" or reduce (not eliminate) the dark shadows (as shown in Figure 1.19) and make them less harsh.

Finally, the rim light (also called a back light, hair light, high light, or when placed low, the kicker) adds highlighting and separation from the background as shown in Figure 1.20. Although nice for portraits, as you can see in this stereotypical setup (shown in Figure 1.21), this three point lighting does not provide very realistic results for most common filming situations. But knowing these lights is crucial to being able to communicate lighting in the world of VFX.

[**Figure 1.22**] Top light creates an otherworldly or godlike presence.

[**Figure 1.23**] Low lighting, pointing upwards, provides the opposite—a much more sinister tone.

[**Figure 1.24**] Side lighting creates dramatic tension popularized in film noir.

[**Figure 1.25**] Placing the camera on the opposite side of the subject from the key light creates a sophisticated off-side key lighting effect.

[**Figure 1.26**] Placing the camera at a very low angle, looking up at a subject, gives the subject an imposing and menacing quality.

[**Figure 1.27**] Placing the camera high and having it look down on a subject gives the subject a sense of inferiority and submissiveness.

By creatively utilizing/adjusting the intensity and positioning of these lighting components, you can create endless combinations of looks and emotional depth, too. For example, place your key light high above your subject and have it point down to provide *top light* and the feeling of an other-worldly or godlike presence (Figure 1.22). Not surprisingly, by placing a powerful key light down low, pointing upwards, you get the opposite, sinister tone that is so familiar to horror movie enthusiasts (Figure 1.23). Placing the key light off to the side (Figure 1.24) creates the dramatic tension popularized in film noir, and placing the camera on the opposite side of the subject from the key light creates a sophisticated off-side key lighting effect (Figure 1.25).

As with placement of the lighting, placement of the camera can also elicit many emotional responses. Any student on the wrong side of William Vaughan's imposing 6 foot 5 inch glare can attest that being at a very low angle, looking up at a subject (Figure 1.26), gives the subject an imposing and menacing quality. Conversely, placing the camera high and looking down on a subject (Figure 1.27) gives the subject a sense of inferiority and submissiveness (not likely with William, unless you happen to be 8 feet tall). Taken to the extreme, placing the camera high in the air and placing the subject in a small portion of the frame (as shown in Figure 1.28) creates the feeling of loneliness and isolation.

These elicited emotions are primal and instinctual. An audience has little control over how it reacts to these visual metaphors. Viewing another creature's eyeline will instantly create feelings and emotions, even when looking at a photo. When a subject's eyeline gaze looks down and away from you,

[Figure 1.28] Placing the camera high in the air and placing the subject in a small portion of the frame creates the feeling of loneliness and isolation.

[Figure 1.29] A subject's eyeline gaze, looking down and away from you, appears non-threatening and friendlier.

[Figure 1.30] A direct eyeline stare is a universal animal kingdom sign of aggression and triggers fear, anxiety, and stress responses.

he (as shown in Figure 1.29) seems non-threatening, friendlier, and even submissive. A direct stare (Figure 1.30) on the other hand immediately sends adrenaline, and fight or flight responses, pumping through your body, amping you up to threat or high-alert status.

The camera's motion can also create emotional responses. The camera may move slowly and transparently, seamlessly starting and stopping to coincide with the movement of on-screen characters, making itself virtually invisible, and allowing the viewer to become immersed in the story. The camera can move slowly and steadily, gracefully, purposefully, or even frenetically. Dizzying or even nauseating real-world simulations can cause a very real, physical manifestation of sensations. The camera can even react to the movie environment (like an explosion, earthquake, or shockwave), making the audience feel as if they are actually in the place of the camera.

Staging, Letter Shapes, and Blocking

As with lighting and camera placement, staging and blocking of the actors, camera, and movement within a scene can also convey a wide spectrum of emotions and responses.

Because many new artists seem to have difficulty with staging and blocking, I've devised a few mnemonic devices to help. A good place to start is to think of staging characters in common letter formations. Staging two actors to form the letter "I" (horizontally across the screen or in depth into the scene) or three in the angular "L" or triangular "A" are good examples of this. If there

[tip]

One of the most important concepts in blocking and staging a movie scene is that you always try to create as much 3D depth as possible to the otherwise flat 2D movie screen. Anything you can do to emphasize the depth of a scene will help draw the viewer into the image, and thus the story.

are significantly more characters you can use "U", "O," or multiple or combinations of other formation staging (such as an "I" with an "L" and so on). You can also enhance visual metaphors by proving *motivations* (or reasons) for lighting, staging, and character or camera movement. Two characters staged in an "I" formation standing face to face covey a very different meaning than they do if they are staged back to back. One character's back turned toward another character's face creates yet another, entirely different, emotion altogether.

You can also use these stagings in depth to metaphorically and subliminally imply the viewer's relationship with characters. The viewer will inherently identify with the character who is closer to the screen and less with characters farther away in depth.

There are many cinematic tricks you can employ to exploit this relationship. Staging characters deep in frame and shifting focus from one to another (called *rack focus*) and using mirrors, foreground reflections, and shadows are also effective techniques for creating identification with a character or emotion in the viewer. Some examples of these letter formation stagings are shown in Figure 1.31.

When blocking the movement of the camera, it helps to think of breaking down a camera move into *keyframes* (a term borrowed from animation that refers to the most important framings). You create a composition and framing of the characters at the beginning and end of the sequence, then plot a creative camera path (and character motion) from point A to point B. It is also possible to *hand off*, or allow the camera to follow an intermediary character, which leads the camera's motion to another character or the end keyframe.

[Figure 1.31]
A few examples of letter-based character staging (shown from left to right these are "I," "L," "A," and a different emotional variation on "I")

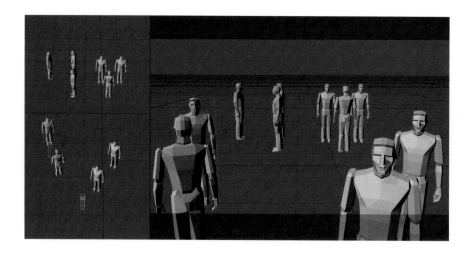

Continuity

It should go without saying that if a character is drinking a bottle of water at the beginning of the scene, and you do multiple retakes of the scene, some-one should keep track of the water bottle to make sure that, in the final edit, the bottle doesn't magically fill up all by itself (unless of course that was the effect, or *gag*). Making sure movie events appear in an uninterrupted and con-tinuous manner is called *continuity* and is the job of the script, or continuity, supervisor.

Screen Direction

It's critical that on-screen movements (or *screen direction*) appear continuous and congruent. If an actor exits the screen's frame moving toward the right, in the next scene, the actor must enter from the left (continuing to move right) in order for the movement to appear continuous and not jarring, as if the actor suddenly changes directions. Likewise, individual shots of two actors having a conversation need to have the actors facing each other or risk having the audience feel as though one actor is talking to the back of the other actor's head.

180-Degree Rule

When a scene is being played out by characters, an imaginary line (called the *line of action*) is created between characters who are talking to or interacting with each other. When filming a scene from one side of this imaginary line of action, characters appear to be facing in a screen direction (usually towards each other). This screen direction appears to reverse if your camera crosses this imaginary line (also called *flopping the line*) during a scene. If this occurs, the actors' screen direction can appear to become reversed and continuity ruined. Therefore, a screen direction guideline known as the *180-degree rule* became a common practice. This guideline states that the camera should always stay on the same 180-degree side of the line of action between charac-ters unless one of three things happens:

1. The camera takes the viewer over the line, filming while crossing the line.

2. An intermediate shot is filmed on the line before crossing it.

3. The geography of the scene is so commonplace that it would be very unlikely that an audience would be confused (as in a courtroom scene, where the judge's bench is commonly known to be at one end of the room and the spectators' seats at the opposite end).

Manipulating Time and Space

Movies, by their nature, manipulate time and space. Who wants to watch a movie about the life of someone in real time? VFX artists manipulate time and space by speeding up a fight or car chase, slowing down an explosion, or compressing the time and distance of a long space voyage. I cover time manipulations and distortions in more detail in Chapter 9.

Parallel Action

In addition to manipulating time, you can even further compress and distort time by running multiple timelines in parallel. This is an excellent technique that can be used very effectively to create suspense, tension, and anxiety in a viewer. Picture in your mind a close-up of a pair of feet walking down a long hallway. Next, picture another scene of a man sitting on his bed with his back to you (the camera). Picture the feet again, but this time, your view cranes up to reveal a gun with a silencer in the man's gloved hand. Cut back to the man sitting on the bed. You (the camera) move slowly toward him as he sits unknowing of your presence creeping up behind him. You cut again to the gun, but now you see the gloved hand picking the lock to a hallway door. Again you're back to creeping closer and closer to the man sitting on the bed. You see the hand turning the door handle and slowly pushing the door open…. You're already hooked and want to know what happens, don't you? This is the power of leaving open-ended visual questions in the viewer's mind—visual metaphor and parallel action.

Composition

There are many excellent guidelines (which are beyond the scope of this book) for interesting compositions; these include the Rule of Thirds, Golden Spirals, Sections and Triangles, Harmonious Triangles, and so on. I highly recommend you explore these and other artistic principles of composition.

Parallax

Hold a finger up very close to your nose and look at it. Open and close each eye independently and notice that your finger appears to jump back and forth, from side to side. Now slowly move your finger farther and farther away from your face while you continue to open and close each eye independently. Notice that your finger jumps less and less the farther away it gets from your face. This apparent movement (your finger isn't actually moving back and forth) is the phenomenon we call *parallax* and it is the effect of binocular, or stereoscopic, vision. Figure 1.32 shows the motion of a camera past two parallel rows of fence posts. Notice how the row closest to the camera seems to be moving faster than the one farther away. In reality, these two rows are identical, as you can see in Figure 1.33. You can experience this similar effect by driving down the highway and watching trees or sign posts appear to be moving at different speeds as you pass at different distances from them. Parallax is one of the visual indicators, or *cues*, that gives us clues about the depth of a scene. I cover parallax in great detail in Chapter 14.

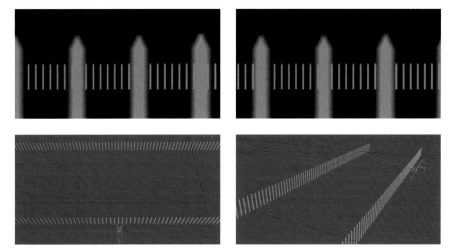

[Figure 1.32]
Fence posts in the foreground appear to move faster than posts in the background.

[Figure 1.33]
In reality, these are two identical sets of parallel fence posts and the camera moves in a simple line parallel to the posts.

Perspective

Another clue (or visual cue) to depth in a scene is *perspective*: the apparent foreshortening of objects the farther away from us they are. The closer objects are, the larger they seem; the farther away they are, the smaller they appear. Figure 1.34 shows a 3D model of the Golden Gate Bridge. Notice how it appears to be smaller and smaller the farther away it gets from the camera.

[Figure 1.34]
Perspective makes the bridge and roadway appear to get smaller and smaller the farther away from the camera it is.

So let's see how all these moviemaking principles were put into action to form the foundations of visual effects.

The Origins of Visual Effects

Though the world of digital and computer special effects is in many ways still in its infancy, the world of special effects in movies has been around almost as long as "movies" themselves—over 100 years.

Many early visual effects were faked newsreel enactments of famous stories. Wars, train and ship wrecks, natural disasters, and other newsworthy events were re-created using models, miniatures, and glass matte paintings.

Thomas Edison and Alfred Clark: Stop Motion

On August 28th, 1895, in West Orange, New Jersey, in Thomas Edison's studio, an employee named Alfred Clark shot the historic dramatization *The Execution of Mary, Queen of Scots*, in what is regarded as the first visual effects sequence in the history of film.

[Figure 1.35] The actress kneels down at the chopping block.

[Figure 1.36] The actress is replaced with a dummy, and then the camera is restarted to complete the grizzly scene.

When the name Thomas Edison is mentioned, surely you think of the amazingly tenacious inventor who invented the lightbulb and the visionary who created the phonograph. But what about Thomas Edison, pioneer of special effects? That's right—he was one of the first!

In 1891, Edison applied for a patent on an invention he named the Kinetograph. *Kinetic* means pertaining to motion. His invention: a motion picture camera. People came from everywhere to experience moving pictures in *kinetoscope parlors*. One at a time, they paid a nickel and peered into a large rectangular box to see the latest "movies." These kinetoscope parlors were the forerunners of today's movie theaters.

Edison also produced movies. By 1893, he had begun manufacturing films and had built the world's first movie studio near his lab in West Orange, New Jersey. Named The Black Maria, this tar paper-sealed structure had a large skylight and was set upon a revolving track to follow the movement of the sun (the bright sunlight was needed for the photographic process). Edison's big one-minute special effects hit appeared in 1895.

In *The Execution of Mary, Queen of Scots*, the short film graphically depicts the queen losing her head on the chopping block. An actress in the film is seen kneeling at the chopping block (Figure 1.35) where she is then beheaded (Figure 1.36). Edison and Clark accomplished this first-ever special effects camera sequence trick by stopping the camera at the moment the axe was to fall, replacing the actress with a dummy, and then resuming the camera rolling to complete the shot with the dummy's head instantly being severed. Audiences were horrified at the gruesome realism.

You can create some amazingly simple stop action effects by having your subject exit one side of the screen, stopping the camera, and then having the actor reappear from the other side (Figure 1.37), which results in an impossible apparent change in direction (Figure 1.38).

Georges Méliès

Georges Méliès is considered by many to be the father of special effects—and even of narrative cinema, for that matter. Méliès, however, was first and foremost a magician. His specialty: fantasy and science fiction.

Between 1896 and 1912, Méliès created over 500 films, combining stage trickery with early optical effects to produce some of the most well-known early special effects films. These include *The Man with the Rubber Head* (1902), *A Trip to the Moon* (1902), *The Dancing Midget* (1902), *The Impossible Voyage* (1904), *The Merry Frolics of Satan* (1906), *The Conquest of the Pole* (1912), and *The Temptation of Saint Anthony*. Méliès was also one of the first filmmakers to utilize storyboards and elaborate pre-production art in order to plan his effects.

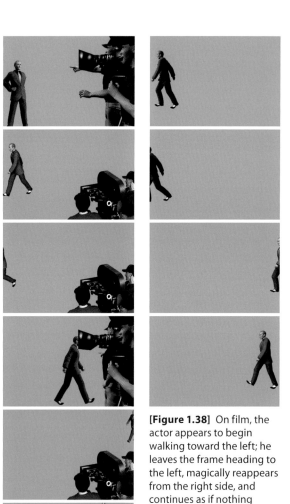

[Figure 1.38] On film, the actor appears to begin walking toward the left; he leaves the frame heading to the left, magically reappears from the right side, and continues as if nothing unusual occurred.

[Figure 1.37] The actor in frame is directed to exit screen left, begins walking, and leaves the frame. The camera is stopped and the actor crosses to the opposite side of the stage. Once the actor is out of frame, the camera is restarted and the actor begins entering from screen right.

Substitution Effect

The early motion picture equipment Méliès used was very prone to breaking down, and film breakage. Like Edison, he soon discovered something important. After he developed the film, it revealed that people walking down a street he was filming seemed to vanish after he had restarted a stopped camera. He called this discovery the *trick of substitution* or *stop action*. Méliès adapted this illusion to create magical transformations on the screen. He'd place an actress in a chair and cover her with a large silk cloth. After filming for a short time, the camera would stop, and Méliès would replace the actress with a skeleton. He would then resume filming. The result was an apparent terrifying metamorphosis (as shown in Figure 1.39). By 1898, Georges was using stop-motion substitution effects regularly.

You can create a variation of this stop-motion effect by having your subject enter a box, only to reappear from another (Figure 1.40), creating an apparent teleportation (Figure 1.41). Or, you can even substitute one person or object for another, to create a basic transformation.

Using stop motion is a great way to do quick, inexpensive effects by themselves or combined with other effects to make exciting new ones. What do you think every new *Star Trek* transporter effect is really, at its core (see Figure 1.42)?

Forced Perspective

Forced perspective is the use of the *appearance* of perspective to trick the mind into believing actual depth is taking place when in fact it is merely an optical illusion. In 1902, Méliès produced two of his most distinguished pieces. In the first, *The Man with the Rubber Head*, Méliès made great use of this effect. In this film, Méliès' head is seen to expand to gigantic proportions after his dim-witted assistant feverishly inflates it using a giant pair of bellows (Figure 1.43).

This devious but simple illusion was executed by constructing a small carriage on a track, which was then moved slowly toward the static camera (as shown in Figure 1.44), thus, from the camera's point of view (POV), enlarging the head (Figure 1.45). An ingenious use of forced perspective (a topic we will cover more extensively in the section "Photography of Miniatures"). Today film-makers employ a track to move the camera in what is termed a *dolly shot*.

[Figure 1.39] *Escamotage d'une dame chez Robert-Houdin* (1896).

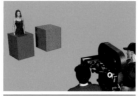

[Figure 1.40] An actor is filmed entering a blue box; she then crouches down into the box until she is completely hidden. The camera is then stopped, and the actor exits the blue box and hides herself in the red box. Then the camera is restarted, and the actor rises from the red box as if she magically moved from one box to the other.

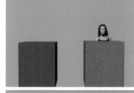

[Figure 1.41] From the camera's viewpoint (on film) the actor appears in the blue box, lowers herself into the blue box until she is completely hidden, and then arises from within the red box as if she had been magically teleported.

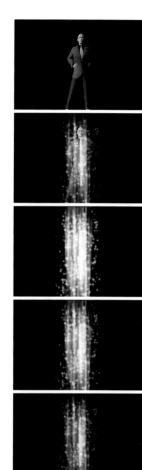

[Figure 1.42] The famous *Star Trek* transporter effect. A sparkly light effect is faded in over the image of the actor being "transported." It becomes so bright that it almost completely obscures the actor. The actor's image is faded out. The sparkly light effect follows, fading out just after the image of the actor, leaving only the background.

[Figure 1.43] Méliès' *The Man with the Rubber Head*, 1902

[Figure 1.44] To achieve the illusion, Méliès used a miniature foreground table set and very simple, but clever, forced perspective cinematography.

[Figure 1.45] The result is a very seamless "inflating head" illusion.

Matte Painting

Méliès is best known, though, for the second movie, *A Trip to the Moon* (1902), which was one of the longest and most elaborate of his trick film epics. The film's elaborate background matte paintings, sets, and clay and papier-mâché make-up effects (shown in Figure 1.46) are legendary.

Dry for Wet

The underwater splashdown shot in *A Trip to the Moon*, revealing live fish (Figure 1.47), was cleverly designed by Méliès (Figure 1.48) with the camera shooting through a glass fish tank (Figure 1.49) in one of the first dry-for-wet effects sequences every created. Méliès took his fantastic voyages even further underwater, too, with a lampoon of Jules Verne's *20,000 Leagues Under the Sea*. His *Under the Seas* features Yves, a fisherman who dreams of a submarine trip to the seabed where he meets the Queen of the Starfish and a slew of mermaids. Before awaking, he is attacked by several sea monsters and a giant octopus. The marine creatures, all created by Méliès himself, again use his dry-for-wet fish tank setup.

[Figure 1.47] Méliès' splashdown sequence used some of the first-ever dry-for-wet effects.

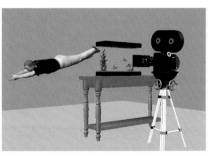

[Figure 1.48] In the film, characters seem to be underwater and surrounded by live fish and other prop creatures.

[Figure 1.49] These clever dry-for-wet sequences were accomplished by filming through a glass fish tank, creating a seamless (and completely "in-camera") effect.

[Figure 1.46] Méliès' *A Trip to the Moon* (1902) made use of extensive background scenic set and matte paintings.

[**Figure 1.50**] I used a variation of this effect in *Anunnaki* to create the effect of actor Chad Ayers submerged in a futuristic medical hydro-recovery chamber.

[**Figure 1.51**] This effect can be combined with model miniatures and fog effects.

I've used this same trick both in a sci-fi scene to portray an actor submerged in a futuristic medical chamber (Figure 1.50) and in combination with model miniatures and fog for underwater submarine effects (Figure 1.51).

A Trip to the Moon was hugely successful, but not as profitable as it should have been. The film was perhaps the most heavily pirated film of its era, and although crowds around the world marveled at its tale of space travel, almost none of this success translated into financial gain for Méliès (pirating isn't such a new problem after all).

Between 1896 and 1912, Georges Méliès' produced and directed almost 500 short films all marked by their rhythm, visually inventive designs, marvelous sense of fantasy, tricks, illusions and detail, and for the time, the cutting edge of special effects.

Oscar G. Rejlander

If we consider Georges Méliès to be the father of special effects, including stop motion, miniatures, forced perspective, and other trick cinematography, then we might well consider Oscar G. Rejlander to be the grandfather of special effects compositing.

In 1857, Rejlander began production on the most technically complicated composited photograph (or combination print, as he called it) of its time. *The Two Ways of Life* (shown in Figure 1.52) was a photograph depicting the

[Figure 1.52]
Oscar Rejlander's
The Two Ways of Life (1857).

two paths one could take in life—good or evil, right or wrong, just or unjust, and so on. The massive effort created a photograph that would have probably been logistically, if not just practically, impossible to have created otherwise; combining over 30 glass negatives.

To make this print, Rejlander started by shooting groups of two or three people each in a small, carefully lit set. He then adjusted each for the size and position he needed them to be in the final print.

This is much the same way that VFX artists do digital crowd replication shots today (as covered in Chapters 6 and 13). You shoot small groups of people in a large stadium or other setting, one small section at a time, taking care to make sure the groups do not overlap but do integrate well. You then composite the small groups together into one large crowd, rather than deal with the logistics and expense of hiring 20 or 30 thousand extras to complete the same stadium, crowd, or battlefield scene.

In some instances, because he needed the subjects being photographed to be smaller in frame, Rejlander photographed their reflections in a mirror, thus increasing the optical distance needed between the camera and subject. This mirror technique can still be used to increase the distance between your camera and subject, to change the apparent direction of the subject's or camera's movement, or even to allow the camera to appear to be in a position that would be far too dangerous or just downright impossible for a camera to be.

The process of printing *The Two Ways of Life* involved selectively exposing each individual piece or negative to a small uncovered section of the photographic paper until all of the required sections had been exposed. This allowed Rejlander complete control over the exposure of each individual portion of the composite.

Although Rejlander used his techniques to see the realization of his particular story and vision, he received much criticism (as many innovators do today) for his use of what his critics cited as "trick" photography and not "valid" or "honorable" artistic expression (this, too, is much the same way many critics talk about new innovations today). Unfortunately, Rejlander himself eventually succumbed to peer pressure and denounced the practice as well, tiring of the public slamming his combination prints. Luckily for us, others continued where Rejlander left off, leading to the development of optical printers, blue and greenscreen photography, and eventually the digital compositing techniques we use today.

In the Beginning: In-Camera Effects

Before there were computers and digital effects, before optical printing and other post-production processes, there were still special effects.

Single-Pass In-Camera Techniques

Without the technology to add effects to the images after they were filmed, early cinematographers had to find other ways to enhance their images. They had to create these enhancements at the same time they filmed (or in a single pass), all within the camera (or in-camera).

Filters

The easiest and most obvious way to do this was to add the effects right onto the end of the camera, where the image was being filmed to begin with. As a result, they began developing and utilizing special lenses and filters. A *filter*, by definition, is a device that allows some or part of something (in this case, some light) to pass through it, while not allowing or modifying another part (or the rest of the light).

Filters can be almost anything imaginable, from frosted glass or a smear of petroleum jelly, to a feather, or even a soda bottle. Filters come in all shapes, sizes, and materials but are most commonly made of glass or resin and are either lens-thread sizes or rectangular shaped to use in filter holders, for example, 3 × 3 or 4 × 4 inches.

Professional cinematographers soon developed a common method of attaching these filters to the camera lens by means of a device that allowed them to easily add, remove, or interchange standard format filters—the matte box and/or filter holder. With this attachment on the end of the camera, cinematographers could easily slide filters in or out depending on their current needs.

Temporal motion

When doctors refer to the temporal lobe of the brain, they're talking about the part of the brain that relates to and processes its conception of time. Let's take a look at the different kinds of time-based motions, how they are created in-camera, and how you can use them in your special effects work.

Normal Speed

Normal speed is any constant speed (keeping in mind the law of persistence of vision, of course) at which a motion picture is both filmed or recorded and projected or played back. This means that if you shoot your film at 24 frames per second (fps), as long as you play it back at 24fps, it will appear to be playing at a speed that is consistent with what we are accustomed to seeing in our everyday life. What about 1,298.65fps? Yep, it doesn't matter… but what an enormous waste of film!

Since it would be very unwieldy to have projectors all over the world running at different frame rates to project movies that have film speed changes, it has come to pass that any film speed manipulations need to be done during the pre-projection phase of filmmaking. To accomplish this in-camera, you simply change the speed at which the camera is filming.

When you are dealing with film speed changes, some of the terminology may at first seem contradictory and confusing. Keeping in mind that the projector is always passing the same amount of film per second through its gate will help you quickly remember the inverse relationship between film speed and apparent motion.

High Speed (Slow Motion)

When you speed up the rate at which the camera is filming (or *over cranking*, as the name was coined in the old days) but play it back at normal speed, the speed of the action being filmed appears to slow down. Back when movies began, motion picture cameras were actually operated by hand cranks. The operator had to try to keep a steady pace to keep the motion as consistent and lifelike as possible. Many times, the camera operator would use a metronome as a reference for pacing himself. In special effects double-exposure shots, the first pass would be filmed while the operator carefully counted the number of cranks or turns he made. He'd then rewind the film the same number of cranks or turns so he could make a second pass. So remember, the higher the frame (or crank) rate, the slower the action.

Slow motion is a great effect for emphasizing action sequences and really heightening the drama of an event. It is also a necessary component of model miniature photography, as the reduction in motion and speed is required to add the apparent size and mass to a miniature object.

Very high speed cameras can also be used to film events or effects that would otherwise happen so fast, their dramatic value would be diminished or lost altogether. Big explosions, crashes, or stunts are good candidates for very high speed photography, many times in excess of 100fps. High-speed intermittent cameras (cameras that arrest each frame for the period of exposure) are capable of speeds of up to 600fps, whereas rotating prism cameras (cameras that utilize a continuous film flow and a rotating prism to project the image on the passing film) are capable of speeds up to 10,000fps for 16mm film. There are faster cameras, but these are used mainly for scientific applications.

Low Speed

Obviously, the opposite of slow motion is fast motion. Slowing the camera and speeding up the action can be very useful for intensifying chase or fight scenes, to make the action appear to be moving faster. Care must be taken not to overdo it (or, er, underdo it) as the effect can become overly noticeable and appear as a scene that was "sped up." It is also important to prevent the relative motion of other subjects in a scene from being *undercranked*. What good would speeding up your hero's car chase be if all of the cars on this highway appeared to be speeding along at the same rate? Carefully pace your actor walking deliberately slowly through a crowd of people, and, upon playback, the result will appear to be your actor walking normally with the entire crowd buzzing around him frenetically. Many early films were shot either cranked at a lower speed than modern projectors, giving them that fast cartoony look you see when projected on modern projectors. C'mon, you didn't think people really moved like that back then, did you?

Stop Frame

Stop frame or stop motion is the manipulation of perceived time by stopping and restarting the camera, depending on the effect you are trying to achieve. This was covered in the earlier section "Thomas Edison and Alfred Clark: Stop Motion."

Time Lapse

Similar to stop motion is time-lapse photography. Time lapse, however, is usually used to denote long lapses in time. Whereas stop motion removes short durations from within a movement or action, time lapse removes minutes, hours, days, months, or even years! The idea is to condense an event that would normally require too much time (not to mention too much film) to record. Imagine sitting and watching 40,000 continuous hours of a tree growing. Eeek! Using time-lapse photography, you can compress this 3- to 5-year event down to a few minutes or even a few seconds. The process is simple: photograph one frame and then wait. After the desired interval of time has passed, photograph another frame… and so on, until the event is complete, or you are too old to complete it. Time-lapse photography can produce amazing images of anything from a flower blooming, to a thunderstorm rolling in, to a structure being built, to a landscape showing the complete cycle of all four seasons in a year—all condensed down to a matter of minutes or seconds.

Reverse

Many cameras, in addition to running at a certain speed, also have the ability to run in reverse. Aside from the comical aspects of everything happening backward, there are some really practical and cool uses for reverse photography, especially for special effects. On the practical side, many effects (especially stunts) are much easier to perform in reverse. For example, it's much easier for your superhero actor to jump down off the roof of a building than it is for him to jump from the ground onto the roof. And, when planned carefully, a reversed action like this can look completely and astonishingly real.

Have your actor shoot his prop gun a few times, then drop it to his foot, all while the camera is rolling in reverse. Then film someone sliding your actor the gun on the floor in correct forward motion. The edited sequence turns your actor into a super spy who effortlessly kicks the gun up into his hands and finishes off the bad guys without batting an eyelash. Another way to use the technique is a variation on the "man in a crowd" theme. Have your actor walk backward through a crowd. When you then play this back running the footage in forward motion, it will appear as if your actor is the only one walking properly while you somehow managed to get an entire city of people to walk all around backwards… on cue!

Bullet Time

From the section on stop motion, remember that a motion picture or animation is really just a continuous series of still images that replace each other quickly enough so that the viewer's brain cannot detect that a substitution has taken place. As a result, the viewer's perception is of continuous motion. Well, if you've gotten your mind around that concept, here's an example of the payoff: Bullet Time.

Bullet Time (the VFX used extensively in *The Matrix*) is an effect that still stumps many people because of its uncanny ability to apparently defy the laws of nature and slow down time while still allowing a natural camera movement to take place. Our perception of motion, is just that—a perception. And as a VFX artist, your job many times is to push and stretch the boundaries of those perceptions. Bullet Time is an excellent example of this concept.

If you have still image after still image of a person moving a little bit at a time and you replace each still fast enough that viewers perceive it to be a moving person, why can't you have still image after still image of the camera moving a little bit at a time while the person is still, and then replace each still fast enough that viewers perceive a moving camera around a frozen-in-time person? "Ahhhh," you say… that's exactly what the basis for Bullet Time is.

Now the complications arise when you start to think about how to simultaneously take however many stills you need to create the desired length of frozen-in-time shot. The math is simple—if you want a 3-second shot of your camera going around your frozen-in-time hero, you multiply 3 seconds times 24 frames per second for film to get 72 stills needed to accomplish your shot. But this means you'll need 72 cameras all firing simultaneously for a true frozen-in-time shot or they'll at least need to fire within milliseconds of each other for the true moving Bullet Time effect. And that's precisely why Bullet Time photography has been so logistically complex and expensive to do.

Superimpositions: Double Exposure (D/X)

In many ways, the great-great granddaddy of all special effects is the double or multiple exposure. It was the forerunner of all combination and composite effects, including split screen, matte photography, miniature composites, and bluescreen photography. It is even the basis for many digital effects we do today. The original in-camera multiple exposure came in two basic flavors: transparent (or ghost effects) and combination (or solid effects).

Multiple Pass (Transparent or Ghost Effects)

The first encounters with multiple exposure effects were likely accidental in nature and undoubtedly of the transparent or ghost-type of effect. All that was required to complete the effect was to accidentally load the same roll of film twice, or more, into the camera and shoot. Obviously, someone got in a world of trouble and at least one director had a really bad day, but once the film was projected, they probably noticed something very interesting—depending on the luminance or brightness of the scenes that were shot, unless one of the scenes was very dark, the images on film appeared "ghosted" over one another. Thus, the means to film ghost and spirit effects was born. Because photographic film has an inherent fixed latency capacity (or maximum ability to reproduce brightness), it can only be exposed so much until the photosensitive chemicals in the film are exhausted, and the negative develops as pure black with no detail at all (meaning the positive develops clear or all white once projected), as one would expect from the repeated adding of light to the film. So, subjects for ghost effects had to be chosen carefully. Darker areas of a background scene would show the second exposed ghost image better than the lighter areas.

It wasn't long before people like Thomas Edison, Georges Méliès, G.A. Smith, and Robert Paul realized that by purposely darkening an area of the frame (by masking it off), they could later expose it with total control, as if it had not been exposed yet.

Multiple Pass (Combination or Solid Result, First Shot Against Black)
Shooting against a carefully selected dark or black area during the first exposure created an un-exposed area on the film which allowed a great deal of control over the second or subsequent exposure. Amazing possibilities opened up with this discovery. It was now possible to film a foreground element and later film the background as a matte painting, miniature, or other location entirely. It was possible to mask or matte off a portion of the screen for split-screen effects or to have an actor interact on the same stage with multiple versions of himself! George Méliès used this technique to great effect in many of his films. The ability to combine two or more elements onto one seamless image allowed virtually anything to be created. Compositing effects for motion pictures were born.

Matte Painting

Since the dawn of time, man has used props to tell a story. Our distant ancestors used rocks, sticks, and animal bones to help their audiences visualize or even feel the hunt (Figure 1.53). A Greek actor in the 4th century B.C. performed in front of panels painted to reflect the location of the story (Figure 1.54).

[Figure 1.53] Early man used bones, spears, and other props to enhance a story.

[Figure 1.54] Greek actors in the 4th century B.C. performed in front of painted panels.

[Figure 1.55] Revolving backgrounds became popular to create extended motion scenes.

Live Composite (Glass Painting)

The first dramatic motion pictures were filmed in front of sets with designs borrowed from theatrical plays.

Painted backdrops and theatrical sets were soon enhanced to include moving or revolving backgrounds, allowing the apparent movement needed for the big stagecoach or train robbery scene (shown in Figure 1.55).

George Méliès was one of the first to realize the power and flexibility he had to create environments for his audiences. Talented painters could hand paint the additions on glass matte paintings—big sheets of glass placed between the camera and the action (Figure 1.56)—to produce epic vistas and perfect imaginary lands (Figure 1.57).

With the advent of process cinematography, all it took was to dress only the area of the set the camera would see, mask off the portion of the frame to be replaced later (Figure 1.58), and shoot the additional location, matte painting (Figure 1.59), or miniature set later using whatever was convenient—and an audience would instantly be transported to magical lands, never before seen (Figure 1.60).

It wasn't long before real photographs and movies themselves were being used as backgrounds: A projector behind the backdrop was projecting the background scenes while a camera in front captured the live action and background together.

[Figure 1.56] Talented matte painters hand painted amazing works of art on large sheets of glass and carefully positioned them to match the set.

[Figure 1.57] The scene was then filmed live, with the effect all taking place in-camera.

[Figure 1.58] Latent image photography allowed a portion of the frame to be masked off…

[Figure 1.59] …and the scenery painted or filmed later, at a different time and/or location.

[Figure 1.60]
The invention of this new process allowed a filmmaker to create rich, new, never-before-seen settings for storytelling.

Photography of Miniatures

One of the main reasons people love going to the movies so much is that movies are bigger than life. The image on the screen is bigger than life, the relationships on the screen are bigger than life, and of course, the action is much bigger than life. How ironic, then, that much of that bigger-than-life action is created using smaller-than-life model miniatures.

Since the beginnings of film, small replicas (or model miniatures) have been a great option for filmmakers who need to do anything that would otherwise be too dangerous, costly, or just impossible to shoot. Whenever a story line calls for something bigger than life to happen in a scene, the producers of a movie are faced with some hard decisions about how to pull it off. Blowing up a city, for example, would definitely not go over well with the citizens who lived there… so what to do? Modern computer graphics visual effects (CG VFX) aside, model miniatures are a great option and can be used in many ways—as sets or environments, scene extensions, props, or even as characters or actors themselves.

Even today, in the age of VFX, it's often cheaper to build a model of a building (when the actual building is situated in some far off location) or a deep-space satellite (to explode) than it is to replicate it in CG; and it is surely cheaper than flying the cast and crew thousands of miles to shoot on location or to destroy a real satellite. Often, a scene or location has almost everything it needs, and a model miniature can complete the scene very cost-effectively. If you were trying to create an ancient medieval walled city, shooting a simple miniature model wall hanging over an existing location would be a very quick and economical solution. This is where forced perspective comes into the picture.

Forced Perspective

When doing an in-camera combination of model miniatures and live action, forced perspective is the trick that allowed Georges Méliès to inflate *The Man with the Rubber Head*. It can make your pint-sized stone model look like the Great Wall of China. *Forced perspective* is using the camera's lack of stereo-scopic vision to your advantage. Let's take a look and see how this works.

Have someone stand close to you with their hand extended and another person stand far away from you (in line with the closer person's hand). Your binocular (or two-eyed) vision tells you that the person in the background (BG) is farther away, so therefore appears smaller, but the camera doesn't have this advantage. It only has one eye, so to speak, or monocular vision.

The camera's monocular vision creates the illusion that the person in the BG is smaller and standing in the larger (or closer) person's hand, as shown in Figure 1.61. By manipulating the distance of the model from the camera, with the proper level of detail, you can make a model appear as big or as small as you want (or, as is the case in *The Man with the Rubber Head*, to be growing or shrinking), all using forced perspective.

When using model miniatures it's important to keep in mind some particular FX cues, namely scale, camera speed, and depth of field.

[Figure 1.61] Forced perspective is the key to elves, giants, and other size-based effects.

Scale: For the best result, when using model miniatures, your models should be as large and close to full size as budget and safety allow. There are a few things that don't scale well as miniatures: fire and water. Since many miniatures are used specifically for these effects, the industry trend is towards the largest miniatures feasible, now called *bigatures*. When a model miniature is to be filmed in motion, in order to appear real, there should be a direct correlation between the model's scale and the camera speed with which the model needs to be filmed.

Camera speed: The smaller a model is, the more compensation has to be made for its lightness or lack of mass. This is accomplished by slowing down the speed of the model's action on film by over cranking the camera. The faster the speed of the film going through the camera, the slower the action will appear when the film is projected, and so the more mass the miniature will appear to have. You can figure out the ballpark camera speed needed by using one of these formulas:

$$F \times \text{the square root of } \frac{D}{d} = f$$

where F is the projected frame rate, D is the dimension in feet of the real object, d is the dimension in feet of the miniature object, and f is the camera frame rate in frames per second.

If you were projecting at 24fps and you photographed a plane that was 20 feet long in reality, but you were using a model that was only 2 feet long, here is how you would calculate the proper frame rate:

$$24 \times \sqrt{20 \div 2} = f$$

which simplifies to

$$24 \times \sqrt{10} = f$$

which means

$$24 \times 3.16 = f, \text{ or } 76 = f$$

In other words, the camera needs to be filming at 76fps.

Another version of this calculation is

$$\frac{(\text{Scale fraction}) \times (\text{portrayed speed}) \times (\text{frame rate})}{(\text{normal frame rate})}$$

For example:

$$1 \div 16 \times 60 \times 96 \div 24 = 15\text{mph (or 22ft/sec)}$$

Be careful not to over crank, or speed up, the camera too much, though, because the slow-motion effect can begin to draw too much attention to itself and start to appear like a miniature shot in slow motion.

The other issue when filming moving model miniatures is the lack of depth of field created by focusing on a small object close to the camera. In order to keep your model in focus and have it best match your full-sized filmed elements, it is helpful to use as small an aperture as possible, even at a high frame rate. This means that shooting in sunlight can make shooting miniatures somewhat easier.

Another challenge is moving a model realistically. Stop-motion has the unpleasant side effect of a sort of jerky or strobing motion, which is created by the lack of natural motion blur that normally occurs when you are filming moving subjects. This issue led to the development of motion control and what became known as go-motion. *Go-motion* is a technique whereby a model's movement is controlled by a motion control computer. The computer can precisely move the model and repeat that exact motion as many times as necessary. This allows you to produce realistic motion blur as well as have the ability to do *multipass photography* (a technique where the same model can be photographed in multiple passes, each time under different lighting conditions) to have much greater control over the final composited image.

Perhaps the single most important concept to comprehend when trying to create photorealistic VFX is that in order for effects to look real, they must contain the imperfections and anomalies inherent in the real world. Motion blur, dirt, chaos, fog, bumps, scratches, and even the inconsistencies and flaws we've grown accustomed to seeing in the mediums of film and video themselves—all of this adds up to the seeming realism of the shot. By adding the imperfection of motion blur to the stop-motion footage, you make the object's motion appear much smoother, familiar to the eye, and… well… real.

Matting for Multiple Exposure

In the early 1900s, another Edison employee, Edwin S. Porter, used sophisticated mattes, double exposures, and other camera tricks to create amazing visual effects in movies such as *Jack and the Beanstalk* (1902), *The Great Train Robbery* (1903), and *Dream of a Rarebit Fiend* (1906). The compositing techniques he used to create moving backgrounds seen through a train car door and train station window in *The Great Train Robbery* are of great significance to VFX artists, because they were some of the first rear-projection effects ever created (shown in Figure 1.62). Rear-projection effects are created by first filming the background scene (as in the example shown in Figure 1.63) and then projecting this footage onto a screen behind the live action (Figure 1.64) while filming both at the same time. The resulting effect is a very convincing combination of the two and is all done in-camera (Figure 1.65).

[Figure 1.62] Edwin S. Porter's *The Great Train Robbery* featured some of the first rear-projection effects.

[Figure 1.63] The background scenery is first filmed and developed.

[Figure 1.64] The live performance is then filmed along with the background footage, which is projected (at the same time) onto a screen behind the action.

[Figure 1.65] The result is a realistic and seamless effect.

During the same time period Méliès was producing his formative work, two British filmmakers, G.A. Smith and Robert W. Paul, were mastering new, multiple-exposure techniques in films such as *The Haunted Curiosity Shop* (1901) and *The Corsican Brothers* (1909). Paul actually developed a device for combining images from multiple negatives several decades before the optical printer was invented.

Probably the most important of the re-photography (literally *re-photographing* a photograph) and optical printing functions to the special effects artist was the ability to matte or block out a portion of the frame by bi-packing (or sandwiching together) the original film with a high contrast matte image that blocked out the portion of the frame to be re-photographed at a later time. In the second re-photography pass, the blocked-out area could then be filled with another image for creating inserts for TV or computer screens, or for dropping in backgrounds, such as matte paintings or model miniature sets. This process has all but been replaced by newer bluescreen and greenscreen photography processes.

It wasn't until the late 1970s that the first computer-generated imagery and digital effects were used in films such as *Futureworld* (1976), *Star Wars Episode IV: A New Hope* (1977), *Star Trek II: The Wrath of Kahn* (1982), *Tron* (1982), *Star Wars VI: The Return of the Jedi* (1983), *The Last Starfighter* (1984), *The Young Sherlock Holmes* (1985), and *The Abyss* (1989).

Traditional Animation

Using the same type of stop-motion camera techniques covered in the "Stop Motion" section earlier, you can animate drawings, paper, sand, fruit, clay, and even create your own Gumby or King Kong. (Remember those old stop-motion monster movies?) Any kind of animated image tracing or painting manipulation you do frame by frame (such as animated lasers, electricity bolts, or light sabers) when making a moving picture is called *rotoscoping*.

Now that you've had a chance to absorb some of the basic principles of motion pictures and VFX, it's time to learn the skill of being able to see the world around you like a VFX artist—and a VFX artist truly does see the world in a very unique way.

VFX Cues

In order to create professional VFX, you must learn to examine and truly match what I refer to as the scene's *VFX fingerprint*. Like a human fingerprint, every scene has unique and identifiable features. You must first identify and define these fingerprints' features and then match these visual characteristics or cues, like a detective. You want all your scene's elements to work together and for the foreground, background, and midground elements to all visually "talk to each other." Among these VFX cues are camera cues, lighting cues, depth and atmosphere cues, and the media itself.

Camera

The best way to understand the visual characteristics you are trying to identify and match is to break down how the mechanisms that create these characteristics operate. Let's start with the camera.

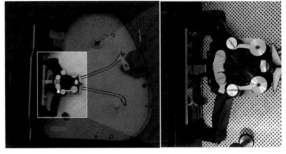

[Figure 1.66] Inside a motion picture camera (and close-up of the film gate)

How a Film Camera Works and Identifying Camera Attributes

A motion picture camera operates by running a long strip of photosensitive film from a loaded spool, around a series of guide and tension posts, through the film gate (shown in Figure 1.66, which precisely positions and holds the film over an opening where the image is exposed to the film), and then back out to a take-up spool. The position on the camera where the film or sensor is exposed is called the *film* or *focal plane* and is indicated on all professional cameras by a small circle with a line running through it vertically (Figure 1.67). This point is very important because it is the point from which measurements must be taken to calculate focal distance and depth-of-field (DOF).

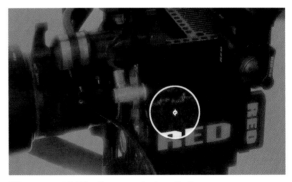

[Figure 1.67] Film (or sensor) plane indicator

On a motion picture camera, a rotating/spinning, adjustable shutter intermittently exposes and then blocks light from hitting the film as it passes through the gate (pulled either by small pull-down claws, sprocketed wheels, or other rollers). This shutter is mirrored on the back side to allow the light to be reflected back to the viewfinder during the portion of the spin when the shutter is over the gate and blocking the film from being exposed. The rate at which each frame is pulled down into position, held in place, exposed, and then pulled down again is called the *film speed* and is referred to in frames per second (fps). Typically normal speed motion pictures are filmed at 24fps.

[note]

Digital cameras frequently use an electronic shutter instead of a mechanical one; however, the effect and results in motion blur are the same.

When a camera's shutter is fully open (resembling a half circle) so that the film is exposed half the time and not exposed the other half (when the next frame is being pulled into position), it's aptly called a 180-degree shutter (literally a 180 degree semi-circle). Having the shutter set to a 180 degrees semi-circle means that the film is exposed for half of each 24fps, or for 1/48 of a second, as the open side of the semi-circle passes the film gate and then "not exposed" as the shutter finishes its revolution and passes in front of the gate. Figure 1.68 shows the shutter closed down to 90 degrees, and Figure 1.69 shows it closing to 20 degrees. Opening or closing down the shutter allows more or less light to hit the film in the same amount of time (because the shutter spins at the same 24fps regardless of the opening size). So a 90-degree shutter will expose the same frame for 1/96 of a second.

When an action is being filmed that is moving faster than the time it takes for the bottom of the shutter to begin exposing a frame to the time the top of the shutter completely blocks the frame (Figure 1.70), this motion is captured

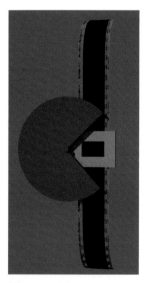

[Figure 1.68] Ninety-degree spinning shutter exposing a frame of film held in the film gate

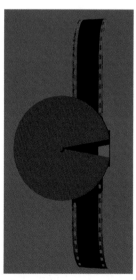

[Figure 1.69] Spinning shutter closed to 20 degrees exposing the same frame of film

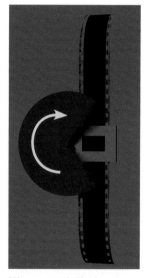

[Figure 1.70] The longer the film remains exposed, the more motion blur is created.

[Figure 1.71] Actual photo of another mirrored spinning shutter configuration

all on the same frame and appears as a smear (or what we call *motion blur*). Figure 1.71 shows another mirrored shutter configuration. The wider the shutter is opened (and the longer the film is exposed), the more motion blur or trailing will be seen on fast moving objects. This motion blur characteristic is critical to match in our motion VFX work.

Identifying Camera Lensing, Focal Length, and Depth of Field

Understanding the effects of what happens in front of the film plane, with the aperture and lens, are equally as important in being able to identify and match the focus and *depth of field* (the distance at which a subject remains in focus) characteristics of a scene. In addition to the shutter controlling how much light hits the film (and therefore creating motion blur), the iris-like aperture (shown in Figure 1.72) can be opened or closed to allow more or less light to enter through the lens.

Because a large aperture allows more light to enter and bounce around from many angles (as shown in Figure 1.73), you can see how subjects might have a more narrow range of "staying in focus" (or depth of field. Conversely, for light to make its way to the film or sensor plane through a small aperture, it must be more directional and focused (Figure 1.74).

[note]

Artists frequently have trouble understanding these relationships, so while not perfectly accurate scientifically, these descriptions are great mnemonic device explanations for engraining the understanding and relationship of these elements in your memory.

f/2   f/4   f/8   f/16   f/32

[Figure 1.72] A camera's iris-like aperture

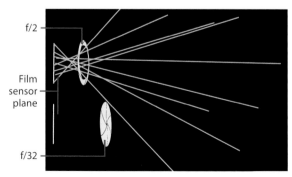

[Figure 1.73] A large aperture allows more light to enter and bounce around from many angles, creating a narrow or shallow DOF.

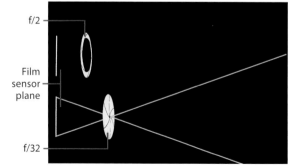

[Figure 1.74] A small aperture requires light to be more directional creating a wider or deeper DOF.

Short focal length—wide angle

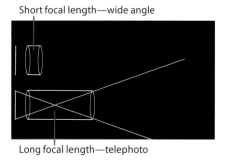

Long focal length—telephoto

Short focal length—wide angle

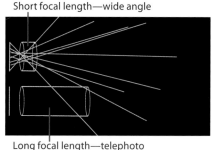

Long focal length—telephoto

[Figure 1.75] A side profile view of a long telephoto lens and the angle that rays of light might need to enter to be able to hit the film or sensor plane

[Figure 1.76] A short focal length, conversely, creates a wide angle of view.

Although somewhat counterintuitive, the longer the lens (or focal length), the narrower the angle of view. The reverse is true with a shorter lens, or focal length, having a wider angle of view. To remember this relationship, think of a side profile view of a long telephoto lens and the angle at which rays of light might need to enter it to be able to hit the film or sensor plane (as shown in Figure 1.75). Using this memory hook, you can easily remember how a short focal length (Figure 1.76) would mean a wide angle of view.

Calculating the depth of field (at what distances things will stay in focus) can easily be achieved using the indicators atop most cameras (most people have absolutely no clue what these are for or do). After looking through the lens and bringing your subject into focus, the center mark on the lens depth of field indicator ring (Figure 1.77) indicates the distance of your subject in feet or meters on the numbered range ring closest to the lens cap—most people also don't realize that this is a range finder. The ring closest to the camera body is the aperture control setting ring. By looking at the depth-of-field range in Figure 1.78, you can see that if your aperture was set to f16, your subject (who is 15 feet, or about 5 meters away) would stay in focus from around 9 feet (or 3 meters) to well over 30 feet (or 10 meters). If your aperture were set to f4, the DOF narrows down to be between only just a little under and a little over 15 feet (or 5 meters, as shown in Figure 1.79). You need to be able to visually recognize the look of these lenses to best estimate your "virtual lens" and other VFX elements to match. Let's take a look at a couple examples.

Figure 1.80 shows two views of the same figure. The one on the left was taken with a wide angle lens from close up (because the FOV is so wide, you need to get much closer to your subject to fill the same frame). Notice

[Figure 1.77] The center mark indicates the distance of your subject in feet or meters on the range finder ring closest to the lens cap.

[Figure 1.78] With the aperture set to f16, your subject would stay in focus from around 9 feet to well over 30 feet.

[Figure 1.79] If the aperture is set to f4, the DOF narrows down significantly.

the wide angle of view of the scene and that everything is in focus. Also notice how a wide angle of view tends to create accentuated depth and distortion. The view on the right side was taken from very far away with a very long (or telephoto) lens. Notice the very narrow angle of view, the very narrow depth of field (everything in front of and behind the subject falls quickly out of focus), and that the depth in the image seems to be de-accentuated, or flattened out. This type of focal length tends to appear more flattering for portraits. Take a look at Figure 1.81 and Figure 1.82. Can you figure out which photo was taken with which lens, how high the camera was placed off the ground, at what angle, and from how far away? Look for VFX camera cues.

[Figure 1.80] The image on the left was taken from close up with a short (or wide angle) lens, and the one on the right was taken from far away with a very long (or telephoto) lens.

[Figure 1.81] If you guessed that this image was taken with a wide angle (or short) lens from very close up, you'd be correct. The accentuated depth and wide depth of field (everything in focus) are the cues.

[Figure 1.82] If you guessed this photo was taken with a long telephoto lens from far away you'd have guessed correctly. The narrow (or shallow) DOF and flattening of perspective or depth are your cues.

[Figure 1.83] An extreme wide angle lens creates a lot of distortion when used close up.

[Figure 1.84] A medium length lens from a little farther away

[Figure 1.85] A long telephoto lens shot from very far away

An extremely wide angle lens creates a lot of distortion and crazy effects on people when it is used close up, as seen in Figure 1.83. The same subject photographed from a little farther away using a medium length lens (24mm–50mm) produces Figure 1.84, whereas a very long telephoto lens used from very far away flattens out the perspective features and creates a very flattering portrait-type images (as seen in Figure 1.85).

Lights

Getting your lighting characteristics to match in a shot is critical to pulling off a successful/photorealistic VFX sequence. Identifying the VFX lighting cues in a scene is usually, but not always, a little more straightforward than identifying camera cues.

Identifying Lighting Attributes

The first cue to determine is usually "Where is the main light source in the scene?" It's helpful to use a two-clock metaphor for describing light position: one to describe the vertical clock orientation and one for the heading or horizontal clock orientation. One clever trick for determining light source direction/location is to examine shadows in the scene. Because light rays travel in straight lines, tracing a ray from the tip of a shadow back to the source that created that shadow will point directly to the light source. You can then notate and describe this as two clock positions. In the first example of Figure 1.86, tracing the tree and trash bin shadows shows the sun position to be at approximately 1:30 vertically (where 12:00 is directly up and 6:00 is directly down) and coming from approximately 4:00 horizontally (where 12:00 is directly in front of you and 6:00 is directly behind you). See if you can guess the sun's orientation in the other three examples in Figure 1.86 without looking at the hints and then check your answers to see how you did (I've provided projected shadow rays, heading, and inclination views with clock overlays to help you get started).

After identifying the main light source's direction/location, make note of any other light sources in the scene, their attributes, and their proportional intensities. This includes color. It is important to keep in mind one of my favorite sayings: "Nothing in nature is perfect, and that is why it's perfect." This applies to everything we do as VFX artists. We are trying to re-create reality, and nowhere are these imperfections more apparent than when it comes to lighting. CG lighting should almost never be a pure color or intensity if it is to appear real (unless you're trying to create a pure white sterile effect). Every

Background plate	Shadow direction	Heading	Inclination

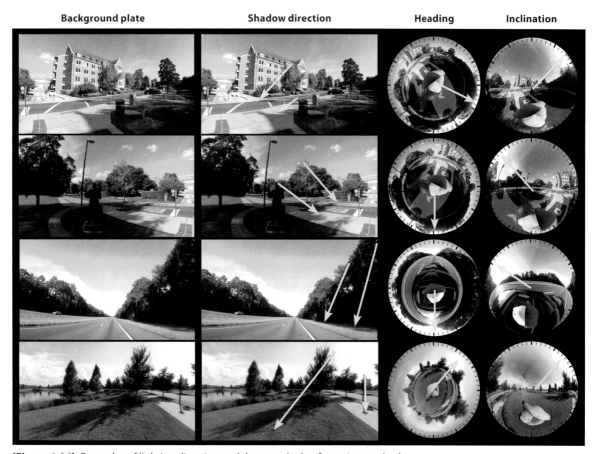

[**Figure 1.86**] Examples of lighting direction and the two-clock referencing method

light in your scene should vary slightly, every color should be off just a bit from pure, every plate on a table should be slightly out of line or misplaced. Learning how to properly "crap up your models and scenes" is probably one of the hardest things new artists have to learn to accept.

Because the human eye is so good at compensating for differences and variances in things, they are very easy for artists to overlook. You might walk into a room and see it as completely evenly lit. But a closer examination will reveal that light is coming in from both a window (daylight balanced light) and from interior light sources (tungsten balanced light), as seen in Figure 1.87. Although the human eye compensates for these differences, film and video are much less forgiving.

We refer to the differences in a light source's color by *color temperature*. This scale was created in the 1800s by Scottish physicist Lord William Kelvin.

[Figure 1.87]
The difference in color temperature between tungsten and daylight

Tungsten 3200 Kelvin   Daylight 5600 Kelvin

[note]

Counterintuitively, colors are commonly referred to in terms of aesthetic temperature, which is the exact opposite of physical Kelvin temperature; warmer aesthetic scene colors (reds) are actually cooler on the Kelvin temperature scale, and cooler aesthetic scene colors (blues) are hotter on the Kelvin scale.

[tip]

Look for neutral-colored objects in a scene to determine color in difficult scenes. Sample white, black, mid-gray, and shadow levels from your BG plate to best match your scene's 3D or VFX elements.

Kelvin noticed that a block of carbon changed color depending on the heat produced as it heated up. Kelvin developed the Kelvin scale as a system of measurement to accurately record color (based on this temperature). Photographic tungsten lights and film are typically rated at 3200 degrees Kelvin, and daylight bulbs and film are rated at 5600 degrees Kelvin. As temperature increases, colors change from reds to yellows to whites to blues, with a bright blue sky being rated at perhaps 10,000 degrees Kelvin. Remember the temperature is referring to the color as a reference and not to an actual temperature of the object, or sky, in this case. Keep this scale in mind when you analyze lighting cues.

In addition to the lighting source's direction, intensity, and color, the light's quality should also be examined. How hard or soft is the light? Is it coming from a large or small light source? Is it constant, intermittent, or interactive? Is it fixed or does it move? A reference "stand-in," such as those pictured in Figure 1.88, can be a great help in determining and recording the lighting conditions on a set.

[Figure 1.88] Lighting reference balls: Matte white, 50% photo gray, and mirror

The Anatomy of a Shadow

Another cue is to again examine shadows for not just direction, but to determine the light source's size, intensity, and quality.

The sharpness of a shadow is directly related to the proportional size/distance of the light source. The farther away from, or proportionately smaller than, the subject the light source is, the sharper the shadow, due to the rays of light becoming more parallel. The larger the light source is (or proportionately closer) to the subject, the softer the shadows are due to the ability of light to bounce and scatter around the subject in an un-parallel fashion, shown in Figure 1.89. When a large light source (providing soft shadows) moves far away from a subject, it becomes (proportionately) a small light source and will, as a result, create harsh or sharp shadows. Figure 1.90 shows just such a shadow.

Shadows are actually composed of multiple components. The *contact shadow* is the portion of the shadow where the subject makes contact with (typically) the ground or another object. It is the point most occluded, or blocked, from receiving light.

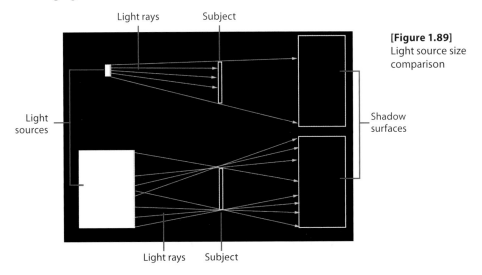

[Figure 1.89]
Light source size comparison

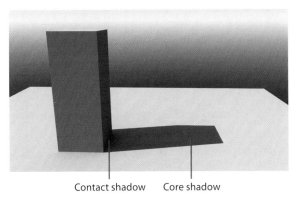

[Figure 1.90]
Components of a hard shadow

[note]

The contact shadow is a critical component to your VFX work. Without it, elements you composite into a scene appear to float or not actually make contact where they are supposed to be in the scene.

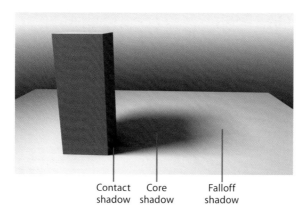

[Figure 1.91]
Components of a soft shadow

Contact   Core   Falloff
shadow   shadow   shadow

The *core shadow* is the main, central part of the shadow that we are all most familiar with and aware of. Finally the *falloff shadow* is the area where a shadow blurs and seems to fade off (Figure 1.91). Seeing a falloff shadow, is an immediate indication of a soft, large, or perhaps close light source, whereas lack of any falloff is indicative of a small, far away, or harsh light source.

Depth and Atmospherics: Identifying Depth and Atmospheric Attributes

Once you know how to place your camera and set up your lights to match the scene, you need to know how to place your subject or element. This requires you to be able to identify the depth and atmospheric VFX cues within the scene.

The simplest VFX depth cue is, of course, *overlap* (or *occlusion*). When one element is directly in front of another (from the camera's viewpoint), it obstructs our view of the farther object, which gives our brains the suggestion of positional relation and depth.

There is a direct relationship between occlusion, the apparent size/scale of an object, the object's placement within the scene, the amount of atmosphere and depth of field seen, and the motion parallax characteristics of that object in the scene. An airplane made very small (with no atmosphere) and positioned on the ground next to a child looks like a toy. That same child, with atmosphere applied and positioned next to a building, appears to be a giant. If you get the atmosphere wrong, they both look like poorly pasted on cut-outs. I cover the use of this relationship in depth in Chapter 8 when I talk about 2.5D atmosphere FX.

Media: Identifying Film/Video Stock (Grain/Noise) Attributes

Finally, you need to examine the media VFX cues related to the type of media you are integrating into and need to match. This could be the frame rate and motion blur characteristics inherent in the media or it could mean matching the physical chemical make-up artifacts of the media, such as film grain or video sensor noise (covered in depth in Chapter 6). To work in these mediums, you should understand how these technologies work. The next section explores just that.

Tech and the Digital Realm: The Binary World and Digital Formats

Human beings are social creatures, and, since the dawn of civilization, in order to communicate with fellow hominids, mankind has searched for effective ways to represent everything in life. Humans used cave painting representations of animals to communicate details of the hunt; cuneiform pictographs pressed into clay tablets to represent words and record business transactions; paintings to represent the beauty they saw; masks to represent fearful dreams they had or beneficent gods they worshipped; telegraph beeps to represent vital messages that need to be transmitted across long distances; phonograph records to represent the music they played; photographs to represent images they saw; motion pictures to more realistically represent the movement they experienced, and now, 3D and virtual reality to represent the other dimensions we live in. In the past, in the "analog" days, each type of representation had its own special medium that was used to record each specific type of event. Paint, brush, and canvas for a painting, stone and chisel for a sculpture, a piano or other instrument for music, magnetic tape and microphone for audio recordings, a camera and celluloid film for visual recordings, and so on. There were almost as many mediums and tools needed to utilize them as there were events themselves. Enter the computer.

With the need for a special, simple, fast, and powerful means of representation for these new calculating machines called *computers* (a name taken from the job an actual human used to fill in financial institutions), they developed a simple language of zeroes and ones. Why zeroes and ones? Well, more specifically, why just two representative digits? Because it is the simplest way to describe the answer to a simple question—yes or no, on or off, right or wrong, black or white, and so on. The genius of it is this simplicity… yet by using multiples of this simplistic representation, we can solve complexities almost beyond our comprehension.

As computers developed, people realized that they could use this binary system to describe images as well as just numbers and letters. A cathode ray tube or (CRT) could be hooked to a computer, and the computer could tell the CRT which picture elements (pixels) should be illuminated and which ones should remain off. The result was a picture represented in zeroes and ones that could be displayed, transmitted, printed, or stored. The next step was to allow more shades of gray instead of just black or white. This was accomplished by simply allowing the voltage/intensity of the CRT to be controlled in incremental steps (from off to brightest). If one digit could only represent zero or one, on or off, black or white, then more places of ones and zeroes representing higher numbers—for instance, 0 would represent 0, 1 would represent 1, 10 would represent 2, 11 would represent 3, 100 would represent 4 and so on—could also represent these incremental increases in brightness, or *shades*. Each place was called a *bit* (binary digit) of data. 8 bits (or places) became a standard—with the highest value possible, 11111111 (or equaling 255). The values from 0 black to 255 white were translated to voltage instructions for the intensity of the CRT to fire. Two hundred fifty-five shades of brightness created some pretty convincing grayscale images. But what about color? Simple… instead of one white CRT electron gun, three were used, each firing a primary light color of red, green, and blue (or RGB), and each having 0–255 values. Voila! Full-color images! Soon audio was represented this same way, then 3D, and then virtual reality… soon, who knows! Maybe one day, everything.

For the VFX artist, this is the greatest thing since sliced bread. Now, instead of having to deal with a zillion different mediums, one person with a desktop or laptop can do almost anything. All it takes is a little patience—alright, maybe a lot of patience—to figure out how to get all of this stuff into and out of your computer. But luckily, the great computer gods have been working feverishly to help hide the complexity from you in each new piece of hardware and software they release… and I'm here to help you through as well. So fasten your seatbelts, and put your seat backs and tray tables in the upright position for takeoff…. I'll see you in the Digital Realm.

Data Transfer, Color Depth, and Compression

Most artists who work with computers have almost no idea of what goes on under the hood that allows their creations to happen. As a result, when things go wrong, they encounter a lot of frustration and needless confusion. If you understand some fundamentals of digital media, you will more easily be able to navigate the minefield of potential problems, solve them when they occur, and create the best work possible.

Data Transfer

I always like to start my high-tech lecture with a low-tech demonstration of how data transfer, file size, and data compression all work. In the old days, I used to do this demonstration on stage with four volunteers, stacks of black and white hanging chips, and three of those large pegged chipboards—the kind you used to find at hardware stores for Formica samples or at the DMV to "take a number" before paper tickets became the norm. I'll use Photoshop here to demonstrate (Figure 1.92).

I start by having volunteer 1 (the sender) take stacks of black and white chips and create a picture on the first 10 × 10 pegboard (with her back to the other volunteers) by hanging the little chips on the pegs to represent the pixels of an image (Figure 1.93). I then ask volunteers 2 and 3 (the receivers) to position themselves by the other of the two identical pegboards located as far from the first, and each other, as possible. I then ask volunteer 4 to be the modem. Volunteer 4 goes back and forth taking one chip at a time (white or black) and delivering it to volunteer 2 with coordinate instructions of where to place each chip (row one, column one, white… row one, column two, white… and so on, as depicted in Figure 1.94). Fairly quickly after the

[Figure 1.92] Two digital pegboards set up on either side of the virtual stage

[Figure 1.93] The simple image is created on pegboard #1 using only white or black chips.

[**Figure 1.94**] Each bit of data (in this case, chips) represents on/off binary pixel data.

[**Figure 1.95**] Individual bits of data being "transmitted" to the receiver via the "modem"

[**Figure 1.96**] An image begins to take shape.

[**Figure 1.97**] The resulting "transmitted" image is lossless and identical to the original.

volunteers get the hang of this, "transmission" speeds up, and an image begins to appear (Figures 1.95 and 1.96).

Ultimately, using this data transmission from volunteer 1 to 2 via volunteer 4, they create an identical image on the other side of the room (Figure 1.97). I then ask the participants to repeat the process, but this time the modem has to go back and forth between the sender and each of the *two* receivers. You can easily see how this slows "transmission" by half (to their relief, I don't make them complete this second transmission). This activity demonstrates packet transmission technology, and you can now see why speeds slow when many people hit the same web page at the same time.

Data Compression

Let's return to my pegboard demonstration to explain data compression. Next, instead of sending my volunteer back and forth for one pixel at a time, I have the volunteers write the instructions for an image in binary code on a sheet of paper to represent a binary file. This file has a 1 wherever a chip is to be on, or white, and a 0 wherever a chip is to be off, or black (Figure 1.98), to coincide with the pixels of the graphic they created (Figure 1.99). This file contains 100 bits of data (since there is a 10 × 10 grid, and there is one bit of data, a 1 or a 0, per pixel). This is, in effect, what a data file is. "But what," I continue, "if we can simplify this file?" Since the top row is all white, we can abbreviate 1111111111 to 10×1, saving six bits on the first line alone. This is what run length encoding (or RLE) compression is, and it is *lossless* compression because all the data remains exactly the same, it's just abbreviated. RLE works great for some images, but it's terrible for images with a lot of detail. Imagine a black and white checkerboard (the first line alone exploding to 1x1, 1x0, 1x1, 1x0, 1x1, 1x0, 1x1, 1x0, 1x1, 1x0—three times the original size!).

Next I explain that we can generalize. For example, they can analyze a small matrix (or chunk) of say 4×4 pixels at a time and say, "The first chunk is mostly white, the second is mostly white, the third is mostly black," and so on (Figure 1.100). This is likely to have them arrive at a reasonable, yet degraded, representation of the image (Figure 1.101). This is considered *lossy* compression—information is lost, and the original data is somewhat degraded in the process.

There have been many advancements in compression schemes and algorithms over the years, and great strides continue to be made to create images that "look" perfect while being the most efficient possible data-wise. One way this is done in motion video is by using color depth sampling compression.

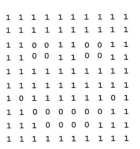

[Figure 1.98] Each pixel of data "digitized" into ones and zeroes

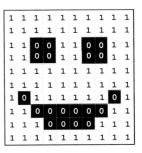

[Figure 1.99] The resulting lossless data file represents the original image exactly.

[Figure 1.100] Averaging areas of the image to conserve data transmission

[Figure 1.101] The resulting lossy compression saves data but degrades the image.

[Figure 1.102]
The number of samples taken determines the reproduction's resolution.

Digital sampling rates

[Figure 1.103] Which color appears the brightest?

[Figure 1.104] The same image showing only brightness (or luminance values)

[tip]

You can now see why bluescreen might not be a good choice when you are using compressed digital video formats. Even though it might look great to the human eye, some of the blue data just isn't there!

Color Depth Sampling and Compression

Sampling is the process of examining something piece by piece in order to re-create it digitally. This could be electric waveforms, sound, or in this case, images and motion pictures. The number of samples taken determines the resolution (or quality). For example, in Figure 1.102, the same waveform is sampled three times, with each sample re-creating an averaged section of the waveform. Notice how the first (consisting of only three samples) barely resembles the waveform. The second (doubled in resolution to six samples) approximates the waveform slightly better. And the third (quadrupling the resolution, yet again, to 24 samples) begins to more accurately re-create the shape of the waveform.

If I asked you to look at Figure 1.103 and tell me which color in the image is the brightest, you would likely choose green. You would then be surprised to learn that the green in this image is, in fact, the darkest of the three colors (Figure 1.104 shows the image de-saturated with only the brightness or luminance data visible). This phenomenon occurs because green is the brightest of the three perceptually to human vision. Because video images are made up of red, green, and blue (RGB), scientists realized that not much quality "appeared" to be lost by reducing the number of times the red and blue values were sampled (or digitized), as long as most of the green/brightness data remained intact.

Full-resolution color is considered to be the ratio of 4:4:4, or four Y (luminance/green) samples, to four Pb (blue) samples, to four Pr (red) samples. File size and bandwidth can be saved by compressing (or reducing) some of the color sampling (or bit depth). Figure 1.105 shows a grid depicting three common color sampling depths: 4:4:4 (full uncompressed color), 4:2:2 (the compression used in high definition, or HD), and 4:1:1 (DV). Other compressions are: 4:2:1, 4:2:0, 4:1:0, 3:1:1, and so on.

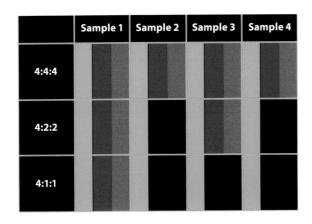

[Figure 1.105]
Common color sampling methods

Formats

There are a wide variety of media acquisition formats, but they can be mainly categorized into two main classifications: analog and digital.

Analog

Film: 35mm, Super 35mm, IMAX, 16mm, 8mm, Super 8mm

Video: D1, D2, D3, D5, D9, 1-inch, 3/4-inch, Beta, consumer/prosumer (8mm)

Digital

The landscape of video manufacturers' latest and greatest is constantly changing, and there are many "flavors" of HD. But digital formats can also be categorized into two main classifications:

Standard definition (SD): Digi-Beta, DV/Mini DV, DVC, DVCPro, DVCPro50

High definition (HD): DVCPro 75, DVCPro 100, Red, Arri Alexa, Thompson Viper

Resolution and Aspect Ratio Comparisons

The differences between all of these formats for VFX artists are mainly in resolution: size, color depth, and aspect ratio.

Size

There are so many sizes and resolutions these days that an entire book could be devoted to the topic, but Figure 1.106 gives you an idea of the majority of most popular media resolutions.

Media Resolutions

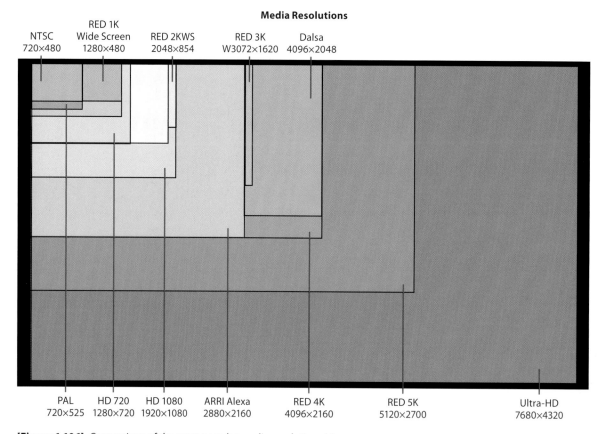

[**Figure 1.106**] Comparison of the most popular media resolutions/sizes

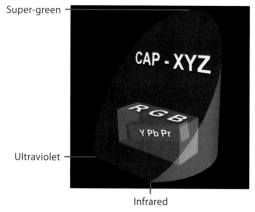

[**Figure 1.107**] Comparison of CAP-XYZ, RBG, and Y Pb Pr color spaces

Color Depth

The amount of visible spectrum color is limited by the format being used, and any color falling outside of that format's gamut limit (or capacity) will be *clipped* (or changed to) the nearest color within that format's capacity. Figure 1.107 shows the comparison between the visible spectrum of light (CAP-XYZ color space), the computer's capacity (RGB color space), and broadcast video's color capacity (Y Pb Pr color space, also known as *component video*).

Aspect Ratio: Screen

In addition to resolution, formats are also commonly referred to by screen aspect ratio (or the ratio of width to height, which is how the final projected or displayed image will be presented). Figure 1.108 shows most of the common screen aspect ratios.

Aspect Ratio: Pixel

Don't confuse screen aspect ratios with pixel aspect ratios (which are the width to height ratios of each pixel). For example, computer monitors typically use a square pixel aspect ratio, whereas NTSC uses a pixel that is slightly taller than it is wide. Common pixel aspect ratios are as follows:

0.90: NTSC. To display frame size of 720×480 (DV) or 720×486 (D1) in 720×540.

0.95: D4/D16 video. To display in 4:3 resolution, 1440×1024 (D4) is displayed as 1365×1024 and 2880×2048 (D16) is displayed as 2731×2048.

1.00: Computer square pixel aspect ratio 1:1.

1.07: PAL. To display frame size of 720×576 (D1/DV) in 768×576.

1.20: NTSC widescreen (anamorphic). To display frame size of 720×480 (DV) or 720×486 (D1) as 864×486 (16:9).

1.33: 4:3 HDV 1080 and DVCPRO HD 720. HDV uses the frame size of 1440×1080 and is displayed at 1920×1080 (16:9). DVCPRO HD 720 uses 960×720 and is displayed as 1280×720 (16:9).

1.42: PAL widescreen (anamorphic). To display frame size of 720×576 (D1/DV) as 1024×576 (16:9).

1.50: DVCPRO HD 1080. The frame size of 1280×1080 is displayed as 1920×1080 (16:9).

1.90: D4/D16 widescreen (anamorphic). To display 1440×1024 (D4) as 2731×1024 and 2880×2048 (D16) is displayed as 5461×2048 (16:9).

2.00: Anamorphic 2:1 video.

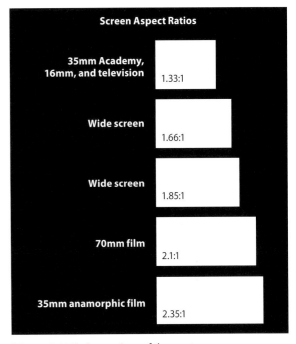

[Figure 1.108] Comparison of the most common screen aspect ratios

The Human Eye vs. Film and Video

The human eye is so much more proficient at resolving (or defining) wide variations in levels of light that it's easy to take this for granted when you are shooting film or video. Figure 1.109 shows the comparison of human vision to film and to video. Note that any image luminance values above the upper limits of each of the film and video curves will be clipped to pure white with all detail lost. Similarly, any luminance values below the bottom curve limits will likewise be crushed to pure black, again with all detail lost. These film and video curves can slide up or down, but any movement to reveal detail in one direction loses it in the other—despite your eyes being able to see detail in both the brightest whites and the darkest blacks at the same time. Figure 1.110 shows the further comparison of latitude between film and video formats.

Shooting Speeds

A wide variety of shooting speeds are common today, ranging from the legendary 24fps for standard movies, 25fps and 30fps for video, and more recently, new higher speed 50fps and 60fps speeds used to capture lifelike high-speed sporting events. Modern variable frame rate cameras have the ability to shoot everything from stop motion and time lapse to ultra-high-speed—cameras that can record at over a million frames per second.

Format Comparisons and "What Is Film Look?"

Most of the time, when you are shooting movies or creating VFX, you are trying to achieve that elusive aesthetic known as *film look*. Let's break down the characteristics of film look into some very tangible and achievable specifics:

Resolution: Film is a very-high-resolution medium. Today it is possible to shoot digitally at the same resolutions as film. If you can't shoot at film resolution, than shoot at the highest resolution possible: 2K, HD 1080, even HD 720 if that's all you can afford.

Frames not fields: Film cameras shoot in full frames (also called *progressive* because of the method by which the pixels are displayed progressively, creating a full frame at a time). Although modern HD video cameras are beginning to adopt the progressive frame standard, many cameras still shoot interlaced. *Interlacing* is a throwback to the origins of television, when CRTs weren't fast enough to draw full frames at a time. The workaround was for the CRT to draw every other line of an image onto a phosphorescent screen,

[tip]

Many times you can achieve the resolution of a much more expensive shooting format if you turn your camera on its side and shoot vertically. As long as you don't need the screen width, you can get close to 4K in size resolution from an HD 1080 camera.

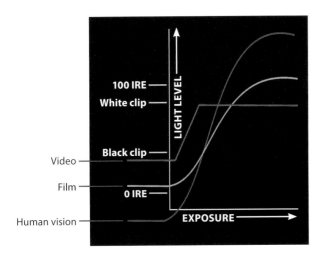

[Figure 1.109]
Comparison of human vision to film and video's ability to resolve detail

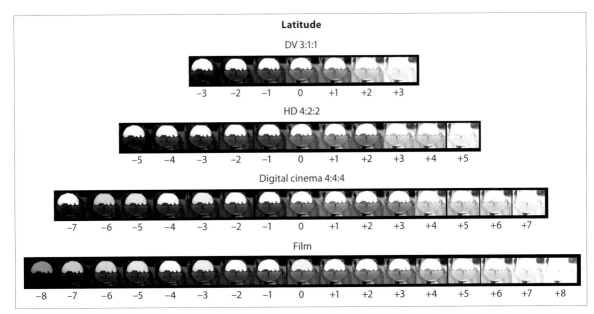

[Figure 1.110]
Comparison of latitude between film and video formats

which retained this luminescence just long enough for the CRT to finish drawing the missing alternate lines. Each image was, therefore, divided into two fields (the half-images consisting of every other line) called upper and lower. An example of an interlaced image of a moving circle can be seen in Figure 1.111. Interlacing can be removed by duplicating, combining, interpolating, or otherwise blending fields.

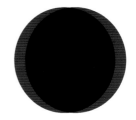

[Figure 1.111] An example of interlacing

Frame rate (speed and temporal differences): Film has traditionally been shot and projected at 24fps. Although other speeds have been used, 24fps is still the standard for film look.

Artifacts of speed (motion blur): Movies on film contain the motion blur associated with a 24fps shooting speed and a rotating shutter of no less than 180 degrees. Modern video cameras with electronic shutters can achieve almost any virtual shutter angle. To achieve a film look, shoot for a similar motion look.

Latitude: As shown in the previous sections, film has a much greater latitude than most video cameras and, as a result, tends to appear to exhibit more contrast. Carefully boosting the contrast (but not losing detail) can help emulate the look of film.

Grain: Film is composed of photosensitive crystals that, when developed, form its signature moving grain pattern. Adding similar grain to video or computer-generated images helps emulate the look of film. I cover adding, simulating, and matching moving grain extensively in Chapter 6.

Is it the format or is it the lighting? Although not inherent to the format of film per se, great care, time, and expense are taken to properly light a movie set. By taking the same amount of care in lighting video, you can achieve surprising, and many times stunning, film-like results.

Camerawork, size, and movement: As in the previous section on lighting, nothing gives away something that was shot on cheap video faster than the camera moving around like crazy. Film cameras are *heavy*! Moving a film camera usually requires a lot of work and equipment, from dollies and jibs to steadicams. Placing your video camera on a rig equipped with 10–20 pounds of weight (or more), or moving the camera via a weighted dolly, will add that sense of scale and grandeur inherent in film camera movement.

VFX Concepts

VFX is a problem-solving occupation. Every new effects sequence presents unique challenges and potential obstacles. Remember, there are always more than 100 ways to solve *every* problem. Get in the habit of mentally stepping outside the box and brainstorming multiple approaches to every shot.

Congratulations! You survived Hell Week! Now that all your newly acquired background information is settling into your memory banks and thought processes, let's get your mindset ready for VFX.

Thinking in Layers

So how do you get your 3D-rendered object to fly behind your live-action actor footage? How do you get your explosions to look as if they are more a part of the scene instead of just pasted on? How do you create set extensions or digital matte paintings for those huge-looking VFX? The basis for these effects lies in what, for the sake of simplicity and ease of understanding, I'm going to call layers.

Layers are a simple concept you have probably used in other applications—like Photoshop, or making a cake… oh, come on, you know, you stack one cake layer on top of another to make a bigger and better-looking cake (Figure 1.112). Well that's what you're going to do—make a bigger and better-looking image. And along the way, you're going to learn some terms that at first might sound foreign and a bit scary but will quickly become familiar.

[Figure 1.112] Think in layers.

Most special effects shots start with what I call a background plate—a *plate* is a term you're going to encounter often in special VFX work—background plates, foreground plates, clean plates, element plates, and so on. The term *plate* comes from traditional cel animation, where an animation plate was used to hold down the layers of cel animation (shown in Figure 1.113). Today, a background plate refers mostly to any footage, photo, or painting that's been scanned and that you will use as the background for a scene or effect (Figure 1.114). In this case, the background plate is this downward-looking shot out the 20th or 30th floor window of a skyscraper (Figure 1.115). Just the perfect place to hang actor Rob Crites to create a cool VFX shot.

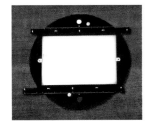

[Figure 1.113] An animation plate

Our foreground picture or *element plate* is this bluescreen shot (Figure 1.116) of Rob lying on a bluescreen material–covered box. The camera is placed low on the floor just under his eyeline to approximate the view you'd have if you were looking down at him (Figure 1.117). If you merely add these two images together to create a double exposure, you'll find parts of both the background and foreground are bleeding through to each other where you don't want to see them, as shown in Figure 1.118. The overall scene has taken on the sickly blue color of your bluescreen, and Rob has a taken on an interesting stucco and asphalt complexion.

[Figure 1.114]
A background plate refers
to any footage, photo,
or painting used as the
background for a scene or
effect.

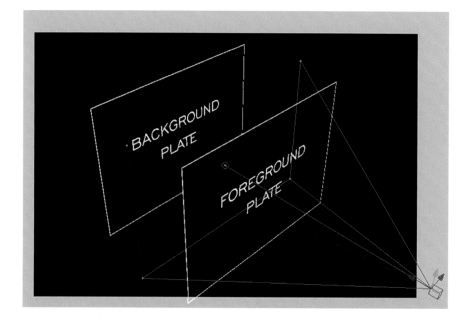

[Figure 1.115] Background plate looking
down out of the window of a skyscraper

[Figure 1.116] Actor Rob Crites, lying on a
bluescreen material–covered box

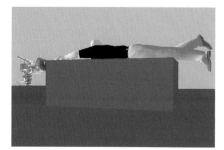

[Figure 1.117] The camera is placed low to
simulate looking down at the actor.

[Figure 1.118] Simply double exposing the
background and foreground does not create
a good seamless composite.

If the background image were a cookie (Figure 1.119), and the image of Rob on the box were another cookie (Figure 1.120), how would you composite (or combine) your cookie scene to get it to look like Rob is on the building without the bluescreen? You might use a cookie cutter (Figure 1.121) to cut away the blue on the foreground cookie, leaving only Rob (Figure 1.122). But to make this cookie seamless, you'd also need to cut out a hole in the background cookie (Figure 1.123) for the Rob piece to fit in. This is not a perfect analogy, but it is an excellent mnemonic device that should forever engrain into your memory the image of the two cookie cuts that need to take place to create a seamless VFX composite (Figure 1.124). This is also an excellent analogy for the way a composite was done in the film world before computers. Actually, it is still very much the same now, except that computers and software simplify the process by hiding and automating some of the complexity from the viewer, as you'll see in Chapter 2.

[Figure 1.119] Think of the background layer as a cookie.

[Figure 1.120] Think of the foreground layer as another cookie.

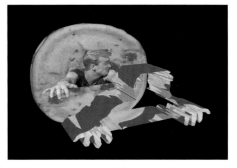

[Figure 1.121] Use a "cookie-cutter" to cut away the blue portion of the foreground cookie...

[Figure 1.122] ...leaving only the actor.

[Figure 1.123] To make this cookie seamless, you also need to cut out a hole in the background cookie...

[Figure 1.124] ...for the piece with the actor to fit in, to create a seamless composite.

Because we're working with computers and software, and a metal cookie cutter makes an awful noise when scraped on a monitor, you need a different kind of cookie cutter. Luckily the omniscient computer gods have given you just such a simple tool: *alpha channels*. Now wait! Get back here and stay on this page! This is actually really quite simple. The great computer gods knew that artist-types aren't very fond of complicated computer things, so the "cookie cutter" they gave us is very simple to use. It's just a black and white and gray image, as shown in Figure 1.125. That's right, you can color with black and white and gray, and wherever the image is white, that part is opaque and stays; wherever it's black, it's 100% transparent and gets cut away; and wherever it's gray, it's semitransparent, depending on the shade of gray (Figure 1.126).

So, if I create an image that's black where the bluescreen is and white where Rob is (Figure 1.127) and make it the alpha of Rob's layer, I get what you see in Figure 1.128. In the old days, we used to have to do both the foreground cookie cut (or matte) and the background cookie cut (or *holdout matte*—Figures 1.129 and 1.130) for each composite, or combined image. But today, most of the time you can simply create, or cut, a matte for the foreground image, and the compositing software simply does an *over process*, meaning it pastes the foreground over the background and simply does the holdout matte for you (Figure 1.131).

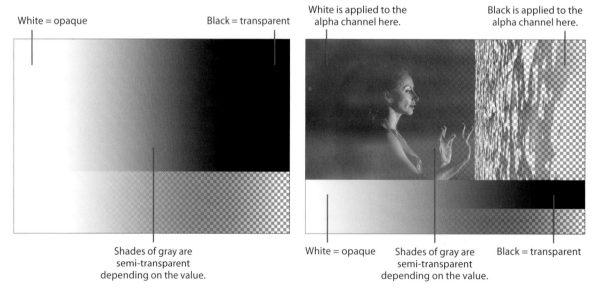

White = opaque   Black = transparent

Shades of gray are semi-transparent depending on the value.

White is applied to the alpha channel here.   Black is applied to the alpha channel here.

White = opaque   Shades of gray are semi-transparent depending on the value.   Black = transparent

[Figure 1.125] An alpha channel is simply a black and white grayscale image that determines transparency.

[Figure 1.126] Wherever the image is white, that part of the image will be opaque; wherever it's black, it will be 100% transparent; and wherever it's gray, it will be semitransparent depending on the shade of gray.

[Figure 1.127] Alpha created of the foreground layer

[Figure 1.128] Blue background cut away using the alpha channel

[Figure 1.129] Holdout matte

[Figure 1.130] Holdout matte cutting away the background layer

[Figure 1.131] Resulting composite of the foreground and background images

Complex and Multisource Operators (Blend/Transfer Modes)

In addition to combining images using alpha channels, you can also combine images using *blend* (or *transfer*) *modes*. With the click of a button, these *complex multisource operators*—a fancy name for combining multiple images using mathematical functions—can combine images or elements in amazing ways, completely automatically. To describe these modes, I will use a simple scene (Figure 1.132) created with image A (a white to black gradient square) sitting on top of image B (a black, gray, and white striped background). Using these modes, the pixel of image A will be combined with (or affected by) the pixel of image B directly underneath it.

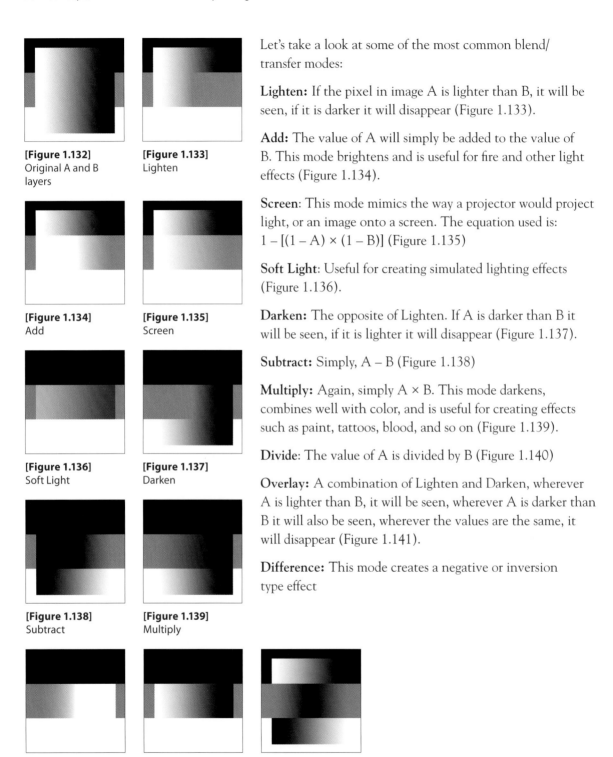

[Figure 1.132]
Original A and B
layers

[Figure 1.133]
Lighten

[Figure 1.134]
Add

[Figure 1.135]
Screen

[Figure 1.136]
Soft Light

[Figure 1.137]
Darken

[Figure 1.138]
Subtract

[Figure 1.139]
Multiply

[Figure 1.140]
Divide

[Figure 1.141]
Overlay

[Figure 1.142]
Difference

Let's take a look at some of the most common blend/
transfer modes:

Lighten: If the pixel in image A is lighter than B, it will be
seen, if it is darker it will disappear (Figure 1.133).

Add: The value of A will simply be added to the value of
B. This mode brightens and is useful for fire and other light
effects (Figure 1.134).

Screen: This mode mimics the way a projector would project
light, or an image onto a screen. The equation used is:
$1 - [(1 - A) \times (1 - B)]$ (Figure 1.135)

Soft Light: Useful for creating simulated lighting effects
(Figure 1.136).

Darken: The opposite of Lighten. If A is darker than B it
will be seen, if it is lighter it will disappear (Figure 1.137).

Subtract: Simply, $A - B$ (Figure 1.138)

Multiply: Again, simply $A \times B$. This mode darkens,
combines well with color, and is useful for creating effects
such as paint, tattoos, blood, and so on (Figure 1.139).

Divide: The value of A is divided by B (Figure 1.140)

Overlay: A combination of Lighten and Darken, wherever
A is lighter than B, it will be seen, wherever A is darker than
B it will also be seen, wherever the values are the same, it
will disappear (Figure 1.141).

Difference: This mode creates a negative or inversion
type effect

Extractions

The main way you remove elements, to combine with other elements or place in other scenes in VFX, is by using some form of extraction.

Optical Printing Extractions

Around 1924, the first color matting (bluescreen) using optical printers came into being. The Dunning Process involved a series of film bleaching, dying, and optical printing steps designed to remove the blue and extract just the subject for compositing onto a background. Today, your computer has taken the place of optical printers, and can perform bluescreen or greenscreen composites with a few mouse clicks. Digital matte paintings have all but replaced nearly all the hand-painted ones, allowing the collaging of real scanned imagery and 3D computer generated imagery into any seamless set, location, or world imaginable.

Digital Extractions

I cover extractions in great detail throughout this book, but I would like to first answer a couple questions I am most frequently asked: "Why use a bluescreen?", "Why use a greenscreen?", "Which one should I use?", and "Does any color work?"

The answers depend on what you are trying to extract. Blue was originally used because it is the least prevalent in human skin (the subject most often being extracted) and is a primary light color. Green became popular for digital because it too is a primary color and is less corrupted in the compression process (due to it being the primary luminance channel).

But what if a person is wearing blue and green? Well, although many software applications are tuned for bluescreen and greenscreen hues, red, orange, pink… in fact, just about any solid, evenly lit, saturated, and contrasting color can work for extractions.

For paint or blood elements, white is a good choice. For fire, explosions, or snow, black is a good background color for extractions. Even a live location or set itself can work as a *difference key*. A difference key is an extraction based on the difference between an image without the subject in frame (called a *clean plate*) combined with the image with the subject in frame, using a difference mode, covered in the next chapter.

With that in mind, let's jump right into basic compositing in Chapter 2.

[note]

In the original Dunning Bluescreen Process, the film interpositive was bleached orange and then composited with the bluescreen foreground image by running it bi-packed (or sandwiched) in an optical printer.

CHAPTER TWO

Introduction to VFX: Advanced Photoshop for 3D, VFX, and Digital Compositing

In its simplest, most distilled definition, creating visual effects, or VFX, is simply either adding or removing something from the original image. To do that, you must first be able to select certain objects in a scene. These may be objects that need to be removed or objects in the original image that need to be replaced back on top of the item or element you are adding to the image. You want it to appear as if whatever you have added is at a proper depth and is behind any appropriate foreground elements already in the scene. This is what will make your object appear to be actually in the image. As you will see, creating the most accurate and appropriate selections possible is probably the single most important fundamental skill required to become a VFX artist.

Designed by visual effects artists in the early 1990s, Adobe's image paint and 2D compositing application Photoshop remains an amazingly versatile tool for VFX work. Compositing with Photoshop is a great way to learn, in a professional environment and application, all the concepts, techniques, and applications you need to make selections for your VFX work. All of Photoshop's selection methods are universal among image editing, visual effects, and compositing applications, so once you learn selections in Photoshop, you can pretty much apply them to any other application.

Photoshop Selection Methods

Photoshop has many prebuilt selection tools. Some are simple and straight-forward, others are complex, and still others are relegated to the categories of *legacy* or *not well documented*. Because many artists tend to shy away from technical stuff, Adobe has hidden much of the inner workings of some of these powerful selection tools under the hood in lieu of creating simple, artist-friendly interfaces and naming conventions.

In order for you, as a VFX artist, to be able to fully understand, utilize, and troubleshoot VFX work, you need to understand all the selection methods and how they work. You need to get under the hood and find out what Photoshop is doing behind the scenes so that you can harness the true power of all of these selection methods. Don't worry, though. This chapter teaches you all this technical information in a very simple, straightforward way. By the end, you'll easily have mastered the power of selections.

Simple Selections

To make simple selections using the basic selection tools, after selecting the tool you would like to use, simply place your mouse pointer at the starting location of whatever you'd like to select, click and hold the mouse, and then drag to the end location and release the mouse.

Marquee Selection

[Figure 2.1]
Marquee Selection tool
pop-out menu

On the Photoshop toolbar, located by default on the left-hand side of the Photoshop interface, the tool second from the top is the Marquee Selection tool. By default, it's the Rectangular Marquee Selection tool. The tiny triangle in the bottom right corner of this tool indicates that a pop-out menu of options is available. Click and hold the mouse button with the pointer over the tool to reveal these options, as shown in Figure 2.1.

As you can see, the pop-out menu reveals three additional Marquee tools you can use to make selections: the Elliptical Marquee tool, the Single Row Marquee tool, and the Single Column Marquee tool.

Each of these Marquee tools has additional, helpful modifier keys that can assist with selections:

- Pressing and holding the Shift key after clicking and dragging the mouse constrains the selection to a perfect square or circle, depending on whether the Rectangular Marquee or Elliptical Marquee is selected.

- Pressing and holding the Alt key after clicking and dragging the mouse creates a selection centered from the point clicked outward (instead of from corner to corner).

- Pressing and holding the Shift key after a selection has been made and then making another selection adds to the selection, meaning both objects will be selected.

- Pressing and holding the Alt key after a selection has been made and then making another selection subtracts from the selection, meaning the second selection will be subtracted from the first selection.

- Holding down both the Shift and Alt keys together constrains a selection and makes that selection from the click point center outward.

[Figure 2.2]
Lasso Selection tool
pop-out menu

Lasso Selection

The next tool button down, as you can see in Figure 2.2, is the Lasso Selection tool.

Lasso Selection allows for freeform drawing of selection shapes. The additional variations within the pop-out menu for this tool are the Polygonal Lasso tool and the Magnetic Lasso tool. The Polygonal Lasso tool makes selections using straight line segments anchored by corners that are placed wherever you click. This feature makes the Polygonal Lasso tool handy for selecting any object with straight edges, such as buildings or street signs. By contrast, the Magnetic Lasso tool "pours" its selection lines, like toothpaste being squeezed out of the tube, automatically finding edges with contrast.

[Figure 2.3]
Magic Wand Selection tool
pop-out menu

Magic Wand Selection

Next is the Magic Wand tool, shown in Figure 2.3, with its Quick Selection tool pop-out option.

Magic Wand tools make their selections based on color values and allow more or less of an image to be selected depending on Tolerance or Brush Size values. These values are based on the pixel that is clicked, or selected; more of similar color values can be selected with higher-tolerance values or larger brush sizes, and less can be selected with lower tolerance or brush sizes, as seen in Figure 2.4.

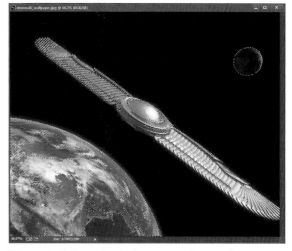

[Figure 2.4] Example of selections made using the Magic Wand Selection tool

Selections in VFX

[note]

All the modifier keys described in the "Marquee Selection" section work equally and the same way with all of these other tools.

These basic selection tools (shown in Figure 2.5) are handy for simple selections. But rarely in VFX are the subjects, or *elements*, you need to select in a scene so simple. In addition, elements in a filmed scene never have a perfectly sharp edge, as you can see in the magnification of Figure 2.6.

The edges of all these selection methods are unnaturally razor sharp, as you can see in Figure 2.7 and 2.8.

Figure 2.8 quite blatantly gives away that an element has been cut and pasted. But your goal as a VFX artist is to create seamless, photorealistic images.

Single Row Marquee   Rectangular Marquee   Lasso tool   Polygonal Lasso tool   Elliptical Marquee

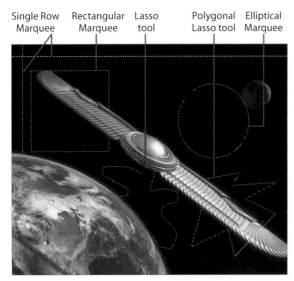

[Figure 2.6] Edges in any kind of photography are never razor sharp.

[Figure 2.5] Examples of selections made with selection tools

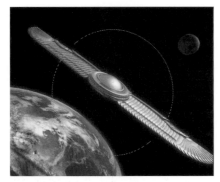

[Figure 2.7] Selections made with selection tools…

[Figure 2.8] …create unnaturally sharp edges when extracted.

At the top of the interface, as shown in Figure 2.9, click Select menu > Modify > Feather. Feather helps produce softer, more natural-looking edges by creating a blurry-edge effect that you can control by setting its Feather Radius. However, setting the Feather Radius is a bit hit or miss. Here's where you need to get under the hood to see what Photoshop is actually doing so you can have more control over the edges.

Alpha Channels

Alpha channels are one of the most important, versatile, and useful tools you will use in VFX.

In this section, if you have Photoshop installed, you can work directly with the same files shown in the figures as you read along. Go to www.peachpit.com/register and follow the directions to register the book. The downloadable files will be listed under the Registered Products tab of your Account page.

Go back to the Select menu (shown in Figure 2.10) and click Save Selection.

Select the New Channel option under Operations in the same Document image you're working on. If you click the Channels tab in the lower right (shown in Figure 2.11), you'll see that in addition to the three RGB (Red, Green, and Blue) channels and the combined RGB Channel layer at the top, you now have an additional black and white image in another channel named Feathered Selection. This is called an alpha channel.

Although the phrase *alpha channel* might tempt the technophobic to immediately run, it's actually quite simple. Where the alpha channel image is white, the image the alpha channel is a part of will be solid or opaque. Where it is black, the image

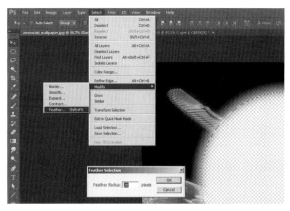

[Figure 2.9]   The Feather tool can be used to soften selection edges.

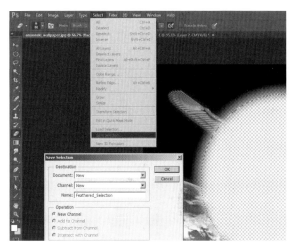

[Figure 2.10]   Save Selection tool found under the Select menu

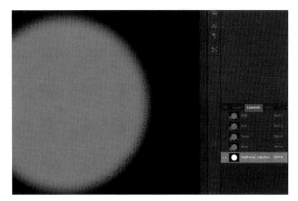

[Figure 2.11]   A new alpha channel created with the Save Selection tool

[Figure 2.12] The Load Channel As Selection tool

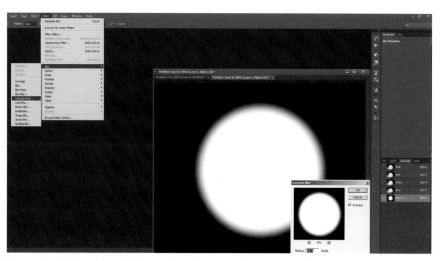

[Figure 2.13] The Gaussian Blur tool applied to an alpha channel

will be transparent or see-through. Where the alpha is a shade of gray, the image will be semi-transparent, or partially see-through, depending on the value of gray. Transparency is determined on a scale of 0–255, with 0 being black (or 100% transparent) and 255 being white (100% solid or opaque).

If you select an alpha channel and then click the Load Channel As Selection button at the bottom of the Channels tab (as seen in Figure 2.12), you will see that any alpha you have selected now loads as a selection!

Let's create a new, perfectly sharp shape selection and perform another Save Selection. After you've done so, select the saved alpha for the sharp shape in the Channels tab.

Click Filters > Blur > Gaussian Blur (shown in Figure 2.13) and adjust the Radius value of the blur slightly. You'll see that you're actually getting the same result as you would using the Feather Selection tool.

This, in fact, is what Photoshop is doing behind the scenes—creating this soft edge. The difference is that by performing the process manually, you have complete control over the quality of the edge and you get instant interactive feedback (you can see it being done right before your eyes as you adjust the Radius Pixel value slider).

Advanced Selections

Unfortunately, most selections you'll need to perform are not simple shapes with simply shaped edges. Most will require more advanced methods, or even

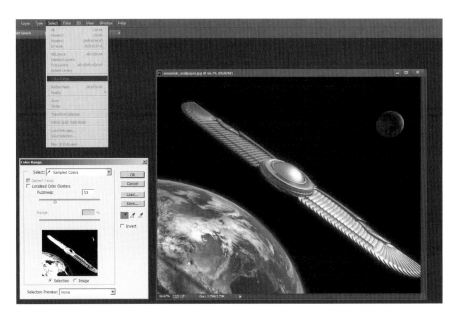

[Figure 2.14]
The Color Range Selection tool creates its selections based on a similar range of color values, selected with the eyedropper.

multiple methods, to arrive at the best possible selection. Photoshop provides a few stock tools to get somewhat better precision over selections, including the Color Range Selection tool (click Select > Color Range), as shown in Figure 2.14.

Notice that the selection of a color value produces a very similar type of result to the one you get with the Magic Wand tool. Notice also that the Fuzziness slider gives you a very similar result to what you get when you raise or lower the Tolerance value of the Magic Wand tool. In fact, it's doing pretty much exactly the same thing! But look at the little selection preview thumbnail image in the tool—does it remind you of anything? Yup. If you save this selection (see Figure 2.15), you'll see that this is just another alpha selection!

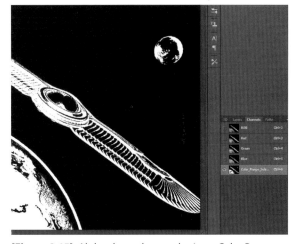

[Figure 2.15] Alpha channel created using a Color Range selection

Levels Adjustment

Among the many tools you'll use in your bag of tricks, one of the most versatile—and one of my favorites—is the Levels adjustment tool (shown in Figure 2.16).

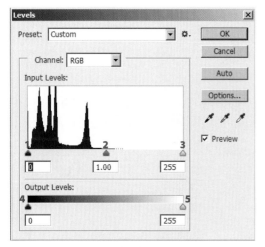

[Figure 2.16]   The Levels adjustment tool

The Levels adjustment tool is found under Image menu > Adjustments > Levels. It has a simple interface with a graphical representation of the values of the image from black to white (called a histogram) and five controls divided into two sections (as numbered in Figure 2.16):

Input

1.   **Black level (shadows):** This controls where on the histogram the image should be black.

2.   **Gamma level (midtones):** This controls where on the histogram the image should be mid gray.

3.   **White level (highlights):** This controls where on the histogram the image should be white.

Output

4.   **Black level:** Where this control is placed on the gradient above will be the darkest black the image can be.

5.   **White level:** Where this control is on the gradient above will be the lightest white the image can be.

By raising the Black Input level and lowering the White Input level, you can effectively increase the contrast and add punch to the image. By raising or lowering the Gamma level, you can increase or decrease the brightness of the image without affecting (*crushing* or *clipping*) the black or white points in the image. By raising the Black Output level and lowering the White Output level, you can decrease the contrast in the image.

Later in this chapter, you'll see how versatile the Levels adjustment tool can be and the many ways in which we can use it to effectively control many different effects.

Channel Ops

Since we now know that the red, green, blue, and alpha channels are all just grayscale images with values ranging from 0–255 in an 8-bit image, what's the difference between them? Absolutely nothing! What does this mean to you, and how can this help you as a VFX artist? Well, it means you can

•   Load any channel or image as a selection.

- Modify or filter any channel or selection as you would any other image.

- Use complex math or interactions between individual or multiple channels within, or even outside of, the image itself to create complex selections.

These are called channel operations or channel ops for short.

To give you an idea of how powerful channel ops are—and how you can use the simple Levels adjustment you just learned about—let's use channel ops to build your own bluescreen (sometimes abbreviated BS) keyer. We'll use this to remove the bluescreen seen in Figure 2.17 from behind the actor and place him into a sci-fi setting.

A keyer or chroma key (or color separation overlay) is a technique for combining or *compositing* two or more images, or frames, together in which a color (or color range) from a foreground (FG) image is removed, or made transparent, revealing the background (BG) image behind it.

To begin, look at each of the individual RGB channels in Figures 2.18–2.20. You're looking for the channels that provide you with the most contrast to work with to help you separate the parts of the image that you want to extract. As you can see, the Red channel has a lot of nice contrast in the skin tones. Let's use that as the first channel in our calculations. The Green channel has the least contrast, so let's skip that one for now. The Blue channel has, not surprisingly, a lot of contrast in the BG (it *is* a bluescreen after all).

Create a copy of the BS footage layer by dragging the layer onto the little sticky note icon at the bottom right of the Layers tab. Select the copy

[Figure 2.17] Actor on bluescreen (BS) background

[Figure 2.18] Red channel

[Figure 2.19] Green channel

[Figure 2.20] Blue channel

[Figure 2.21]
Result of Calculations
procedure

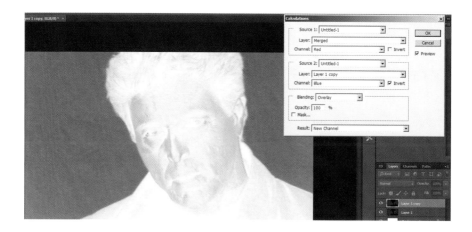

[note]

Your eye should always be on the edge and you should take great care not to lose detail in the fine edges, such as hair, wherever possible. You can always fix the black BG or fill the white FG with garbage or core mattes (discussed later in this chapter), but you can never regain detail lost in the edges! For right now, don't worry too much about losing the edges—you're just getting to know the tools.

(you *always* want to work on a *copy*, never the original… just in case!). Select the copy layer and then choose Image menu > Calculations from the top of the interface to bring up the Calculations dialog box, as shown in Figure 2.21. For Source 1, select Red in the Channel box. For Source 2, choose Blue and select the Invert checkbox. For Blending Mode, select Overlay (make sure you have the Preview checkbox under the Cancel button checked) and set the Result to New Channel (you should see a result that looks something like Figure 2.21), then click OK.

You can see from the result that there's great contrast between the actor and the BG, but it's not quite strong enough (remember, grays will give you semi-transparencies—you're shooting for black transparencies and white opacities). Not to worry, Levels adjustment to the rescue!

By sliding the little triangular controls, bring the Black Input levels up to where the BG is crushed to black, and then bring the White Input levels down to where the actor is crushed to white. Figure 2.22 shows the Levels Histogram settings before any adjustment and Figure 2.23 shows the Levels Histogram adjustment settings and the resulting alpha (or matte).

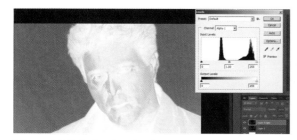

[Figure 2.22] Before Levels adjustment

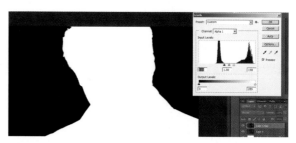

[Figure 2.23] Result of the Levels adjustment procedure

Once you have a solid alpha/matte, simply select the new alpha/matte in the Channels tab and load it as a selection using the Load Channel as Selection button. Press Ctrl+Shift+J to cut the actor out, as shown in Figure 2.24, and place him on his own layer. Then load the BG image into a layer below the actor (Figure 2.25).

Congratulations! You just built your own keyer! You may notice a little blue halo around the actor. That's called *spill*. I address cleaning up spill in Chapter 6. Feel free to experiment with this process and different transfer/blending modes as well as using different, or even all the same, channels to get different results.

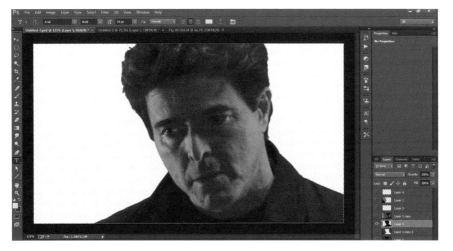

[Figure 2.24]
Actor extracted from BS into his own layer

[Figure 2.25]
The extracted actor composited over the background (BG) image

Application of Selection Methods: Grunge and Grime Maps

You can use many of these same steps and techniques for all kinds of cool VFX including the creation and use of grunge and grime maps. I have a saying that I teach my students: "Nothing in nature is perfect, and that's why it's perfect!" To make things in VFX look *real*, you need to mimic the way they are in *reality*—not in the computer. In nature, there is no such thing as a perfectly straight line, a perfectly saturated or pure color, a perfectly flat surface, or perfectly symmetrical body parts or leaves. Everything—everything—has a certain bit of imperfection. That's what makes it perfect, natural, and real.

A sure sign of a beginning 3D or VFX artist is a scene with perfectly white lights, perfectly straight edges, perfectly smooth motion, perfectly symmetrical dinner plates placed around a perfectly round table with a perfectly 255,0,0 red, wrinkle-free, spotless tablecloth. In reality, everything has a bit of imperfection and grunge to it. Although many artists choose to hand paint these kinds of detail, I am of the firm belief that no one can create the complexity of nature like nature herself. I also firmly believe in not wasting time. Why spend countless hours trying to re-create nature's complexity when you can just steal it? Visual effects is one of the few professions where cheating is not only okay, it's encouraged. (I'm not referring to copyright infringement or plagiarism here—I'm talking about saving time and money by taking an easier, better, cheaper, faster way out if it's available and makes for a better product.)

My favorite demonstration of this technique is to create something photorealistic out of something completely *not* photorealistic using grunge/grime maps extracted out of only one image. After doing this exercise, you will never look at dirt, grime, rust, or other such textures the same way. You can thank me or curse me when someone laughs at you for taking a photo of some really amazing rust or grunge while everyone else is taking snapshots of the tourist attraction.

Procedural Extraction of Grunge and Grime Maps

The first thing you need to do is extract some of nature's complexity to use for your grunge/grime maps. When I'm referring to nature, I'm including dirt, residue, and other grunge that accumulates naturally or from man-made processes, such as industrial dirt, residue, debris, and so on. For this example,

[**Figure 2.26**] Grungy warehouse floor image

[**Figure 2.27**] Desaturated grungy warehouse floor image

we'll use one of my favorite images of a grungy warehouse floor, shown in Figure 2.26. (Download the image from www.peachpit.com/register and follow the directions to register the book. The downloadable files will be listed under the Registered Products tab of your Account page.) I took this photo right after the company moved a piece of machinery. You should've seen the look on their faces when I said, "Wait! I'll be right back! I gotta get a photo of that!"

When I refer to a procedural extraction, I mean a method of extracting what you need by way of a series of procedures, as opposed to hand creating.

To get a good idea of how versatile this technique is, you're going to pull a few different, but matching and relational, grunge and grime maps, all from this one image. As always, make a copy of the original to keep as a backup just in case you need it.

First get rid of the color information because, in this case, what you're really interested in is the texture and not the color information. (There are a few ways you could also use the color to extract some different variations, but for now, let's keep it simple.) The first procedure, then, is to desaturate the image. Select Image menu > Adjustments > Hue/Saturation and desaturate (reduce the saturation) all the way down to nothing. Make three more copies of this desaturated version (shown in Figure 2.27).

With the first one selected, you're going to try to extract the large, thick dirt patches and scratches. Add our best friend, the Levels adjustment. Bring the Black levels up, the White levels down, and the Gamma up a little until the large thick dirt patches are the most apparent things you see; then click OK. There's no right or wrong to this, it's all to taste. You should have something like Figure 2.28.

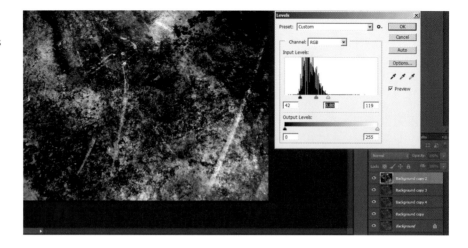

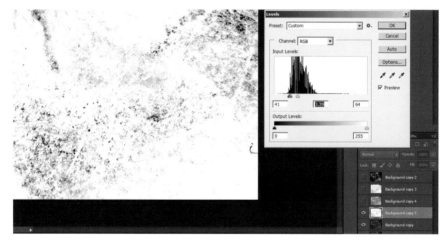

Temporarily turn off the visibility of the first copy by clicking the eyeball icon to the left of the layer to toggle visibility on/off and select the second copy. For this one, you're going to try to extract the finer, grittier dirt. Again, add a Levels adjustment. Bring the White levels almost all the way down to the bottom of the histogram, the Black levels up to the base or foot of the curve, and the Gamma levels toward the Black levels to get a fine gritty result like in Figure 2.29; then click OK.

Hide this Layer and move to the third. For this one, you'll just bring the White levels down to the front end of the curve and leave the rest alone, which should look something like Figure 2.30; then, again, click OK.

For the fourth copy, add a Levels adjustment, bring the White levels down about half as much as in the previous copy, and then apply Filter menu >

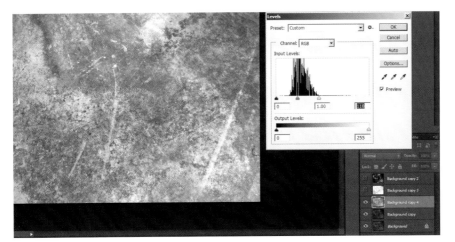

[Figure 2.30]
Levels adjustment to bring the White levels down to the front end of the curve

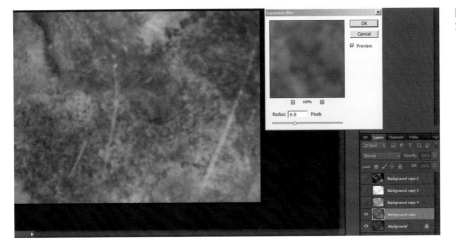

[Figure 2.31]
Slight Gaussian Blur added

Blur > Gaussian Blur of about 7 pixels or so, which should give you something that looks similar to Figure 2.31.

That's it! Now let's put them to use.

The Five Magical Uses of Grunge and Grime Maps

The most amazing demonstration of how procedurally extracting grunge and grime maps can add realism to your VFX is to take the most unrealistic samples you can find and then make them look photo real. You usually (but not always) want to use grunge maps that are appropriate for what you're trying to create. That is, for wood, you'd use a wood-based extraction; for peeling plaster, use peeling plaster; and so on. Since we're using dirty concrete floor grunge and grime maps, we'll take a completely unrealistic logo and make it look like it could actually be a real one on a concrete floor. Use whatever unrealistic and perfect colors you'd like for this example (colorful vector logos work well for this, too—a simple web search for "vector logos" will give you hundreds of great examples).

Create a new file and follow along. For this example, I'll fill the entire screen with a perfect 0,0,255 Blue. Next I'll type some big thick letters using a perfect 255,0,0 Red, which gives me what's shown in Figure 2.32.

Yuck, right? Remember, *nothing in nature is perfect, that's why it's perfect.* There's no such thing as *perfect* colors, so let's desaturate each of the blue and red graphic layers a bit using the Hue/Saturation tool, as seen in Figure 2.33.

Now let's use grunge and grime maps to demonstrate these five magical uses.

[Figure 2.32]
A very unnatural perfect 0,0,255 (Blue) and 255,0,0 (Red) image

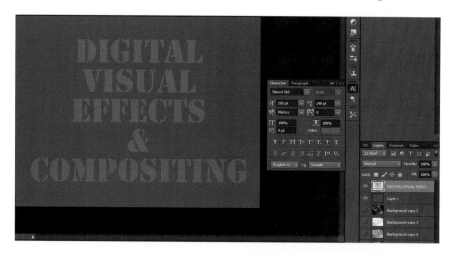

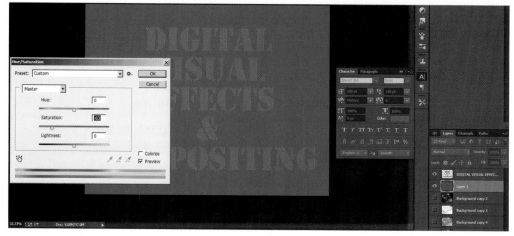

[Figure 2.33] Desaturated layers using the Hue/Saturation tool

1. Stripping Paint and Surfaces

The first magical use is to strip paint and surfaces. For this, I want you to be light-handed at first. Remember from the "Alpha Channels" section of this chapter that the darker or lighter the alpha, the more strongly it is either opaque or transparent—or more accurately in this case, the more or less it is selected. First select your text layer and then turn the visibility of everything off. Turn on the visibility of the darkest grunge map (this will select the *least* amount).

Switch to the Channels tab, choose any channel, and then click the Load Channel as Selection button. The grunge map loads as a selection, as shown in Figure 2.34.

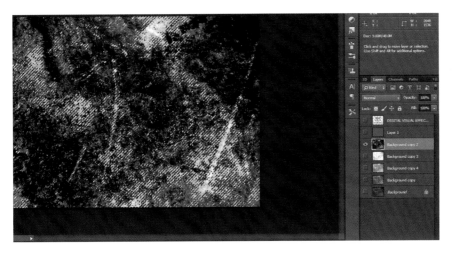

[Figure 2.34]
Grunge map loaded as a selection

Turn your logo images back on and make sure the top layer or lettering is selected (press Ctrl+H to temporarily hide the "marching ants" selection indicator). Then press Delete. You should notice some of your logo or lettering disappears as if worn away. Press Ctrl+H to unhide the selection and then Ctrl+D to deselect everything.

Make a duplicate of your BG color layer and add a Hue/Saturation, desaturating a little more and darkening the bottom of the colored layers. Repeat the previous process and strip away some of the upper solid layer. You should have something that looks like Figure 2.35.

You can repeat this process as much as you'd like or even perform it again with other grunge or grime maps.

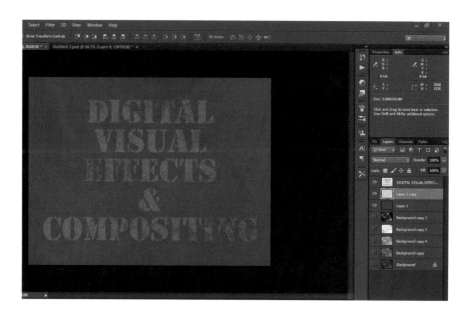

2. Dirtying Down

Next, you'll use grunge maps for dirtying down your textures. Select a grunge map you'd like to use (in this case, I'll try the really light one) and make a copy of it by dragging it down to the Create New Layer icon. Drag this copy to the top of the stack and set its Blend mode to Multiply, which should give you something that looks like Figure 2.36.

You can also adjust the Opacity slider to taste. Experiment and add another grunge or grime map, trying different Blend modes to see how they affect the results.

3. Randomizing Maps

You can also use grunge and grime maps to break up and randomize other textures that may repeat or not have enough variation. In this case, you have plenty of variation, so we can skip this one.

4. Using Grunge and Grime Maps as 2D Texture Displacements

Notice how, even with all of that paint/texture stripped away and dirt added, the text is still relatively perfect, with perfect edges everywhere. That's gotta go. Turn off the visibility of everything except the blurred version of the grunge map you created, and then save this file as a "copy" .psd (make sure to uncheck layers). Next, select your text or logo layer and select Filter menu > Distort > Displace as you see in Figure 2.37. When prompted, select the blurred grunge map you saved. You can also add another Levels adjustment to the blurred grunge map file you're using to increase the effect. If you'd like more of a harsh tearing and displacement, save out an unblurred copy. Try the default values of 10, 10, and then experiment until you get the effect you want. The result should slightly displace the lettering, similar to what you see in Figure 2.38.

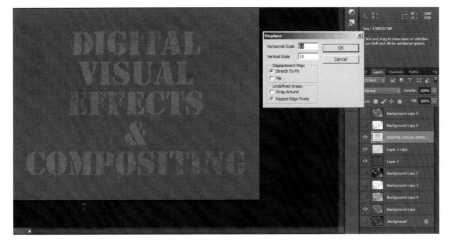

[Figure 2.37] Before layer displacement

When you're done experimenting, turn the visibility of all the dirt layers back on. Your result should now look similar to Figure 2.39.

[Figure 2.38] After layer displacement

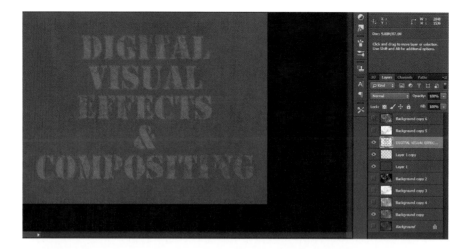

[Figure 2.39] Dirt layer visibility turned back on

[Figure 2.40] Another desaturation added

Press Ctrl+A to Select All, then choose Edit menu > Copy Merged, and then paste once or twice (if you want a backup) by choosing Edit menu > Paste. This will paste a copy of the entire texture so far. Feel free to add another desaturation (Figure 2.40) if you feel it's still looking a little too bright and colorful.

5. Using 3D Lighting Bump Maps and Displacements

Finally, the last magical step. Choose one of the medium gray grunge maps and turn off the visibility of everything else for a moment. In the Channels tab, drag a copy of one of the channels of the grunge map into the Create New Channel icon (the same as the Create New Layer icon, but on the Channel tab). This creates a copy of the grunge map and places it as the alpha in the scene. (Feel free to click the name of the channel to rename it for easier identification if you'd like.)

Reselect RGB and go back to the Layers tab. Turn on one of the merged copies and select it. From the top menu select Filter menu > Render > Lighting Effects. Change the Light type to Spotlight and the color to White. Rotate and widen the light using the little circle handles on the light to get a glancing angle across your texture. Make sure Gloss is turned off and increase the Ambient to around 50–65.

Now the magic! Under the Texture tab, select the copy of the grunge map alpha you copied in the Channels tab and raise the height (I've found that around 2 or 3 is a pretty good starting point, but feel free to experiment). You should see something like Figure 2.41 appear—a really nice textured surface!

[Figure 2.41]
Lighting applied using alpha as Texture

After you're satisfied, click OK to accept and feel free to add additional desaturation (Figures 2.42 and 2.43), Levels adjustments, or even copies you've added together with blend modes to get the effect that you're looking for.

The finished texture is shown in Figure 2.44.

[Figure 2.42]
One last desaturation—
before…

[Figure 2.43]
…and after

[Figure 2.44]
The finished texture

Other Matched Texture/Layer/Element Sets

The preceding tutorial shows that you can do amazing things with just these different types of basic grayscale images. But the fun doesn't end with alphas and grunge maps. You can utilize these same types of grayscale images to affect and represent many other types of image data that you can use for 3D texturing and VFX work.

In a typical 3D modeling/rendering application, there are many different types of maps you should know about in order to fully understand how light is reacting with your model in the virtual 3D world and why your image looks the way it does. These maps include the following:

Color

- **Color map:** A color or image map that determines what color will be seen (and where); one of the few maps that actually uses color information.

Luminance

- **Luminosity map:** A grayscale map that determines what parts of a surface should appear to be self-illuminating.

- **Glow map:** A grayscale map that determines where a surface should appear to *glow* or radiate light (as opposed to being just self-illuminated).

Reflectivity

- **Diffuse map:** A grayscale map that determines where a surface's raw color reflectance will be shown or not. If a color map is associated with the texture, this channel will dictate how much of that color/map/image will be seen.

- **Specularity map:** A grayscale map that dictates where a surface's reflective hotspot will be seen (to give the impression that the surface is reflective). This channel should be balanced with the Diffuse map, as both are actually two sides of the same reflective-quality coin (meaning as one increases, the other should theoretically decrease and vice versa; the idea being that the more a surface is shiny, the more reflective it becomes, hence, the less diffuse).

- **Specularity Breakup map:** A grayscale map that mimics the way dirt, smudges, fingerprints, and so on dampen the apparent reflectivity of a reflective surface, causing it to be less reflective wherever dirt is present.

This creates a more realistic-looking surface. Perfectly clean, shiny, smudgeless materials are rare in the real world.

- **Glossiness map:** A grayscale map that determines how small or tight the specularity hotspot will be. A surface such as brushed aluminum will have a very low value (close to black), whereas a surface such as porcelain or lacquer or a liquid such as water will have a very high glossiness value (closer to white).

Transparency

- **Transparency map:** A grayscale map that dictates where a surface is transparent or see-through (such as glass). One hundred percent transparent, clear, or see-through would be white; non-transparent or not see-though would be black.

- **Opacity map:** Some applications use an Opacity map instead of a Transparency map. They're the same thing, just opposite. An Opacity map determines where a surface is opaque, or not see-through. White would be completely 100% opaque, and black, 0% opaque, or completely transparent.

- **Refraction map:** A grayscale map that shows where a surface is refractive or not. *Refraction* is the bending of light and is used to show the light-bending properties of surfaces such as liquids, crystal, or other transparent, but light-bending, materials.

- **Translucency map:** A grayscale map controlling where a surface is *translucent* (allowing some light to show through, but not necessarily transparent). The light glowing through a lit candle and the light showing shadows glowing through a closed curtain are good examples of translucency.

Bump

- **Bump map:** A grayscale image that controls the *fake* 3D shadowing/modeling properties of a surface (*fake* because no real surface distortion is happening—it is, in fact, just a lighting trick). A bump map does a good job of adding the subtle appearance of 3D to a surface without adding actual complexity to a 3D model, making it an efficient cheat in many circumstances.

- **Normal map:** An RGB image that creates a bump map–like effect but calculates the effect using more data (the red, green, and blue channels) and the *surface normal direction* creating a more detailed "bump" look.

Displacement

- **Displacement map:** Unlike its bump map counterpart, a displacement map actually does modify the surface to create complexity, bump, and distortion. Displacement modeling is a powerful technique. I cover it in great detail in Chapters 14 and 15.

No matter how complicated the texture or composite is as a whole, at its core it is still a simple grayscale image representing 0% to 100% of *something*. Whether that something is a color channel, alpha (or level of transparency), specularity (or the hotspot associated with shininess), or Z-depth (distance from camera), at its core, it is still just a 0% to 100% (or 0 to 255 in 8-bit) of *something*. And this something will be perfectly aligned with every other layer of something above and underneath it to create a representation you can fine-tune and adjust each parameter for.

Let's take a look at a few of the other grayscale images/channels in the matched set that makes up the image shown in Figure 2.45. You can see that we can use grayscale images/maps to determine where the color of our diffuse lighting (Figure 2.46), specular highlights on all the metal and glass reflective surfaces (Figure 2.47), specular breakup where dirt and smudges break up those highlights (Figure 2.48), transparency of the glass materials (Figure 2.49), and others will be seen, all using the same principles of 100% where the grayscale image/map is white, 0% where it's black, and proportionately wherever it is a degree of gray.

[Figure 2.45]
Render of a steampunk blimp

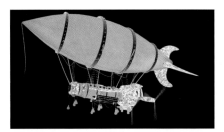

[**Figure 2.46**] The Diffuse channel

[**Figure 2.47**] The Specular channel

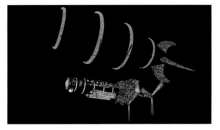

[**Figure 2.48**] A Specular Breakup channel

[**Figure 2.49**] A Transparency channel dictates where a surface should be transparent or opaque. In this image, you can see that the glass electrode tubes and windows are mostly white (or mostly transparent).

Cloning

No, don't worry, we're not going to get into any kind of philosophical debate here…. I'm referring to *image* cloning. In the world of VFX, sometimes nothing can get you out of a bind quicker than a little image cloning. *Cloning* is the process of copying pixels from one position on an image, or from another image entirely, and pasting them into a different area of the same or other image, as shown in Figure 2.50.

Cloning techniques can be used to remove or replicate elements and help create digital matte paintings (Figure 2.51).

You can use cloning to remove blemishes and flaws while doing beauty work, or repair dust and scratches in old film footage (*dustbusting* is shown in Figures 2.52 and 2.53).

You can even use cloning to do crowd and object replications (Figures 2.54 through 2.57).

[Figure 2.50]
Cloning an actor with a positional offset from within the same frame

[Figure 2.51]
Cloning concrete cracks, damage, and debris onto a clean street to create a post-apocalyptical setting

[Figure 2.52] Frame with large dust particle near actor

[Figure 2.53] Dust particle removed by cloning from nearby clear area

[Figure 2.54] Aerial shot of parking lot with cars; more cars needed to be added digitally

[Figure 2.55] Grid created with Vanishing Point Clone tool to allow cloning in perspective

[Figure 2.56] Cars being cloned/added to empty part of parking area

[Figure 2.57] Finished parking area with cloned additions

Basic Cloning Techniques, Tips, Tricks, and Strategies

There are two main strategies to help you when cloning. They are your best friends when you have to either remove or replicate elements in a scene. For simplicity's sake, and as a good memory hook, I'll call them randomness and order. Which one you should use depends on the content of the image itself. After determining what element in the image needs to be removed or added, examine the surrounding image features and decide whether they are more random or orderly. Random features include things like grass, bushes with many small random leaves, large bodies of water, and so forth. Orderly features would include things like walls with straight edges, buildings or elements with linear or repeating features or patterns, and so on.

To use the Cloning tool, we select the Rubber Stamp icon from the toolbar on the left, Alt+click the point on the image or area where you want to clone from (called the *source*), and then move the cursor to where you want to copy the source pixels to (called the *target*) and simply start painting with the offset pixels.

Randomness

If you determine that the surrounding features to the element you need to remove are random, you will want to use this randomness to fool the eye or camouflage the element. You use pieces of surrounding randomness the way a sniper adds twigs and branches to his ghillie suit to blend into the surrounding foliage. In this case, I've pieced together two images to create a seamless panoramic background plate for an effects shot. The problem is, the two sky plates don't match very well—they leave a nasty, very obvious seam. This is what we need to blend (Figure 2.58). You'll use bits and pieces of the randomness of the surrounding clouds to paste over and obscure the seam (Figure 2.59).

Make sure you take large enough samples of the surrounding sky that you don't create repeating patterns (which the human eye is expert at recognizing). Make certain that the areas being cloned lie in the same general Z-depth as the area being covered to assure there are no inconsistencies in size and perspective.

After finishing the cloning of the seam and other nearby elements, and generally color correcting the shot, the finished, seamless sky is complete (Figure 2.60).

[Figure 2.58] Offending seam created by combining two different sky plates

Blend

[Figure 2.59] Bits and pieces of random nearby clouds are cloned over the seam using a soft-edged clone brush to allow for the better blending of the edges.

Blend

[Figure 2.60] The finished seamless panoramic BG plate

Finished clone shot

Order

When there is no randomness to help you mask your cloning work, you look to your other friend, order. In this example, again I've combined two images into a panoramic BG plate for the effects shot. This time, however, there are no random features to hide the seam. Everything from the straight edges of the buildings to the repeating windows and concrete texture is orderly (Figure 2.61).

Figures 2.62 and 2.63 show that a better seam location might be the edge of the elevator shaft portion of the building jutting off the side.

Two photos
overlap here

Bad seams

[**Figure 2.61**] Offending seam created by combining two different building plates

[**Figure 2.62**] Bad seams

Good potential
seam location

[**Figure 2.63**] Better
potential seam location

Eliminating
the seam

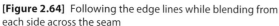

[Figure 2.64] Following the edge lines while blending from each side across the seam

[Figure 2.65] The finished, blended shot

When using order as your guide, you can use a technique I call *follow and continue*. This means you find features that are linear, or that repeat in a pattern, and then you simply follow them and continue them, taking care to use the same position, spacing, and so on, while still blending from nearby areas on either side (Figure 2.64) using a soft brush as in the random example.

The finished shot (Figure 2.65) is a seamless panoramic blend.

2D Visual Effects

When you're not dealing with 3D VFX, and you're in the realm of 2D VFX, you're mainly dealing with paint (which includes cloning), matte and roto work, and compositing. Let's take a look at each of these.

Paint: Wire and Rig Removal

In the old days of VFX there was a lot more 2D paint VFX animation. These animations were hand-painted, rotoscoped (frame-by-frame) animations used for effects, such as electricity arcing, light sabers, and even cartoon animations traced over live action movies and then painted on animation cels. Today, most hand paint work consists of removing unwanted elements from a scene or performing hand extractions of difficult elements that need to be replaced back on top of a filmed or computer-generated (CG) element.

[Figure 2.66] Super hero on bluescreen

[Figure 2.67] Wires still remain after the key extraction.

[Figure 2.68] Our super hero, flying free thanks to roto clone wire/rig removal

In VFX, one of the most frequent uses of 2D paint work is to remove wires, rigs, and harnesses used to protect actors and stunt men and women during dangerous VFX stunts. Let's take a look at the ubiquitous flying super hero shot, one of 2D paint work's simplest forms. Figure 2.66 shows one frame of the original footage shot on a bluescreen with wires suspending our super hero. But even after extracting the bluescreen (BS), you can see there's still a problem—the wires remain (Figure 2.67).

In this scenario, the only choice is to do a wire/rig removal using frame-by-frame roto cloning techniques (whether by hand painting or using spline-based roto tools). Once the wires are removed (see Chapter 9 for information on wire removal), the super hero can fly free (Figure 2.68).

Matte and Roto

You may have already deduced that, since an alpha channel used to extract an actor or element is simply a grayscale image, it's entirely possible to create and/or modify an alpha channel or matte completely by hand, painting each frame one at a time. This may sound like a daunting task—and it definitely can be (it's the way it was done for many decades and through the optical FX printing days)—however, it is still is a viable option, and sometimes it's your only one.

When it comes to extracting actors or elements, your first line of defense should always be to use some relatively self-matting method. I say *relatively* because the extraction process, on a professional level, is rarely if ever a one-click automated process. Nevertheless, there are some tried-and-true techniques you can use to get the best results with the least expenditure. The following sections discuss some of these.

[tip]

The best strategy in VFX should always be to approach any VFX shot using the most efficient means possible. That means using the most efficient means cost-wise, time-wise, and resource-wise, including manpower. I teach my students to have "multiple, preplanned lines of defense." Here is what this means: form a strategy known and proven to be very effective and efficient and take that course of action first; if it fails or becomes too time/cost/resource consuming, jump to the next line of defense; and so on.

[**Figure 2.69**] Actor Chad Ayers filmed on a bluescreen stage

Self-Matting

By *self-matting* techniques, I'm usually referring to some form of chroma key extraction method. The subject is filmed against a (hopefully) evenly lit, highly chrominant (color saturated) and consistently colored background (BG), like the bluescreen (BS) shown in Figure 2.69.

Keying software is used to "pull" the best possible extraction, retaining as much detail as possible in the subject or element, particularly at the edges. Although a one button–click solution may sound attractive, unfortunately, it is rarely ever the case. You can, however, help this process go as smoothly and efficiently as possible if you follow the method the top-end pros use: Your eye should *always* be on the edge.

Garbage Mattes

There's no reason to make the keyer work to remove areas of the image that are nowhere near your subject, even if your footage has a well-lit bluescreen or greenscreen. So your first step is *always* to create a garbage matte. A *garbage matte* is a matte loosely created around the subject that literally cuts out the "garbage" in the scene or frame, as shown in Figure 2.70.

The result leaves just a small amount of actual bluescreen around the subject for the keyer to have to contend with, shown in Figure 2.71.

However, as you can see in Figure 2.72, when you apply the keyer, select your key color to extract, and then look at the alpha channel in the viewer, you can see that, although you've retained a good amount of detail around the edge—remember the most important factor is to *always* keep your eye on the

[**Figure 2.70**] A garbage matte cutting away stage flags, C-stands, the ladder, and everything not in the immediate vicinity of our subject

[**Figure 2.71**] The garbage matte leaves only a little bluescreen around the actor for the keyer to have to extract.

[Figure 2.72] Initial key extraction leaves too many gray (transparent) areas in the actor (he was wearing a light blue shirt as well due to scene scheduling issues, so we knew we'd have to contend with this).

[Figure 2.73] Trying to crush the matte to get rid of the transparency (gray) in the alpha/matte results in losing tons of edge detail.

[Figure 2.74] A core matte fills in any unwanted "holes" or transparency in the alpha/matte.

[Figure 2.75] The finished combined (garbage matte, key matte, core matte) alpha/matte

edge to make sure you don't lose that precious edge detail—there is quite a bit of non-white area inside the actor that will result in him being transparent. Remember, gray in our alpha channel equals partial transparency. We definitely don't want that.

If you try to get rid of that stuff by crushing the matte using the keyer controls, you will crush and lose all your edge detail, as Figure 2.73 shows.

Core Mattes

In this case, you'll undo those keyer controls and get rid of that unwanted transparency using the opposite of the garbage matte, called a *core matte*. Normally, you'd create a core matte out of multiple shapes (as you'll see in Chapter 3), but for clear illustration purposes, I've created a single-shape core matte (shown in Figure 2.74) so that you can easily see and understand the concept here.

The combined matte is perfectly solid on the inside and perfectly transparent on the outside (see Figure 2.75); only the edges having any semi-transparency where the fine details like hair require it.

Edge Mattes

In addition to mattes that address the outside and inside of the subject, you can also create mattes to fine-tune the edges of your mattes. These are, not surprisingly, called edge mattes. Edge mattes can help you fine-tune

[note]

Always check your extraction mattes for holes or other errors by temporarily applying a gamma adjustment in the viewer. This will allow you to see any areas that might otherwise be too faint to see.

The goal of this process is to create a matte that you will then use or combine with the original clean footage to accomplish a pristine extraction, and not to use the keyed footage that is the result of the keyer (as many people tend to do). Most keyers inherently degrade the original footage considerably, so using the created matte to extract the original pristine footage ensures the absolute best quality.

everything from edge softness (like we did with the alpha blur at the beginning of the chapter) to light wraps (specialized mattes that give the illusion of wrapping the FG element in the light of the BG plate). You'll dive into edge softness and light wrap in detail in Chapter 6.

Fine-Tuning Mattes

You can use many of the steps and techniques from the beginning of this chapter to fine-tune selections on your alpha/mattes as well. You can add blur to soften them, clamp the blurred version using a Levels adjustment to erode or dilate them, add filters and effects, and a whole lot more. Chapters 5 and 6 explore some of these cool concepts.

Compositing

Once your key is pulled and you have an acceptable alpha/matte, you're left with the actor alone on a transparent BG, as seen in Figure 2.76. To place him into another image or environment, you need to composite, or comp, him into another image, as shown in Figure 2.77.

Not surprisingly, to do compositing, you will need to use a compositing application, or compositor.

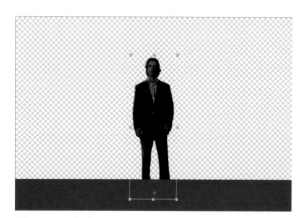

[Figure 2.76] The actor extracted and all alone on a transparent BG

[Figure 2.77]
The actor comped into his new BG

Compositing Applications

A *compositing application* is a piece of software that allows you to combine, process, manipulate, animate, and apply effects to images or motion footage. Many compositing applications are available on the market today. They all have different strengths, weaknesses, features, bells, and whistles, but the core functionality of all of them is pretty much the same. They generally fall into one of two categories: layer-based compositing or nodal-based compositing. These two categories approach compositing using slightly different method-ologies, but again, with core functionality that is pretty much the same (see Figure 2.78).

After Effects: Layer-based compositor

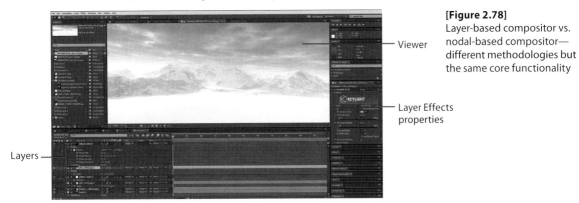

Layers

Viewer

Layer Effects properties

[Figure 2.78]
Layer-based compositor vs. nodal-based compositor— different methodologies but the same core functionality

Nuke: Nodal-based compositior

Nodes

Viewer

Node properties

Layer-based Compositors

Layer-based compositors combine their elements by stacking them up, layer on top of layer, on a timeline. Adobe's After Effects is among the most popular in this category. The strength of a layer-based compositor is in working with long duration composites that have many components that need to be synchronized very precisely in time. The ability to lay all the components out on a timeline and cut and paste them—like in a word processor—while compositing, allows for a speedy workflow for long projects where there are not many people working on each shot. Layer-based compositors also tend to be very intuitive to work with, especially for those accustomed to working with photo or video editing software. The layer-based compositors' weaknesses are in dealing with huge composites, especially in a professional feature film environment where enormous file sizes and very complex composites can easily bring a layer-based compositing application to a crashing halt.

Nodal-based Compositors

Nodal-based compositors combine elements and add effects by *piping* together (or connecting using string-like pipes or noodles) a series of modules, or *nodes*. You can think of nodes as little containers that hold a tool. Each node (tool) is represented by a small graphical icon that is placed in one of the application's work areas or grids and then connected to other nodes to create the finished composite. A project consisting of nodes is called a *node-flow* or *script*. The Foundry's Nuke is among the most popular and widely used in this category. At first glance, a huge node-flow can look extremely intimidating for the uninitiated, but a nodal-based compositor really works in much the same way as a layer-based one. They both have viewports, timelines, and parameter/property controls for each effect or function added. They both combine and animate images, and both use alpha channels and mattes, and so on. They're just packaged differently and take a little getting used to. I highly recommend learning both.

The advantage of a nodal-based compositor is its efficient use of elements, assets, and data, which allows it to work very efficiently on much larger, more complex composites. Nodes allow you to reuse an asset by simply piping another pipe off of a node and into any other node or node tree you want, as opposed to having to reload a copy of the asset to put into another layer. This allows for fast, flexible work with massively complex node-flows and excellent collaborative environment pipelines such as in large VFX studios, where hundreds of artists might all be working on different aspects of the same complex

VFX shot. Nodal-based compositors' weakness is that they are difficult to very quickly sync and align complex, long-form, timing-intensive composites.

Keyer Types and Concepts

Many of the keyers used in compositing are available on many applications and platforms. Keyers such as Keylight, Primatte, and Ultimatte are available on both layer-based and nodal-based compositing applications and can be divided into three general categories.

2D Color Space Keyers

2D color space keyers, such as Keylight, work primarily by allowing you to select a key color (usually by means of an eyedropper tool selection) and to expand and modify the selection based on tolerance levels that are centered on a 2D color space selection method (see Figures 2.79 and 2.80).

[Figure 2.79]
The key color is selected in 2D color space

2D color space keyer

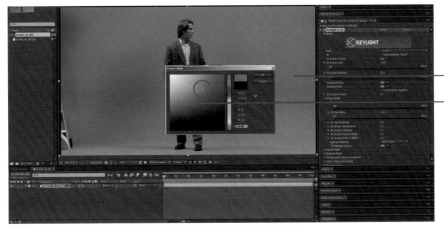

[Figure 2.80]
Tolerance ranges expand or contract in 2D color space around this key color.

2D color space keyer

Key color in 2D color space

3D Color Space Keyers

3D color space keyers, such as Primatte, work by allowing you to select a range, or volume, of key colors (usually by scrubbing an area with a tool selection). You can then expand and modify your selection based on tolerance levels centered on this 3D color volume selection in 3D color space (see Figures 2.81 and 2.82). This allows you to make very precise selections that group and expand into neighboring color values.

[Figure 2.81]
The key color is selected in 3D color space.

3D color space keyer —

[Figure 2.82]
Tolerance ranges expand or contract in 3D color space around this key color.

3D color space keyer —

Key color in 3D color space

Advanced Keyers

Whereas 2D and 3D color space keyers work by allowing you to choose key colors and then expand and modify your selection based on tolerance levels centered on these selections in either 2D or 3D color space, advanced keyers, such as Ultimatte and Nuke's Image Based Keyer (IBK) also add the ability to load and analyze real (or create fake) clean plates (see Figure 2.83). These clean plates allow for the additional comparison of *difference* value data between the original and clean versions of the image to be added into the calculation and extraction process, for even greater precision of extractions, and the amazing retention of edges, shadows, reflections, and transparency.

Creating selections, cloning, and keying are some of the most common procedures you will perform in creating VFX. In the next chapter you will learn three more powerful tools for your VFX arsenal: rotoscoping, motion tracking, and 2D matchmoving.

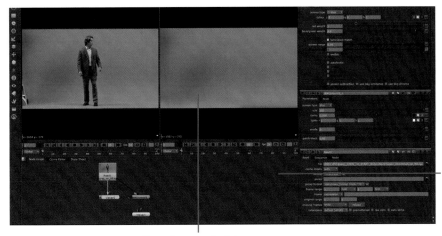

[Figure 2.83]
The creation of a fake clean plate allows for the image difference comparison data to be added into the extraction calculation process.

Advanced keyer

Key color + created clean
plate difference

CHAPTER THREE

Rotoscoping, Motion Tracking, and 2D Matchmoving

In addition to selections, extractions, cloning, and compositing, the other three most important skills in a visual effects artist's arsenal—which you will need to understand and become proficient with—are rotoscoping, motion tracking, and matchmoving. Rotoscoping allows us to very accurately modify frames of a sequence or animation on a frame-by-frame-accurate basis. By motion tracking footage, we can precisely follow the motion of a subject in frame, or the sequence as a whole, and then do a wide variety of things with the tracking data we obtain—everything from attaching a 2D or 3D object and stabilizing and destabilizing the image, to semi-automating our roto, paint, or cloning work.

Introducing Roto

Perhaps one of the most important and most misunderstood terms in VFX is the term rotoscoping, or, more commonly these days, roto for short. The term is derived from the old days of cel animation in which artists who wanted to create lifelike motion in their animated characters would use a machine called a rotoscope, which projected filmed images onto the animator's animation plate (yes, the same plate we derive our VFX terms from, such as background plate, foreground plate, clean plate, and so on). The animator would then trace, draw, or paint over the image onto a glass or acetate animation cel (celluloid made of cellulose nitrate and later cellulose acetate). This process became known as rotoscoping. The job of painting frame-by-frame became rotopaint.

As the use of computers emerged onto the animation and VFX scene, it became more efficient to create a shape frame-by-frame on a computer screen and simply move the shape, rather than repainting it every frame as had been previously done. To make things even more efficient, the use of spline-based tools to create shapes quickly became the state of the art because splines (which are mathematically created) could, additionally, be modified periodically (or keyframed) and the computer would automatically create (interpolate) the in-between or tween shapes. The job of rotopaint quickly gave way to the new form, rotosplining (rotoscoping using splines, which interpolate between keyframes).

Rotoscoping has since become synonymous with anything that is done on a frame-by-frame basis, from the hand painting of mattes to clay and stop motion animation. All of these have come to be known collectively as roto.

Rotoscoping Mattes

One of the most basic uses of roto is in the creation of mattes. As you saw in Chapter 2, to most efficiently perform key color extractions for compositing, it is critical that we use garbage and core mattes to allow us to retain as much detail as possible in the fine edges of our image. Because our image is likely moving, rotosplines will be the tool of choice to create our mattes. When rotoing, you will be able to move entire rotospline shapes and combine them into the final matte instead of having to paint entire mattes by hand every frame, which is very tedious and time consuming. The computer helps you by drawing all of the frames in-between (or tween) your keyframes. You draw a frame of your rotospline, set a keyframe, move the timeline to another position, and set a new keyframe, and the software creates and animates all the tween frames.

There is much disinformation as to the strategies for placing keyframes while doing roto work—continually halving the number of frames, placing keyframes at each halfway mark, placing keyframes every ten frames, placing keyframes every *x* number of frames, and so on. All of these are poor, inaccurate, and wasteful strategies for doing roto and will usually create far too many keyframes, resulting in much more work than is necessary, as well as poor matte motion.

Roto Basics: Types of Rotosplines

To get started with a roto project, you first need to decide which is the best type of rotospline to use for the particular task at hand. The two most common types of rotosplines used for roto work are the *Bezier* curve and the *B-spline* curve.

Bezier

Bezier (pronounced bez-ee-ay) curves are parametric curves created by placing points, or *vertices*, which are then automatically connected by rubber-band–like line sections. Simply placing points will give you sharp-pointed, or *cusp*, corners, like those you see in Figure 3.1, whereas clicking and then dragging the mouse will pull out two tangent handles from the point that can be controlled together and used to form a smooth curve, like the top point in Figure 3.2.

[note]

Roto work is still a very patience-intensive job. A good way to approach roto is to get into the proper mindset for the task. You will be spending a lot of time doing very repetitive and detailed work, so being in a rushed or impatient mood will no doubt result in frustration. Get relaxed, pour a cup of coffee or tea, perhaps (for some people) put on some relaxing music you enjoy. Roto is much more enjoyable if you can get into a groove or "flow" (the Zen-like state of relaxed free-flowing concentration).

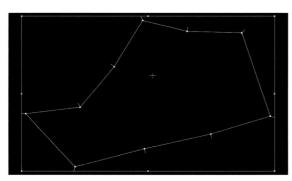

[**Figure 3.1**] Sharp-edged, or cusp, Bezier curve

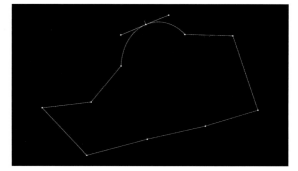

[**Figure 3.2**] Tangent handles pulled out to create a smooth curve

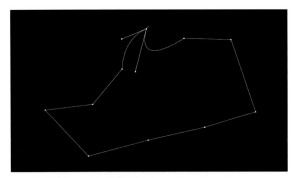

[Figure 3.3] Tangent handle broken to create sharp or obtuse angles

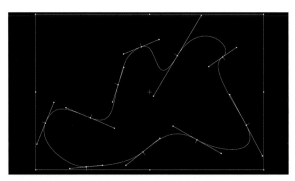

[Figure 3.4] All vertices converted to smooth

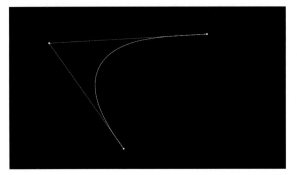

[Figure 3.5] B-spline curve interpolated between three points

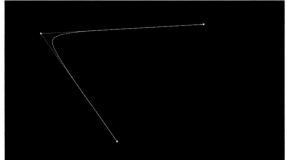

[Figure 3.6] Center point weight/tension increased to create sharper curve

These tangent handles can also be broken and controlled individually to create sharp or obtuse angles and curves, as seen in Figure 3.3.

Because Bezier curves are parametric, their vertices can easily be converted back and forth from curves to cusped, and tangent handles can be animated or modified at any time, as seen in Figure 3.4.

B-Spline

B-spline curves, unlike Bezier curves, require three points, or vertices, to create a curve. A B-spline uses these three points to interpolate a smooth curve between them as you can see in Figure 3.5.

Although B-spline curves don't have the tangent handle controls that Bezier curves have, they can be more accurately controlled by adjusting the weight or tension of each vertex. You can think of this weight/tension as being like gravity. The stronger the weight or tension is, the stronger the pull of gravity on the curve toward the vertex, as shown in Figure 3.6.

Deciding Which Type of Curve to Use

Each type of curve has its advantages. For rotosplining hard surfaces with straight edges, Bezier curves are much faster because they are straight by default until the tangent handles are pulled out from a point. I prefer the workflow for using them for most everything, since once you get the hang of them, creating almost any shape or following virtually any edge is fast and intuitive.

On the other hand, many artists prefer B-splines and feel they are faster using a "put the points down quickly and come back to refine them after" workflow. B-splines are particularly good for rotoing organic shapes because they are always perfectly smooth by default. You can think of the two different types of splines as almost opposite workflows, Bezier splines are sharp edged by default, but you can make them smooth, and B-splines are smooth by default but you can make them sharp edged.

Advanced Spline Features

Although rotosplines are great at creating sharp and smooth curves, the principles we discussed in Chapter 2 should instantly come to mind. Almost nothing in reality has a perfectly sharp edge. Fortunately, most high-end applications have solutions for this exact challenge. First, and simplest, is the same technique we used in Chapter 2—a feather or blur. Most professional applications provide for not only an edge feather/blur control but for various types of falloff as well. In addition, the best roto apps provide a double-edged rotospline, which allows for a second, and attached set

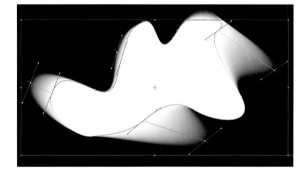

[Figure 3.7] A double-edged rotospline showing varying amounts of edge feathering

of curves to be pulled from the first, allowing for very precise feathered edges that can be custom tailored to your subject to account for varying amounts of motion or blur, as seen in Figure 3.7.

The Golden Rules of Roto

When rotoing, a definite set of Golden Rules should be followed to ensure the best and cleanest possible matte with the least amount of edge vibration or chatter. Engrain these Golden Rules in your memory; they are critical to good roto work:

1. Create your shapes with as few points as possible (the more points you have to deal with, the greater the chance of matte chatter).

2. Create your mattes using multiple individual roto shapes for every part of the subject that will move or change shape in profile within the sequence. (Although you may be tempted to create your mattes using one big roto shape, as in Figure 3.8, this will very likely end in disaster as soon as a part of the subject disappears into the body of the shape and reappears out the other side, as when an actor turns from side to side.) Creating your mattes using multiple individual animated shapes for each moving part (as seen in Figure 3.9) allows for whole shapes to be moved without individual points needing to be manipulated, thus reducing matte chatter.

[**Figure 3.8**] Bad roto—do not use one big shape like this.

[**Figure 3.9**] Good roto—proper break-up of shapes into small shapes that can be articulated as a whole

3. Think of creating a "paper puppet" when rotosplining people or subjects with moving parts; create rigid shapes for each part that doesn't change shape (i.e., for a person, you'd create a shape for the upper arm, connect it to a shape for the lower arm, connected to a shape for the hand, fingers, and so on). This allows for the simple rigid animation—via translation, rotation, and scale—of entire shapes without having to do extensive single point adjustments.

4. When animating shapes, find the frame where the subject moves farthest away from the rotoshape's position before either changing direction or

moving back toward the original position. That is the point at which you want to place your keyframe. In Figure 3.10, we see actor Chad Ayers at the forward most position in frame 1; by frame 50, he is at the farthest point back; and he has moved forward again toward his beginning position at frame 100. Frame 50, his farthest point, is where we will place the first keyframe. After this, we find the next farthest point he moves to before either changing direction or starting to move back toward this position, and place our keyframe at this frame. We continue this process until the spline is locked to the motion.

Frame 1 position

Frame 50 position
(keyframe)

Frame 100 position

[Figure 3.10]
Best frame at which to place
a roto keyframe

5. The object is to set as few keyframes as possible. This will deliver the cleanest and smoothest animation possible.

6. It is perfectly correct and common to start from the beginning and work forward, start at the end and work backward, start in the middle and work forward, then backward, and so on. Many times you will have to work in small segments as well.

7. When moving rotoshapes, your first line of defense is to try to move all, or as many of the shapes as possible, together by translating, scaling, and rotating them as a single unit.

8. If this isn't possible, try to move as many individual whole shapes as possible by translating, scaling, and rotating them as a single units.

9. If this isn't possible, try to move as many points together as possible by translating, scaling, and rotating them as a single unit.

10. Only as a last resort after all of the above are exhausted should you move individual points in a spline.

[note]

These procedures are critical to good roto work; they are not just suggestions!

[Figure 3.11] Matte created from rotosplines in Figure 3.9

Isolated Roto for Keying

In addition to utilizing rotosplines to create mattes for extractions, you can use rotosplines to isolate areas of an image that are particularly difficult to extract for one reason or another. In Figure 3.11 you can see the matte created from the combined splines seen in Figure 3.9. Notice how it would be extremely difficult to create a matte of the actor's hair using this method; you'd be trying to create individual shapes for each hair or set of hairs. For this, you can use an *isolated roto matte*, like the one in Figure 3.12, just to isolate and then key a specific feature—in this case the hair; you'd then combine the matte created with that key with the ones you created previously using rotosplines.

In Figure 3.13 you can see the matte created by using a *luminance key* (a key based on luminance or brightness) isolated with the matte from Figure 3.12. If we combine this matte with the roto matte in Figure 3.14, we get a very nice fully matted actor, complete with fine hair details, as seen in Figure 3.15.

[Figure 3.12] Isolated roto matte created to key only actor's hair

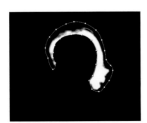

[Figure 3.13] Detailed hair matte created by luma keying hair isolated with matte from Figure 3.12

[Figure 3.14] Combined roto matte and overlay of isolated roto key area

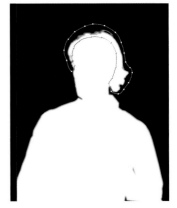

[Figure 3.15] Finished matte, created by combining mattes from Figures 3.11 and 3.13

Roto Applications

Although there are dedicated applications for sophisticated roto and tracker-assisted roto work, such as Imagineer's Mocha Pro (seen in Figure 3.16) and Silhouette, almost all compositing applications (including Nuke, After Effects, Fusion, Shake, etc.) will have very capable roto tools, which all work basically the same way.

[Figure 3.16] Mocha Pro planar tracking and roto application interface

2D Motion Tracking

Modern VFX artists don't have the luxury their early VFX predecessors had—using still, or *locked off*, VFX footage (where great care was taken to ensure that the camera didn't move at all to allow VFX elements to be more easily and perfectly aligned and integrated). Today, most VFX shots are going to be moving, and because of this, you have to have a way to integrate your VFX element using the same motion that is happening in the footage or it will be painfully apparent that your fake VFX element is floating awkwardly onscreen looking as if it were just poorly pasted on.

To ensure your VFX elements match and integrate perfectly, you will need to *motion track*, or track the motion, in the footage or sequence to which you will be adding an effect. In its simplest form, 2D motion tracking analyzes a specific set of pixels (which you identify) and then tries to follow those throughout the duration of the footage while recording the horizontal and vertical, or X and Y, coordinates. You can then use and reuse this set of data to move your VFX element in the scene to match the original camera's motion, or to make it easier to integrate other features.

Anatomy of a Motion Tracker

A motion tracker will almost always consist of three parts (as seen in Figure 3.17):

- **The pattern area:** This is the area defining the pattern that the motion tracker is to try to follow.

- **The search area:** This is the area or distance that the tracker will limit its search to, for the pattern defined in the pattern area, on any given frame.

- **The anchor target:** This is the point that any data will actually attach to.

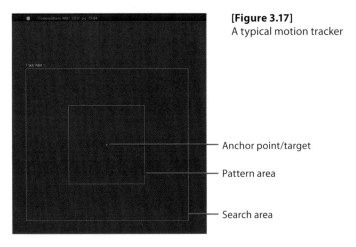

[Figure 3.17]
A typical motion tracker

Anchor point/target

Pattern area

Search area

Types of 2D Motion Tracking

There are a few different types of 2D motion trackers, each with its own purpose (and sometimes as a necessary fallback for another, when one doesn't work).

1 Point

The simplest of 2D tracks is a *1 point track*. A 1 point track uses one motion tracker (as seen in Figure 3.18) to track one pattern. This allows for the attachment of an element to the translational motion of the pattern being tracked in the horizontal and vertical, or X and Y, motion planes and is the go-to workhorse tracking method for simple tracks or when all else fails.

[Figure 3.18]
A 1 point track

[Figure 3.19]
A 2 point track

2 Point

Adding a second tracker, as seen in Figure 3.19, adds two functionalities:

- The added ability to track relative rotation between the two trackers

- The added ability to track relative (faked) scale between the two trackers as they move closer together or farther apart

[Figure 3.20]
A 4 point cornerpin track

4 Point Cornerpin

Tracking with four trackers, as seen in Figure 3.20, adds

- The ability to *pin* or stick an image to common flat plane targets such as billboard signs, computer screens, and so on

- The added ability to warp four corners of an element to add perceived (faked) perspective

The Golden Rules of Motion Tracking

Just as in roto, there is a definite set of Golden Rules that should be followed to ensure the best and cleanest possible track with the least amount of *noise* or *drift*. Like the Golden Rules for roto, engrain these Golden Rules in your memory; they are critical to good tracking and matchmoving work:

1. When selecting your pattern area, choose a pattern that has as many of these attributes as possible:

   - Has high contrast

   - Doesn't change shape during the course of the footage

   - Doesn't change lighting appearance (reflective, flashing, etc.)

   - Isn't occluded during the footage

- Contains distinct high-contrast corners or angles or is completely surroundable as is the case with a circle or sphere

- Doesn't contain long, continuous, unbroken lines or repetitive or similar patterns seen elsewhere in the scene

2. When selecting your pattern area, choose a pattern that is positioned

   - For a 1 point track—as close to the position where the CG or VFX element will appear as possible (especially in depth, or Z-space)

   - For a 2 point track—as far apart onscreen as possible but in the same depth or Z-space

   - For a 4 point cornerpin track—as close to the corners of the area where the CG or VFX element will be placed in the scene

3. When selecting the search area, make sure to first analyze the footage to determine how far the point to be tracked moves on any given frame:

   - Creating a search area that is too large will waste a lot of calculation, resulting in long track times, and is likely to lose the track mistaking something else in the image for the pattern area.

   - Creating a search area that is too small will quickly lose the track as the pattern area to be tracked moves outside of the area to be searched.

   - Creating tiny pattern or search areas can result in the tracker thinking film grain or video noise is motion and tracking it, thus resulting in a very jittery or noisy motion track.

4. Although the anchor point *may* be in the middle of the pattern area, it doesn't necessarily have to be. A common mistake is to assume it is the center. The anchor point can be placed anywhere in the scene (even outside of both tracking boxes) and is the point to which the motion data will be attached.

5. It is perfectly correct and common to start tracking from the beginning and work forward, start at the end and work backward, start in the middle and work forward, then backward, and so on. Many times you will have to work in small segments because the subject you are tracking becomes occluded in areas.

Comparing Good and Bad Tracking Targets

Take a look at Figures 3.21–3.28 in which you can compare a few good and bad tracker targets.

Figure 3.21 shows an example of a good 1 point tracker location. It has high contrast, is singular, and has a well-defined vertical and horizontal angle pattern with a search area that is not too large or too small.

Figure 3.22, on the other hand, shows poor 1 point tracker placement. In this case the tracker has been placed along a straight edge. Although this pattern area does have high contrast, there is nothing to lock onto vertically, so the tracker will not lock on and will slide around on the horizontal edge.

[Figure 3.21]
Good 1 point tracker location

[Figure 3.22]
Poor 1 point tracker placement

Figure 3.23 shows an example of good 2 point tracker placement. This location has both high contrast and well-defined vertical and horizontal angle patterns, has the trackers placed a good distance apart, and has search areas that are not too large or too small.

Though the 2 point tracker placements in Figure 3.24 have high contrast and well-defined vertical and horizontal angle patterns with search areas that are not too large or too small, this would be considered an example of poor placement because the trackers are placed too close together and rotational errors will be hugely amplified (see the following section, "2 Point Tracker Placement: Rotation and Scale Error Amplification").

[Figure 3.23]
Good 2 point tracker placement

[Figure 3.24]
Poor 2 point tracker placement

Figure 3.25 is also an example of poor 2 point tracker placement. It does exhibit high contrast and well-defined vertical and horizontal angle patterns, and trackers that have been placed fairly wide, the search areas are too large and will cause long tracking times and tracking errors. The trackers will likely jump to very similar looking nearby bridge pylons that are also within the search area boxes.

Although at first glance the tracker placement in Figure 3.26 might appear to be a good 1 point motion tracking target for an element to be placed in the distance near the palm tree, and although this example is high contrast and fairly "surroundable," remember that palm trees sway in the wind, which will likely result in erroneous tracking data. (You wouldn't want your CG building swaying, would you?)

[Figure 3.25]
Another example of poor 2 point tracker placement

[Figure 3.26]
A good example of a 1 point tracking target—or is it?

Figure 3.27 shows another poor example of 1 point tracker placement. In this image, the leaves on the tree are far too similar to all of the leaves in the entire group of trees. These leaves are also likely to move randomly in the wind, which will result in a very inaccurate, noisy/jittery track and data.

Figure 3.28 shows one more example of good 1 point tracker placement for an element that will be placed near the light pole in Z-space. Like the palm tree in Figure 3.26, this is a good high-contrast target, but it is in fact much better than the palm tree because it also contains almost perpendicular angles and is a fixed target that doesn't move.

[Figure 3.27]
A further example of poor 1 point tracker placement

[Figure 3.28]
Good 1 point tracker placement

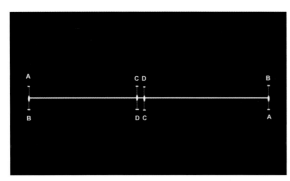

[**Figure 3.29**] A simple scene for 2 point tracking with error distance points A, B, C, and D, all exactly the same distance from the center line.

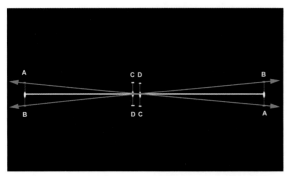

[**Figure 3.30**] With trackers set far apart, the total rotational error is about 10 degrees in this particular example, which would impart a slight rocking of the element to which you attach the tracking data.

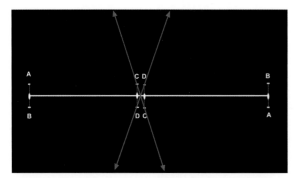

[**Figure 3.31**] With trackers set close together, the total rotational error skyrockets to about 140 degrees in this particular example, which would have the element you attach the tracking data to rotating wildly.

2 Point Tracker Placement: Rotation and Scale Error Amplification

When approaching a 2 point tracking shot, it's critical to understand the concept of *error amplification*. If you select tracking points for a 2 point track on a simple scene like the one shown in Figure 3.29, and you place your tracking points as far apart as possible (in this case, the first tracker at the center point between the left A and B and the second tracker at the center point between the right A and B) where the distance between each A and B is assumed to be the distance of error in the track, you get an error rotation up of (for argument's sake) 5 degrees and down of approximately 5 degrees, totaling about 10 degrees of rotational error. Any element we attach to that tracking data will rotate through that 10 degrees of error, as illustrated in Figure 3.30.

If we place the tracking markers very close (at the point between the leftmost C and D and between the rightmost C and D) with the same distance of error, we now have a rotational error of plus and minus 70 degrees, or about 140 degrees of total rotational error, as shown in Figure 3.31, which would have our element rotating wildly. This error amplification effect works the same way with scale. In instances where you have no choice but to use tracking points that are close together, it's a good idea to disable the tracking of scale, rotation, or perhaps even both.

2D Motion Tracking Applications

Most good compositing applications contain capable 2D trackers and all follow similar conventions as to the design and functionality of the look and operation of motion trackers.

After Effects

After Effects has a great 2D motion tracker that is very fast to use with its *pickwhip* ("drag and connect") functionality (shown in Figure 3.32).

Nuke and Fusion

Nuke (Figure 3.33) and Fusion, which are both nodal-based compositors, contain excellent 2D tracker nodes that look and operate almost identically to the ones in After Effects.

[Figure 3.32]
After Effects' motion tracker

[Figure 3.33]
Nuke's motion tracker

Planar Tracking

As you have seen, most of the 2D trackers rely on a definite high-contrast "pattern" so they are able to track a subject. One exciting and relatively new spin on tracking has appeared in a technology called *planar tracking*. True planar tracking differs from point tracking in that it tracks entire planes, every pixel, and thus it can do an amazing job of sticking to a track when point trackers fail.

Mocha Pro

One such specialized planar tracker is Mocha Pro (seen in Figure 3.34). Mocha Pro uses X-Splines to surround and define a pattern of pixels on a plane and then tracks every pixel in that pattern to obtain amazing results. New versions of Mocha Pro are also able to determine some 3D planar tracks that are calculated from multiple 2D planes on a different axis.

[Figure 3.34]
Mocha Pro's planar tracker with an X-Spline outlining pattern to be tracked

Tracker Assisted Roto

One huge advantage of breaking up subjects to be roto'd into many separate individual shapes is that they can be attached to tracking data to assist in semi-automating the rotoscoping process. For example, if you needed to rotoscope the bottom section of the boat in the background in Figure 3.26, you could roto the boat and keyframe the rotoshapes by hand, or you could create just one shape for the boat as seen in Figure 3.35 (since it is a fairly rigid object), 1 point track the scene, as seen in Figure 3.36, and then simply apply that tracking data to the shape, as seen in Figures 3.37 and 3.38.

[Figure 3.35]
Simple rotoshape for the bottom portion of the boat in the background

[Figure 3.36]
1 point track of the corner of the boat window

[Figure 3.37]
Rotoshape attached to 1 point tracking data

[Figure 3.38] Almost perfectly automated animation of the roto via tracker assist

2D Matchmoving

2D tracking, of course, is only the first half of the task at hand. The whole reason for tracking our scene is so that you can place something into the scene that moves along with the scene as if it was there when the footage was originally shot. You will do this by the process known as *matchmoving*. In the old days, matchmoving was done entirely by hand. A *matchmover* would literally match the move of the footage. In those days, matchmoving was an entire profession (and still is in very high-end VFX companies). Today, however, it is very common for a VFX artist to have to do his own matchmoving.

The process of matchmoving is part technical, part art, and some would argue, part magic. If you have done a perfect track, a matchmove is almost an automatic process. If you haven't, or if a good track isn't possible, then it becomes anything from a clever work of art to a complete point-nudging nightmare. The point here is that every step in the process is cumulative. If you take great care to do your tracking well, the matchmove goes smoothly. The opposite is also true, of course.

For a simple example, let's build some quick sunglasses out of nothing but rotosplines, track the original footage, or plate, of our actor (seen in Figure 3.39), and then matchmove the sunglasses to his movement. Since the shape of these doesn't have to be animated, we can create them with just two shapes: an outside frame shape and an inside lens shape (created by just scaling down the outside shape and applying a slight bevel effect and a little transparency, as you can see in Figure 3.40).

Next, we'll track his eyes using a 2 point track. Since he isn't moving toward or away from the camera, we won't be tracking for scaling, only position and rotation.

[Figure 3.39] Actor Chad Ayers filmed against a bluescreen

[Figure 3.40] Our quick and dirty rotospline sunglasses

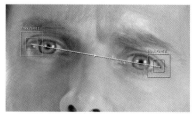

[Figure 3.41] 2 point trackers set to track corners of eyes

Tracking an actor's face can be tricky as many parts of the face can move (such as the corners of the nose, mouth, ears, eyebrows, etc.). It's best to try to stick to areas of the face that are pretty much anchored, conveniently in this case, like the corners of the eyes as shown in Figure 3.41. This gives us a pretty good track with only position and rotation keyframes, which you can see as small diamonds on the timeline in Figure 3.42.

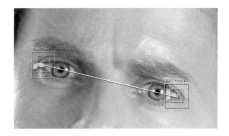

[Figure 3.42] 2 point track with keyframes on the timeline

Now, all that's left to do is to position the layer with the sunglasses onto our actor (Figure 3.43) and then attach the tracking data from our 2 point track to the layer with our rotospline sunglasses for them to be matchmoved (as shown in Figure 3.44).

Stabilization

If you think of the data we obtain from tracking an object in a scene with a 2D motion track as merely finding the position of that object at each frame and then recording that information in a series of numeric XY coordinate data (which it literally is), you can take that process one step further. You can apply the inverse, or negative values, of that data to the entire sequence, which will move the footage, or plate, in the opposite direction of the object's movement every frame, thus *stabilizing* the plate around the object. The object will appear to be perfectly still, whereas the entire plate appears to move and float around it.

[Figure 3.43] The sunglasses layer positioned into place

[Figure 3.44] Our quick and dirty sunglasses matchmoved onto our actor made out of nothing but rotosplines

Stabilization is very handy for doing complex shots on footage that additionally has complex camera movement embedded in it as well. Stabilizing the plate allows us to work on what appears to be a locked-off shot.

Destabilization

Once we've completed any VFX work on a stabilized shot, we will need to replace the original camera movement back into the shot. This process is known as *destabilization* and is performed by simply reapplying the original motion tracking data back to the entire plate again (reversing the stabilization back to the original camera motion, but with the VFX now added and appearing to move as if it was part of the original photography). This is a very powerful technique that we will cover in more detail in many later chapters.

Advanced 2D Tracking Strategies

Sometimes, trackers just don't work. No matter what you do, there's just not enough to lock onto, or something keeps occluding the frame and throwing the tracker off, or there's just nothing to track, as in the case of Figure 3.45, where you can see a sequence shot on greenscreen with no tracking markers. At first glance it may seem like there is nothing on the background wall to track. But if you use the same trick you learned in Chapter 2 to pull your grunge maps and add a new trick, we can make this work.

First, you will need to look through the individual RGB channels (Figures 3.46–3.48) to see which has the most information for the background greenscreen wall.

You can see that the green channel, of course, has the most data for the greenscreen background. Add a levels adjustment to the green channel, crush the black levels and lighten the gamma a little, the same way we did in Photoshop to pull the grunge maps from the dirty warehouse floor in Chapter 2. Lo and

[Figure 3.45] Actors shot against greenscreen with no tracking markers or clearly definable high-contrast features

[Figure 3.46] Red channel

[Figure 3.47] Green channel

[Figure 3.48] Blue channel

[Figure 3.49] Crushing the black levels and raising the gamma reveals the drywall seam on the greenscreen background.

[Figure 3.50] Cross formed from drywall seam

behold, the drywall seam in the greenscreen background emerges, forming the cross you see in Figure 3.49 and Figure 3.50, as if by magic!

Now, this feature still isn't quite defined enough for a tracker to follow, but it is definitely defined enough for our human eyes to discern and follow. So get ready to get down into the trenches. We're going to have to do this one by hand.

Hand 2D Matchmoving

There are many techniques that can be used to perform hand tracking. Hand tracking is basically just hand keyframe animating—yes, the same type of keyframe animating that you did creating the rotosplines! Consequently, the same rules apply when determining what frames to make your keyframes:

- When you are animating a hand track, find the frame in which the subject moves farthest away from your tracker's position before either changing direction or moving back toward the original position. That is the point at which you want to place your keyframe. After you've placed your keyframe, find the next farthest point the target moves to before either changing direction or starting to move back toward this position and place your next keyframe at this frame. Continue this process until the track is locked to the motion.

- The object is to set as few keyframes as possible. Doing so will deliver the cleanest and smoothest animation possible.

- It is perfectly correct and common to start from the beginning and work forward, start at the end and work backward, start in the middle and work forward then backward, and so on. Many times you will have to work in small segments as well.

[**Figure 3.51**] Grid method of hand tracking—using a grid overlay to line up features of a drywall seam

"But what," you are surely asking "do I use to actually *do* the tracking with?"

Some people recommend using a layer with a grid to overlay your scene, keyframe animating that layer (matching lines and intersections on the grid to features in the scene you are hand tracking as seen in Figure 3.51) and then using that data as your tracking data. The data you are recording when setting keyframes on a layer *is* the same type of XY position data the tracker is recording. Over the years, I've devised a very clever trick which works much better and is a lot more precise. I call this "Using the footage to track itself"!

The way this works is to take a frame of the footage—one that contains the most detail, has the best contrast, has the most features in frame, and so on (you can use multiple frames as well)—and copy this still frame onto another layer.

Set the duplicate layer on top of the footage you want to track and set this layer's transfer or blend mode to a *difference* blend mode. The screen should go completely black. That is exactly what you want! If it doesn't go completely black, you need to line up your still's position in the timeline until it matches exactly and goes completely black. It's going completely black because you have its blend mode set to *difference* and there is no difference at this point. Set your first keyframe at this completely black frame (Figure 3.52) and then move ahead in the timeline following the guidelines for where to set your keyframe at the widest point of divergence. At that point, your frame should look like a strange negative with ghosted areas like the ones in Figure 3.53.

Simply look for your target (in this case the cross formed by the drywall seam), move the layer back until it lines up perfectly and goes black again, then repeat the process until all your keyframes are done and the footage stays black throughout the entire process. Anywhere it drifts or you see ghosting, you'll need to go back and set another keyframe at the new widest divergence point.

Using this "widest divergence" method of keyframe placement helps prevent unnecessarily keyframe-heavy tracking and animations and should be applied to any keyframe animation activity you do.

[Figure 3.52]
Perfectly aligned still
(tracking frame layer)

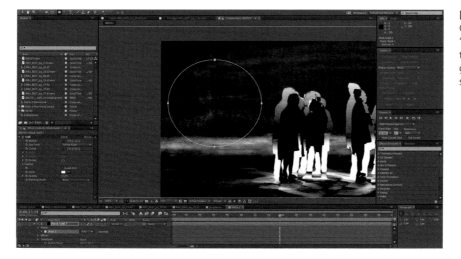

[Figure 3.53]
Ghosting reveals the
"difference" in position of
the tracked features of the
greenscreen wall from the
still tracking layer

Once hand tracking is completed, the VFX element can simply be parented
or connected to the keyframed still layer, or the positional animation data
can be copied and pasted to the target element.

Now that you have a good idea of what you'll need in the way of 2D skills, it's
time to jump into the third dimension of 3D for VFX!

CHAPTER FOUR

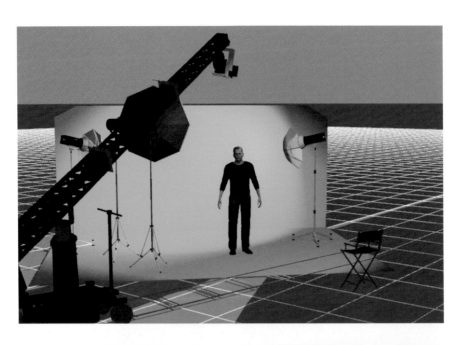

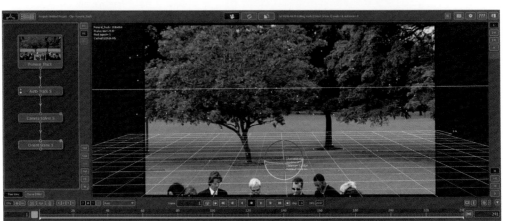

3D for VFX

VFX have advanced tremendously since their humble stage beginnings as practical special effects in the late 1800s and early 1900s. With the rapid advancements in computer graphics technologies and techniques in the late 1990s and early 2000s, those models, miniatures, and puppets rapidly gave way to the world of 3D CGI (computer-generated imagery). In 3D, anything can be created—from props and digital prosthetics to entire sets and even full 3D worlds.

How 3D CGI Is Created

At the heart of 3D CGI is the concept of representing the 3D world on a 2D screen. To do this, computer software must somehow calculate and simulate points in space in the 3D world in order to draw (or render) points (also known as *vertices*) and surfaces (whether polygons, surfaces, normal vectors, also called normals, or faces). We VFX artists use a common mathematical 3-axis system to describe our virtual 3D world.

We call this the XYZ coordinate system. Typically X represents the horizontal axis, Y represents the vertical axis, and Z represents the in and out or depth axis. If you are unfamiliar with the XYZ coordinate system, an easy way to remember it is to hold your fingers like a child pretending to shoot a gun, but with your middle finger sticking out at a 90 degree angle (perpendicular) to your pointer finger, as seen in Figure 4.1. With your fingers in this configuration, as silly as it might look to those around you, your middle finger is the X axis, your thumb is the Y axis, and your pointer is the Z axis.

[Figure 4.1] Fingers representing the XYZ coordinate system: middle finger (X), thumb (Y), and pointer (Z)

[note]

Different 3D applications sometimes assign these axes differently (i.e., Z is assigned to vertical instead of Y), but aside from the naming convention, the concept is exactly the same.

There are a few different methods of creating 3D models, or *meshes*, but they all work pretty much the same way.

Points (vertices) or curves (also known as *splines*) are created or placed in the virtual 3D environment (see Figure 4.2). These points or curves are then connected to create edges (Figure 4.3). Edges and splines are then closed to create polygonal faces (sometimes referred to as patches), as shown in Figure 4.4.

Primitive 3D shapes can also be created, modified, and combined to more quickly create complex objects, as shown in Figure 4.5.

For creating hard surface models such as buildings, furniture, computers, and so on, this method of building 3D models works very well. In cases where more curved or fluid shapes are required (called *organic modeling*), rough or blocky polygonal models' faces, as shown in Figure 4.6, can be smoothed (or subdivided) to create even more complex shapes and models. This method of creating rough blocky polygonal models and then subdividing them into smooth organic shapes is referred to as *subdivision surface modeling*.

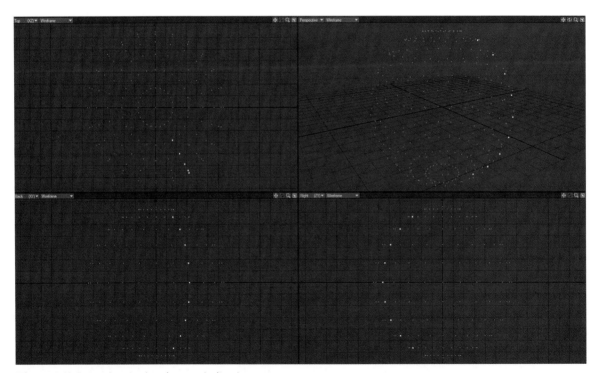

[Figure 4.2] Points (vertices) and curves (splines)

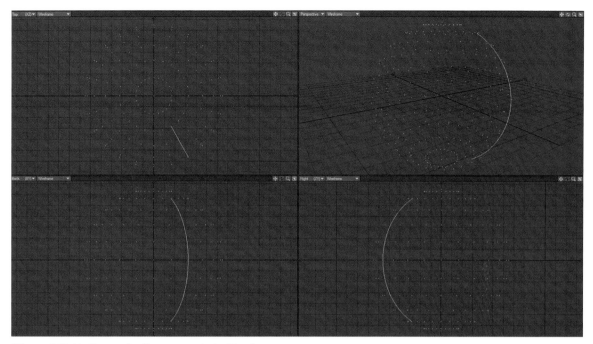

[Figure 4.3] Vertices and splines connected with edges

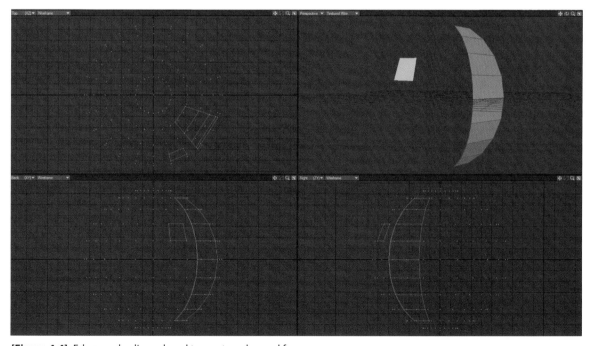

[Figure 4.4] Edges and splines closed to create polygonal faces

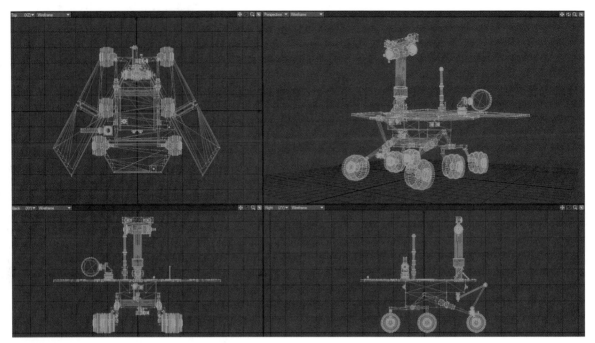

[Figure 4.5] Primitives combined to create complex meshes

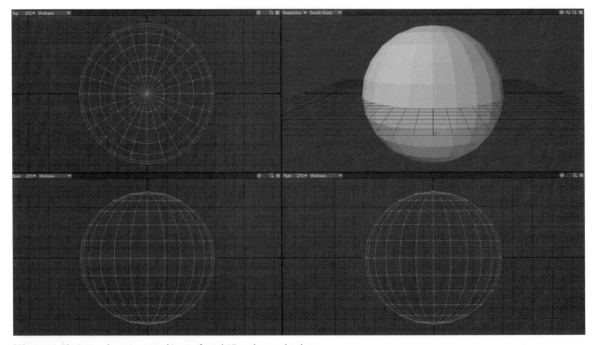

[Figure 4.6] A simple untextured/unsurfaced 3D polygonal sphere

Once faces, or polygons, are created, they can be textured (or *surfaced*) to create the appearance of real or fictional objects. These textures (or *maps*) can be any combination of colors, images, or mathematical procedural operations, as discussed in Chapter 2 in the section "Other Matched Texture/Layer/ Element Sets." Textures can then be layered and combined to form complex materials (or *shaders*).

Texturing (or surfacing) is both an art and a science. The most important skill required for great texturing or surfacing is refining your observational skills. Let's take a look at a couple examples.

In Figure 4.6 you can see a simple 3D sphere.

By carefully observing the details and attributes of the surfaces of other spherical-based objects, you can easily modify the textures and surface attributes of this simple sphere, changing it into many completely different objects.

First, for a simple one, let's create the texture of a billiard ball. Billiard balls are colored and have a high-gloss finish. By setting the value in the color channel—in this case, to blue—and the diffuse channel to 90% (which will give the ball 90% of its reflected color from the blue base color in the color channel), the ball will take on a nice, bright, saturated blue finish (as seen in Figure 4.7).

Because a billiard ball is also very shiny from the highly polished finish, you want to turn the specular value up very high as well (in Figure 4.8, the specular channel is set to 100%).

Notice that the *specular highlight*, or *hotspot* (the white spot reflection of the light source), is very broad and spread out. The tight molecular structure of a billiard ball's high-polish finish creates a very tight highlight spot. To simulate this, you can also increase the glossiness channel to 100%, as shown in Figure 4.9.

[note]

Although every 3D application has a slightly different approach to texturing/ surfacing, the core concepts are identical and ubiquitous among all 3D applications.

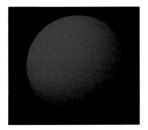

[Figure 4.7] 3D sphere with Blue selected in the color channel and the diffuse channel set to 90%

[Figure 4.8] Specular channel set to 100%

[Figure 4.9] Glossiness set to 100%

[Figure 4.10] Mirrored gazing ball reference image

[Figure 4.11] A 180-degree spherical image of a park loaded into the environment reflection channel

[Figure 4.12] The finished 3D CGI mirrored gazing ball

That gloss finish means that it is partially reflective. So you can also add a slight amount of reflectivity to the reflection channel, which gives a nice re-creation of a billiard ball's texture. Of course, for a production, as discussed in Chapter 2, you would want to add the number decal and many imperfections to the surfaces, such as dings and dents in the finish and even chalk marks and fingerprints to dull down the finish in some areas for added realism.

Next, let's look at the mirrored gazing ball reference image in Figure 4.10.

From the very first glance you can see that the gazing ball really has no color of its own, but instead, because it is so highly reflective, it gets it color from the reflection of whatever is around it—in this case an outside park scene. By turning the diffuse map to black (or zero), you turn off any base color the sphere would have. You can also set the color map to black since there isn't any. It too is shiny and glossy, so those aspects should be set high, similar to the way they were set for the billiard ball. Finally, you will want to set the reflection channel to 100% (or close to it) since a mirrored ball is definitely reflective. But something's wrong! So far your sphere is just a shiny, glossy black. Actually, the only thing that's wrong is that there's nothing for your mirrored ball to reflect. When you load the image of the exterior park scene (Figure 4.11) where the reference image was taken into the environment or reflection channel, the 3D mirrored ball instantly springs to life, as you can see in Figure 4.12.

Now the ball has become a very accurate re-creation of the original. As with the first example, for a production quality model you would want to add all of the similar "reality imperfections."

Finally, for a completely different spin, let's create a pumpkin. We'll push in the top and bottom of the sphere and reset all of the map parameters; then, using the same technique and dirty warehouse floor texture we used in Chapter 2, we'll create a dirty, desaturated orange texture (Figure 4.13).

Next, since a pumpkin reflects a lot of its own orange color, set the diffuse channel high, to about 80% (to taste of course), the specular channel to about 20% (to give a wide highlight), and the glossiness to between 30 and 40% to emulate the shiny waxy-like surface of a pumpkin. This will give you something that looks like Figure 4.14.

It's always important to *think* about a texture or material thoroughly, the same way you thoroughly need to think through every VFX you create, as described in Chapter 1. If a pumpkin were to have the dirty discolorations that the dirty warehouse floor texture has, it most definitely wouldn't be as shiny on those spots as on the waxy orange surface of the pumpkin skin itself. To simulate this, you can load a matching copy of one of the dirt/grunge textures used to create the orange skin texture into the specular channel to "knock down" the amount of specularity in those spots, as shown in Figure 4.15. This is called *specularity breakup*.

You can now see that those dirty spots are less shiny than the cleaner skin areas. But this still looks more like a partially deflated dirty orange beach ball than a pumpkin. The magic happens in another channel. This channel isn't actually a "texture" channel per se in the material/surface sense, but instead, it is a texture channel used by the modeling engine to *displace*, or push, points/vertices around based on the values of a map (yes, the same kind of map we've been using for textures. This one we just need to think through to use for 3D displacement instead of 2D displacement). As with a bump map, a displacement map pushes the vertices in the 3D geometry down, or in, wherever the map is darker and up, or out, wherever it's lighter. Because

> **[note]**
>
> There is no exact science to texturing/surfacing. All of the surface settings described here are starting points and recommendations. Material and texture will always be dependent on the particular model, scene, and requirement and will need to be fine-tuned to taste.

[Figure 4.13] A dirty desaturated orange texture

[Figure 4.14] The diffuse, specular, and glossiness settings are set.

[Figure 4.15] Specularity breakup added to the specularity (spec) channel

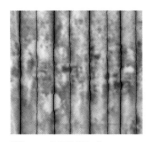

[Figure 4.16] Displacement map created to simulate the vertical ridges on a pumpkin

[Figure 4.17] The finished, displaced geometry pumpkin

[Figure 4.18] Autodesk's Maya user interface

a pumpkin has organic linear stripe-like vertical indentations, a map with wavy dark vertical lines that gradually fade to white and then gradually back into another wavy black line will push the geometry of the sphere in or out at those vertices on the geometry, respectively, based on how dark or light the map is at any given point. Once this map (Figure 4.16) is loaded into the displacement channel, the deflated sphere magically transforms into a natural looking pumpkin! (Figure 4.17)

3D Applications

There are many 3D applications, and each has its own strengths, style, workflow, and conventions—but the principles for modeling, texturing, lighting, animating, and rendering are all the same. This section introduces the most widely used 3D applications in the industry.

Maya

Originally spawned from Alias | Wavefront's Power Animator, Autodesk's Maya (www.autodesk.com), shown in Figure 4.18, is one of the most popular, high-end 3D applications in the VFX industry. Maya has a steep learning curve, but has powerful animating and simulation tools and is almost infinitely extensible with its plugin and customization capabilities.

3ds Max

Autodesk's 3ds Max (www.autodesk.com) (Figure 4.19) is also part of the
Autodesk family of products. 3ds Max has very strong roots in both architectural and gaming 3D but is widely used in many facets of VFX.

LightWave 3D

NewTek's LightWave 3D (http://newtek.com) (Figure 4.20) spawned from
NewTek's Video Toaster in the early 1990s and, because of its speed, flexibil-
ity, and superb renderer, it quickly gained a foothold in television and film
VFX, especially in many popular sci-fi series such as *Star Trek* and *Babylon 5*.

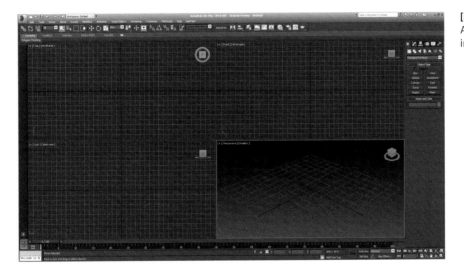

[Figure 4.19]
Autodesk's 3ds Max user
interface

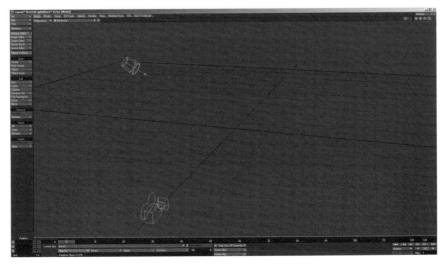

[Figure 4.20]
NewTek's LightWave
3D user interface

Cinema 4D

German-based Maxon also released Cinema 4D (www.maxon.net) in the early 1990s (see Figure 4.21). Cinema 4D, though not too popular in those formative years, has quickly grown into a powerhouse 3D application fully capable of stunning 3D and VFX work.

Modo

In the early 2000s, some senior management and developers from NewTek, wanting to take 3D software in a different direction, formed Luxology. Their 3D application, Modo (www.thefoundry.co.uk), shown in Figure 4.22, quickly became a leader and favorite in the industry for its innovative workflow and features.

[Figure 4.21]
Maxon's Cinema 4D Lite user interface

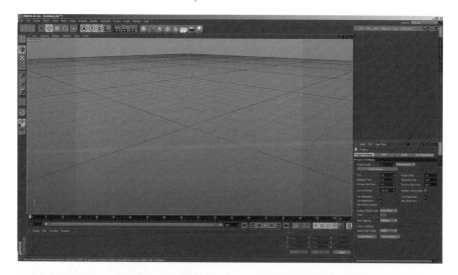

[Figure 4.22]
Luxology's Modo user interface

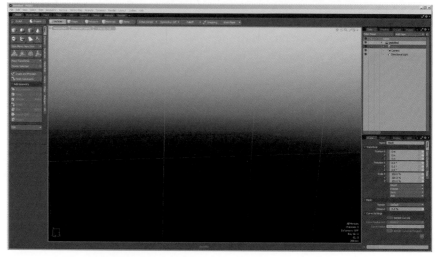

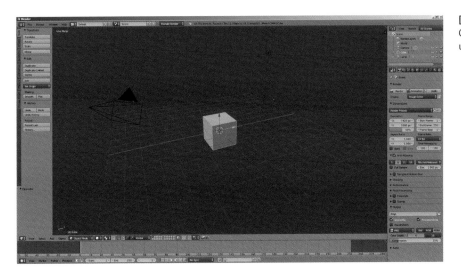

[Figure 4.23]
Open source Blender
user interface

Blender

Originally created by Dutch animation studio NeoGeo and Not a Number
(NaN) Technologies as an in-house 3D application in 2002, Blender (www.
blender.org) (Figure 4.23) was released as a free and open source 3D computer
graphics software product under the GNU General Public License. Blender
has been used in many areas of VFX production and continues to develop
amazing innovative features—and all for free!

3D Motion Tracking

In Chapter 3, in the discussion of 2D motion
tracking, you saw how to track one, two, and even
four points on an image to record and utilize the
positional/translational, rotational, and *apparent* scaling data. I say *apparent* because what we
are actually tracking is the points moving closer
together, as shown in Figure 4.24, simulating scale,
which will sometimes suffice for creating simulated
Z-depth movement.

[Figure 4.24] Simulated scaling as an object moves closer
to or farther away in depth (Z-space) from the camera

Many times this will be sufficient enough data to allow you to lock your element to the plate so you can create a seamless integration. But what happens
if the camera is orbiting around or within a scene, or is moving through a
scene at an angle, allowing you to see *around* objects in the scene as you pass
them? New VFX artists frequently want to know the dividing line between

when a 2D track is enough to make a shot work and when a 3D track is required. Well, this is it. Any time the camera *orbits* around or within a scene or translates/passes objects within a scene in Z-depth close enough to reveal the 3D nature of a subject or object (or reveal a portion, or portions, of those objects that weren't seen originally)—as the examples in Figures 4.25–4.28 illustrate—a 3D track and solution is required.

Unlike 2D tracking, which derives its data from the X and Y motion of pixels on a flat screen, 3D tracking utilizes much more complex triangulation calculations to determine objects' actual position and motion in 3D space. If you want to be able to integrate a 3D object into a scene where the camera is moving in three dimensions, you need to be able to re-create this camera's motion in 3D and have your virtual camera repeating this same motion in order for your element to integrate seamlessly.

To be really good at 3D tracking (and to avoid the needless frustration many artists encounter), it's important to understand how 3D tracking works.

The origins of 3D tracking technologies lie in the science of *photogrammetry*, the scientific method of calculating positions and distances of points referenced

[Figure 4.25] XY translation-only camera movement that would work well with a 2D track

[Figure 4.26] Z Translation-only camera movement that would work well with a 2D track

[Figure 4.27] Orbital camera movement requiring a 3D track

[Figure 4.28] Camera translation close to subject and on an angle so that the 3D nature of the object or subject is revealed.

[Figure 4.29]
Points in two images being
triangulated to determine
camera position

in one or more images. By comparing and triangulating the position of points referenced in multiple images (as seen in Figure 4.29), or consecutive frames of a motion image, the position of those points, as well as that of the camera, can be calculated using trigonometry and geometric projections.

3D Motion Tracking Application Technique

A 3D tracker does its mathematical magic in a series of well-defined steps:

1. A mass (usually automated) 2D track, or *auto track*, of the scene is performed, tracking many (sometimes hundreds or thousands) high-contrast *candidate* (or potential) points in the scene. This first track is almost identical to a 2D track except that it is done on a mass scale on the entire image, as shown in Figure 4.30. During this process, complex software algorithms sift through all of the tracked 2D points to weed out and

[note]

When doing the auto track, it is important that you mask out any objects in the scene that are creating extraneous motion using the masking tools in the 3D tracking application. These tools create an alpha channel that tells the tracker what areas of the image to ignore and exclude from tracking and calculations.

delete any of those that fall below a user set *confidence threshold* (meaning how confident the software is that the point being tracked is the same on each frame or range of frames).

[Figure 4.30] The first step in a 3D track is a mass, automated 2D track.

2. Next, a complex 3D *camera solve* is done. A solve is an exhaustive series of calculations wherein the motion of every point tracked is compared and triangulated on a frame-by-frame basis (usually both forward and backward) to determine its position as well as the camera's position and any movement within each frame, as shown in Figure 4.31. The more information known about the camera used and its motion and environment, the more accurate the solve will be.

[Figure 4.31] 3D camera solve

3. Once the 3D tracking application completes its solve, it will display
    the resulting 3D camera, motion track, and *point cloud* (cluster of points
    representing solved candidate points). The camera's position and track,
    at this point, are relative to the point cloud and not necessarily aligned
    with the real world X, Y, and Z axes (as shown in Figure 4.32), so the
    next step is to *align*, or *orient*, the scene. Most 3D tracking applications
    have scene orientation tools that allow you to designate a point in the
    scene as the X, Y, Z, 0, 0, 0 origin. Additional scene orientation can be
    refined by using tools that allow you to designate certain points as being
    on a common plane, or that allow you to manually translate, rotate, and
    scale the entire scene into position by eye, or by aligning to reference
    grids, as shown in Figure 4.33.

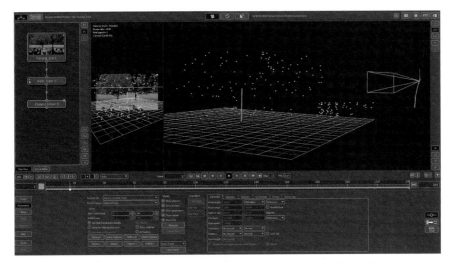

[Figure 4.32]
3D camera, track and point
cloud

[Figure 4.33]
3D orientation and
alignment of camera track
and point cloud scene

4. At this point, most 3D tracking applications will allow you to place test objects into the scene to determine how well they follow the track (or *stick*), as shown in Figure 4.34.

[Figure 4.34]
3D test objects inserted into
the 3D tracked scene

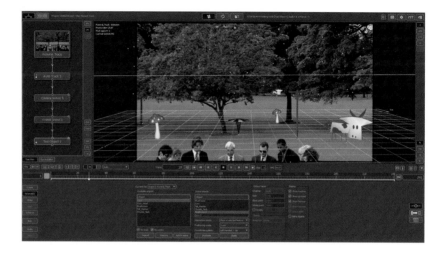

5. If there are any errors or errant motions in the track, you can apply mathematical filters to smooth the tracks motion. Averaging, or Butterworth, filters are common filters to accomplish this. Isolated errors or motions may also be edited or removed manually by editing, adjusting, or deleting track motion keyframes, as shown in Figure 4.35.

[Figure 4.35]
Editing 3D camera motion
track keyframes

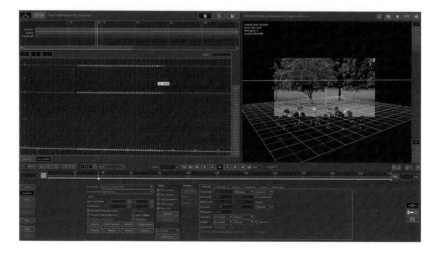

6. Once the 3D camera track proves to be solid, the data can then be exported in a variety of file and scene formats to other 3D and/or compositing applications for use.

3D Motion Tracking Applications

There are many 3D motion tracking applications, some which come as integrated solutions in other applications, as well as the standalone application variety. Although their workflows and methodologies vary somewhat, they all contain the steps outlined in the preceding section (whether obviously or under-the-hood in the case of completely automated versions). This section introduces some of the most popular 3D tracking applications.

PFTrack

Originating from the University of Manchester's Project Icarus, PFTrack (www.thepixelfarm.co.uk) (see Figure 4.36) and its sibling applications have grown into some of the most powerful and widely used 3D tracking applications in the VFX industry.

[Figure 4.36]
PFTrack user interface

Boujou

Vicon's Boujou (www.boujou.com) was one of the first almost fully automated 3D tracking applications and still offers a great set of powerful 3D tracking tools, as shown in Figure 4.37.

Nuke and After Effects

3D tracking has become a commonly integrated feature in compositing applications, which continue to grow and blur the lines between VFX job descriptions. Recently, compositing applications such as The Foundry's Nuke (www.thefoundry.co.uk) (Figure 4.38) and Adobe's After Effects (www.adobe.com) (Figure 4.39) have also integrated 3D tracking capabilities.

[Figure 4.37]
Boujou user interface

[Figure 4.38]
The Foundry's Nuke 3D
tracking interface

[Figure 4.39]
Adobe After Effects' 3D
tracking interface

Mocha

Even Imagineer Systems' planar tracker Mocha Pro (www.imagineersystems.com) (as seen in Figure 4.40) has been given a turbo boost with its ability to extrapolate 3D camera tracking motion from multiple 2D planar tracks, resulting in some very impressive output where some standard 3D trackers fail.

SynthEyes

One of the first affordable, low-cost, 3D tracking applications, SynthEyes (www.ssontech.com), shown in Figure 4.41, has also grown in capability and features to become a powerful and widely used 3D tracking solution.

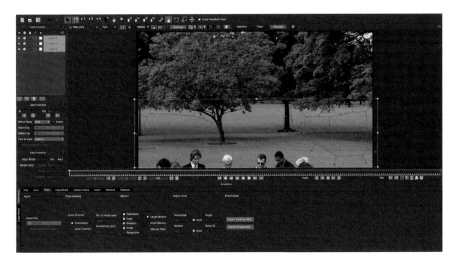

[Figure 4.40]
Imagineer Systems' Mocha Pro user interface

[Figure 4.41]
SynthEyes user interface

Voodoo

The University of Hannover's Laboratory for Information Technology developed this free non-commercial 3D camera tracking software. Voodoo (www.viscoda.com) (Figure 4.42) is an excellent tool for beginners to use to experiment with 3D camera tracking at no cost.

3D Matchmoving

Once a solid 3D tracking solution is exported from a 3D tracking application, creating a 3D matchmove involves little more than setting up a scene and importing the solution into your 3D or compositing application of choice, as shown in Figure 4.43 and Figure 4.44. (See Chapter 3 for much more on matchmoving.)

Advanced 3D Tracking Strategies

There are many times when it is extremely helpful to know some advanced 3D tracking strategies as well.

Hand 3D Tracking and Matchimation

Unfortunately, as is usually the case in VFX, 3D tracking is often not quite as simple as autotrack, autosolve, autoorient, and export. Tracks contain too much noise or too many errors or they just downright fail altogether. In these cases, as with 2D tracking and matchmoving, you need a fallback strategy.

[Figure 4.43]
3D tracking solution and point cloud in PFTrack

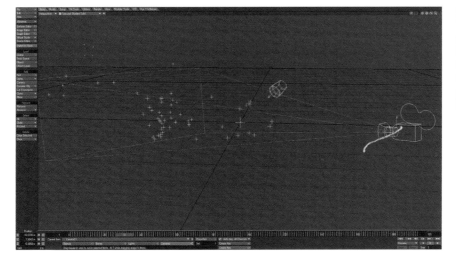

[Figure 4.44]
The same 3D tracking and point-cloud solution imported into a 3D application (which depicts tracking points from the point cloud as null objects in the 3D application)

Very similar to the hand-tracked 2D track in Chapter 3, when all else fails, you can hand track, or *matchimate*, a 3D track as well. *Matchimation* is derived from the combination of *matchmove* and *animation* and refers to the process of manual frame-by-frame or keyframe matching a track.

To hand track a 3D scene, you first want to create 3D reference stand-in objects for any scene elements with known sizes and/or positions. You are basically trying to replicate key elements of the scene in your 3D application. Elements nearest to the 3D CG object you intend to place into the scene are the most important to place, if possible. In Figure 4.45 you can see a dolly shot sequence filmed on a bluescreen set, which will become an air traffic control radar monitoring station in this example.

[Figure 4.45] Bluescreen VFX sequence to be hand 3D tracked

Load the footage into the background of your 3D application, making sure the footage size and aspect ratio is set correctly in both the background and the scenes camera. Set your 3D models to wireframe view mode so that you can easily see through them to the footage behind as well as the wireframe edges outlining your elements.

Since I know that we cut the tabletop portions of the "radar stations" to 30 inches wide and left them at their full 8 foot, plywood length, there is a base measurement to start with to build a reference object in your 3D application. In Figure 4.46 you can see two of these, laid end to end, to represent the two workstation countertops. Let's eyeball the height of these countertops and place them at about 27 inches (the height of my workstation desk, which seems about right). Next, using the camera VFX cues you can ascertain (discussed in Chapter 1), set your camera to a fairly wide focal length and place the camera's starting position at about 30 inches off the ground and approximately 10–12 feet away from the subject, as shown in Figure 4.46.

Align the wireframe with the counter at whatever point in the shot you choose. Remember, it's perfectly acceptable to work from beginning to end, end to beginning, middle forward and back, and so on. Keep in mind the information you can deduce from the scene—such as that the camera appears to be on a dolly so will likely translate in a straight line, even if it pans about on its Y axis. Move the camera in a straight line on its local axis until the end (or furthest point) of the shot and pan the camera until the counters and the wireframes align, as shown in Figure 4.47. Set your camera's first keyframe here.

[Figure 4.46] Camera placed at guesstimated starting height and position

[Figure 4.47] Camera aligned with scene element

From here, it's the same procedure you followed for the hand 2D track, only in 3D. You will move your camera along the guesstimated path to the point where the 3D scene element you're tracking diverges the farthest from the wireframe before either beginning to return or changing directions. This will be your next keyframe position, and you will realign your camera until the stand-in and on-screen element are aligned, then set your next keyframe, and so on (Figure 4.48).

Then simply repeat this process until the wireframe and scene elements are locked throughout the duration of the shot.

Once this is completed, any object added to the scene—once composited and properly integrated, color corrected (covered in Chapter 5), and rendered—should composite and integrate nicely, follow the motion of the scene, and appear to actually exist within the scene, as shown in Figure 4.49.

[tip]

Make sure to move only your camera and only the way in which you believe the camera moved on set. Do not move the scene elements to match (unless they moved in real life) and do not move the camera in such a way that it didn't or wouldn't have moved on set.

[Figure 4.48]
Camera aligned with scene element to next keyframe position

[Figure 4.49]
Integrated 3D air traffic radar workstation set piece

3D Object Tracking

If we defined 2D *stabilization* as simply 2D motion tracking data of a piece of footage, inverted and applied back to that footage, you can think of the inversion of 3D camera motion track data as *object tracking*. Where the output of a 3D camera track is a static scene and a moving camera, the output of an *object track* is a static camera and a moving object or scene. This technique is particularly useful in cases such as adding 3D prosthetics or props to moving characters, covered in detail in Chapter 7.

Motion Control and Motion Capture

Finally, no discussion of matching camera movements would be complete without discussing motion control and motion capture.

Motion control is the utilization of computer-controlled robotics (Figure 4.50) to very precisely create, record, and repeatedly play back camera movements over and over again. This allows for the combination of complex slow motion, or *replication shots*, such as adding clones of the same character to the same scene all within a continuous moving camera shot. On the pro side of this technique, motion control shots are very precise, align perfectly, and allow amazing seamless integrations. On the con side, motion control robots are expensive, huge, slow, and unwieldy and take a lot of time to set up, rehearse, and tear down.

[Figure 4.50]
3D illustration of a motion control camera rig

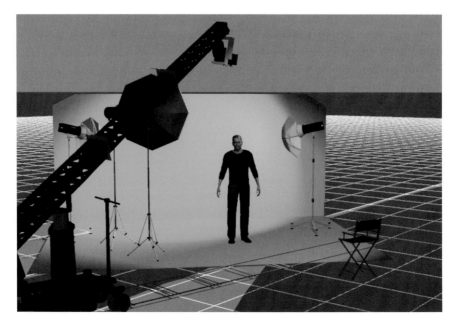

Similarly, *motion capture*, though not actually camera tracking either, is the capture of object motion data (as you would get with an object track) via various forms of data capture ranging from optical to wireless sensor arrays, as shown in Figure 4.51.

Motion capture is mainly used for the recording of lifelike organic character motions and interactions, and although used extensively in VFX for 3D CGI character and digital doubles, it is more in the realm of 3D character animation than VFX and compositing.

Now that you understand the basics of VFX, 2D, and 3D, let's jump right in and begin integrating some CG VFX in Chapter 5.

[Figure 4.51] Wireless motion capture sensor camera rig

PART TWO

Visual Effects Techniques

CHAPTER FIVE

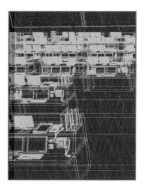

VFX Techniques I:
Basic Integration VFX

Lighting is, by far, one of the most critical components in creating a photoreal-istic VFX shot. When creating the elements to be integrated into a VFX shot, whether CG or live action (filmed against a bluescreen or greenscreen), match-ing all the VFX lighting cues covered in Chapter 1 will be the deciding factor that makes all the difference between a VFX effect that looks seamless and real (as in Figure 5.1) or one that looks like a poor attempt or "pasted on" garbage (as in Figure 5.2).

Although many artists feel a disconnect between the lighting of live action elements filmed in front of a keyable background and the lighting of a 3D CG model rendered in a 3D application, the strategies and techniques used to light both components of a good seamless VFX shot are actually identical.

[Figure 5.1] A well-lit 3D object, integrated into a live action plate

[Figure 5.2] A poorly lit object, not integrating well at all due to the mismatched lighting

CG/VFX Lighting and Integration

The first step in creating excellent lighting for a VFX integration is *not* actually doing any lighting at all, but carefully analyzing the image, footage, or plate into which the element will be composited or integrated. When analyzing a background plate, you should ask yourself the following questions, take note of the answers, and figure out what you need to do to make your lighting match:

- **Where is the main source of lighting in the scene coming from?**

  Key light placement, distance, and direction

- **What is the *quantity* of the main light source?**

  Key light intensity level

- **What is the *quality* of the main light source?**

  Key light harshness or softness

  Shadow density and falloff

  Key light color and temperature

- **Is there any fill or secondary lighting in the scene?**

  Placement, distance, and direction

  Intensity

  Shadow density and falloff

  Color and temperature

- **Is there any rim, highlight, or back lighting in the scene?**

  Placement, distance, and direction

  Intensity

  Shadow density and falloff

  Color and temperature

- **Are there any interactive or moving lights in the scene?**

  Placement, distance, and direction

  Intensity

  Shadow density and falloff

  Color and temperature

- **Are there any special shadowing considerations in the scene?**

  Size, shape, and type (tree leaves, window mullion, rain, shadows from interactive scene elements, and so on)

  Placement, distance, and direction

  Intensity

  Shadow density and falloff

  Color and temperature

Once you have carefully analyzed the scene's lighting, it's time to light the foreground element that you want to film and integrate into the scene.

Method and Technique for VFX Element Lighting

Whether you are integrating a live action element (which was filmed in front of a blue- or greenscreen) or a 3D CGI element (created in your 3D application of choice), the method and procedure for lighting these elements are the same:

1. First, kill all of the light in the scene! Yes, you read that right. Although many artists tend to start with setting an ambient light level, that method inadvertently leads to having to add more and more lights, leading to over lighting and *light spill contamination* (lights spilling onto areas where they are not wanted or needed). Ideally, your scene should be completely dark or black. In a 3D computer graphics application, killing the lights simply means turning off all lights in the scene and setting the ambient intensity to 0%.

2. Make sure to have your element adequately far from your background (if shooting a live bluescreen/greenscreen element). *Adequately* means it's far enough away that light projected onto the background won't reflect, or *spill*, onto the foreground subject. *Flags* are devices used in lighting to block light, cast shadows, provide negative/dark fill, or protect the lens from a flare. You can use flags or curtains to block off foreground lights from contaminating the background and are very helpful when lighting small areas. Ideally, when your foreground is lit and the lighting on the background is turned off, the background should be completely black (as in Figure 5.3). When the background lights are turned on and the

[tip]

A great trick to getting excellent matched lighting results is to run a "feed" from your camera into a real-time keying application that can do either real-time full, or rough, key extractions over a sample of your background. A few examples of these include plugins for compositing applications, such as Frischluft's Lensfeed (www.frischluft.com), and even standalone stopframe animation software, such as AnimatorHD.

foreground lights are turned off, the foreground should be completely black and silhouetted against the bright and evenly lit background (as shown in Figure 5.4) with no spill or cross contamination of either. Professional lighting directors affectionately refer to this as "wrangling the beam."

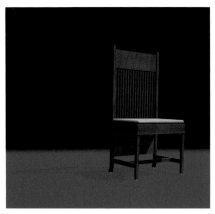

[**Figure 5.3**] Foreground object lit with background lights turned off

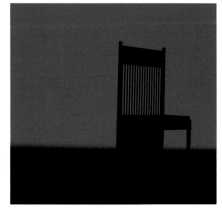

[**Figure 5.4**] Foreground object's lights off and silhouetted against lit background with no spill or contamination

3. Next, you will place your *key light* (or main light source). From your careful examination of the background image (and the tips and tricks covered in Chapter 1), you should have a good idea of where to place your key light, at what height and angle, what type or quality of light it should be (harsh or soft), and its basic color and intensity (or quantity), as shown in Figure 5.5.

4. Once your key light is in position and set, it's time to set up any *fill* or *bounce lighting* affecting the object you are filming. Again, by carefully analyzing the plate, you should be able to see where bounced/reflected lighting is *filling* in and lighting up (*lifting*) the shadow (or *shadow density*) levels. You should also have a good idea of where to place your fill lights, at what heights and angles, what type or quality of lights they should be (harsh or soft), and the basic color and intensity of each. You should perform constant monitoring and comparison, checking to make sure that the lighting and shadow levels, direction, quality, quantity, and color continue to match the reference as each light is added and adjusted (see Figure 5.6).

[note]

It is very common to have more than one, or even many, fill lights in a scene. In an exterior scene, fill lights could emulate the light being bounced off of the sky and clouds, ground, nearby walls or objects, and so on.

[tip]

It is extremely important while adding each light to take great care to isolate these lights' output and avoid each of these lights spilling onto or contaminating the background.

[Figure 5.5] Object lit with key light only   **[Figure 5.6]** Fill lights added

5. After adding your fill lighting, place any rim or highlight lights (Figure 5.7), taking great care that these rim lights do not spill or reflect anywhere except where they are directed. Because these lights are commonly high-intensity lights, take great care that flags used to block the lights from spilling or causing lens flares don't inadvertently reflect and backspill light onto the background or backdrop (this is also common with lights that aren't completely light sealed on the back side of the lamp housing).

6. Finally, once your element is lit to match the lighting and shadows in the background footage or live action plate, it's time to light your background or backdrop. There are many theories about the best way to light a back-

[Figure 5.7] Rim lights added

drop, including specific light meter readings to ascertain specific exposures. I find that as long as you've carefully and correctly done the first five steps in this exercise and have perfectly isolated your foreground and background lighting to contain no spill or cross contamination, simply lighting the background with even diffuse light to a normal exposure level will yield excellent results, as shown in Figure 5.8.

Many people recommend keeping your bluescreen or greenscreen exposed one F-stop over. Although this does tend to make keying easier, it also increases on-set lighting and frequently results in having to add more and more light to the foreground, eventually (like trimming your hair too short on one side, then having to trim the other side more, back and forth, again and again) resulting in over-lighting the set.

[Figure 5.8]
Fully lit object and background with no spill contamination

2D Motion Tracking and CG Integration

One of the most basic and most commonly needed VFX is the integration of a filmed bluescreen/greenscreen or 3D CG–rendered element into a 2D motion-tracked live action plate.

To illustrate this technique in a very bold way, we will 2D track and integrate a large 3D CG building into the background of seemingly common driving footage (shown in Figure 5.9), which was shot overlooking a city, from a moving car on a highway overpass. The footage was shot with a handheld camera and, as a result, is moving around quite a bit.

The creation of this type of VFX can be roughly distilled down to five basic steps.

[Figure 5.9]
Moving footage shot from overpass

Step 1: Analyze the Shot, Elements, and VFX to Be Created

Your first step—as always, when approaching a new VFX shot—is to carefully analyze the footage and determine what factors you are dealing with, the footage's attributes, the lighting, and what you will need to do to create the desired effect.

Step 2: Light the Live Action Bluescreen/Greenscreen or 3D CG Element to Be Integrated

Using the methods and techniques for lighting elements covered in the previous section, we will open the building model in a 3D application and kill all the lights in the scene. As you can see from the footage/background plate, the main light source, the sun (using the two-clock description method covered in Chapter 1), is coming from approximately 5 o'clock (behind us) on a horizontal clock (where 12 o'clock is directly in front of us, 6 o'clock is directly behind us, 3 o'clock is 90 degrees to the right, and 9 o'clock is 90 degrees to the left), and about 2 o'clock on a vertical clock (where 12 o'clock is directly up, 6 o'clock is directly down, and so on). In the background image, you can see that it is a fairly bright day, so we want to make sure the intensity of the key light source is set to a match with a similar-in-appearance value (as shown in Figure 5.10).

[Figure 5.10]
3D building lit with key light to match color and intensity of sunlight in the scene

Once the key light is set, you can place and set your fill lights. You can set as few or as many as you'd like, but I highly recommend adopting the methodology of always using the fewest lights possible that get the job done. The fewer variables you have to contend with, the more control you have over the scene and, ultimately, the final results and output. At a bare minimum, in this scene you will need one fill light to emulate the bounce lighting from the sky (which will, of course, be blue-tinted) and one fill light to emulate the color of ground reflection or bounce (which in this case will reflect the colors of gray buildings, roads, green grass, greens and browns from trees, and so on). Using the eyedropper or color picker tool in Photoshop, you can get the exact value of the sky colors to ensure that your light color matches perfectly (see Figure 5.11).

[Figure 5.11]
Fill lights added to the 3D CG building model to match values in the background plate

Though, many artists prefer to use distant or infinite lights to light their 3D scenes, and there is no definitive right or wrong when lighting, I prefer and recommend spotlights and point lights. Spotlights and point lights do require a little more work and tweaking due to their cone angles, radii, and falloffs, but ultimately, they allow the same kind of fine-tuned control that you want to have with real lights on a sound stage or in a studio—the ability to control your lights and prevent spill and contamination.

Step 3: Track the Live Action Background Plate

Because this footage is handheld and contains quite a bit of rocking and rotation, you'll want to track both position and rotation (meaning a 2-point track will be required). Scrub the footage to get a general idea of the camera's motion and to see how far the background elements travel from side to side throughout the duration of the clip. Doing so will help determine the best features to track—obviously, ones that don't drift off-screen. As you will remember from the 2D tracking guidelines covered in Chapter 2, you want to select high-contrast features that are on the same approximate Z plane (or approximately the same distance from camera). For this example, you will be integrating the CG building quite far into the distance. Place the first tracking point on a feature in the far distance on one side of the footage and the second tracking point the same approximate Z-depth from camera as far to the other side of the screen as possible. In Figure 5.12 you can see I've chosen clumps of trees on the horizon, which contrast nicely against the light sky.

[note]

It is critical that you track areas of the footage in the same Z-depth as the depth of the element that you are going to integrate will appear. Although this is not always 100% possible, the nearer the better. The farther away from the Z-depth you track, the more drift and sliding your element will do, and the more hand adjustment and fixing you will have to do later.

[Figure 5.12]
Trackers set to track distant trees on either side of the background plate

Step 4: Composite and Matchmove Foreground Element over Live Action Background

Once you have a solid track, import a still render of the lit 3D building with its alpha into your compositing application and do a simple composite of the foreground over the background, as shown in Figure 5.13. In a layer-based compositor like After Effects, this means simply placing the foreground layer above, or on top of, the background layer; in a nodal-based compositor like Nuke or Fusion, it means creating a simple merge node, piping the foreground into the "A" input and the background into the "B" input and setting the merge node to a simple "A over B."

[Figure 5.13]
Simple A over B composite

Sometimes, when tracking data is applied, you will find that you might need to do a last-minute placement adjustment of your foreground image or that there are a few places where keyframes may slip and need to be corrected. By creating a new layer or merge and making it the parent of the one with the tracking data, you can, in essence, create an overriding "cheat" control, which you can use to make any fine-tune placement or keyframe animation adjustments.

Next you will apply the tracking data to the foreground image using whatever method your compositing application uses to apply tracking data. Depending on your compositing application, this may be done by using a pickwhip tool to parent the foreground element to the tracking data layer, or *null* (non-rendering helper object/layer), by copying and pasting the tracking data, or by using *expressions* (mathematical equations that allow variables, which can be used instead of specific input values). Once you have successfully applied your tracking data to the foreground element, it should be moving along with the footage nicely.

Step 5: Fine-tune Color Correct (CC) and Finish Composite Adding Grading, Grain, Atmospherics, Artifacts, and More

Finally, once your CG element is locked into place, it's time for the final integration tweaks. We'll start with a handy procedural color-matching technique I've refined over the years for myself.

With the composite in the viewer and the foreground element selected, toggle on the color channel view to look only at the first color channel—in this case, the Red channel (see Figure 5.14). You should see a black and white grayscale image of the composite representing the Red channel. Notice that the foreground image doesn't really look like it *belongs* in, or is part of, the background image. You will now apply a levels adjustment to the Red

Although being color-deficient or color-blind will require you to always double-check your color corrections with someone who has good color vision, this method will help you get "most of the way there" to an excellent color correction and match. This method has helped countless artists I've taught who previously thought they were incapable of achieving such great results.

[Figure 5.14]
Red channel view of comp

[Figure 5.15]
Matching black/shadow
densities

channel only and follow this procedure until it looks like it is integrated and
actually a part of the background scene.

First, you want to match your black levels (or *shadow density*). Using the black
input level control to darken the black levels or the black output level control
to lift the black levels, match the darkest darks in your foreground image to the
darkest darks in the background image. This might mean darkening them or
brightening them (lifting the black levels), as shown in Figure 5.15.

Next, do the same thing for the white levels (or *highlights*). Starting with the
white level input control, brighten the whitest white levels in the foreground
image to match the whitest whites in the background image. Or, using the
white output control, darken the whitest whites to match the background's
whitest whites, as shown in Figure 5.16.

[Figure 5.16]
Matching white/highlight
densities

[Figure 5.17]
Matching gamma levels

After your black levels and white levels match, adjust your mid gray, or
gamma, levels, using the middle gamma input control to match the overall
mid gray level look of the image. Once the foreground image looks well
integrated into the background plate, repeat the process individually with
each of the Green and Blue channels, adjusting each with its own single color
channel levels adjustment (as shown in Figure 5.17).

[Figure 5.18] Black output and white output controls pushed too far will create very bad
color issues.

Once the individual channel levels adjustments are completed, an overall RGB levels or curves adjustment can be done to further refine the integration.

After your colors and densities are all matched (see Figure 5.19), you can add one more level of integration detail by adding in a layer of atmosphere, or *aerial perspective*. To do this, you can simply use the color picker or eyedropper tool to select a color in the atmosphere at the horizon or closest to where your CG element will be placed in the scene (see Figure 5.20).

[Figure 5.19]
Matched density/color levels

[Figure 5.20]
Color picker used to select atmosphere color

Then add a solid layer, or *constant*, using this color and apply the alpha of the 3D or keyed element to have it affect only this element (see Figure 5.21).

Finally, adjust this layer's opacity until the underlying CG element appears to take on the correct amount of atmosphere and blend perfectly into the scene (Figure 5.22).

Congratulations! You have successfully completed your first CG integration VFX.

Roto VFX: Energy Weapons and Effects

In this section, you will tackle two techniques at once: the creation of a roto-based VFX and the creation of an energy weapon VFX. *Roto-based VFX* are any effect that uses rotosplining or frame-by-frame animating as the main tools to create the effect. This can include anything from light saber effects (similar to what we are doing here) to digital amputations and wire and rig removals. *Energy weapon effects* include a wide range of effects but are mainly focused on those that appear to be created by high concentrations of energy: electricity, plasma, explosives, lasers, and so on. These types of VFX are very important to VFX artists because, well, creating dangerous-*looking* effects that will be placed in very close proximity to highly paid actors is a great deal of what we do. These effects are also critical to understand because knowing the structure of such weapons and the principles and techniques used to re-create them gives you the knowledge to tackle almost any energy-based effect (because in the real world they all respond photographically in a similar manner and have similar visual components and structure). We'll begin by examining the components of an energy weapon.

Components of an Energy Weapon or Effect

At the heart of every powerful energy weapon or discharge is its core, or source. As discussed in Chapter 1, when you create VFX, you're not always necessarily creating an exact replica of reality. More often than not, you're re-creating what *a camera would see* if it were filming the effect. In the case of a high-energy source or weapon, the limitations in latitude of photographic film and video sensors would likely cause the core of that energy source to *blow out* or *clip* the upper limits of the recording medium's ability. This would result in what would look like a pure white, RGB 255, 255, 255 origin that would take on the vague shape of whatever was producing it. In the case of a light saber, it would be a long, straight, sword-like core; on a ball of plasma, a sphere; and in the case of lightning, the familiar treelike branching. Because the energy produced from this type of weapon or discharge is so great and in flux (moving), it will usually appear as a glowing, soft-edged structure and will not be perfectly well defined (unless it is to be contained within some kind of structure).

Emanating outward from the core will be a hot, glowing area of highly charged or heated air. This is the area that begins to take on the energy's color characteristics, if it has any. And dissipating outward from this area will be the *falloff* area—the region where the charged particles, or air, taper off and return back to normal. You can see examples of these in Figure 5.23.

This example uses footage of actor Steve Roth, shown in Figure 5.24, portraying the sun god Ra. The footage was shot with helmet- and staff-tracking markers in front of a greenscreen.

For this example, we will create Ra's energy staff. Later, in Chapter 7, we'll add Ra's headpiece when we cover 3D object tracking and replacement.

Because the staff is a solid object and doesn't change shape, in this case, we can get away with using only one simple rotoshape for the core. Start by creating a rotoshape for the staff (using the roto guidelines covered in Chapter 3), as shown in Figure 5.25.

Because you will cover the entire shape with the energy weapon effect, you can save yourself some work by completely encompassing the staff within the rotoshape. Keyframe the shape to animate along with the character's motion (see Figure 5.26), following the technique and guidelines in Chapter 2.

[**Figure 5.23**] Examples of high-energy discharges

[**Figure 5.24**] Greenscreen footage of actor Steve Roth with tracking-markered helmet and staff

[**Figure 5.25**] Rotoshape of staff

[**Figure 5.26**] Rotoshape keyframed

For those few frames where there is significant motion blur, it is okay in this case to animate the entire shape of the rotospline to widen, for those few frames, to encompass the entire blurred shape, as shown in Figure 5.27.

Use this rotoshape on a solid white layer or constant to create an animated core, as shown in Figure 5.28.

Because this will no doubt be too sharp, feather the edges of the rotoshape outward, as shown in Figure 5.29. You may need to expand or dilate the shape slightly to maintain complete coverage of the stand-in staff.

It is also perfectly valid to use a blur on the shape instead of using an edge feather. Our guiding rule and principle in VFX applies here: "If it looks right, it's right."

After your core is complete, duplicate this shape (or layer), place it behind (or under) the core layer, expand or dilate it outward slightly, and then lower this layer's opacity. This layer will be used to create your energy weapon's glow, as shown in Figure 5.30. (You may need to further feather this layer's edges as well.)

[**Figure 5.27**] Rotoshape widened to cover motion blur

[**Figure 5.28**] White solid/constant used to create core

[**Figure 5.29**] Rotoshape feathered and dilated slightly to soften and widen energy core

[**Figure 5.30**] Duplicated layer expanded and made more transparent for glow

Next, duplicate the glow layer (placing it under or behind both previous layers) and repeat the process of expanding, feathering it slightly, and again lowering the opacity. You will use this to create the energy weapon's glow falloff, as shown in Figure 5.31.

Once you have this base energy weapon set up, you can add slight animated noise or displacements to each of the layers and/or their alphas to create pulsing effects, and slight color corrections to the glow layers to create color variations, as shown in Figure 5.32. You can add other glow, filter, and lens flare effects to this effect framework as well for finishing touches (see Figure 5.33). In Chapter 13 we will also learn to add fake interactive lighting to the character in this type of effect (which we would naturally expect to occur from the light being emitted from such a weapon).

And that's all there is to it. You can create almost any type of imaginable energy effect using this layering (core, glow, falloff) methodology—from suns, lasers, and plasma to photon torpedoes, light sabers, and lightning!

[Figure 5.31] Glow falloff added

[Figure 5.32] Pulse and color effects added

[Figure 5.33] Glow and lens flare finishes

Tips and Tricks for Energy VFX

Here are some tips and tricks to keep in mind and follow when creating energy-based weapons and effects. You want to avoid the common pitfalls that often ruin the results of beginning VFX artists creating these types of effects.

- When creating roto-based energy weapons and trying to follow stand-in objects that move quickly, there are two basic philosophies/methods as to how to approach and address dealing with motion blur. Neither is necessarily right or wrong; it all depends on the effect you are trying to achieve and how much time you have to achieve it.

  The first method is to ignore the motion blur and cover the entire area with a solid roto shape. This is the easiest and most painless way to go and gives a look very similar to that of the light sabers in the original *Star Wars* movies (see Figure 5.34).

  The second method is, perhaps, more technically accurate but much more difficult to control and get perfect results from. In this method you create a roto shape of the original stand-in object and then try to match the motion blur using motion blur control, shutter frame, and bias settings (see Figure 5.35).

- The core of an energy weapon is hot and thus emanates brilliant light. Color from falloff areas *cannot* appear in front of this light (as in Figure 5.36) because it is less brilliant. Core energy should *always* be the topmost layer or effect, with falloff light or color emanating from behind the source. You will almost always want to use Add or Screen blend modes for these types of effects.

[Figure 5.34] Solid rotoshape covering motion blur

[Figure 5.35] Motion blur added and adjusted to rotoshape

[Figure 5.36] Incorrect placement of color falloff on top of hot core effect

- Energy by its nature is moving and, like everything else in nature, not sharp or perfect edged. Energy weapons and effects should always have slightly feathered, natural glowing edges (though not too feathered). Adding slight noise or motion to the shapes of the core and outer layers will also add naturalistic effects.

- High-energy discharges are usually caught by photographic recording mediums as pure white, fading off to a color. When adding color to your energy weapons and effects, keep colors subtle and at the outer glow areas of the effects. *Do not* use candy-like saturated colors (as in Figure 5.37) and definitely *do not* color the core (unless you are specifically required to do so).

- When two energy sources overlap or collide (in the case of light sabers, crossing electrical branches, or overlapping fire or explosions), they are light sources and additive, meaning they combine to form white. They *cannot* shadow one another, and the glow of the frontmost source will combine and disappear into the core and glow of the rearmost effect. Correct and incorrect are shown in Figure 5.38.

- When two high-energy sources meet, they tend to arc or flash. Again, in a real photographic situation this would tend to completely overwhelm the photographic response and latitude of the recording medium, resulting in a completely blown out (or clipped to white) frame. You can use this phenomenon to your advantage to create seemingly super-powerful weapons and effects by creating lens flare elements at the point of crossing and then by simply placing a full white frame or two at the frame of impact. The result makes viewers feel that the impact was so intense it blew out the frame and overwhelmed the camera! Clever, huh?

[Figure 5.37] Coloration too saturated

[Figure 5.38] Correct (left) and incorrect (right) energy effect

Basic 2.5D VFX

There are times in VFX when creating an entire 3D scene is just too time and resource consuming. There are also those times when a 2D scene or composite just isn't enough. No discussion of VFX would be complete without exploring one of the VFX world's best kept and most closely guarded secrets… that mystical realm known as two and a half D (2.5D)!

Basic 2.5D VFX

2.5D truly captures the essence of VFX's "do whatever you have to do to get it done" spirit and comes in many forms, configurations, shapes, and flavors. In its most basic definition, 2.5D is any combination of 2D and 3D that isn't purely one or the other.

This could mean 2D layers stacked and spaced out in 3D space to allow parallax between the flat layers or a 3D scene with 2D cards instead of 3D geometry. Or it could mean 2D planes extruded into 3D to allow *just enough* parallax to pull off a 3D conversion. More often than not, it's some combination of any or all of these. 2.5D is the epitome of guerrilla production creativity, ingenuity, and resourcefulness and is a shining example of the filmmaking spirit.

2.5D is covered in many aspects and great detail in Chapters 6, 8, 10, 13, 14, and 15, but let's take a quick look at a few different, clever ways you can use 2.5D to create fake shadow and reflection effects.

2.5D Fake Shadows and Reflections

When you create VFX such as energy weapons, it's easy to overlook small details that are needed to make your results look realistic. When you create a light saber, for example, you also need to create the effect of the interactive light that this weapon emits. It's even easier to overlook the shadows and reflections that this interactive light would create as well.

Chapter 1 discussed the components of a shadow, which are important to VFX artists. The structure of shadows is very similar to the structure of the light of an energy weapon, only somewhat in reverse: contact, core or *umbra*, and falloff or *penumbra*. Creating fake shadows and reflections are vital skills you will need as a VFX artist. Let's take a look at two completely different methods to use 2.5D to create fake shadows and reflections. The first we'll call the 2.5D Card Method, and the second we'll call the 2.5D Projection Method.

2.5D Card Method of Creating Fake Shadows and Reflections

The advantage that creating 2.5D fake shadows and reflections has over just plain 2D fake shadows and reflections is that, using 2.5D, you can actually create realistic perspective. Shadows and reflections falling on an actual wall or ground plane and take on the more realistic foreshortening and falloff appearance that a simple 2D distortion cannot easily provide.

To create a simple fake 2.5D shadow or reflection, follow these steps:

1. Create a 2D plane in 3D space and apply a copy of the shadow or reflection's source image and alpha. This should give you a duplicate of your subject (in this case, our actor extracted from a bluescreen), as shown in Figure 5.39.

2. Move the pivot point of the 2D plane/card to the very bottom and then rotate the card 90 degrees on the X axis until it is laying down in the desired position, as shown in Figure 5.40.

[Figure 5.39] Duplicate plane

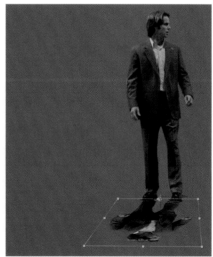

[Figure 5.40] Pivot point moved and card rotated 90 degrees on X axis

3. Apply a hue/saturation to the shadow object and remove all saturation, as shown in Figure 5.41.

4. Next, lower the brightness all the way to 0 to create a completely black shadow, as shown in Figure 5.42.

[Figure 5.41] Image desaturated

[Figure 5.42] Brightness lowered to black

[Figure 5.43] Blend mode set to multiply and opacity lowered

[Figure 5.44] Blur added to create falloff

5. Set the blend mode to multiply and lower the opacity until it matches the density of surrounding shadows in the scene, as shown in Figure 5.43.

6. Finish the shadow by applying blur (or a gradient mask with blur) to create a fake, but realistic falloff, as shown in Figure 5.44.

2.5D Projection Method of Creating Fake Shadows and Reflections

Whereas the previous method uses a 2D plane to simulate the look of a shadow with the shadow basically pasted on it, the effect falls apart if the shadow has to fall upon any uneven geometry, such as angular walls or stairs. For such a situation, you can use a slightly more sophisticated method and setup to actually project a shadow onto the desired geometry.

To begin, follow these steps:

[Figure 5.45] Silhouetted black shadow caster

1. Repeat steps 1–4 of the previous section to create a black silhouette of the shadow to be projected. This will be your *shadow caster* (shown in Figure 5.45).

2. Create stand-in geometry using 2D cards or basic 3D geometry for any areas of the background image scene that you'd like shadows to fall upon. Align these with the image and set their material and color to all white. These cards or objects (shown in Figure 5.46) will be your shadow catchers.

3. Create a spotlight in your scene like the one shown in Figure 5.47 and position it to project its light to cast a shadow from the silhouette card onto the stand-in geometry.

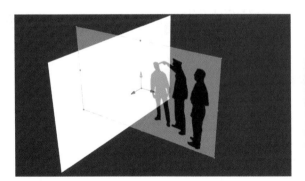

[Figure 5.46] White shadow catcher object

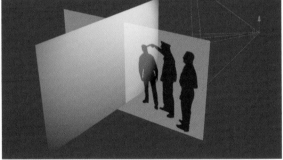

[Figure 5.47] Spotlight added and positioned to cast shadow

4. Set the spotlight to raytrace or cast shadows and the stand-in objects and materials to receive shadows (see Figure 5.48).

5. Set the shadow caster's object/material properties to cast shadows, seen by rays but set to unseen by camera. This will allow the object to cast shadows, using the alpha of the actual motion footage, onto the shadow catcher objects, yet not be seen itself in the scene, as shown in Figure 5.49).

[Figure 5.48] Materials set to receive shadows

[Figure 5.49] Shadow caster set to cast shadow but to be unseen by camera

6. As in step 5 of the previous section, setting the shadow catcher planes/objects blend mode to multiply and then lowering the opacity allows the shadows to blend nicely and naturally onto the contours of the underlying geometry and to appear to actually be in the scene, as shown in Figure 5.50.

7. Also as in the previous section, blurs can be applied to soften the shadows to match the background plate (see Figure 5.51).

Now that you've done a simple integration, in Chapter 6, we'll dive into some more sophisticated VFX and learn some more advanced techniques to further fine-tune your composites and integrations.

[Figure 5.50] 2.5D shadows appear to be casting onto image properly

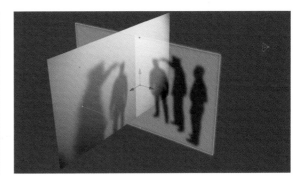

[Figure 5.51] Fine-tune blur added to soften shadows

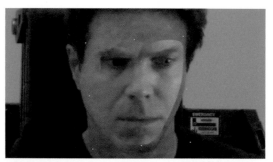
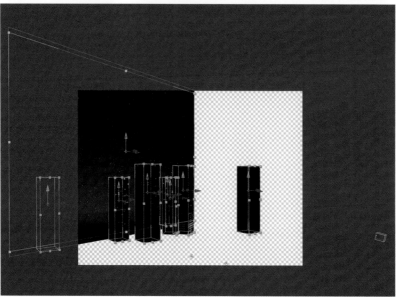

CHAPTER SIX

VFX Techniques II: Advanced Integration and Card Trick VFX

It's sometimes helpful to think of the VFX creation process as being done in stages, levels, or waves of refinement, with each pass refining the quality, look, and integration of the shot further and further.

After your tracking is solid and your integration is matching well, you'll want to dig down to the next level of refinement, matching the grain or noise characteristics of the acquisition medium and further integrating the foreground into the background plate by applying a VFX trick called a *light wrap*. A light wrap gives the look and appearance of light from the scene actually wrapping around your composited foreground element the way it would if it had actually been in the original scene.

Fine-Tuning Integration: Film Grain/Video Noise Matching and Light Wraps

Many compositing applications have built in or semi-automated grain-matching tools. However, to be truly masterful at integration, and to quickly be able to deal with anomalies and problems when they arise, a professional VFX artist must know how to match and create these fine-tuned details from scratch.

Matching Film Grain and Video Noise

As you remember from Chapter 1, film grain is the result of the interaction of light with the film emulsion's layers of silver halide crystals and the chemical processes used to develop those granules in the film. Similarly, video acquisition has noise artifacts created from the exposure of the photosensitive CCDs or CMOS chips to light. When you composite a CG element that has no inherent grain or noise (or other element with different grain/noise characteristics) into a film or video background plate that *does* have grain or noise, in order for these elements to integrate seamlessly, you need to match and add grain or noise to this added element. You probably won't have a grain/noise plate that perfectly matches every scenario, but you can easily create a simulated matching grain or noise. Though the characteristics of film grain and video noise are slightly different, they are similar enough that you can create a reasonable facsimile from scratch, using very basic tools and techniques, which will be indistinguishable from the real thing to the average viewer.

Upon closely examining an area of a piece of footage with film grain or video noise, you will notice that grain and noise are not static—they move and evolve. One of the biggest flaws in a VFX shot that can instantly give away that it is a composited 3D CGI element or bluescreen/greenscreen footage addition is the lack or mismatch of moving grain or noise.

When adding an element to a piece of footage that has film grain or video noise, you have to choose how you will apply this grain or noise. You basically have three options:

- Add grain or noise to only the new composited element.

- De-grain the entire footage and then add back grain or noise to the entire composited composition.

- Add grain or noise over the entire composition without de-graining the original plate.

Each of these methods has its advantages and disadvantages.

Applying grain to only the added element is usually the easiest and quickest way to go. The disadvantage to this method is that you have to very closely match the grain in the original plate or risk the added grain looking as noticeably bad as an element without grain at all.

Although de-graining the entire plate and adding back grain to the entire composite may sound like the purest way to go, the process of de-graining a plate inevitably leads to some softening of the footage and therefore may yield some unacceptable results with some footage.

Adding grain to the entire plate, although also a seemingly easier option, leads to effectively doubling the amount of grain on the areas of the plate that originally had grain to begin with, so again, it might lead to unacceptable results.

Video noise is usually a little more blocky and granular. Film grain tends to be softer with grain appearing as random blotchy patterns of the developed photosensitive granules. You will also notice that grain and noise have color to them (because they are the RGB-filtered photochemical granules or individual RGB pixels). They are not black and white like video snow. In fact, the color is usually perceptually biased toward the blues and greens, meaning it usually appears slightly more blue and green than red.

To create your own grain or noise layer, again as with all VFX, start by analyzing the footage and what exactly it is that you are matching.

Look at dark and mid-gray, or neutral-colored areas of the footage and zoom in to more clearly be able to see the shape, structure, definition, clarity, and color of the grain or noise pattern. Figures 6.1 through 6.3 show zoomed-in examples of film grain from three different Kodak film stocks. You can also scrub the timeline to get an idea of its motion.

In Photoshop, or the image-editing application of your choice, create a mid-gray (or approximately RGB 128, 128, 128) solid or constant, as shown in Figure 6.4.

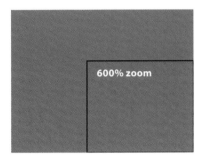

[Figure 6.1] Kodak 5245 EXR 50D Color Negative Film

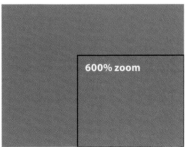

[Figure 6.2] Kodak 5218 VISION2 500T Color Negative Film

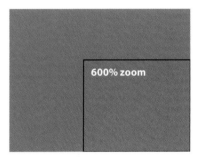

[Figure 6.3] Kodak 5217 VISION2 200T Color Negative Film

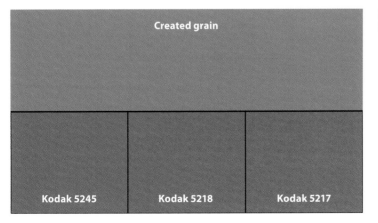

[Figure 6.4]
Mid-gray RGB 128, 128, 128 solid

Create a duplicate of this gray layer and apply motion Gaussian noise to it. Make sure to use color noise, and not monochromatic noise, and set the size or intensity high enough to best match the size and strength of the grain or noise in the footage. Figure 6.5 applies a color Gaussian noise of about 4%, zoomed in, and includes small comparisons of the actual film grain close-ups.

If the size of the grain is too small, you can always scale the layer up in size afterward.

Add a blur to the grain/noise layer and adjust the value to match the softness of the grain or noise in the footage. Usually, only a fraction of a pixel or so is sufficient. Figure 6.6 shows the results of a 0.5-pixel blur, again compared to the actual film grain close-ups.

[Figure 6.5]
Color Gaussian noise at approximately 4% applied to the duplicate 50% gray solid and compared to the actual film grain samples

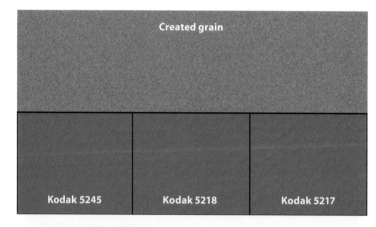

[Figure 6.6]
Gaussian blur of 0.5 pixel added and compared to the actual film grain samples

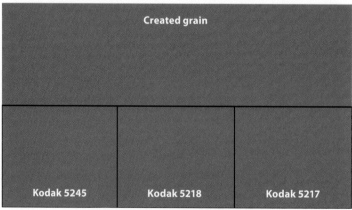

As you can see, you have a very close match to the grain in real film. To use this grain (or real film grain samples), simply switch the grain/noise layer's blending mode to overlay or soft light. Which one you choose will depend on

[Figure 6.7]
Before and after example of fake film grain added to a plate

how it looks and which looks better when applied to the footage. Then dial back the opacity to get the closest match to real film possible, as shown in the before and after example in Figure 6.7.

As a final tweak, you can apply a levels adjustment to your element to add more of a film-like contrast. You can add another curves adjustment to your grain layer by pulling the middle of the curve slightly negative in the red and green channels and boosting this same area of the curve slightly in the blues to better match the color characteristics of the grain or noise in your original plate if necessary. Your grain should now match very closely to the grain in the original plate and should help to integrate your foreground element nicely.

So how does adding this fake grain/noise help you? By adding matching grain or noise, you create a number of subtle consistencies to the shot that otherwise might not exist:

- The added blanket of grain/noise helps cover and normalize slight color and edge inconsistencies between the foreground elements you add and the original background plate.

- The moving grain/noise also helps add a level of motion refinement and consistency, better integrating elements that may not have originally been filmed at all but rendered instead and thus containing no inherent grain or noise.

Next, let's take a look at how to procedurally create light wraps to further refine and integrate your VFX shot.

Creating Procedural Light Wraps

When you shoot a photo, film, or video of a subject in a real-world lit environment, light from that environment hits that subject from all angles. This light then reflects off of the material properties of the subject—depending on whether that material is shiny, reflective, light absorbing, and so on. This light appears as a slightly lit rim around the edges of the subject. With a human subject, in a sunny exterior environment, the blue from the sky may be cast on the edges of the hair and shoulders; green from the grass might reflect up onto the shoes and pants; or a reflection of the sun off of a bright glass or metal object behind the subject might bloom and flare around the subject's edges. All these interactions of light are visual cues to the observer that the subject or object being viewed is actually *in* the scene.

You can simulate and fake this effect of light by using a technique called a *light wrap*. As with film grain, some plugins can create light wraps—but again, to be able to troubleshoot and harness the true power of this technique, you should learn to create this little bit of VFX wizardry yourself from scratch.

[Figure 6.8] Bluescreen shot of actor Chad Ayers

[Figure 6.9] Sunny park background used to show mirror ball comparison in Chapter 4

The key to creating a light wrap is creating a special alpha channel or matte called a *light wrap matte*.

To create a light wrap matte, begin by following the same steps you would use when doing a standard key composite (covered in Chapter 2). Your procedural light wrap matte will use the alpha from your keyed subject to, conveniently and semi-automatically, create the moving matte. In this example, you will key a bluescreen shot of actor Chad Ayers (Figure 6.8) over the sunny park background example (Figure 6.9) used in Chapter 4. Though the shot of Chad wasn't originally lit to be composited onto this background, as it would have been in a production, the disparity between the two will help illustrate and emphasize the power of this technique.

Following your usual key-extraction procedure, garbage matte (as shown in Chapter 2) the area to be keyed (Figures 6.10 and 6.11).

[**Figure 6.10**] Garbage matte spline

[**Figure 6.11**] Resulting much smaller bluescreen area left to be keyed only near subject

[**Figure 6.12**] Key extraction

[**Figure 6.13**] Slightly blurred background to simulate narrower DOF

[**Figure 6.14**] Simple composite/merge of actor over background

Then extract the subject by selecting a blue background color near the actor, as shown in Figure 6.12.

As you can tell from the VFX camera cues discussed in Chapter 1, this is a long lens shot, so you need to slightly blur the crisp in-focus background to simulate a narrower depth of field (DOF) (Figure 6.13).

After a simple composite/merge and quick color correction of the subject onto the background (Figure 6.14), you can see that the actor's edges don't have the kind of brightness or halo/glow you'd expect to see in such a bright sunny environment. This is where the light wrap comes in—to help ease this type of disparity.

Next you will take the alpha from the keyed foreground, by using a set channels effect or shuffle node, and set each of the red, green, and blue channels to use the alpha. Doing so gives you the black and white alpha also in the RGB channels, as shown in Figure 6.15.

[note]

For advanced artists, this process can all be done in the alpha channel alone without copying the alpha information to the RGB channels. But many applications make manipulations of just the alpha channel difficult to see, keep track of, and use. Unless you are very familiar with complex alpha manipulations, this method is easier and more straightforward and "visible" for all artists.

[note]

In some cases, you may have to matte out some additional small pieces of the light wrap matte where the edge of the screen or other unwanted barriers may create unwanted light wrap. In these cases, simply create small feathered mattes to match the blur used for the light wrap matte and "cut away" those unwanted areas.

[tip]

Many artists misuse the light wrap matte by directly applying it over the subject using a screen or add blend mode. Although doing that may help the scene somewhat, it merely applies an unnatural whitish glow to the subject and does not truly harness the power of this technique.

Next make a copy of this black-and-white RGB matte image and apply a blur to it. How much you blur is up to you and is adjustable to taste once you apply the effect, so add a healthy amount to start, as shown in Figure 6.16.

Simply laying the blurred image over the original will yield what looks like a glowing alpha channel, as shown in Figure 6.17.

That's partially what we want, because we want it to look like the light from the scene is glowing *onto* the subject, but not *outside* of the subject, as this method gives you so far. Luckily, you have the original, non-blurred alpha image that already defines the limits of where you want this effect to appear. All you need to do now is apply the alpha again using a silhouette luma blend mode, track matte, or another merge to achieve the finished alpha limited version of this matte, as shown in Figure 6.18.

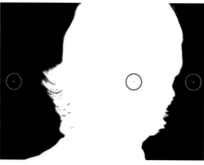

[Figure 6.15] The RGB channels set to the alpha channel using a set channels effect or shuffle node

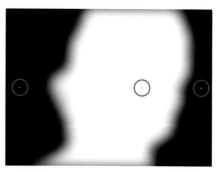

[Figure 6.16] Blur added to copy of black and white RGB

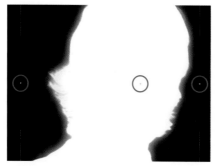

[Figure 6.17] Blurred version overlaid onto original unblurred matte

[Figure 6.18] Finished light wrap matte

[Figure 6.19] Blurred copy of background plate merged/placed over top of composite

[Figure 6.20] Blurred image masked by light wrap matte

It's time to use your light wrap matte.

To properly use the light wrap matte, create another copy of the background image (in this case the sunny park image), merge it on top of the entire composite, and blur it until small features are basically unrecognizable, as shown in Figure 6.19. Because you've already blurred this image to create the narrow depth-of-field effect, it should be okay as is, but feel free to add more blur to taste.

Next, you mask this blurred image using the light wrap matte as a luma matte, which will give you a result similar to Figure 6.20.

Notice how, unlike the light wrap matte alone, the image in Figure 6.20 takes on all the brightness and color information of the background image and applies it *only* to the edges of the foreground subject's edges. You can completely control how much or how little this light wrap wraps around your image by adjusting the blur amount in the original light wrap matte blur.

To apply this light wrap to the foreground image, simply set its blend mode, usually to either screen or add, but other blend modes will also work well in particular cases. I've used this technique with dark images and blend modes set to multiply as well for a darkening, shadow-type effect. Figure 6.21 shows the before, and Figures 6.22 and 6.23 show applied and exaggerated applications of the light wrap to better illustrate its effects.

Figure 6.24 shows added film grain, some desaturation, and a final couple of color corrections to get a better integrated, cooler, more filmic look.

[Figure 6.21] Base composite before light wrap

[Figure 6.22] Small amount of light wrap added to actor's edges

[Figure 6.23] Exaggerated amounts of light wrap added to actor's edges for better illustration

[Figure 6.24] Film grain, desaturation, and final color corrections added for a more stylized look

2D and 2.5D Crowd Replication

One of the coolest VFX tricks is to take small groups of small quantities and use them to create large quantities, or crowds—of people, animals, vehicles, arrows,… anything. When used for people, this kind of VFX shot is referred to as a *crowd replication* shot.

In its simplest form, this kind of effect is a simple 2D composite in which you matte and stitch together small groups, or *pods*, of people into one seamless image. Perhaps the most important factor when creating a podding-style crowd replication is the way in which it was shot to begin with. It is extremely important that the series of pod shots be carefully photographed with each pod of people in each shot placed in a distinct area, isolated from overlapping each other pod shot as much as possible to help prevent manual roto masking work. Preferably all pods should be lit under the same lighting conditions. That can be easier said than done, especially in extremely large crowd pod scenes, such as an arena or stadium, where exterior lighting conditions may change between pod shot takes.

For this example, I've illustrated a concert crowd scene shot with about 20 extras who will be podded and used to represent a crowd of a few hundred. To control the lighting as much as possible, I shot this on a small greenscreen stage and side lit as much as possible to try and get mainly silhouetted figures in the foreground audience crowd. In Figure 6.25 you can see the compilation of the 10 or so positions in which the pod of 20 people was placed. Starting at the front left, a couple-minute take was filmed of the crowd cheering, then moving everyone to the right and repeating the process, being as careful each time to prevent each pod from overlapping the next. Once the width of the stage had been covered, the process was repeated, starting in a position back behind where the first had been filmed. Again, this was repeated across the stage and then back one more position. Finally, one last take was done with the small crowd directly camera center in front of the camera.

In the compositing application, a render of a 3D stage (with composited performers) was placed at the bottom, or back, of the composite. Each small pod of crowd members was imported and (starting from the frontmost pod and working toward the back of the crowd, towards the camera) garbage matted, keyed, and positioned until the full crowd was achieved, as shown in Figure 6.26.

[Figure 6.25]
Compilation of ten pod positions of small group of extras filmed on greenscreen

[**Figure 6.26**] Pods imported, garbage matted, keyed, positioned, and composited into the full crowd scene

To take this technique a step further, each of the pod layers (as well as the background stage) can be mapped to a 3D plane, or *card*, and pushed back into Z-space. You can then offset each card to create a hybrid 2D/3D or 2.5D composite, as seen in the top images in Figure 6.27. This method allows you to make camera moves in 3D with real motion parallax, add interactive animated relighting (concert spotlights in this case), and atmospheric and depth-of-field blur effects.

The sequences shown in Figures 6.28 and 6.29, created by two of my students, show how amazing, convincing, and versatile this effect can be. Figure 6.28, created by Michael Keith, shows the application of this method for the creation of a 2.5D angry mob. Figure 6.29, created by Emmy-nominated Ed Ruiz II, shows this method taken to the extreme—to create a Persian army of more than 100,000 for the Battle of Thermopylae shot created for the TV show *Deadliest Warrior*.

[Figure 6.27]
Pods layers pushed into Z-space and offset to create motion parallax, depth-of-field, and interactive relighting effects

[Figure 6.28] 2.5D crowd replication used to create an angry mob, created by Michael Keith

[Figure 6.29] Crowd replication taken to the extreme, created by Ed Ruiz II using the same technique

2D Face Replacement

Many times, VFX artists are called upon to do some visual surgery to help, or even sometimes save, a production. Face replacement is quite common—replacing the face of a stunt double with the actor's face. Sadly, a few times in recent history we have lost an actor before the wrap of a production. In those cases a double was filmed and that double's face was replaced throughout the remainder of the production using this technique.

As with all VFX, the key to a great face replacement is the similarity of actors' facial structures, accurate matching of the lighting and camera and, optimally, positioning and movement. Unfortunately, these things are not always achievable, and you have to work with positioning that is off, actors with very different facial structures, and lighting that often doesn't quite match. There is a lot you can do, though, to remedy these VFX maladies.

To illustrate face replacement, we'll start with a greenscreen shot of actor Steve Roth in an aircraft prop seat, as shown in Figure 6.30.

[**Figure 6.30**] Actor Steve Roth filmed on greenscreen sitting in an aircraft prop seat

[**Figure 6.31**] Actor Chad Ayers, also filmed on greenscreen sitting in an aircraft prop seat, but in a different position and with slightly different lighting

His face will be replaced with actor Chad Ayers, also filmed in the seat but in a different position and with different lighting, just to make it a little trickier (Figure 6.31).

Because it is impossible for a human to hold completely still, you must stabilize both actors' faces to create a solid replacement. The corners of the eyes is a good location to 2 point track for this type of facial stabilization and is done exactly the same way as described in the 2D tracking lesson in Chapter 3. The only difference is that instead of applying the tracking data as a matchmove, you will apply it inversely to *stabilize*. I highly recommend using only position and rotation and not scale in this case, because tracking errors amplified by the close positioning of the tracking markers tend to make a face replacement go haywire.

Once both plates are stabilized, move the pivot point of the actor's face—the one you will be using as the replacement—to the center between the actor's eyes. This will allow you to precisely align, rotate, and scale the face to make the best match possible. Reduce the opacity of the plate to about 50% and position the two plates until the inside corners of the eyes are aligned, as shown in Figure 6.32.

[**Figure 6.32**] Pivot point moved to center between actor's eyes, and plates aligned to match the position of the inside corners of the eyes

Next, rotate and scale the plate until the eyes, nose, and mouth line up. The best way to know when is to look for what I call the creepy factor.

[note]

If the integration is particularly difficult or the actor has distinctive facial features, scars, or other distinguishing characteristics, you may reduce the full face mask shape around the eyes, nose, and mouth to be as small as you need to resemble more of a "monkey face mask." Doing so will show a lot more of the original actor's face and less of the one replacing it, but it is usually sufficient enough to allow the replacing actor to be able to do his/her performance with the required facial expressions.

The *creepy factor* is the moment when the two faces seem to blend into some creepy combination (as shown in Figure 6.33).

The appearance of "the creepy factor" indicates that it is time to begin blending the two faces. Create a mask in the shape of… well … a mask (the full-face ones like the famous drama mask decorations you might have seen before—see Figure 6.34).

Now make the replacing actor's plate 100% solid (opaque) to see where you are (Figure 6.35). You want this mask to be razor sharp on the edges for now so that you can best identify the areas of mismatch in the plates.

You can also create a dip in the mask around the actor's right eye (like I have in the example) to cut out the hair that was dangling over it.

Next, go channel by channel, using a levels adjustment and the procedural color-matching technique covered in Chapter 5. In the red channel (Figure 6.36), you can see the noticeable difference between the lighting on the two sides of the face.

[Figure 6.33] Plates rotated and scaled until they align and exhibit the creepy factor

[Figure 6.34] Spline mask creating facial mask shape

[Figure 6.35] Replacing plate made 100% solid/opaque

[Figure 6.36] Red channel

Ideally, you want the seam between the two plates to completely disappear, as you can see indicated by the yellow arrow in Figure 6.37. Unfortunately, in this example, making the seam on one side disappear as you'd like it to causes the other side of the face's seam to get worse.

In this case, your best bet is to "split the difference" between the two sides, as shown in Figure 6.38. Next, repeat the process with the green and blue channels, as shown in Figures 6.39 through 6.42.

[**Figure 6.37**] Seam between two plates disappearing

[**Figure 6.38**] Splitting the difference in the red channel levels adjustment match

[**Figure 6.39**] Green channel

[**Figure 6.40**] Splitting the difference in the green channel levels adjustment match

[**Figure 6.41**] Blue channel

[**Figure 6.42**] Splitting the difference in the blue channel levels adjustment match

Once the color match is done, return to the full RGB view, as shown in Figure 6.43.

As you can see, it looks okay, but not that great. Well, here's where the magic happens! Go into the mask properties for the spline that's creating the mask and turn up the edge feather or blur. Like magic, you should suddenly see a great integration happen (like the one seen in Figure 6.44) right before your very eyes!

Zooming back out to full view (Figure 6.45) reveals quite a convincing and natural-looking face replacement using quite mismatched source plates.

[Figure 6.43] RGB view of color corrected/matched face replacement plate

[Figure 6.44] Turning up the edge feather/blur on your mask spline suddenly creates a great integration, almost like magic.

[Figure 6.45] Zooming back out to full view reveals a nice result from less-than-perfect source footage.

Card Tricks: Outside-the-Box Strategies

Although it may now be obvious to you, from seeing how we were able to map pods of people onto simple 3D planes/cards (or *billboards*) to create stunning crowd VFX, there is a lot more you can do to expand this technique and create some pretty incredible VFX with very little in the way of actual 3D geometry, all with just these simple 2D cards.

It's time for me to teach you how to use some outside-the-box thinking strategies to create some amazing VFX, which I affectionately call *card tricks!*

The Grid

Chapter 1 discussed how VFX are meant to save money, time, and resources. It should always be at the forefront of your mind to approach a VFX shot with this mindset. Far too often, I see VFX artists believing they are in some way "purists" to some imaginary art form that they have deemed the holy grail of VFX technique. I've seen it happen with 3D modelers, 3D animators, 3D sculptors, and particle and simulation artists, each believing because it is their favorite or specialty, that it's the *best* way to approach a VFX shot. All too often, I watch them get sucked into the black hole vortex of time, emerging after the shot could have been completed a dozen times with a simpler, more straightforward approach. Remember, you only need to create what is going to be seen and nothing more. Nowhere is this more applicable than in a shot such as our previous concert example, which may require extensive and intricate trussing, scaffolding, or other supportive gridwork.

Let's say you have been told you need to create a theater stage. You will need to create a complex grid of lighting support trusswork that will be tucked away in the rafters above the stage. Many 3D artists would jump right in and get started modeling in their favorite 3D package—wasting millions of needless polygons, many rendering hours, and too much production time. We will use a little outside-the-box thinking to save you tons of work and time. First, we will consider that this trusswork is tucked away in the rafters, so we will never really be getting that close to it. We'll only get close enough to see the form and the parallax that occurs between sections of the trussing.

If you think of a truss in its simplest form, it is a series of metal rods or tubing welded together to form flat planes, which are then connected with welded crossbeams to form solid geometric shapes such as cubes, n-gons (a polygon with n or "any value" number of sides), or grids.

Knowing this, open Photoshop (yes, Photoshop) and create a solid black square large enough for a decent texture (1024×1024 or 2048×2048 should be fine). Select the Gradient tool, click the small gradient thumbnail to open the Gradient Editor, and choose a black to white gradient, as shown in Figure 6.46.

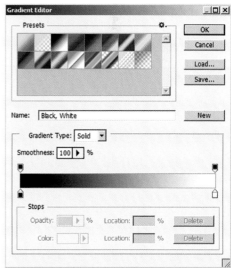

If you remember from Chapter 4 a bump map and displacement map are, like most other maps, just grayscale alpha maps. If you were to create a rod or tube using such a map, all you would really need to do to represent it is to have the tube start at black, gradate to white at the closest point to us (the viewer), and then round back to black again as the other edge of the tube falls away from us. To simulate this, open the Gradient Editor again and slide the bottom white color marker to the middle of the gradient. Click at the far

[Figure 6.46] Gradient Editor with black to white gradient selected

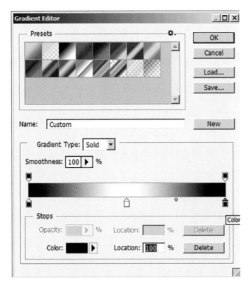

[Figure 6.47] Gradient Editor with black to white to black reflective gradient created

right (where the white color flag originally was) to create a new white color flag. Double-click this flag and then the tool's Color swatch at the bottom of the Gradient Editor tool and then select black. You should now see a *reflective gradient* (one that seems to mirror itself on each side) that looks like the one in Figure 6.47.

Next, after you make sure you've selected the Gradient tool from the toolbar, start about a quarter of the way from the top of the image and while holding down the Shift key (to constrain your tube or pipe to a perfect angle), click and drag vertically a small distance (about the thickness you want your piping to be). You should see a nice resemblance to the top support tube, similar to Figure 6.48.

Next create another solid black layer, and this time, starting about a quarter of the way from the bottom, repeat the above steps to get the bottom support tube. Now, using a little of the blending mode magic you learned in Chapters 1 and 2, set the blending mode to Lighten. You should now see both the top and bottom support struts, similar to Figure 6.49.

[Figure 6.48] First tube, or pipe, created with the Gradient tool

[Figure 6.49] Lighten mode allows both layers' struts to appear

Repeat this process again, adding another layer, but this time carefully draw your gradient line at an angle, creating a crossbeam. When you change the blending mode of this layer to Lighten, in addition to now being able to see all your tubing, you will see that the Lighten mode, together with the gradient you created, nicely (and automatically) creates the look of a complex metal join or weld, as seen in the yellow circled areas in Figure 6.50.

Experiment with placing and creating tubes and joins and then create an open-ended, tileable truss pattern like you see in Figure 6.51 and save this out as your color map.

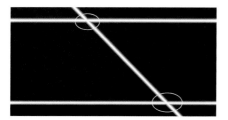

[Figure 6.50] Joins, or welds, automatically created when Lighten mode is selected

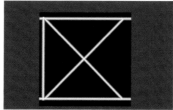

[Figure 6.51] Open-ended, tileable truss pattern

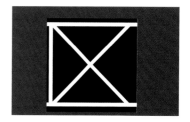

[Figure 6.52] Matching truss alpha map

Next, you want to be able to see through the open areas of the trusses (now black), so you will create a simple matching alpha channel/map to do this. Click Select menu > All, Edit menu > Copy Merged, and then Edit menu > Paste to quickly create a copy to the entire set in one layer. This will be your color and/or diffuse map. Duplicate this layer and then, with this layer selected and the Shift key held down, select each of the black areas using the Magic Wand tool (you may have to adjust the Tolerance level—somewhere around 10 or 20 should work well) until the only thing not selected are the trusses. Click Select menu > Inverse (this will select all of the truss areas that you want to be solid or opaque). Click Edit menu > Fill and fill these areas with 100% white, which will give you your matching alpha map (similar to Figure 6.52). Then save this out as your alpha map.

Now it's time to create your geometry. No fancy 3D models are needed here. In your 3D application (or even in your compositing application—this will work as well, just without as many texture controls), create a simple, long, flat rectangle, as shown in Figure 6.53.

[Figure 6.53]
Simple, flat, rectangular plane

Next, duplicate this plane and push it back into Z-space so that it sits where you would expect the next truss to be in a series. Repeat this process as many times as you'd like (as shown in Figure 6.54).

Place a light in the scene and a camera below the rectangles looking up, as you would if you were looking up at a ceiling (Figure 6.55).

[Figure 6.54]
Duplicated and offset truss rectangles

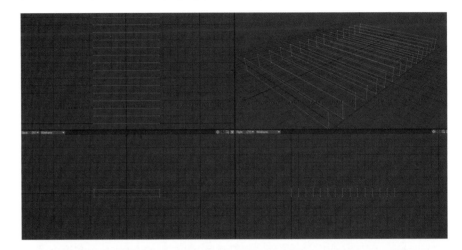

[Figure 6.55]
Light and camera placed in scene

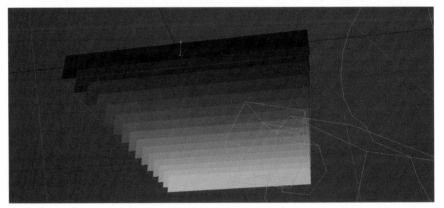

Feel free to replicate these truss rectangles some more and rotate them vertically, as in Figure 6.56, or however you'd like to add more complexity.

Now apply the color map into the color channel, diffuse channel, and bump channel (you can use this same map as a displacement as well), as shown in Figure 6.57, and load the alpha you created into the alpha, or transparency/opacity, channel.

All that's left to do is to click Render! You should now have a complex grid of trusswork similar to Figure 6.58 (all with about 45 polygons in this case).

[Figure 6.56]
Two more sets of rectangles
duplicated then rotated
vertically

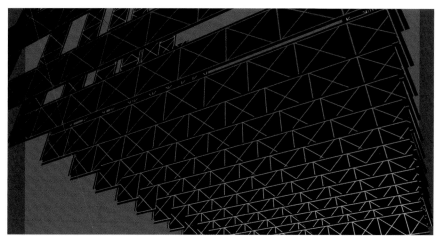

[Figure 6.57]
Color map loaded into color,
diffuse, and bump channels

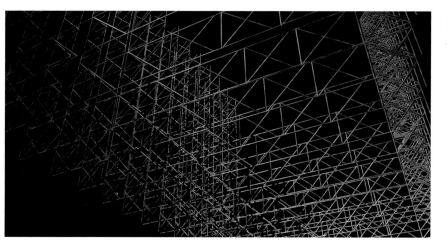

[Figure 6.58]
Rendered trusswork using
only 45 polygons or planes/
layers

House of Cards

Let's take this card concept in another direction and one step further, using it to quickly put together simple structures. This entire example will use only two images: a background night sky (Figure 6.59) and a cropped face of a high-rise building (Figure 6.60).

[**Figure 6.59**] Background night sky image

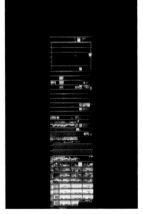

[**Figure 6.60**] Cropped face of high-rise building image

Load the sky image onto a card and place it way in the background. You will likely have to scale it up so that it fills the frame after you move it so far into the distance.

Next, map the high-rise image onto a simple rectangular card. Duplicate this card and move the pivot point to one side edge. Doing this allows you to easily rotate the duplicate 90 degrees while keeping its edge aligned with the original. Repeat this process until you've made a cube with the four identical cards, as shown in Figure 6.61.

Next, group these planes into one group or object, duplicate it a few times, and distribute the duplicate copies around the scene however you'd like, rotating them and moving them in Z-space, as shown in Figure 6.62.

Finally, place a camera, a few lights, and some color correction and/or post effects (in this case I've only added a bloom effect, nothing else) to create another amazing shot, as shown in Figure 6.63, with only 29 polygons in this case!

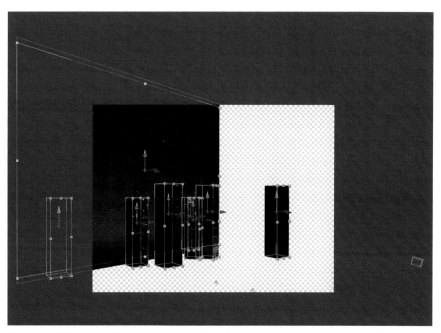

[**Figure 6.61**] Four identical image planes rotated and arranged into cube

[**Figure 6.62**] Grouped image cards distributed around the scene, rotated, and offset in Z-space

[**Figure 6.63**] Finished shot with only 29 polygons and one bloom effect

[note]

A bloom effect creates a glowing effect to (usually) bright areas of an image. A tolerance control determines what point on the histogram will be considered "bright" and therefore bloomed. It is also possible to bloom dark areas instead of bright areas of an image.

[Figure 6.64] Image of dove in flight used as basis for card trick

[Figure 6.65] Back wing element

[Figure 6.66] Body element

[Figure 6.67] Front wing element

For the Birds

Now that you probably have some great ideas for how you can use these card tricks with alphas to create trusses, railings, distant trees, signs, scaffolding, vents and grills, simple buildings, and a myriad of other handy elements, I'm going to blow your mind and show you how you can put these card tricks into motion to create flying birds! Now, you might be asking yourself why you would want to create birds at all, right? Well, because everyone inherently knows what a bird looks like and can gauge an average bird's size. Birds are one of those clever little VFX secrets that can be used to add scale to a 3D environment or miniature set piece, lead the audience's attention, and focus and direct them anywhere on the screen you would like them to be looking. This trick instantly brings a matte painting or 3D environment to life that might otherwise appear completely lifeless. Simply add some flying birds in the distance, and *voila!*—the scene instantly springs to life.

Although it is entirely possible to just sketch or roto basic bird shapes for birds that will appear in the distance, I always prefer to work with photorealistic sources wherever possible. In this example, you will create a flock of doves using an image of a dove (Figure 6.64) in flight as the basis for this 2.5D card trick.

First, cut the dove into pieces (yeah, I know how that sounds). You want to create separate back wing (Figure 6.65), body (Figure 6.66), and front wing (Figure 6.67) elements. These will require a little cloning work to patch and extend areas so that they are seamless and overlap properly.

Next, as with the buildings we did earlier, you will map each image to a flat 3D card and move the pivot points of the wing cards to the point on the card/image where they would attach and rotate from in real life. This may not be the exact same place on each card, and that is perfectly fine—remember: "in VFX, if it looks right, it's right." Rotate and translate them to intersect the body card as you would a paper bird (see Figures 6.68 and 6.69).

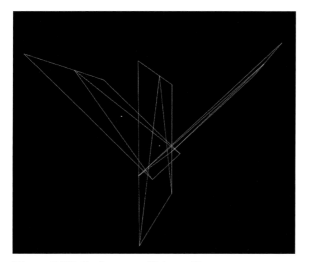

[Figure 6.68] Cards arranged into position

[Figure 6.69] Cards arranged into position with color maps applied

Keyframe and loop the animation of each wing to rotate from the upmost position (Figure 6.70) to the downmost position (Figure 6.71) over about five frames. Keyframe the wings back to the starting position over about four frames. The total rotation should be around 135 degrees, depending on the type and wingspan of the bird, of course.

Enabling motion blur at these flapping speeds should give you a nice, natural-looking, flapping motion blur (see Figure 6.72).

Next, as you did with the buildings, group these layers together and replicate them into a small group of ten or so. Offset their motions in time so that their wings flap at different times (Figure 6.73).

[Figure 6.70] Wing in upmost rotation position

[Figure 6.71] Wing in downmost rotation position

[Figure 6.72] Natural-looking wing motion blur created by keyframed rotation

[Figure 6.73] Small group of birds with wing motions and positions offset and randomized

You can also add a slight noise or randomization *expression* (a mathematical equation, procedure, or variable) to the position of each bird so that they drift around slightly while still basically maintaining formation.

You can now replicate this group into larger flocks, as shown in Figures 6.74 and 6.75, and keyframe an overall motion path.

For finishing touches, you could add a lens flare to simulate the sun over the birds (Figure 6.76) and then drop in a background, as shown in Figure 6.77. You could also scale the flock layer down and put them in the distance, as shown in Figure 6.78, to add life and a sense of depth and scale to a static image or matte painting.

[Figure 6.74]
Small group duplicated into large flock—wireframe box preview

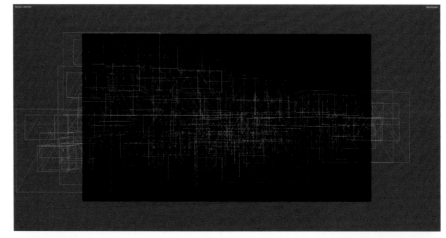

[Figure 6.75]
Small group duplicated into large flock—textured preview

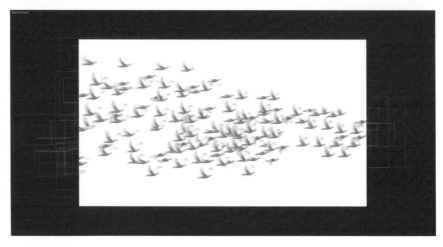

[Figure 6.76] Lens flare sun added

[Figure 6.77] Flock of animated 2.5D doves with background added

[Figure 6.78]
Flock of animated 2.5D doves scaled down to provide scale and depth to scene or matte painting

Now that you've had a chance to explore some great 2D and 2.5D tracking and integration VFX, you will see that there are times when you just can't quite get a 2D or 2.5D tracking solution to work. In those cases, you will have to turn to a full 3D tracking and integration solution. And that's exactly where you will start in Chapter 7.

CHAPTER SEVEN

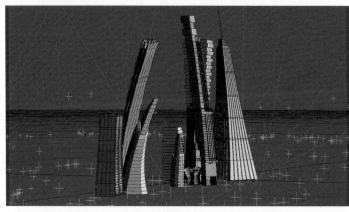

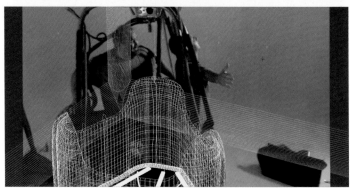

VFX Techniques III: 3D VFX

Many VFX shots can be accomplished using only 2D and 2.5D techniques, but there are definitely those times when only a fully 3D solution will get the job done. At some point, almost every VFX artist I've trained has asked me, "How do I know when I need to do a 3D track instead of a 2D track?", "When does a VFX shot have to actually be 3D and not some 2D or 2.5D cheat?", and "Where is the line between the two?" After having to answer these questions and discussing all of the variables so many times over so many years, I've distilled the best answers down to one simple, easy-to-understand, concept:

Whenever the movement in a VFX shot is not just a slide straight up and down, left and right, or forward and back, but instead moves in any kind of orbital or rotational motion through a scene or around an object, which allows you to see parts of that object that were previously self-occluded or which would reveal that a 2D solution element was merely a flat plane in the scene, you will then need a 3D solution (as seen in the example of 2D bookcase cards in Figure 7.1).

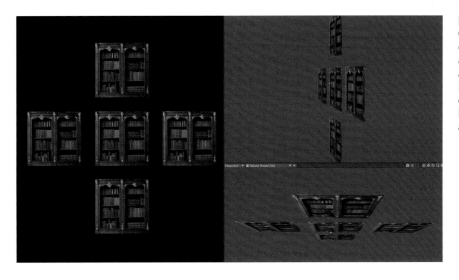

[Figure 7.1]
On the left, 2D bookcase cards seen from front view and moved up, down, left, and right; on the right, the illusion is being broken by orbital camera movement horizontally (upper image) and vertically (lower image)

3D Tracking and Matchmoving CG

There is something truly magical about the first time you see a VFX shot you've completed that includes a 3D motion track and matchmove. Traditionally, a VFX shot always had to be locked down or completely motionless in order to be accomplished at all. There was even a very specific camera, the Mitchell, which was used especially for VFX work due to its rock-solid handling of film through the film gate, preventing even the slightest gate weave. But the development of sophisticated algorithms in the scientific computer vision, space exploration, and architectural research communities has allowed the creation of truly incredible 3D tracking software that has made the moving VFX shot, even the wildly moving VFX shot, the standard in the industry. By triangulating rays projected from common feature points in multiple images, the positions of those points, other relative points in the scene, and even the camera's position can be calculated and plotted in 3D space. The motion of the camera through the scene can be tracked, recorded, and re-created (*3D camera tracking*), and from the generated point cloud, geometry of objects within the calculated area can also be created (*3D photogrammetry*). A VFX artist now has to be able to take just about any piece of moving footage and be able to track and matchmove it to allow for the integration of 2D and/or 3D VFX elements.

As with every skill discussed so far, to be truly great at this fine science/art of 3D tracking and matchmoving, you need to fully understand what a 3D track is, know how it is accomplished (under the hood), and arrive at the best approach and implementation of the techniques involved.

You create a 3D camera track and matchmove in a number of well-defined steps. For this example, we will use a camera shot similar to the one used in the 2D tracking example, except in this one, the camera passes in a curved motion over a lower overpass that runs almost perpendicular to the camera's path, creating an orbiting camera motion path around a stretch of roadway.

3D Tracking

To begin, carefully review and analyze your footage. Enter any known data about the camera, its lens, and movement into the 3D tracking software. The more known information you provide to the software, the more accurate the 3D track calculation will be. In this example, the exact camera and lens information is unknown, but you can determine that the focal length remains constant throughout the shot so you should enter that information as well.

You can also see that the camera does not simply pan around a fixed point (as it does when it is on a tripod) but moves freely through the scene, so you will set this camera motion calculation to be a *free move*.

As discussed in the overview in Chapter 4, the first thing a 3D tracking application does is an automated mass 2D track of the entire moving scene. Whereas in a normal 2D track you might think that the more solid tracks, the better, in a 2D track *you* select the high-contrast patterns and search areas for your one, two, or four point tracks to follow, not the software. The automated mass 2D track that begins a 3D track *automatically* identifies and tracks tens, hundreds, even thousands of whatever points it determines are worth tracking, capped only by the limit number and confidence tolerance value you set.

Although it would seem that tracking hundreds of points completely auto-matically would be just fantastic, remember that *any* high-contrast point will be tracked, even if it isn't relevant to the motion of a scene. Consider, for example, a camera shot where the cameraperson handholds the camera and simply walks forward down a sidewalk. Any car pulling out of a drive-way, person or dog walking past the camera in another direction, and so on will be tracked and included in the solve, creating an absolute mess. Many 3D tracking applications have the ability to filter out tracks that seem to go against the majority of motion data points, but it's always better to mask out these types of distractions before starting a 3D track. Fortunately, most 3D tracking applications have excellent masking tools created specifically for this purpose—to tell the trackers what areas to completely ignore.

In this case, I've used keyframable roto Mask tools in the Pixel Farm's PFTrack to mask out the barrier wall in the lower foreground of the shot, as well as most of the sky and car window pieces in the upper portion of the frame (Figure 7.2)—remember, clouds move and evolve, so they are not good tracking targets. Once any elements in the scene that might obviously cause miscalculations are masked off, an auto track of the scene can be started, as shown in Figure 7.3.

After the mass 2D track is done (note that many tracking applications will track both forward and then again backward in this process), the software analyzes the track points for confidence level to determine which might be good candidates for inclusion into the solve equation. *Confidence* means, literally, the confidence the software has that this tracked point or pattern is the same throughout all or part of the duration of the shot. Tracked feature

[note]

It was only a few years ago that 3D camera tracking software required 7 to 12 solidly tracked points to arrive at an accurately calculated solution or *camera solve*. Today, with the advancements in technology, many 3D tracking applications can create a decent solve from as few as 3 to 4 solidly tracked points.

[Figure 7.2] Roto Mask tool masking off bottom foreground barrier wall and top of frame sky and car window edges

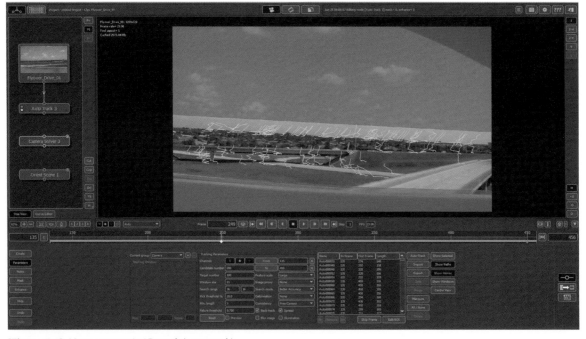

[Figure 7.3] Mass automatic 2D track (auto track)

points that fall below the set level of confidence threshold are automatically filtered out and eliminated. Keep in mind that the software needs only the minimum number of candidates on any one contiguous frame, meaning that *active* candidates can change between frames as long as at least the minimum number is maintained frame to frame. The longer the duration of a candidate point's consistency, of course, the better and more solid the solve will be.

Once the 2D auto track is done, the next step is to set the software to actually perform the camera solve for the 3D track. This process used to require an exhausting waiting period while the computer chugged away at a mind-bending number of calculations. Today's new powerful software and hardware can blaze through these calculations at blistering speeds compared to those of just a few years ago.

When the solve is complete, a 3D point cloud will be produced (Figure 7.4) that shows the solved tracking points as well as the camera and the camera's motion path. This 3D scene can be navigated as in most other 3D application scenes to better analyze the results (see Figure 7.5). You can scrub

[Figure 7.4]
Camera solve of track, showing the solved tracking points, grid, and horizon line

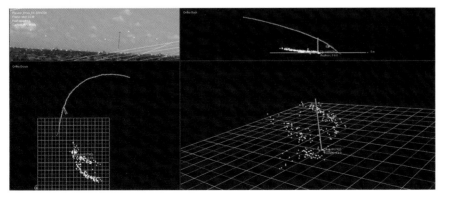

[Figure 7.5]
3D view of camera solve showing tracked points, camera, and camera motion path in standard 3D-application-style orthogonal views

the timeline to see the 3D camera's motion (as shown in Figure 7.6 and Figure 7.7), to check the track's solidity in the 2D view, or to navigate the scene in 3D to verify candidate points and recognizable feature structures.

The camera solve may appear slightly, or extremely, off axis and may even be upside down. This is because the software has no point of reference other than the way the pixels of the moving image correlate to one another and so this disorientation is not a problem at all. To correct this, you can simply rotate the entire scene once you bring it into your 3D application. Or, more conveniently, you can use one of the excellent scene orientation features included in most 3D tracking applications. These allow you to set one of the candidate points as the 3D scene's origin (XYZ 0, 0, 0), determine which points lie on similar planes, or even just tumble or fly the scene into proper orientation.

After the scene is properly oriented, most 3D tracking applications allow you to place test objects. These are simple 3D objects that can be placed within the 3D point cloud. They can then be viewed along with the original

[Figure 7.6]
Timeline scrub of track result at frame 275

[Figure 7.7]
Timeline scrub of track result at frame 399

[Figure 7.8]
Sample of test object at frame 290

[Figure 7.9]
Sample of movement and object lock at frame 330

footage to verify a solid track and identify any possible problems such as drift or motion path jitter or noise, as seen in the test objects, pins, and tacks in Figures 7.8 and 7.9.

If the track is solid and the 3D motion looks good with the test objects inserted into the scene, the solve is ready for export as a 3D scene to most 3D and compositing applications' native scene file formats.

[tip]

Most 3D tracking applications also provide motion smoothing and filter features, as well as manual keyframe editing, to correct any such errors.

3D Matchmoving CG

When the 3D track scene file is opened in the 3D or compositing application, it should very closely resemble the result in the 3D tracking application—with the exception that the candidate points will likely be converted to, and replaced with, non-rendering null objects (see Figure 7.10).

The scene file will include the tracking points as nulls, the camera (and camera's motion path), and a scene master null or controller (to orient and move the entire scene as a whole if necessary), as shown in Figure 7.11.

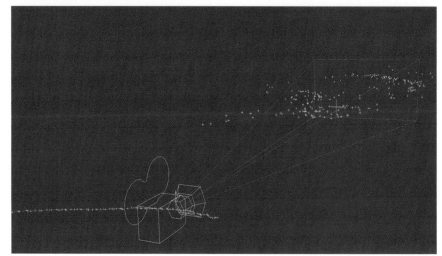

Next, you will load your 3D object into the scene (as seen in the oddly shaped 3D buildings placed in Figure 7.12) and light it to match the scene using the same lighting techniques covered in Chapter 5 for CG lighting and integration.

The easiest method for placing a 3D object in a scene consisting of only a point cloud is to determine the 3D position of one of the tracker/null objects in the scene that is on or near the location where the CG object is supposed be. Then simply cut and paste, or manually apply, that positional data to the CG object, which should place it close enough to easily tweak its position

[Figure 7.12]
3D buildings loaded into scene

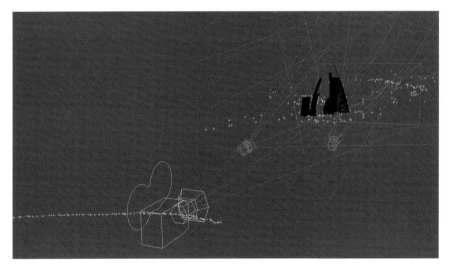

[Figure 7.13]
3D buildings positioned at location of tracker/null on underpass ramp

manually. Some 3D applications will allow you to *parent* a 3D object to another, instantly snapping it to the second object's position without having to cut and paste or manually apply any data at all. In this example, the building models have been placed at the position of a null on the underpass (see Figure 7.13), allowing for an odd scene but an excellent example.

Next you should check the position of the 3D object in the scene for accuracy and *lock* (to make sure the 3D element is locked to the plate). Tweaking the 3D object's positioning may be required, as any misplacement in the X, Y, or Z will manifest itself in the model, causing the object to appear to float, drift, or slip off the background plate. The best method of curing such errors is to make sure the correct tracker/null was selected in the 2D viewing area with the background footage in view, then view the 3D object and point cloud in all 3D orthogonal and perspective views to ensure it is placed properly, and finally nudge the model little by little until a perfect position and lock is achieved. It should be noted that the 3D objects being integrated may (at this point) still overlap things they shouldn't, such as the overpass guardrails in this example. This will be addressed in the final compositing steps.

Once the object is locked perfectly to the background plate, you should render it out along with its alpha (or using a file format that has the alpha embedded).

In the compositing application, you should load the original background footage and the rendered 3D CG element, making sure to set the 3D element's alpha to straight alpha and not premultiplied.

Note the difference in real perspective change as we pass the true 3D buildings. If we were to compare this to placing images of the buildings on 2D cards and try to do a 2D or 2.5D cheat with this camera motion, the flattening of the plane and loss of believability would be apparent, and the illusion would be broken, revealing that the buildings were simply 2D cards. You can see this in the final frame of the sequence in Figure 7.14 with the buildings mapped onto a card and then scrubbed back to the beginning frame in Figure 7.15.

Finally, all that's left to do is for you to composite the 3D CG buildings over the background plate using simple roto masks to remove any areas (such

[Figure 7.14] A building element, mapped to a 2D card to illustrate the need for a 3D solution in this case. Shown is the end frame of the sequence.

[Figure 7.15] Scrubbing back to the starting frame reveals that the buildings are merely a big, flat 2D card.

[**Figure 7.16**] 3D tracked and composited buildings at beginning of shot

[**Figure 7.17**] 3D tracked and composited buildings at middle of shot

as those overlapping the overpass guardrails) that would be hidden or occluded. You can then use the same color matching, fake shadow, and light wrap techniques covered in earlier chapters to arrive at a convincing result, as seen in Figures 7.16 through 7.18.

[**Figure 7.18**] 3D tracked and composited buildings at end of shot

Hand 3D Tracking: Matchimation

As discussed in Chapter 3 with 2D tracking and matchmoving, no matter how much control you think you have over the shooting environment or how well you plan and prepare for a VFX shoot, there are always going to be those times when "surprises" happen and leave you with a shot that your 3D tracking application just won't have anything to do with and that just seems to be impossible to track. This is that type of scenario where everything covered in this book about going "under the hood" and "guerrilla VFX" comes to save the day.

This example is from the short comedy film *Balloon* that I co-produced and directed with actors Rob Goodman and Sabrina Kurzman. We arrived on-set to find that the painters had taken down and disposed of almost all of our proper tracking markers and had left us with a much-less-than-perfect green-screen paint job. Because we only had this small soundstage set, jib/operator, and rented hot air balloon basket for a very short amount of time, we had no choice but to make the best of it. We placed some tape for markers as high as we could reach and just started shooting. The shot we will examine is a jib/crane shot mimicking the famous "I'm the king of the world!" *Titanic* shot. The camera starts from a low angle looking up at actor Rob Goodman in the balloon basket, as seen in Figure 7.19.

The camera cranes up toward, and then past, Rob (Figures 7.20 and 7.21), continuing upward but tilting down to reveal the character's wife (played by actor Valerie Zach) who is terrified and huddled in the bottom of the balloon's basket (as seen in Figure 7.22). This camera angle and view give us what will be a panoramic view of them and the landscape far below. As you can see from these first three frames, in the majority of the shot there are really no consistent high contrast points on the greenscreen background to track (none stay on-screen for more than a few frames), and the balloon basket and actors occlude virtually every trackable background object, as well as each other, during almost the entire shot.

[Figure 7.19] Start of VFX jib/crane shot—low angle, looking up at actor Rob Goodman

[Figure 7.20] VFX jib/crane shot continues toward actor Rob Goodman.

[Figure 7.21] VFX jib/crane continues past Rob.

[Figure 7.22] VFX jib/crane shot continuing up and then tilting down to reveal actor Valerie Zach cowering in the balloon's basket

In Figure 7.23 we get a glimpse of one of the only frames where the tracking tape markers are actually visible. One clever technique we can use to squeeze something trackable out of the footage is to use the technique you learned in the grunge map section of Chapter 2. By finding the channel that has the most contrast on the background—in this case, obviously the green channel, (seen in Figure 7.24)—we can use the same levels adjustment technique used with the grunge maps to crush the levels and literally squeeze out some high-contrast, trackable features (as shown in Figure 7.25). Although a 3D tracking application will likely still have trouble tracking such features (because increasing such small differences in contrast will also increase the amounts of noise), the bad paint job turns out to be extremely helpful in this case; it gives us many small, high-contrast features (even cross-shapes, as seen in Figure 7.26) that the human eye can see very well to track manually by hand.

[Figure 7.23] Continuation of VFX jib/crane shot. A few tape tracking markers can be seen on the greenscreen.

[Figure 7.24] The green color channel of Figure 7.23 reveals slight contrast details in the poor paint job.

[Figure 7.25] Crushing the levels with a severe levels adjustment reveals high contrast details where none previously existed.

[Figure 7.26] These high-contrast light and dark spots and angles can be 3D tracked by hand, and then the non-destructive levels adjustment can be simply turned off after the track is completed.

As with an automated 3D track, the more info you have, or can deduce, the better. To do the manual hand 3D track or *matchimation* for this example, first construct a three-walled *cyc* (short for *cyclorama,* the seamless, curved, walled backdrop used in photography and movie productions) or any other known features in your shot's environment in your 3D application (as seen in Figure 7.27) to approximate the configuration of the one used in the shoot. Many times you won't have any specific information about the dimensions of the set cyc actually used, aside from eyeball guesstimates. The only thing we need, though, as you will see, is for the walls of our 3D cyc to be flat and perpendicular, like the real ones.

If there are enough trackable features on the walls and floor of the shot, that's all we really need. But in this case, the basket and actors occlude just about everything in the frame. Since the actors move around, the balloon's basket is our best bet to hand track and use as an additional stationary object to matchimate (literally *match + animate*) to in this case. So, we will build as close a replica to the basket as possible and position it as accurately as can be guesstimated if we don't know the exact measurements. You can see why having a comprehensive and accurate survey, reference photos, and so on of the set or location can be extremely helpful and save tons of time. In a case like this, where we are dealing with an uncommon subject, a little research goes a long way. When researching different balloon baskets to find one that closely matched the one on-set, I was able to find a close model and even some dimensions that helped me build and place a rough model of the basket on the 3D cyc (as shown in Figure 7.28). Again, it doesn't have to be perfect, but the closer, the better, and the more time it will save you when you're animating.

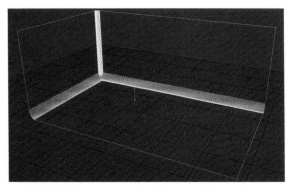

[Figure 7.27] Three-walled cyc built in 3D to best approximate and match the one used to film the shot

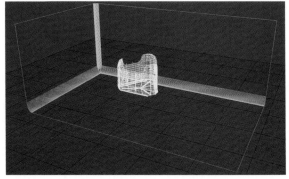

[Figure 7.28] Rough model of balloon basket, placed on 3D cyc

Once all your rough 3D set pieces are built and placed as accurately as possible, it's time to place the camera. Create a camera and enter any known information about the camera into your 3D application, such as the film back, angle of view, lens information, and so forth. Load your footage into the background of your 3D application and set your view to the camera's view and the viewing mode to wireframe, point, or any other easy-to-see-through mode. When your camera is created, it will be placed in the scene in some default position, as in Figure 7.29.

You can start at whatever frame has the easiest vantage point and the most features available to track. You can work beginning to end, end to beginning, middle forward and then middle backward—whatever works best. There is no right or wrong way. Move the camera until it's in the closest matching position for the frame you are on. In this case, I've started at the end, at frame 338, as seen in Figure 7.30.

[Figure 7.29]
3D application with footage in background, looking through camera set to Wireframe view mode, in default position

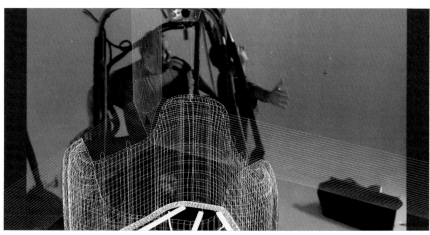

[Figure 7.30]
Camera is positioned to match its real-world counterpart and make the cyc wall and balloon basket align as perfectly as possible.

[n o t e]

While tweaking the placement and positioning of scene elements, make sure they stay aligned with reality. Don't position scene elements in a way they would not exist in reality simply to make alignment easier (buildings set floating off the ground, leaning at angles, and so on).

It's important to understand that once you set all your scene elements into their final position, you will *only* move and keyframe the camera—nothing else. Tweaking the position of your scene elements is fine to get the best possible starting frame before you start, but once you've started keyframing, only touch the camera and nothing else.

You can see from Figure 7.31 that the camera and scene elements are positioned as you would imagine them from seeing the footage frames. Always double-check your 3D scenes in all orthogonal and perspective views, as seen in Figure 7.32.

[Figure 7.31]
Perspective view of scene showing camera, cyc, and basket in plausible realistic positioning

[Figure 7.32]
Checking all orthogonal and perspective views of scene to assure camera, cyc, and basket are all in plausible, realistic positions

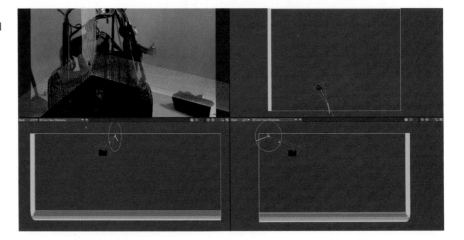

Now for the secret to this method: *transitive relation* (if A = B, and B = C, then A = C). In Figure 7.33 you can see that the tracking tape markers are on the walls. You don't know exactly where, in the X, Y, or Z, on the walls they are, but you do that they are there… on the walls. By that train of logic, if your 3D cyc is aligned with the one in the scene, and you place a null (marker) exactly on the face of one of the 3D cyc's walls aligning it with the marker in the footage (as seen in Figure 7.34), and you duplicate this marker and place the additional duplicate markers on the same plane (and they too align with the footage), as long as they line up on other frames when only the camera is moved, you should have a relatively accurate match. Figure 7.35 shows additional markers duplicated and aligned onto the same plane/wall and then onto the adjacent perpendicular wall (which again follows this same logic).

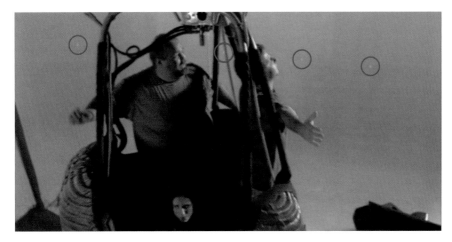

[Figure 7.33]
Tape tracking markers visible on walls

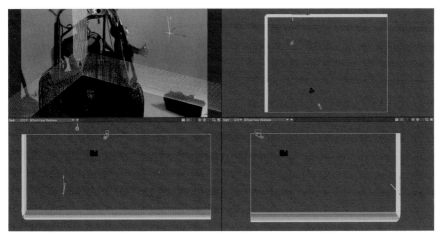

[Figure 7.34]
Null placed on 3D cyc model wall aligned with tape tracking marker visible on real studio wall

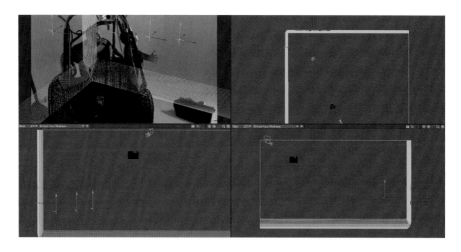

In Figure 7.36, you can see the camera wireframe view with the basket and wall null/markers aligned to match. Figure 7.37 shows the disparity when the time slider is moved back 28 frames to frame 310. Notice how the nulls and basket no longer align properly. The only thing left for you to do is to keyframe the camera into the new position, following all the same keyframe animation rules covered in the roto section of Chapter 3 (easier said than done, I know, but with practice, you will get the hang of it). In Figure 7.38 you can see the camera repositioned to realign the tape tracking markers and balloon basket. When markers fall out of frame, use the basket to estimate camera placement and alignment; when the basket is out of frame, use the tape markers, and vice versa, with other known scene elements and stand-in geometries, as seen in Figure 7.39, where no tape wall markers are visible and only the basket is used for camera positioning.

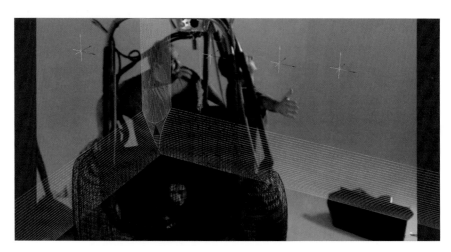

[Figure 7.37]
Nulls and basket become unaligned with their respective real-world counterparts as time slider moves to an earlier frame

[Figure 7.38]
Camera repositioned and keyframed to realign wall nulls and basket

[Figure 7.39]
3D balloon basket aligned with real-world basket since no tape tracking markers are visible anywhere in the frame

[tip]

When adding 3D elements to your 3D hand tracked scene, it's vital that you remember to place these objects where they would appear in the scene in the real world in order to get correct camera movement look and parallax.

Once your keyframed camera sticks throughout the shot, and you have completed your 3D hand matchimation track you can add 3D objects to the scene, as usual, for rendering.

3D Object Tracking and Replacement

Until now, I have discussed tracking the camera through the scene to place objects in the scene. But what if you want to place an object on something moving *within* the scene, such as on a moving person? There are many methods of accomplishing this, including the same kind of simple matchimation covered in the previous section. Many new 3D tracking applications also have geometry and object-tracking features that allow for just this task. These features basically do the same things as the steps we are about to do, except they add a semi-automated geometry or object build at the end of this process, which basically just inverts the camera motion data in the same way inverting 2D camera tracking data creates a stabilization. But for the sake of those who don't have such a newfangled tool, you will accomplish this effect in true guerrilla VFX fashion, using a method that any 3D tracking application is capable of.

This example uses footage of actor Steve Roth (seen in Figures 7.40 through 7.42), portraying the Egyptian god Ra looking down at his worshippers and then victoriously holding up his spear, shot on a greenscreen. Steve is wearing a helmet and holding a broomstick affixed with reflective tracking markers for an experimental rig I created using a high-powered LED diode attached to the top of the camera lens hood. This allowed the tracking markers to glow and reflect the diode's light while not being bright enough to cast any visible

[Figure 7.40] Actor Steve Roth portraying the Egyptian god Ra

[Figure 7.41] Actor Steve Roth portraying the Egyptian god Ra looking down over his worshippers

[Figure 7.42] Actor Steve Roth portraying the Egyptian god Ra victoriously holding up his spear

light on the actor or the background. A stone hawk head will replace Steve's head and helmet, and a matching spear will replace the broomstick.

Because many 3D tracking applications can accomplish a good camera solve with only a handful of points, you want this track to be as simple as possible. Rather than using an auto track to do the primary 2D track, in this case, you will use a handful of user-defined user tracks instead. Selecting one user track at a time, place a tracker on each of the handful of helmet markers and track them (as shown in Figure 7.43). These work just like normal 2D trackers in any compositing application. You can see the trackers and their paths' movement in Figures 7.44 and 7.45. Tracking each marker individually allows you to ensure that each tracker has a solid track throughout the move and even allows you to pause, keyframe, and make fine-tuning adjustments as the track progresses.

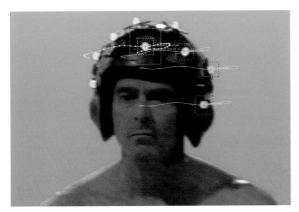

[Figure 7.43] User tracks placed to track individual reflective helmet markers

[Figure 7.44] Movement paths of each user track

[Figure 7.45] Accuracy and positioning of each marker can be seen in the lower tracker zoom window, allowing for precise placement and adjustment

Once you complete all the 2D user tracks, solve them as usual for a 3D track. You can review the resulting camera movement in the 3D views. The motion of the helmet is being interpreted as a camera moving around a stationary helmet instead of the other way around. This is very helpful in many cases because it allows you to work with a stationary object as the replacement, providing for some very complex VFX to be created quite simply. Any 3D object you place in front of the camera will appear to move whereas the camera will appear to be stationary. The 3D camera track seen in Figure 7.46 locks very well but contains a lot of noise or jitter. Run a *refining* solve by smoothing or filtering the camera's motion path, which results in a smoother, more natural-looking motion and path, as shown in Figure 7.47. Then export the 3D camera track as a scene file to your 3D application of choice, as you did at the beginning of this chapter.

After you open the scene file in the 3D application, import the 3D objects that will be replacing the helmet and broomstick and place them to align with the tracking nulls, as shown in Figure 7.48. Be careful to check the

[Figure 7.46]
Camera solve seen in 3D. Notice the noise and jitter in this solve.

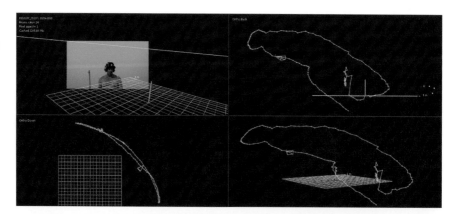

[Figure 7.47]
Refining solve done with smooth/filter enabled to smooth path

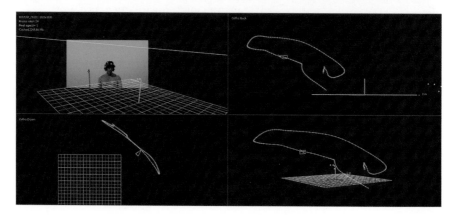

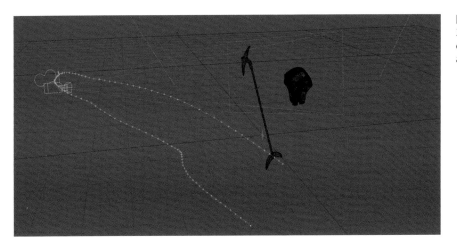

[Figure 7.48]
3D headpiece and spear elements imported and aligned with tracker nulls

[Figure 7.49]
Checking the alignment of the 3D objects from the camera's perspective in Wireframe mode to more easily see the location of the tracker nulls

alignment of objects in all 3D and camera views in wireframe mode (as shown in Figure 7.49) to ensure that the 3D object aligns properly to where the original tracking markers were. An offset or mismatch will result in the 3D object sliding and floating off its desired position.

Next, light the 3D objects to match the footage, and then check the motion of the solid textured objects for both position and lighting matches, as shown in Figures 7.50 through 7.52. Because the motion of the spear is quite basic, matchimate it by hand using the same method as in the previous section—creating a null to match the position of the broomstick marker and then keyframing its position to match. Once these look great, you can render out the 3D elements with their respective alpha channels, as shown in Figure 7.53.

[Figure 7.50] 3D elements lit to match background footage and motion checked at the beginning of motion frame 319

[Figure 7.51] Lighting and motion checked for match at widest motion frame 377

[Figure 7.52] Lighting and motion checked for match at actor's end motion frame 489

[Figure 7.53] 3D elements rendered by themselves along with their alpha channels

[Figure 7.54] Greenscreen footage of actor Steve Roth

[Figure 7.55] Render of 3D ancient temple background element

[Figure 7.56] Rectangular roto mask to remove broom handle and second roto shape created to roto out hand to place back over 3D spear element

After you render the 3D elements, bring the background plate and the element plates into your compositing application for integration. Composite the greenscreen footage of Steve Roth (Figure 7.54) over the 3D rendering of an ancient temple (Figure 7.55).

Because you want the spear to appear in Steve's hand, you need to remove the broomstick from the background plate. You can do this using a simple rectangular roto mask, as shown in Figure 7.56, and create a second roto mask to cut out the part of Steve's hand that needs to be placed back over the spear shaft. Figure 7.57 shows Steve keyed from the background greenscreen, color corrected to match, and composited over the ancient temple render.

[**Figure 7.57**] Actor Steve Roth keyed and color corrected to match background element

[**Figure 7.58**] 3D elements composited over, and color corrected to match, actor and background

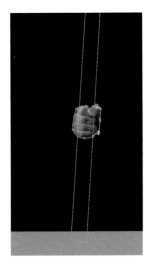

[**Figure 7.59**] Hand element roto extracted from copy of original greenscreen plate

[**Figure 7.60**] Hand element composited over 3D spear element to complete the illusion of the spear being in the actor's hand

Next, the 3D elements are composited over the actor greenscreen plate and color corrected to match (as seen in Figure 7.58). The hand element can then be composited (Figure 7.59) over that in order to place the spear in Steve's hand (Figure 7.60).

Add a shadow to the headpiece (Figure 7.61) using the techniques covered in Chapter 5, and add fire (Figure 7.62), smoke, and glow elements (Figure 7.63) to the CG temple.

[Figure 7.61] Fake shadow added on top of actor greenscreen plate and under 3D headpiece element

[Figure 7.62] Torch fire and smoke elements composited over 3D background ancient temple element

[Figure 7.63] Copies of fire elements, scaled up, blurred heavily, and composited over temple using additive blend mode to create fire glow effect

[Figure 7.64] For final polish, a final color correction, film grain, and a vignette are added to impart a more dramatic look to the shot.

For a final polish add a final color correction, film grain, and a vignette to impart a more dramatic look to the shot, as shown in Figure 7.64.

You can see that the 3D elements all move and work together nicely in the final shots, as shown in Figures 7.65 through 7.67.

Now that we have covered 2D and 3D VFX, it's time to explore that mystical realm between the two… 2.5D VFX.

[Figure 7.65]
First frame of finished shot

[Figure 7.66]
Frame showing actor's widest range of motion

[Figure 7.67]
Frame showing actor's final position

CHAPTER EIGHT

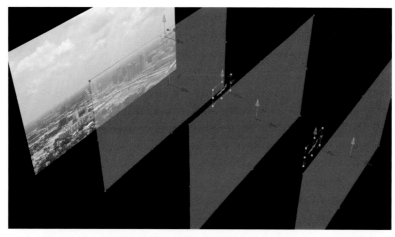

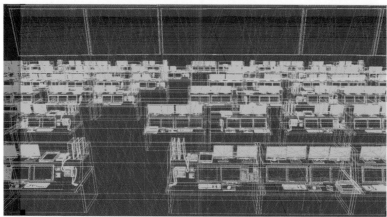

VFX Techniques IV: 2.5D VFX

By far, some of my favorite VFX techniques involve 2.5D VFX. Combine their speed, efficiency, excellent results, and just downright cleverness, and you have the VFX artist's proverbial "ace in the hole" for too many situations to even list here. Let's start with some of the most commonly used, effective, and quickest-to-deploy 2.5D VFX.

2.5D Atmosphere FX

As you'll recall from our discussion of VFX cues in Chapter 1, there is a direct and proportional relationship between an object's apparent size, position in frame, and the atmosphere or aerial perspective seen in that object. One of the best examples of this—which I like to use to demonstrate this principle—is a simple setup using an aerial background and a 3D CG jet airplane.

Let's start with the aerial photo shown in Figure 8.1, which I shot from a helicopter overlooking downtown, and a 3D model of a jet airplane.

[Figure 8.1] Aerial photo for use as background, overlooking downtown

The jet is lit to match the background image using the 3D light matching technique covered in Chapter 5 and four lights (one for the key sun light, two to emulate sky fill, and one to emulate bounce from the ground, as seen in Figure 8.2).

This simple controlled lighting setup provides a very nice result, as seen in Figure 8.3, with the base lighting matching fairly well.

If you do a simple composite of this (now 2D) jet over the aerial background image, duplicate the jet two times, then offset and scale each of the two jet copies down smaller and smaller and position them properly for their scale to emulate the look of the two copies being consecutively farther and farther away (see Figure 8.4), you can see that something definitely still looks *off*.

[Figure 8.2]
3D jet model lit with four lights: a key sun light, two sky fills, and one ground bounce

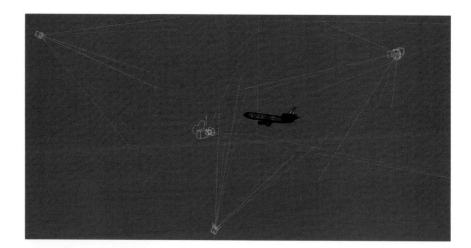

[Figure 8.3] Jet rendered with simple four-light setup

[Figure 8.4] Composite of jet and two copies over background aerial photo

The composited jets, while placed appropriately and scaled smaller, aren't really blended with the image. They look like the flat, pasted-on cards/billboards they actually are (Figure 8.5). In addition, when the camera moves, there will be no realistic parallax motion between the aircraft, which will definitely reveal the scene for what it is—a fake.

If we undo the scaling so that all three jets are the same size (you can do a little cheating in scale, but the less the better) and actually push the background and 2D image planes into Z-space (Figure 8.6), we can not only get a realistic motion parallax between the scene elements when we move the camera, but we can achieve depth-of-field blur and Z-depth atmospheric effects as well.

[Figure 8.5]
Jet images scaled for size but all on one 2D plane

[Figure 8.6]
Jet images actually moved in depth into Z-space to achieve realistic apparent perspective size differences

[Figure 8.7] Colors of atmosphere chosen from heaviest accumulation of atmosphere on the horizon

[Figure 8.8] First atmosphere card/plane placed in front of rearmost jet

[Figure 8.9] Second atmosphere card placed in front of middle jet

To realistically integrate the jets into the background plate, though, you will definitely need to address the disparity in atmospherics or aerial perspective. There are two basic components to doing this: first, adding the look of the color and density that atmospheric particles accumulate and impart with distance and, second, correcting the black (shadow) and white (highlight) densities of each aircraft image to properly emulate the way atmosphere scatters light and reduces apparent contrast with distance.

First, to address the aerial perspective, a clever 2.5D solution is to create 2D cards/billboards of colored atmosphere (chosen by using any color selection or info tool to select the color of the heaviest level of accumulated atmosphere on the horizon) for each element in front of the background plate. Figure 8.7 shows the areas sampled and the color chosen for these atmosphere planes. One of these planes is then placed in front of each foreground element, as shown in Figures 8.8 through 8.10. Next the opacity is reduced on each plane to simulate the buildup of atmosphere (as shown in Figure 8.11).

Although this does an excellent job of simulating atmospheric buildup and would be great for creating/simulating heavy fog or smog, the atmosphere cards accumulate atmosphere on each other and even the background (we presume the background is shot the way it was supposed to appear and is not supposed to be altered), so each card's atmosphere value needs to be limited to only the jets. Fortunately, there are already alpha channels for each jet, so applying each jet's alpha to the corresponding atmosphere plane in front of it limits the atmosphere effect of each card only to its respective aircraft (also allowing precise individual control of the application of aerial perspective to each element) and prevents it from affecting the background plate at all, as seen in Figures 8.12 and 8.13.

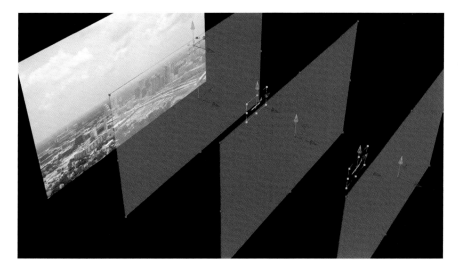

[Figure 8.10]
Third atmosphere card placed in front of closest jet and then opacity/transparency of all planes turned down to simulate atmospheric buildup

[Figure 8.11] Opacity of all atmosphere cards reduced to simulate atmospheric buildup

[Figure 8.12] Each jet's alpha is applied to the atmosphere card in front of it, allowing for precise individual control of the amount of atmosphere applied to each jet as well as preventing any additional atmosphere from contaminating the background plate.

[Figure 8.13]
3D view of individual atmosphere applied to each jet

[tip]

When doing element integration, an excellent methodology and habit to get into is always checking and correcting shadow density match (black levels), highlight density match (white levels), and then gamma match (gray levels), in that order.

Finally, the opacity of each atmosphere card is adjusted to match the atmosphere buildup at each jet's distance. A levels adjustment is also used to lift the shadow densities and lower the highlight densities, using the color matching and integration technique discussed in Chapter 5, to arrive at a natural-looking atmosphere for each plane's apparent Z-depth, as seen in Figure 8.14.

2.5D Smoke: Cloud FX

Building upon the techniques used to create 2.5D atmosphere, we can add a few steps and create convincing 2.5D smoke and cloud FX. If you happen to have real smoke footage that works with the desired effect, by all means use that. I always prefer to use real footage whenever possible. But for those times when none is available, many times, a simple image will do.

This example uses an image of dark smoke (see Figure 8.15). If your smoke image doesn't already have an alpha, by simply manipulating a copy of the image by simply manipulating a copy of the image (by inverting and/or levels adjustment), you can usually create a quick alpha/luma matte.

First, create a 2D plane/card from the image. Immediately center and move its pivot point to the base of the smoke. This is important because we will be animating the apparent billowing and upward evolution of the smoke column from and around this pivot point, as shown in Figure 8.16.

[Figure 8.15] Smoke image with transparency

[Figure 8.16] Smoke card with pivot point centered and moved to base

[Figure 8.17] Smoke card scaled down to beginning size

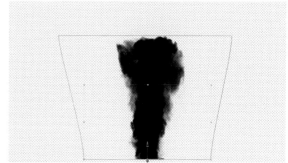

[Figure 8.18] Smoke card's top two vertices keyframed to scale up slowly while preventing base of smoke column from expanding

Next, scale the smoke down to whatever beginning size you feel works best (see Figure 8.17). Keyframe the scale of the top two vertices of the card up and outward to create the ending height and size of a slow-rising smoke column, as shown in Figure 8.18 (keyframing/animating only the two top vertices keeps the base of the smoke column from expanding).

To create a natural billowing effect, you will use a distort tool. Using a large brush (see Figure 8.19) and a rotation distortion (many other types of distort tools will work for this as well), keyframe outward puffs of the smoke to

[Figure 8.19] Large brush used to rotate-distort outward puff of smoke column

[Figure 8.20] Outward puff of smoke keyframed to slowly rotate-distort as column of smoke rises

[Figure 8.21] Larger brush used to slowly bulge-distort smoke column outward as column of smoke rises

slowly rotate-distort (as seen in Figure 8.20) while the image is also scaling upward. Next, use an even larger brush to slowly animate a bulge distortion of the smoke column in the upper areas to simulate billowing growth (see Figure 8.21).

Apply the same techniques used in the previous section to integrate three copies of the smoke and different apparent depths in our aerial jet scene. Again, as in Figure 8.22, place three copies of the same smoke in the scene and move them to different depths behind each of the jets. (If this were an actual production, you could also offset and animate/distort the motions of each of the columns of smoke to look completely different.) Mask off each smoke column at the bottom with a feathered mask to conceal the straight frame's edge and animate each to slowly rise (see Figure 8.23). Use the same atmosphere and color correction techniques covered in the previous section to add atmosphere and color correct the smoke columns to integrate, as seen in Figure 8.24. Make sure to choose the colors of the atmosphere cards for the smoke columns by using a color selection/eyedropper tool to select neutrally colored objects at the same guesstimated Z-depth where each element appears.

[Figure 8.22] Three copies of smoke column effect applied to flat cards and pushed into Z-space behind each jet card

[Figure 8.23] Smoke columns at their highest animated growth

[Figure 8.24] Smoke columns color corrected and atmosphere applied to integrate each at its respective apparent depth in the scene

Faking Z-Depth and Ambient Occlusion

In the real world, light is blocked or obstructed by objects. We call this *occlusion*. If you look at a real image—as in the bluescreen shot of actor Chad Ayers shown in Figure 8.25—you will notice objects in the scene occlude some of the light in the scene from hitting any objects they come into contact with, as well as parts of themselves. In this case, Chad partially occludes the floor and parts of himself, as shown in the close-up Figure 8.26.

Fake Ambient Occlusion (AO)

You can emulate this effect in a 3D application using a 3D model and 3D lights to create what's called an *occlusion map* or to render an *occlusion pass*, as seen in Figure 8.27. If only ambient light is used for this pass, it's called an *ambient occlusion* (or AO) pass. These occlusion passes are characterized by soft pools of floor shadows and soft gradations of shadow that appear to

[Figure 8.25] Bluescreen shot of actor Chad Ayers

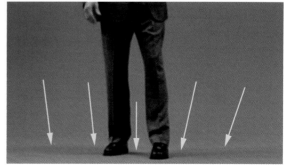

[Figure 8.26] Close-up of real-world occlusion

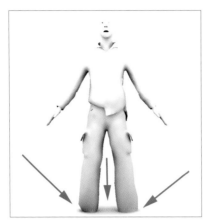

[Figure 8.27] Occlusion pass rendered in a 3D application

[Figure 8.28] Crowd replication with no AO appears cut and pasted

accumulate and become more dense the farther out of the light source's direct line of sight they get (as can be seen in the 3D model's shadowing getting denser the closer it gets to the floor).

When creating many effects, such as crowd replications, using source footage that does not contain these occlusion shadows runs the risk of having elements look cut and pasted on, as the little crowd replication of Chad demonstrates in Figure 8.28.

You can fake this effect to help bring the scene closer to reality using a few clever masking and gradient tricks.

To begin this example, as with all extractions, garbage matte (Figures 8.29 and 8.30), key (Figure 8.31), and place the bluescreen footage on an all-white background (Figure 8.32). Using a heavily feathered elliptical roto mask, composite a black solid or constant behind and at the base of the subject, as shown in Figure 8.33. This simulates the *falloff* floor shadow.

Next, duplicate the extracted subject and use a hue/saturation to desaturate and make the subject completely black. Add a blur and a mask to allow only the very bottom of the dark image to be seen (as shown in Figure 8.34). Add a directional blur horizontally to emulate the slightly heavier *core* shadow (see Figure 8.35). What makes this trick so clever is that if you have a character who is, say, running, each footstep will appear to make proper contact with the ground completely automatically, in the proper place, and with the proper timing. This does not require additional animation because the shadows are being generated procedurally using the original extracted bluescreen footage source material to generate them.

[Figure 8.29] Rotospline used to create garbage matte closely around subject to be extracted

[Figure 8.30] Garbage matte removing all but a thin area of bluescreen to be keyed

[Figure 8.31] Bluescreen keyed and subject extracted

[Figure 8.32] Subject composited over plain white background

[Figure 8.33] Elliptical rotospline used to mask black solid to create fake falloff floor shadow

[Figure 8.34] Fake shadow trick (covered in Chapter 5) masked off with a feathered rectangular mask to reveal only a little more than floor contact point

[Figure 8.35] Horizontal directional blur added to create convincing, moving ground core shadow

[Figure 8.36] Keyed actor composited over ground shadow

You can stack and/or blur additional copies at varying degrees of opacity and blur to get any desired density or falloff effects. You can also translate them a few pixels down to reveal them slightly from under the subject and use them to create a dense contact shadow. Figure 8.36 shows one possible blend of these shadows.

The only part of the shadow that's missing is the falloff onto the subject from the other replicated copies of the subject in the crowd replication. You can easily create this effect by duplicating one of the other shadows, lessening the blur, moving the mask upward on the subject, and increasing the feathering to get a nice soft gradation, as shown in Figure 8.37. You can then multiply this new gradient shadow over (with adjustable transparency) copies of the subject that sit behind other copies. Examples of this can be seen in the before and after images shown in Figures 8.38 through 8.41, and in the 2.5D perspective view in Figures 8.42 and 8.43.

[Figure 8.37] Additional copy of original fake shadow masked with a very feathered/blurred mask to create a smooth gradient falloff

[Figure 8.38] Extraction of actor with fake floor shadow but no AO over him

[Figure 8.39] Actor with fake AO added/multiplied over him. Notice the darkening of the lower half of his body that would occur if another person were standing in front of him blocking the light from reaching the lower portions of his body.

[Figure 8.40] Crowd replication with no AO appears cut and pasted.

[Figure 8.41] Crowd replication with fake AO appears more realistic.

[Figure 8.42] Crowd replication before AO appears cut and pasted.

[Figure 8.43] Crowd replication after fake AO appears more realistic.

Fake Z-Depth

Another amazing effect you can achieve, using a similar faking method, is creating fake Z-depth. This technique allows you to do many effects, including depth-based atmosphere and depth-of-field blurs. It's also the primary concept and technique behind creating 2D-to-3D stereoscopic conversions, which are covered in depth in Chapter 14.

A depth map is another simple grayscale map that plots the distances from the camera in shades of gray. These depth maps can use either black to delineate "farthest from camera" or, more typically, white. An example of a depth map generated in the 3D CG scene (shown in wireframe in Figure 8.44 and fully rendered in Figure 8.45) can be seen in Figure 8.46.

[Figure 8.44]
Wireframe of 3D interior
environment scene

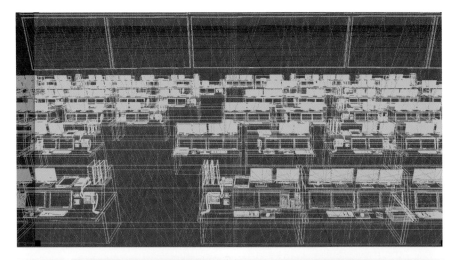

[Figure 8.45]
Render of 3D interior
environment scene

[Figure 8.46]
Z-depth render of same
interior environment scene.
Notice how the scene falls
off in gradation from black
(closest) to white (farthest)

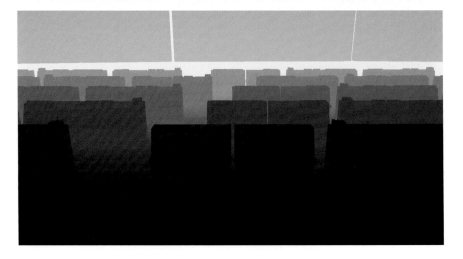

As with the previous example, begin with a simple extraction of your subject. Next, use a channel Shuffle or Set Channels tool to set all of the RGB channels to the alpha matte creating a solid white silhouette of your extraction, as shown in Figure 8.47.

The trick now is to create 2.5D planes that will represent floors, walls, ceilings, objects, and so on and color them all just off pure white to start.

In this example, I create a simple floor plane, replicate our subject into a small crowd, copy the color versions, and set all their RGB channels to alpha. When you position these elements, make sure they all actually touch the ground plane and are not floating. I then applied a simple gradient to the floor plane that transitions from almost black (nearest camera) to almost white (farthest point from camera), as shown in Figure 8.48. From the camera's perspective (Figure 8.49), it's hard to see where each of the subjects is. That's okay, because we are going to address that right now.

When you create a fake depth map, whether for an atmosphere, depth-of-field (DOF) blur effect, or even more importantly, when doing a 2D to 3D stereoscopic conversion—it is *critical* that your subjects make proper contact with the ground plane at the appropriate level of depth. And because the only thing determining depth in a depth map is the shade of grayscale, your subjects' value *must* match the value of the spot on the ground plane exactly where they are supposed to come into contact with it. If they do not, the effect will be broken, and the subjects will appear to be at the wrong depth or float.

[Figure 8.47] A channel Shuffle or Set Channels tool has been used to set all RGB channels to alpha to create a solid white silhouette of the extraction.

[tip]

You always want to create your depth maps just short of pure white and pure black. Doing so allows you a little room for depth adjustments later, which you can accomplish using levels, curves, grades, lookups, and so on.

[Figure 8.48] The floor plane transitions from almost black (nearest the camera) to almost white (farthest point from the camera). The subject has been replicated into a small crowd, with all of their RGB channels set to alpha.

[Figure 8.49] From the camera's perspective, all the subjects seem to blend together.

This might sound intimidating, but have no fear. I've developed a quick and easy trick for you to make sure that your subjects are at the right Z-depth for your scene. Add a hue/saturation, grade, or lookup to each white subject layer (any of these will work). And now for my little trick! As you adjust the brightness control to darken each subject plane, one at a time, watch carefully for where the bottoms of the feet touch the ground plane. At the adjustment point where the feet seem to disappear and blend into the ground (as in Figure 8.50), you know you have the exact correct depth! Simple, right?

[Figure 8.50] When the feet seem to blend in with the ground at the depth they appear, you know you have set the correct value of grayscale.

For those times when you can't quite tell, I have another trick for you. I modified this technique from my earlier days as a recording artist, editing audio. I call this "rocking the reels." When you're having trouble identifying the exact shade to match, try "rocking" the controls overboard (way too much/way too little) both ways— too bright, then back to too dark, back and forth, back and forth, each time less and less extreme until you start to easily see the area that's right "in the groove." You can also use the color picker tool to check the actual numeric values for a perfect match. Once your depth map is completed, it's time to put it to use.

[Figure 8.51] Small crowd replication with no effects

In Figure 8.51 you can see our small crowd replication. By just overlaying the depth map onto the image (see Figure 8.52), you can already see how it begins to add what appears to be fog-like atmosphere. Using this depth map as a luma matte for a blurred copy of the plate, with the original unaltered plate underneath, you can achieve a very cool depth-of-field blur effect, as shown in Figure 8.53. By adding a simple colored solid or constant and using the same map to limit the effect (as its alpha), you can achieve a wide variety of atmospheric effects. In Figure 8.54 this is applied

[Figure 8.52] Depth map overlaid and transparency slightly reduced, creating apparent atmospheric fog effect

[Figure 8.53] Depth-of-field blur effect using depth map as a matte for a blurred copy of the plate

[Figure 8.54] Eerie red fog effect using depth map as a matte for a simple red constant/solid

with a simple red constant (of course, all kinds of noise, fractals, and even photographic elements could be used for more complex effects as well). You can adjust and animate all of these effects by applying levels, grades, curves, lookups, and so forth to the matte, which can move the near, far, and mid densities, as shown in Figures 8.55 through 8.57.

[Figure 8.55]
Depth map with no levels adjustment applied

[Figure 8.56]
Depth map with gamma lifted slightly to move atmospheric effect back in Z-space

[Figure 8.57]
Depth map with gamma crushed way down to move atmospheric effect far forward in Z-space

Displacement FX: Water, Heat, Cloak

The next set of VFX tricks and techniques is an extremely versatile group we'll call *displacement FX*. These effects all rely on the grayscale displacement map discussed in Chapter 2 and can be used to create animated water effects for matte paintings, heat distortion/shimmer, and cloaking effects.

[Figure 8.58] Still image with lake in the foreground

[Figure 8.59] Close-up of lake. Note the wave ripple pattern on the water's surface. This is what you will try to match.

To start with a basic version of the effect, let's look at a simple simulated water displacement animation. As with all VFX you do, your first step is to always carefully analyze the source material to see exactly what it is you're trying to match or create. In this case, we want to carefully examine the still image water plate we are going to animate, as shown in Figure 8.58. If you look closely at the water (Figure 8.59), you can see that its surface has a very particular look or *grain* to it. This is the wave pattern we need to try to simulate as closely as possible. The closer we get to this wave, or grain, pattern, the more realistic the water motion will appear.

Create a square white solid and fill it with monochromatic noise (see Figure 8.60). Next, add a decent amount of blur to get a look similar to that of the fake film grain we created in Chapter 6 (Figure 8.61). Add a horizontal directional blur until the noise is spread into "waves," matching in size and length as closely as possible to the reference (see Figure 8.62). This blur can lower the contrast,

[Figure 8.60] Plain white solid filled with monochromatic noise

[Figure 8.61] Blur added to noise

[Figure 8.62] Horizontal directional blur added to blurred noise

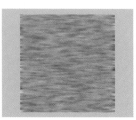

[Figure 8.63] Contrast increased with a levels adjustment to bring back contrast

so you can add levels, curves, or grade (as seen in Figure 8.63) to bring back however much contrast is required. Finally, the entire composition can be scaled down vertically or stretched horizontally and then cropped to even more closely match the waves in the reference image (see Figure 8.64). Now, let's use this displacement map to animate the water in the still image.

Bring this displacement map into your compositing application and scale it up a little to allow some room to slide it within the composition. From the reference image, determine which way the water should be moving from and to and push the displacement map off to that respective side and slightly up or down. The up or down depends on whether the water will be moving toward the top or bottom of the frame; it will usually be the bottom.

Keyframe the displacement map to move very slowly, slightly raking a little more horizontally and in the same vertical direction as the waves should be travelling, as shown in Figure 8.65. Only two keyframes should be necessary: one at the starting position and one at the ending position.

Once you have keyframed/animated the displacement map, create a duplicate of the background image containing the body of water to be animated. Apply a displacement effect to it and use the displacement map you just created as the displacement. You can adjust the strength of the displacement using the effect controls or by increasing the contrast of the displacement map. Adjust the speed of the water by moving the end keyframe of the displacement motion in time. You will notice that many parts of the image that are not water are also displacing. That is why we created this on a separate copy of the footage. Simply roto mask this copy to show only the water, as shown in Figures 8.66 and 8.67, and composite this moving water onto the original full background image (see Figure 8.68). The result is a seamless composite and almost magically moving water… from a still image!

[Figure 8.64] Entire composition scaled down vertically to best match grain of water wave pattern

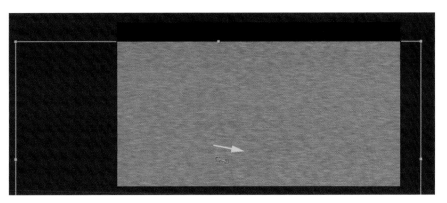

[Figure 8.65] Displacement map keyframed to animate very slowly in basic vertical direction of wave movement, but raking slightly more horizontally to create wave development motion in the displacement

[Figure 8.66] Displaced water layer roto masked to only the water element

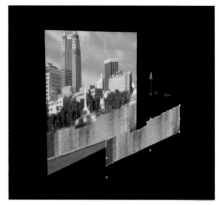

[Figure 8.67] 2.5D composite to show water element being composited back on top of original still image plate

[Figure 8.68]
Final seamless composite, looks exactly the same except the water is now moving

To take this technique one step further, let's use it to create a heat displacement effect. This example uses a still image of a missile I roto masked from a photo of a military jet I shot footage of at a local airshow, composited on top of an aerial landscape I shot from a commercial jet (Figure 8.69). For the missile's flame, I used an element of a Bunsen burner I shot against a black backdrop (Figure 8.70). I then added a directional motion blur to both the missile and flame to give them a sense of speed. (In motion, you would accomplish this by keyframing the missile and trail to actually move across the frame, and add a pixel-based motion blur to get an actual motion blur, very similar to this effect, as shown in Figure 8.71.)

[Figure 8.69] Roto masked missile composited onto high altitude aerial photo shot from plane

[Figure 8.70] Bunsen burner element shot against black backdrop

[Figure 8.71] Missile and burner elements composited over background with slight horizontal directional blur added for motion effect

Heat distortion can best be described, and re-created, as being composed of two parts. The heat emanating from a source not only appears to displace what's behind it, but the light-scattering effect it has tends to blur whatever is behind it as well. So we will combine these two effects to achieve a realistic heat distortion.

Like the water displacement effect, this effect begins with a noise, blur, and directional blur combination, as shown in Figure 8.72. To create the billowing effect of hot air (into the surrounding cooler air), you can also add animated turbulence or cloud filters (as seen in Figure 8.73). In this case, because a rocket trail moves very quickly and would cause a lot more turbulent air movement than, say, a heat stack, you can overlay another, finer-grain layer of turbulent noise on top of the first one to get finer details (see Figure 8.74). As with the previous example, add this displacement map as a distortion

[Figure 8.72] Monochromatic noise with blur and directional blur added

[Figure 8.73] Cloud filter added

[Figure 8.74] Finer grain turbulent noise added for smaller displacement details

[Figure 8.75] Background displaced using combined displacement map

[Figure 8.76] Blur added to displacement to complete heat distortion effect

displacement to get a result similar to Figure 8.75. Finally, add a blur using the displacement map and a roto mask as an alpha to limit the area of the blur to just where you want to see the heat effect. This should achieve a final subtle, but realistic, heat distortion effect shown in Figure 8.76.

A cloaking effect is almost exactly the same effect except that it is more displacement, only a very slight amount of blur, and the effect is masked by the alpha of the subject being cloaked. In this example of a jungle background (Figure 8.77), the keyed actor subject (Figure 8.78) is the source of the alpha that's used to mask the displacement map (Figure 8.79) to create the cloak effect. Figure 8.80 shows the effect overdone to allow the effect to be seen in print, since this effect is usually only visible because of its motion in the scene, which obviously cannot be seen in print form.

[Figure 8.77] Jungle background

[Figure 8.78] Jungle background showing actor placement. The actor's alpha will be used to mask the displacement and blur effects.

[Figure 8.79] Displacement map used

[Figure 8.80] Very exaggerated blur used in this cloak effect example so that it can be seen without motion in print

As you can see, these 2.5D VFX are so versatile, they're used all the time in our workflow (or *pipeline*). Chapter 9 covers VFX that you will use for almost every production you work on. They must be part of your VFX arsenal. These VFX are needed so often, I call them "Bread & Butter VFX."

CHAPTER NINE

VFX Techniques V: Bread and Butter VFX

Some VFX are so common and have to be done so often, they should be a requirement in every VFX artist's skill set. Many times, as far as the jobs that bring in the bread and butter go, you will find that being well versed at these will make you the indispensable "go to" artist, a position that you always want to occupy in this competitive industry.

This chapter takes a look at two different ways you can do sky replacements (which are extremely common in movies), turning daytime scenes into nighttime, summer scenes into winter scenes, creating full-motion, high-tech 3D heads-up displays (HUD), and doing wire and rig removal to make a bungee jumper appear to be plummeting to earth with no attachments. We'll also explore the very popular time-ramping effect used in many action movies, and the chapter wraps up with the breakdown of advanced multi-pass rendering and compositing.

Sky Replacements

It's amazing how many times VFX artists are called upon to replace skies, and it's even more amazing how important this job is. Yet if it's done well, the audience will never know it's been done at all. Skies are extremely important for any scene in any production because they set the entire mood and tone. Imagine a scary horror story on a bright sunny day or a summer beach scene with flat, gray, overcast skies. Directors and producers want to set the mood of the scene and emotionally bring the audience into the story by showing the environment in the best way possible. Unfortunately, Mother Nature doesn't care about shooting preferences, actors, or schedules and does not always cooperate. On the day of shooting, when the sky isn't what the shot called for, guess who's going to be called in to fix it... yup... you.

Sky replacements fall under the huge category of *invisible VFX*. These are the VFX no one ever really talks about, the audience never notices (unless they are done poorly), and are arguably the majority of all VFX done in movies and TV today.

Let's look at two different methods of sky replacement. The first technique I call the *reverse sky replacement method*, and the second, the *extraction method*.

Reverse Sky Replacement Method

I chose the name *reverse sky replacement* for this method because it's actually doing almost the reverse of removing and replacing a sky. It's really *adding* a better sky to the existing sky.

This method is an amazingly fast and effective way of doing a sky replacement (or probably more accurately, a sky augmentation), but it can only really be best used as a complete solution under particular circumstances—namely, when the sky needing to be replaced is very flat and solid in appearance. A clear blue-sky day, a flat, gray, overcast day, or even a jet black night are all excellent candidates for this technique. You can use this method for other sky conditions, but flat and solid skies are the easiest and fastest, and they provide the best results with the least amount of roto work.

[Figure 9.1] Background plate of desert highway for drive-by shot

In Figure 9.1 you can see a background plate for a desert highway drive-by shot. Unfortunately, the weather was *too good*—there's not even one nice, little, puffy cloud in the sky. The director wants picture-perfect clouds going out into the distance, all the way to the horizon. Fortunately, we have just such a sky in the ocean plate, shown in Figure 9.2. The perfectly flat, clear sky in the desert scene is a perfect candidate for the reverse sky replacement technique.

[Figure 9.2] Foreground sky plate of ocean scene

Simply composite the sky plate over the desert plate, reduce the opacity temporarily to help position the sky plate over the background plate properly, and then create a simple big rectangular mask, cutting the new sky off just before the background sky touches the ground (as seen in Figure 9.3). Figure 9.4 shows the result of the composite with the unnaturally hard edge that's created (indicated by the two arrows). This is simple enough to fix by adding a little matte edge feather or alpha blur. In Figure 9.5 you can see what a great job this does creating really great, dramatic skies. By turning down the opacity, you can get more subtle effects (as seen in Figure 9.6).

[Figure 9.3] Sky plate matted with simple, big, rectangular mask

[Figure 9.4] Composite showing the unnaturally sharp edge between sky and desert plate

[Figure 9.5] Matte edge feathered/blurred to create seamless composite

[Figure 9.6] Opacity of sky turned down to create more subtle hazy clouds

[Figure 9.7] Cloud plate flopped to correct incorrect sun (key light) direction

Let's test your eye for VFX cues. Although this composite looks really good, and many people would call it a day at this point, there's something technically wrong with it. Can you tell what it is? Look very closely and think about all the VFX cues covered in Chapter 1.

It's the sun. In the desert shot, the sun is coming from the opposite direction. Look at the shadows of the signs on the highway. In the cloud plate, the clouds' shadows are on the opposite side. You can easily fix this by *flopping the plate*, or flipping it horizontally, as in Figure 9.7. In the end, which way the cloud plate should face is a judgment call by the higher-ups, but always do your best to be the expert, reliable artist who makes sure these types of details match.

To show how easy and versatile this technique is, let's do another, completely different shot. In Figure 9.8 we have a dusty desert shot with a camel and some people in the foreground. The director has called for a dramatic sky. The current sky is *not* at all dramatic. However it *is* flat, and so it is an ideal candidate for the reverse sky replacement technique. Figure 9.9 is indeed a dramatic sky complete with volumetric *godrays*. Simply mask this sky as in

[note]

Godrays, or crepuscular rays, are rays or columns of sunlight that stream through gaps in clouds and appear to radiate from the point in the sky where the sun is located.

[Figure 9.8] Dusty desert plate with flat sky

[Figure 9.9] Dramatic sky plate with volumetric godrays

the first example (Figure 9.10) and feather or blur the matte edge to get just the kind of sky the director is looking for (see Figure 9.11). Using the 2.5D atmosphere technique covered in Chapter 8, I sampled the color of the sand on the horizon and added it as a transparent solid to the sky. Then, using a color blend mode, I imparted to it a little of the sand dust color to help it blend more convincingly with the scene. You can see the results of this in Figure 9.12.

Of course, not all skies are perfectly clear or flat, and not all horizon lines are so simply defined. In those cases, you will need to do roto, paint, or procedural extractions (or some combination thereof) to matte the sky and foreground. Let's take a look at the latter, using a procedural extraction to create a mask for a sky's edge.

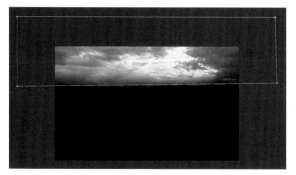

[Figure 9.10] Sky plate matted with simple big rectangular mask

[Figure 9.11] Seamless composite with feathered/blurred matte edge

[Figure 9.12] Sand-colored 2.5D atmosphere added to better integrate composite

Extraction Sky Replacement Method

This second method of sky replacement is for those times when, well… let's face it… most of the time when the sky you need to replace is anything other than flat and solid. This second method requires the procedural extraction skills you learned in Chapter 2, the roto skills you learned in Chapter 3, the color-matching skills you learned in Chapter 4, and the light wrap skills you learned in Chapter 6.

In this example, the director has given us the sky (Figure 9.13) and the foreground plate (Figure 9.14) that have been chosen for a "dark and stormy London" establishing shot. In an extraction, wherever there are well-defined straight or smooth-curved edges, you can use roto to create those shapes. Wherever there is a well saturated or constant flat color or brightness difference, you can use a color or luma key. As a last resort, you can use hand roto painting or tracker-assisted roto/paint to extract the elements you need. But in this case, there are some definite contrast and hue differences between the buildings and the gray sky, so we'll opt for the most efficient means possible: the calculations extraction method covered in Chapter 2.

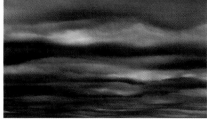

[Figure 9.13] Dark and stormy sky plate

[Figure 9.14] Foreground plate of London is definitely not dark and stormy.

Using the calculations extraction method to get a base extraction of the city and then applying a simple core matte to get rid of any holes in that matte (using the concepts and technique covered in Chapter 2), I created a matte for the city (Figure 9.15). I slightly blurred the matte to soften the edges just a little so it better matches the softness of the cloud plate. When it's all quickly composited together in what is called a *slap comp* (Figure 9.16), you can see that a lot of work definitely needs to be done to make the foreground plate match the sky and for this to *sell* (or be believable) as a "dark and stormy" set.

[Figure 9.15] Procedural extraction plus core matte used to create matte for the city

First I did a color correction using the color-matching techniques from Chapter 6 and added a slight blur to the city to help better match the feel of the cloud plate (see Figure 9.17).

[Figure 9.16] First slap comp

[Figure 9.17]
First color correction and slight blur of city to better match sky background

[Figure 9.18]
Grain added to foreground to match cloud grain and bluish hue tint wash added to entire plate to help integrate plates further

This starts to bring the foreground plate more into range, but the two plates still don't seem to "talk to one another," as I discussed in Chapter 1. So, in Figure 9.18, I added grain to match the cloud plate and a bluish hued tint as a wash to the whole plate to help integrate then two plates a bit more.

Because rain builds up in the distance, as atmosphere does, I used a very basic version of the atmosphere/fake Z-depth technique covered in Chapter 8 to add rain/atmosphere in the distance. I applied the light wrap technique covered in Chapter 6 to the foreground buildings to wrap a little more of the atmosphere and rain around them, as shown in Figure 9.19. You can see that you can use these techniques for many purposes—in this case, using the light wrap technique to "wrap" atmosphere and rain around the edges instead of sunlight or reflection.

Finally, I added and composited footage of rain over the entire composition (Figure 9.20) to add motion to the scene and for the finishing touch.

[Figure 9.19]
Distant atmosphere/rain/ aerial perspective added to composite

[Figure 9.20]
Final rain footage plate added over entire composite as finishing touch

Day for Night and Summer for Winter

In addition to the reasons for the frequent necessity of sky replacements discussed so far, the high production costs of lighting sets at night demand that, many times, we have to shoot nighttime scenes during the day and winter scenes during the ... well... not winter. Creating day-for-night and summer-for-winter effects can be challenging, but they can also be quite a lot of fun. Let's take a look at some techniques for creating each of these types of effects.

Day for Night

To create a day-for-night scene, first it is important that you *define the problem* or know a little bit about what you are actually trying to create or match. Are you trying to create the way night looks recorded with a film camera? With a video camera? The way a movie would portray night? Or are you trying to re-create the human visual experience of night? The answer is, perhaps, a little of each.

In human vision, the photoreceptor cells of the eyes—the rods and cones—are the cells responsible for the transmission of visible light into chemical/electrical impulses sent to the brain that we interpret as vision. The rod cells are the most sensitive to light, but they do not contribute color information. Most people have three main types of cone cells (though there have been verified reports of people with four or more). Each type of cone has a different pigment and, therefore, is sensitive to different wavelengths of light. The L-cones (long wavelength) peak in sensitivity at a reddish color, the M-cones (medium wavelength) peak at a greenish color, and S-cones (short wavelength) peak at a bluish color. The S-cones are the most light-sensitive of the three, so, not surprisingly, the less light there is and the more the rods begin to take over responsibility for vision, colors diminish toward the most sensitive of the cones (the S-cones) and toward the blues.

In most situations where there is still visibility, it's not that you don't see color at all, but that your ability to distinguish color diminishes. To create a convincing day-for-night scene, then, you want to emulate this apparent diminishing (but not complete loss) of color saturation. You don't want a completely black and white scene, you just want to reduce saturation and bias the hues toward the blues.

In addition, there is a phenomenon I call *movie reality expectation*. What this means is that people watching a movie *expect* to see things the way they are used to seeing things portrayed in a movie almost as much as they're expecting to see something that replicates reality. Machine gun muzzle flashes in real life appear as a continuous flame emanating from the barrel, not the intermittent flashes we're used to seeing in a movie, which are caused by the camera shutter. Explosions in reality usually last a split second and BANG they're over—they are not drawn out for 30 seconds in slow motion. Morgues these days rarely have the wall of drawers you probably imagined when you read the word *morgue*—they almost all use commercial walk-in coolers like you'd find in a restaurant these days. So, we have to temper reality with the audience's movie reality expectation. And don't forget the artistic license of the directors, producers, and others who are trying to make movie magic, *not* necessarily re-create reality precisely.

One of the very first and biggest mistakes beginning VFX artists commonly make when trying to
create a day-for-night shot is to try to tackle it all
at once and just darken the shot down and color
it blue as one big element. A much more effective
way to address this type of shot is to first split the
scene into parts, addressing the sky, walls, rooftops,
ground, and so on independently and separately.
If you go outside on a dark night, you will notice
that each of these elements usually appears different. The ground may be dark, walls partially lit
or in shadow, and the sky glowing or ramped with
a gradient.

[Figure 9.21] Jungle shot with added muzzle flashes

Like a sky replacement, there are simple (reverse) and complex (extracted)
methods for doing day-for-night VFX. To begin with a simple example, let's
take an interesting daytime image—Figure 9.21, a jungle shot with added
muzzle flashes—and duplicate it. You will use one copy for the base image
and one for any areas that would be lit by lights (it's already lit in those areas
in the original image, so why have to try to create something that's already
done for you?).

You'll use the Curves adjustment tool extensively for this example, so let's
take a quick look at how this tool works.

Curves Adjustment

A curves adjustment is almost identical to, and can be substituted for, a levels
adjustment, but it has one important difference, especially in this case. A
curves adjustment allows for the non-linear adjustment of points on the histogram anywhere on the curve and not just linear adjustments like a Levels
adjustment does.

Like the Levels adjustment, the Curves adjustment is an extremely versatile
tool in your bag of tricks (shown in Figure 9.22).

In Photoshop, the Curves adjustment is found under the Image menu >
Adjustments and also has a simple interface with a histogram—basically the
same five controls as the levels adjustment, though placed and implemented
slightly differently, as numbered in Figure 9.22. The five controls are divided
into input and output:

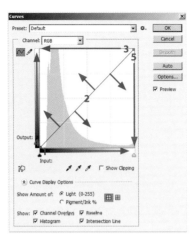

[Figure 9.22]
The curves adjustment tool

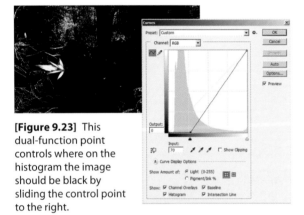

[Figure 9.23] This dual-function point controls where on the histogram the image should be black by sliding the control point to the right.

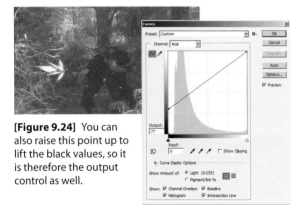

[Figure 9.24] You can also raise this point up to lift the black values, so it is therefore the output control as well.

Input

1. **Black level (shadows):** This dual-function point control where on the histogram the image should be black by sliding the control point to the right (Figure 9.23) the same way you would with the Levels control. However, you can also raise this point up to lift the black values (as seen in Figure 9.24), so therefore it's the output control as well.

2. **Gamma level (midtones):** This is where the controls differ. You can add a point or multiple points anywhere on the line (Figure 9.25) running from the black input to the white input. You can lift specific shadow values or drop any specific highlight value's gain almost completely independently of any other point you might add(with a smooth curve automatically interpolated in between points). In many applications' curve tools, you can freely draw a curve by hand as well. This elegant set of controls allows you to adjust multiple, very specific values in a scene very precisely.

3. **White level (highlights):** This dual-function point control where on the histogram the image should be white by sliding the control point to the left (Figure 9.26) the same way you would with the Levels control. However, you can also bring this point down (as seen in Figure 9.27) to lower the white values. Therefore it's the output control as well.

Output

4. **Black level:** This is the same dual-function control point as the Black level input. However, it's also used for the output, so wherever this control aligns with the gradient running vertically on the left is where the darkest black of the image can be.

5. **White level:** This is the same dual-function control point as the White level input. However, it's also used for the output, so wherever this control aligns with the gradient running vertically on the left is where the lightest white of the image can be.

By raising the Black level input (sliding the black point to the right) and lowering the White level input (sliding the white point to the left), you can effectively increase the contrast and add "punch" to the image. By raising or lowering areas on the line (see Figure 9.28), you can increase or decrease that respective value on the histogram without affecting (crushing or clipping) the black or white points in the image. By raising the Black level output and lowering the White level output, you can decrease the contrast in the image.

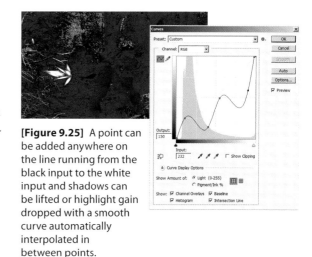

[Figure 9.25] A point can be added anywhere on the line running from the black input to the white input and shadows can be lifted or highlight gain dropped with a smooth curve automatically interpolated in between points.

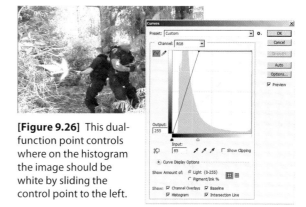

[Figure 9.26] This dual-function point controls where on the histogram the image should be white by sliding the control point to the left.

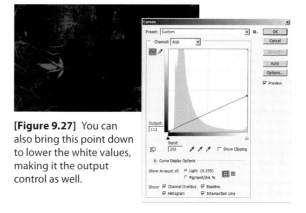

[Figure 9.27] You can also bring this point down to lower the white values, making it the output control as well.

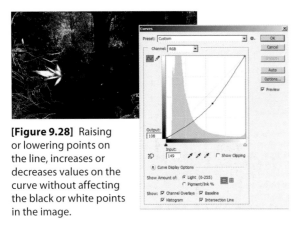

[Figure 9.28] Raising or lowering points on the line, increases or decreases values on the curve without affecting the black or white points in the image.

Add a curves adjustment to the first copy and bring the white point from the top of the screen straight down to darken the light areas of the image. Go into each of the individual Red, Green, and Blue channel drop-down selections and add a middle point (pulling the reds and greens down slightly but pushing the blues up a bit, until you get a result similar to Figure 9.29).

Add a gradient from black at the top to white on the bottom over the image and set it to Multiply (Figure 9.30) blend mode, which will help darken the top of the image.

Now for the magic! Since our original plate is already "lit" with natural sunlight, all that's really needed is to punch a hole (so to speak) through the darkened image and reveal the original one underneath through the hole. To do this, you can create a simple roto, or in this case, a quickly hand-painted, mask (see Figure 9.31) to show areas of the jungle that would be lit by the muzzle flashes as well as areas of the actors' bodies and faces. The masked layer should reveal something that looks like Figure 9.32.

With the two composited together, a cool nighttime jungle battle scene starts to take shape (Figure 9.33). I had to keep the night look a little lighter than usual so it would reproduce acceptably in print. You can download this image file from the book's product page on www.peachpit.com (see the Introduction for instructions on downloading files).

[Figure 9.29] Result after curves adjustments

[Figure 9.30] Gradient from black at the top to white on the bottom added over the image and set to multiply blend mode to help darken the top of the image.

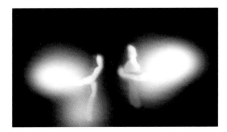

[**Figure 9.31**] Roto mask created to punch hole in darkened image

[**Figure 9.32**] Masked layer reveals original daylight image

[**Figure 9.33**] Composited nighttime jungle scene

[**Figure 9.34**] Daytime footage of a cobblestone side street

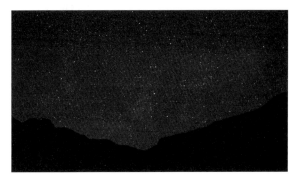

[**Figure 9.35**] Starry nighttime sky plate

For a more complex and detailed day-for-night VFX shot, let's take daytime footage of a cobblestone side street (Figure 9.34) and convert it to a nighttime scene (inserting the starry sky plate in Figure 9.35).

As with the detailed sky replacement, this example begins by creating a procedurally extracted (with roto'd core matting) matte of the foreground to allow us to replace the sky, as seen in Figure 9.36.

[**Figure 9.36**] Procedurally extracted (with roto'd core matting) matte of the foreground so sky can be replaced

[tip]

In these exercises, think of the steps presented as a palette of tools to use however best suits your need.

Next you need to create all the mattes you will need. There is no one right answer or process for this. Pick and choose whichever of these steps work for your particular footage and situation. Create as many mattes as you will need to do whatever it is you have decided to do.

In this case, I've created mattes for the ground (Figure 9.37) and building walls (Figure 9.38). I created them separately so they can be used by themselves or combined (Figure 9.39).

Using rotosplines, I selected all the windows (Figure 9.40) and saved these selections to create window mattes for all of the street-facing windows (Figure 9.41). I did the same with the glass in the streetlamps (Figure 9.42).

With the extraction of the sky completed (Figure 9.43), I did a Hue/Saturation adjustment to the foreground plate to lower the saturation of color (Figure 9.44). I then did a Curves adjustment to decrease some of the contrast in the scene (Figure 9.45). Figure 9.46 shows the result so far.

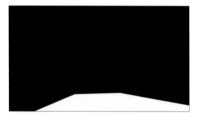

[Figure 9.37] Ground matte

[Figure 9.38] Building walls matte

[Figure 9.39] Combined ground and walls matte

[Figure 9.40] Rotosplines are used to select all of the windows

[Figure 9.41] Window mattes for all of the street-facing windows

[Figure 9.42] Mattes for street lamps

[Figure 9.43] Sky extracted

[Figure 9.44] Hue/saturation added to desaturate scene

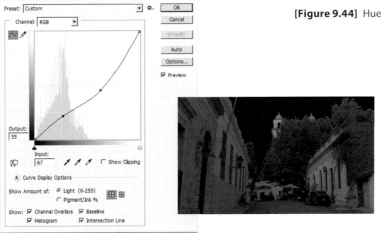

[Figure 9.45] Curves adjustment to decrease some of the contrast in the scene

[Figure 9.46] Result so far

[Figure 9.47] Hand painted/roto'd gradient of darkness

[Figure 9.48] Dark desaturated bluish solid is multiplied over the entire plate

At night, streetlight usually falls off (diminishes) the higher up you look, so a hand-painted or roto'd gradient of darkness (similar to how we did the previous example) is multiplied over the upper structures, areas of the walls, and trees, as shown in Figure 9.47. I also multiplied a dark desaturated bluish solid (Figure 9.48) over the entire plate to help blend it a little more and to further bring it down in brightness. I added another curves adjustment to the RGB in a slight "S" curve to darken it some more while further reducing contrast (Figure 9.49).

To bring in the apparent night vision bluish hue, I did three individual curves adjustments as with the previous example, reducing the gamma of the reds (Figure 9.50) and greens (Figure 9.51) and boosting the gamma of the blues a little (Figure 9.52). We've got a nice nighttime look now (see Figure 9.53), but it's time to add some lights.

Figure 9.54 shows a soft matte I created to keep the lights from falling onto the sky. It's also handy for adding more darkness to the upper walls and sky if needed.

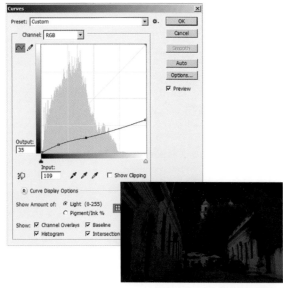

[Figure 9.49] Another curves adjustment is added to the RGB in a slight "S" curve.

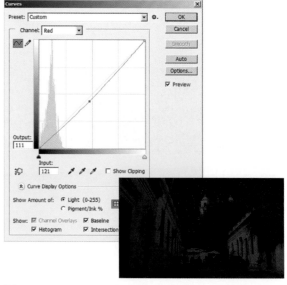

[Figure 9.50] Curves adjustment slightly reducing gamma of red channel

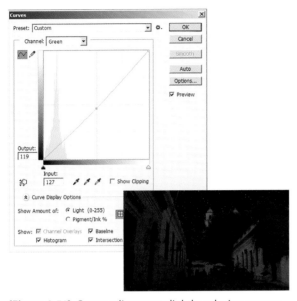

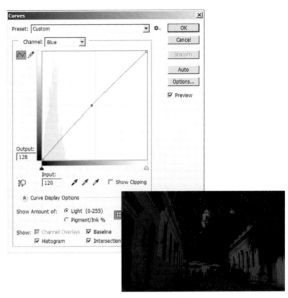

[Figure 9.51] Curves adjustment slightly reducing gamma of green channel

[Figure 9.52] Curves adjustment slightly increasing gamma of blue channel

[Figure 9.53]
Nice nighttime look

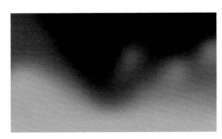

[Figure 9.54] Soft matte is created to keep the lights from falling onto the sky or adding more darkness to the upper walls and sky

[**Figure 9.55**] Lights rendered in 3D application onto stand-in geometry for reference and/or use as luma matte

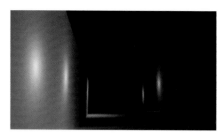

[**Figure 9.56**] Colored solids matted with above matte to create fake reflected light

[**Figure 9.57**] Matte created in Figure 9.54 multiplied onto to scene

[**Figure 9.58**] The window matte is used to add a warm colored solid to the window areas using an Add blend mode.

If you were to render lights in a 3D application onto stand-in geometry as a reference (see Figure 9.55) to see how light would fall in this scenario, you would see how and where the lights tend to fall off in pools throughout the scene. If this render and the original image were matched up precisely, you could actually use this as a luma matte for colored solids to create fake reflected light as well, as shown in Figure 9.56. Figure 9.57 shows the matte created in Figure 9.54 multiplied onto the scene to further darken the upper areas before adding the lights.

Figure 9.58 uses the window matte to add a warm colored solid to the window areas using an Add blend mode. You can Add a blurred copy of this same layer (Figure 9.59) on top of these additive solids, which produces a very nice and convincing softly glowing light effect. You can add fake cast or reflected light elements using the same technique (the result is seen in Figure 9.60).

Figure 9.61 shows the final composite with light elements added over the darkened scene for a convincing nighttime effect.

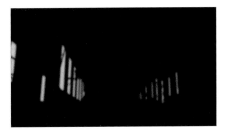

[**Figure 9.59**] Adding another blurred copy of this same layer

[**Figure 9.60**] Adding Figure 9.58 and Figure 9.59 results in a very nice and convincing softly glowing light effect.

[**Figure 9.61**]
The final composite with light elements added over the darkened scene for convincing nighttime effect

Summer for Winter

So production planned a perfect warmhearted Christmas scene, only Jack Frost overslept this year and there's no snow (Figure 9.62). Guess who's getting a phone call? Yup, the VFX crew. Time to turn summer into winter.

First we need to extract as many separate elements as we can—winter and snow are a bit more complex than the dark and nighttime. As always, begin by making plenty of backup copies of the original.

[**Figure 9.62**] Original summer plate

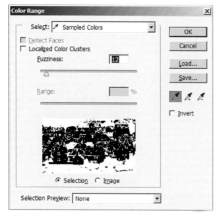

[Figure 9.63] Selection of green areas with Color Range tool

The grass, shrubs, trees, and other green areas can be selected procedurally or using a tool such as the Color Range tool (see Figure 9.63). This type of selection gives you a matte (Figure 9.64) that, hey, conveniently looks a little like snow cover! Let's cut these out and place them on their own layer so we will be able to treat them separately (Figure 9.65).

Do the same thing for the rooftops, which also need snow. Create a matte for them (Figure 9.66) and cut them out onto their own layer as well (Figure 9.67).

Because these selections are not perfectly precise and tend to select elements that shouldn't be selected (snow tends to accumulate on horizontal surfaces like roofs and grass and not on vertical surfaces such as the walls of buildings), we need to roto the walls and vertical faces of all the buildings (see Figure 9.68) and create a matte so we can easily extract them (Figure 9.69).

[Figure 9.64] Matte created with selection of green areas

[Figure 9.65] Green areas cut out onto their own layer

[Figure 9.66] Rooftop matte

[Figure 9.67] Rooftops cut onto their own layer

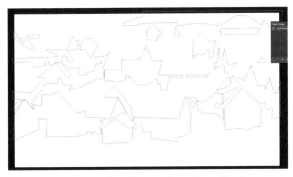

[**Figure 9.68**] Vertical surfaces such as the walls of buildings roto'd

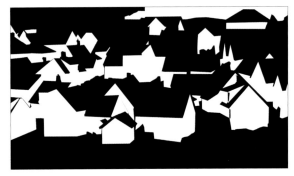

[**Figure 9.69**] Matte created of vertical walls

Like nighttime scenes, winter landscapes are less saturated than their summer counterparts. Add a Hue/Saturation to each of the layers (foliage, roofs, and walls) and desaturate the colors of the scene (Figure 9.70).

[**Figure 9.70**] Plate desaturated

Next, add a harsh curves adjustment to the foliage and roof layers, crushing the white point until you achieve something that resembles snow (Figures 9.71 and 9.72). Compositing these two layers together begins to produce a wintery look (Figure 9.73), but the vertical surfaces need to be toned down. Adding back the unaffected wall layer in (Figure 9.74) helps bring the scene into the realm we're looking for, but we're missing some key visual cues that it is winter. One cue is icicles, which form on roof ledges and corners.

[**Figure 9.71**] Harsh curves adjustment added to the foliage layer, crushing the white point to simulate snow cover on foliage

[**Figure 9.72**] Harsh curves adjustment added to the rooftop layer, crushing the white point to simulate snow cover on rooftops

[Figure 9.73] Figure 9.71 and Figure 9.72 composited together

[Figure 9.74] Desaturated walls added back using vertical wall matte

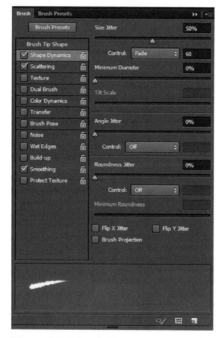

[Figure 9.75] Brush Shape Dynamics; set Control to Fade to create "icicle brush"

[Figure 9.76] On the Brush tab, set Scattering to randomize icicle thickness

To create these, we'll create a custom Photoshop brush. Select a small, round, hard-edged brush and open the Brush Properties panel from the Window menu. Under the Shape Dynamics panel, set Control to Fade and the amount to whatever number creates a realistically sized icicle for you in the image you are working with—in this case, 60 (Figure 9.75). In the Scattering panel, change the Scatter setting until you get a nice icicle-like effect in the preview at the bottom of the panel (in Figure 9.76, 30% worked well). Now, starting

[Figure 9.77] Icicles created on rooflines and gutters

[Figure 9.78] Frost layer extracted

on a blank layer, begin drawing icicles sporadically on the edges and corners of roofs, as shown in Figure 9.77. Note that I've shown this layer against a black background so you can see it more easily, but it should be white icicles on a transparent layer. By adjusting the size of the brush using the square bracket ([and]) keys and the Fade amount (with each brush size adjustment), draw different-sized icicles and make them smaller to simulate perspective the farther back the rooftops are. Additionally, you can isolate some of the walls and procedurally extract them to create a frost plate, as shown in Figure 9.78.

Next we'll create the snow that accumulates along roof edges and gutters, along the bases of houses, on bushes, and so on. To do this, turn off the Fade control and increase the size of the brush. Follow along the edges of roofs, the roof gutter angles, the bases of houses, and the tops of bushes and window sills to add a plate of the snow that tends to pile up in winter (as seen in Figure 9.79).

With two gradients used to create the atmospheric look of snow (Figure 9.80), a snow plate (Figure 9.81), and light smoke plates for the chimneys (Figure 9.82), we get a nice-looking winter scene (Figure 9.83) from a summer plate.

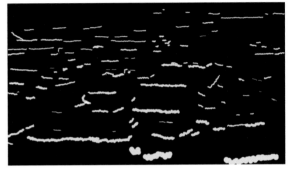

[Figure 9.79] Snow piles/buildup created by increasing brush size and turning off the Fade control

[Figure 9.80] Snow atmosphere gradient

[Figure 9.81] Snow plate

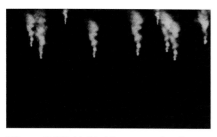

[Figure 9.82] Light chimney smoke plate

[Figure 9.83] Finished summer-to-winter scene

Digital 3D HUD Creation

There are so many instances, and types, of digital HUD (heads up display) effects required for movies, TV, and even print, that a complete book could be dedicated to just this topic. From simple, everyday digital displays, such as thermometers and speedometers, to uber-futuristic, haptic 3D interfaces, such as those seen in movies like *Avatar* and *Minority Report*, it is almost a guarantee that as a VFX artist you will be called upon to do one of these VFX at some point in your career.

HUD displays can range from very simple flat LCD readouts to complex true 3D projected models. HUD effects can usually be categorized into eight or so types (discussed shortly). You can see three of these (gauge, map, and alphanumeric displays) from left to right in Figure 9.84.

Figure 9.85 explodes out a number of these effects so you can see what the individual components look like and how they are created and animated. The main common feature of each is that they are all tinted to the common display theme color and then are placed either over black or with an alpha.

Here's a brief explanation of the different types of HUD displays and how they work:

1. **Alphanumeric:** Simple letters or numbers that can be either hand animated or generated with plugins or scripts to show preformatted or random values.

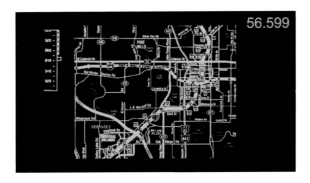

[Figure 9.84]
Gauge, map, and
alphanumeric displays

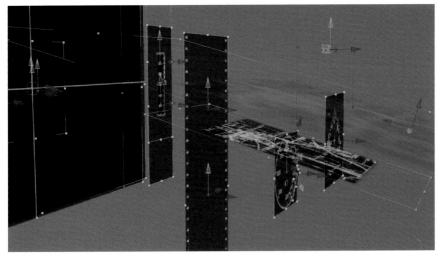

[Figure 9.85]
Various HUD display types
exploded into 3D side view
to see composition

2. **Dial:** Picture or vector-graphic–based frame, with a simple animated pointer or hand.

3. **Gauge:** Picture or vector-based frame with matted animated sliding value indicator.

4. **Target:** Simple picture or vector crossing lines and target reticle animated by hand or by parenting/attaching to a simple 2D XY coordinate track.

5. **Scrolling:** Like the gauge, scrolling displays are simply sliding displays, usually used to represent heading or pitch movement.

6. **Indicator:** Simple on/off lamps or graphic based with on/off picture components (such as aircraft missile arming).

7. **Map- or picture-based:** Usually pictures or maps can easily be extracted for use in a HUD using the same methods covered in Chapter 2 for grunge map extraction.

8. **3D:** These are actual 3D models, usually rendered in wireframe and simply colored for use in a HUD.

To create a moving 3D HUD—in this case, on a futuristic aircraft cockpit (Figure 9.86)—I first did a standard 3D track of the moving scene. I exported the track to a 3D application, as shown in Figure 9.87 (as explored in Chapter 7). Take special note of the specific nulls in the areas where the HUD will be placed (Figure 9.88). Place the instrument panels, or in this case, simple floating planes placed in 3D layers at the positions of those nulls (Figure 9.89). Figure 9.90 shows the panels textured in place and then rendered in Figure 9.91.

Figure 9.92 shows the rotational movement of the cockpit and green tracking markers on the edge rails, which need to be painted out and covered

[Figure 9.86] Overhead original plate of futuristic cockpit

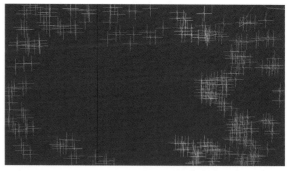

[Figure 9.87] Nulls of 3D track solve brought into 3D application

[Figure 9.88] 3D track nulls superimposed over original plate to locate where 3D HUD displays will be composited

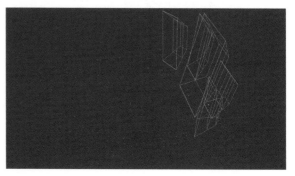

[Figure 9.89] 3D planes placed in proper position according to tracking nulls used as feature markers

(Figure 9.93). When composited over the live action plate using a simple Screen or Add blend mode (Figure 9.94), these simple layers of interface spring to life as a complex futuristic HUD, as shown in Figure 9.95. You can also use full 3D models rendered out in wireframe, instead of flat planes, for even more complex effects.

[**Figure 9.90**] Textured 3D planes

[**Figure 9.91**] Rendered 3D planes

[**Figure 9.92**] Live action cockpit with tracking markers

[**Figure 9.93**] Tracking markers removed via cloning after 3D track is completed

[**Figure 9.94**] 3D HUD composited onto live action plate

[**Figure 9.95**] Finished 3D HUD VFX shot

Wire and Rig Removal

Like HUD, wire and rig removal is another staple in the VFX artist's bag of tricks. These removals can be as simple as a spoon hanging from a wire or as complex as a puppeteered animatronic with dozens of wires, cables, and armature controls that need to be removed. Some great semi-automated wire/rig removal tools and plugins exist on the market, but let's examine a tried-and-true, under-the-hood method for doing one manually.

In this example, you see a bungee jumper, wearing a harness and bungee cord, jumping from a bridge (Figures 9.96 through 9.98). If the jumper were only falling against a clear blue sky, you could use the sky as a bluescreen and simply key the jumper using a standard keying method. But as luck would have it (and as is probably more common than not), here the jumper falls against the background of varied trees and forest.

Most wire/rig removal shots rely on some form of clean plate as the basis for the removal, and this shot is no exception. This example uses what I refer to as the *window method*. If we were to merely cut away the thick bungee cord and harness, it would leave a hole behind in the plate. This is the "window" that this technique derives its name from. The only problem is this: what to fill it with? There are many methods of creating a clean plate for the missing background that needs to be replaced, but by far one of the simplest and most convenient these days is to use the automated power of Photoshop.

Because the bungee jumper is falling and the camera follows the movement by tilting down, a different area of the background is revealed at different

[**Figure 9.96**] Bungee jumper, wearing a harness and bungee cord, jumping from a bridge highest position

[**Figure 9.97**] Bungee jumper, wearing a harness and bungee cord, jumping from a bridge mid position

[**Figure 9.98**] Bungee jumper, wearing a harness and bungee cord, jumping from a bridge lowest position

[Figure 9.99] "Window" method of wire/rig removal, showing matted live action plate in front of 2D tracked still clean plate

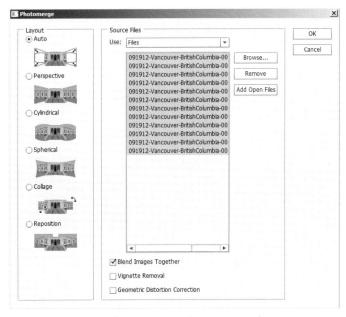

[Figure 9.100] Photoshop's amazing Photomerge tool

times in the sequence. The key here is that the bungee jumper is *not* at certain areas we need cleaned at certain times in the sequence. By taking snapshots of the sequence at frequent intervals when the jumper is at many different locations in the camera's view, you can stitch the interval stills together to create one giant plate encompassing all the camera positions and the jumper easily cloned out from them. Then animate the motion of the giant clean plate back in by using a 2D track or hand track to match the position of the foreground, so everything lines up in the windows properly, as shown in Figure 9.99.

After you capture frequent individual overlapping frames from the sequence, you can load these stills into Photoshop's File > Automate > Photomerge function (Figure 9.100) and just manually paint retouches to a few of the layer masks where needed. With this technique you can achieve a surprisingly good, full, clean plate in a matter of minutes (Figure 9.101).

[Figure 9.101] Finished clean plate after Photomerge and a little hand painting into layer masks

In Figure 9.102, you can see a close-up of the jumper, and in Figure 9.103, some simple painting and cloning has been performed to remove the harness straps. Since the right arm is occluded by the bungee, you can copy the upper left arm, flop and rotate it to get the piece you need (Figure 9.104). After slightly warping it to match the size of the right arm (Figure 9.105), blending the edges (Figure 9.106), and cloning away the rest of the bungee (Figure 9.107), you can achieve a clean plate of the jumper (Figure 9.108).

[Figure 9.102] Close-up of falling jumper

[Figure 9.103] Harness cloned/removal

[Figure 9.104] Right upper arm re-created by duplicating and flopping left upper arm

[Figure 9.105] Arm shape warped to match

[Figure 9.106] Edges of upper arm blended

[Figure 9.107] Rest of rig removed via cloning

[Figure 9.108] Clean plate of jumper

You can create simple rotosplines for each section of the bungee cord and animate them to follow along to cut out the support (Figures 9.109 through 9.111).

After you've roto'd the holes in the foreground plate, feathered them (to hide the edges), and tracked and animated the clean plate to move in sync, the bungee cable is removed, and the jumper appears to be free falling with no safety (Figures 9.112 through 9.114), even in front of the complex line of trees.

After you track and retouch the jumper with the clean plate (Figure 9.115) and add back a little fake motion blur, the shot is complete (as seen in Figure 9.116).

[Figure 9.109] Bungee rig rotos, highest position

[Figure 9.110] Bungee rig rotos, mid position

[Figure 9.111] Bungee rig rotos, lowest position

[Figure 9.112] Bungee rig removed via window method with clean plate showing behind, high position

[Figure 9.113] Bungee rig removed via window method with clean plate showing behind, mid position

[Figure 9.114] Bungee rig removed via window method with clean plate showing behind, low position over trees

[Figure 9.115] Jumper's harness removed with clean plate

[Figure 9.116] Slight pixel-based motion blur added

Time Ramping

Just about every action movie will depict an explosion slowed down, a fight scene sped up, or—the new trend—both, one immediately after the other. Made popular in many action movies' fight and car chase scenes, this super-fast to super-slow to super-fast effect is known as *time ramping*.

Although the effect itself is fairly simple to accomplish, you should be aware of, and understand, a few important nuances and technicalities.

Figure 9.117 shows actor Chad Ayers in a full-on run. To create the time ramp look, you simply add the time ramp, or time remap, effect, set keyframes at the start and end points at which the effect should occur (Figure 9.118), and then move these keyframes. Think of them as being like pushpins in a rubber piece of film: If you move them apart, the time is stretched, and it takes longer for the action to occur and so the motion slows down; if it's squashed together, time is compressed, and the action speeds up.

An important factor to consider is that when time is stretched, frames have to be created in between, or *tween*, the existing frames to slow the motion down. If tween frames weren't created the motion would just stutter from the repeated existing frames. Software can do this in a number of ways. At its most basic (and lowest quality), adjacent frames can be simply blended together (see Figure 9.119), but this results in a blurry, ghosting look that doesn't appear very natural.

[Figure 9.117]
Live-action plate of actor Chad Ayers running

[Figure 9.118]
Time ramp/time remap effect added and keyframes set at the start and end points at which the effect will occur

[Figure 9.119]
Results of "frame-blend" tween frames

At its best and the highest quality, your compositing software can be set to use the technology known as optical flow (or pixel flow) to analyze every pixel and creates new, in-between pixels for every frame. With this method, you can achieve some stunning realistic results (Figure 9.120), but it is important to understand, and look out for, the limitations of these technologies. In this case, when the feet get close together, optical flow has difficulty determining which leg is which, and a strange smearing can occur, as shown in Figure 9.121. Many times you can control and correct these errors by or masking off these the offending components, time ramping them individually, and then compositing them back together.

To complete the effect, set multiple keyframes along the timeline and precisely squash and stretch them, as seen in Figure 9.122, to achieve the effect of ramping from fast to slow and vice-versa.

[Figure 9.120]
Results of "optical flow"/"pixel flow" tween frames

[Figure 9.121]
Errors that can occur with extreme time ramps using optical/pixel flow

[Figure 9.122]
Multiple keyframes added
for multi-speed time ramps

Multi-pass Rendering and Compositing

You will find that in every major VFX studio workflow, or *pipeline*, the output
of any kind of 3D—whether small 3D elements to integrate into a live action
plate or full 3D animation or environments—is broken out into many separate components of the scene, or *passes*, and then composited back together.
These processes, called *multi-pass rendering* and *multi-pass compositing*, are
done this way to allow for maximum flexibility in look and integration all the
way up until the very last stages of post-production.

Renders on a complex production can take hundreds, or even thousands,
of hours. One element needing to be re-rendered because of a small change
or flaw is wasteful and could even be devastating to the deadline of a production. For this reason, and so that changes are possible on the fly up until
the very end, a multi-pass workflow is the standard (or the nearest thing to
a standard).

These individual passes are commonly automatically or semi-automatically generated by 3D and rendering applications, but you can also create
them manually.

Which *passes* do you need? Well, there is really no one right answer.
The answer is: whatever the production requires or demands.

Let's take a look at a few examples. Figure 9.123 shows the render of a steampunk airship. At the top is the final composite. Here are the passes that were created for this render:

1. **Beauty pass:** Includes most or all of the color and lighting

2. **RGB pass:** Contains only the RGB color information but with no lighting/shading

3. **Key Diffuse pass:** Contains only the diffuse lighting for the key light

4. **Key Specular (Spec) pass:** Contains only the specular lighting for the key light

5. **Sky Fill Diffuse pass:** Contains only the diffuse lighting for the light being used to emulate bounce lighting from the sky

6. **Sky Fill Spec pass:** Contains only the specular lighting for the light being used to emulate bounce lighting from the sky

7. **Ground Fill Diffuse pass:** Contains only the diffuse lighting for the light being used to emulate bounce lighting from the ground

8. **Ground Fill Spec pass:** Contains only the specular lighting for the light being used to emulate bounce lighting from the ground

9. **Electricity FX pass:** Contains the electricity arcing effects used in the glass engine tubes

10. **Electricity Alpha pass:** Contains a matte to limit an electricity effect that engulfs the entire ship

In this particular case, the passes rendered allow almost complete relighting of the ship, since the opacity of each lighting pass can be adjusted to reveal either more or less of the pass. But they are somewhat limited with regard to other controllable tweaks because the surfacing on these passes is pre-rendered, or *baked*, into the lighting pass renders. While it is entirely possible to do, the surfacing attributes here are not separate passes unto themselves.

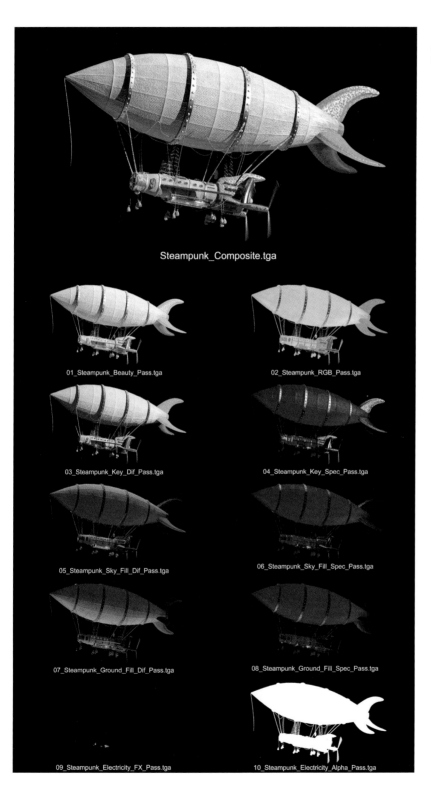

[Figure 9.123]
Multi-pass render of
steampunk airship

The second example (Figure 9.124) shows a digital set of a NORAD war room created for my movie *Anunnaki*. Rendered passes for this set include the following:

1. **Composite:** All of the passes composited together.

2. **Geometry pass:** Indicates the relation of the angle of the polygon's surface normal and the direction of the camera. The brighter the surface, the more it faces the camera directly.

3. **Diffuse Shading pass:** Indicates the amount of light reflected toward the camera from a surface, including the effects of shadows cast onto the surfaces.

4. **RGB pass:** Contains only the RGB color information but with no lighting/shading.

5. **Shaded Diffuse pass:** Contains shaded elements and the diffuse lighting for the scene.

6. **Shaded Specular pass:** Contains shaded elements and the specular lighting for the scene.

7. **Shading pass:** Represents the lighting effects for shadows, as well as specular and diffuse.

8. **Shading matte:** Matte for shadows.

9. **Luminosity pass:** Indicates the intensity of luminosity on a surface.

10. **Normal pass:** Surface normal information.

11. **Depth pass:** Indicates the relative distance of items from the camera. The further away an item is the brighter it is represented.

12. **Specular Shading:** Indicates the amount of specular light reflected toward the camera from a surface, including the effects of shadows cast onto the surfaces.

The final example (Figure 9.125) shows a complex 3D multi-pass render. In addition to many of the passes in the previous example, rendered passes for this set also include diffuse and specular map passes, diffuse and spec passes for every light in the scene, and 3-color RGB diffuse and spec lighting passes. In a 3-color RGB pass, mattes can be extracted for any light simply by selecting the corresponding red, green, or blue color channel and then loading it as a luma matte.

[Figure 9.124]
Multi-pass render of 3D
digital interior set

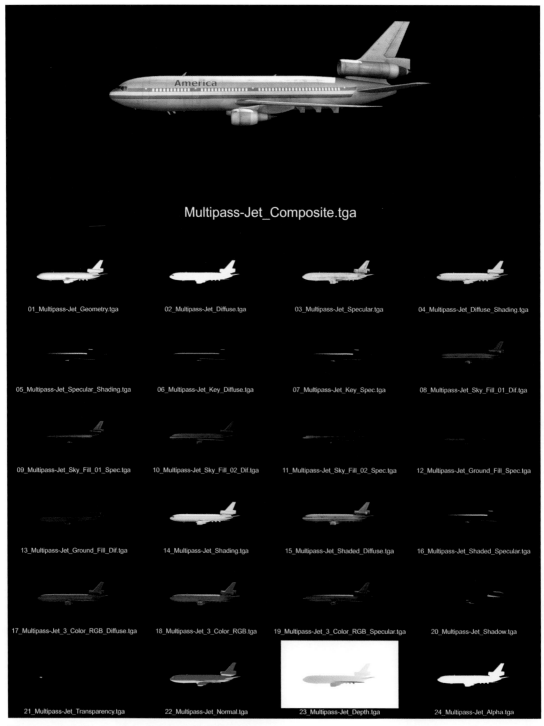

[Figure 9.125] More complex multi-pass render of jet

Having all of these passes allows for the complete relighting, and even retex-turing, of the 3D element… and all *after* it's been rendered!

Compositing all these elements back together may seem like a daunting task at first, but it merely requires stacking each pass on top of the next using a merge or layer and then setting the blend mode (or using a matte to limit the effect). An example of a multi-pass composite of the jet using eight of the passes can be seen in Figure 9.126.

By using multi-pass compositing and rendering, you achieve the maximum in creativity and flexibility while avoiding the need for wasteful additional renders at the end of the production pipeline.

Nowhere is this more critical than when creating complex full 3D digital sets and natural environments, which we jump into next in Chapter 10.

[Figure 9.126] Compositing multiple individual passes into a finished composite

PART THREE

Advanced Visual Effects Techniques

CHAPTER TEN

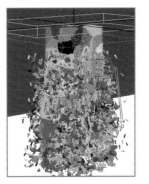

Advanced VFX Techniques I: Digital Matte Painting and Environment VFX

Although creating 3D objects, cloning, extractions, and other VFX wizardry might be impressive, something is inherently downright astounding about creating entire environments from nothing. Perhaps it's the practical flexibility, or maybe it's the complete god-like control you can have over creating entire worlds or even universes. Being able to create anything you see, think of, or dream can be a very liberating and inspiring facet of the art and science of VFX.

This chapter takes a look at the many different methods of creating environment and set VFX.

2.5D Compositing

Some of the cleverest creations of environment VFX are in the realm of 2.5D compositing. You can use 2.5D to take a simple 2D composite, such as the one seen in Figure 10.1, and pull the background plate out into 3D depth (as shown in Figure 10.2) to achieve more realistic background motion or parallax. Or you can create surprisingly realistic, fully lightable and navigable 3D environments (shown in Figure 10.3) made from nothing but the 2D card tricks you learned in Chapter 6, as shown in Figure 10.4. The combinations and possibilities for these clever tricks are almost endless.

[Figure 10.1]
Simple 2D composite from the movie *Balloon*

[Figure 10.2] Background plate pulled out into 3D depth to achieve more realistic background motion parallax

[Figure 10.3] Full photorealistic 3D hallway

[Figure 10.4] Three-quarter view reveals the simple "card trick."

For example, in the case of the bluescreen shot in Figure 10.5, my crew created a complex 3D set in a 3D application (Figure 10.6) and rendered it (Figure 10.7). Once an acceptable look is achieved for a complex 3D environment like this, the huge 3D set can be rendered down into a simple 2D plate and then composited behind the extracted bluescreen plate to achieve a convincing 3D-looking shot (as shown in Figure 10.8) while being, efficiently, nothing more than 2D planes (Figure 10.9).

[Figure 10.5] Original bluescreen plate from the movie *Anunnaki*

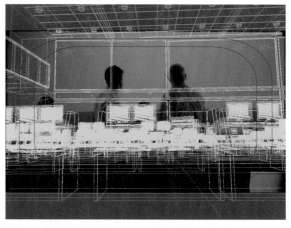

[Figure 10.6] NORAD set created in 3D application

[Figure 10.7]
Rendered 3D set

[Figure 10.8]
Finished composite

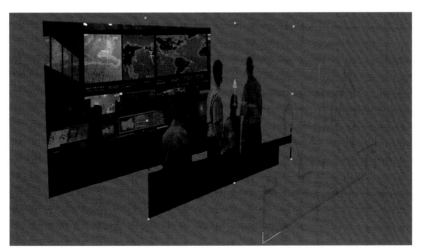

[Figure 10.9]
Exploded composite scene

[Figure 10.10] 3D space shot pre-viz

In a complex animation, such as the space scene in Figure 10.10, you can save enormous amounts of time and achieve amazing effects by combining real 3D objects in front of moving 2D planes as backgrounds (Figure 10.11).

And at the most complex end of the spectrum, you can create simplified 3D geometry to match complex environments (as shown in Figure 10.12), set up virtual cameras in a 3D application to frame the desired composition to your liking (Figure 10.13), and then project textures onto the geometry from the camera's POV (point of view) to achieve lightning-fast realism (see Figure 10.14).

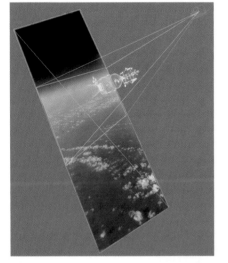

[Figure 10.11] Three-quarter view reveals 2.5D trick, showing 3D objects in front of 2D card space background

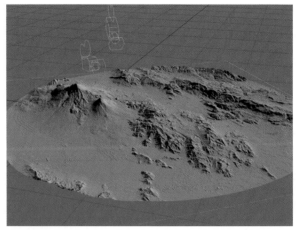

[Figure 10.12] Mt. Ararat, DEM displacement modeled, using the technique covered in Chapter 14

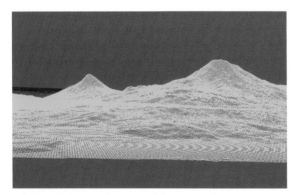

[Figure 10.13] Wireframe model composed in 3D application

[Figure 10.14] Finished camera projected texture

There are so many combinations and variations to these amazing effects that the most important concepts to become familiar with are the Zen-like state of fluidity and thinking outside the box for you to achieve any permutation that gets the job done in the most efficient manner possible.

Let's take a look at a few combinations and variations to these effects as they would apply to creating environments, matte paintings, and set extensions.

Digital Matte Painting and Set Extensions: 2D, 3D, and 2.5D

In the first example we take a look at what at first seems like a simple bluescreen replacement. In this shot from my movie *Anunnaki* (Figure 10.15), we needed a large office for a high-ranking general and lower-ranked workers in a huge area behind his office. The only problem was we had no way of getting to such a location on our tight shooting schedule. We did happen to be near a very large penthouse conference room downtown, however, which was available. We decided to shoot in the conference room and use rolls of bluescreen material to matte off whiteboards that were on the walls; we'd replace them in post with the back office space and workers.

The large back office was created entirely in 3D (Figure 10.16), allowing us the flexibility to get a good camera angle match (Figure 10.17) no matter what we required. Figure 10.18 shows a shaded wireframe view of the scene, and Figure 10.19 shows the rendered 3D environment created exactly to our specs.

[Figure 10.15] Original bluescreen plate

In Figure 10.20, we brought the rendered plate into the compositing application and color corrected and positioned it to better match the foreground bluescreen plate. At another location and date, on a bluescreen background we filmed actors posing as workers. These actors' bluescreen plates were brought into our compositing environment as 2D cards (Figure 10.21), keyed (Figure 10.22), blurred slightly (Figure 10.23) to better match the background plate's softness, and then color corrected (Figure 10.24) to match. We added more workers using the same steps and techniques (Figure 10.25).

[Figure 10.16]
3D back office
environment model

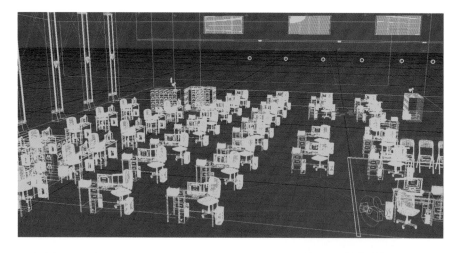

[Figure 10.17]
Wireframe composed to
match foreground plate
angle and perspective

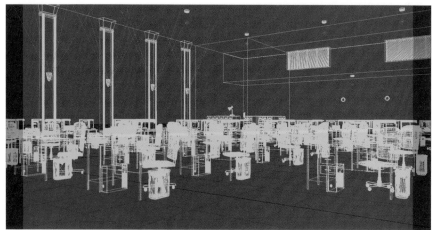

[Figure 10.18]
Shaded wireframe view
of scene

[Figure 10.19]
Rendered 3D back office
scene

[Figure 10.20] Color corrected and positioned render in composition

[Figure 10.21] Bluescreen workers added on 2D cards

[Figure 10.22] Bluescreens keyed

[Figure 10.23] Slight blur added

[Figure 10.24] Worker elements color corrected

[Figure 10.25] Additional worker cards added using same techniques

[Figure 10.26] Foreground plate bluescreens keyed

[Figure 10.27] Actor's hand and glass roto masked from original plate and added back in

With the background assembled, the foreground plate's bluescreens were keyed (Figure 10.26) and the foreground actor's hand and glass were roto'd back in separately (Figure 10.27) to allow finer keying control over the transparent glass.

Figure 10.28 shows the background composited into the space where the bluescreens had been. Notice that the workers in the background (and the room in general) are almost as in focus as the foreground, taking our attention away from the foreground actor and making the scene a bit busy and confusing to the eye. In Figure 10.29, a little more blur has been applied across the entire background, helping to move the viewer's attention back to the foreground. To help add even more distinction, we added a window tint layer, shown in Figure 10.30, which helped provide even more separation between foreground and background elements.

[Figure 10.28] CG background composited in behind foreground plate

[Figure 10.29] Additional blur added to background elements

[Figure 10.30] Window tint layer added to reduce background scene brightness

[Figure 10.31] Reflections added to office windows

We added window reflection elements to our fake glass (Figure 10.31) and to the actor's glass (in Figure 10.32) to help subliminally imply the unseen area behind the camera. In a 3D application, we created simple window vertical blinds (as shown in Figure 10.33), positioned them using the foreground plate as reference (Figure 10.34), and then rendered them (Figure 10.35).

In Figure 10.36, we composited the vertical blinds into the scene and added fake shadows for the blinds (Figure 10.37), using the simple fake shadow method covered in Chapter 5. Finally, we added a grain pass and final color correction to finish the shot (Figure 10.38).

[Figure 10.32] Same reflections added to actor's glass

[Figure 10.33]
3D model of vertical blinds

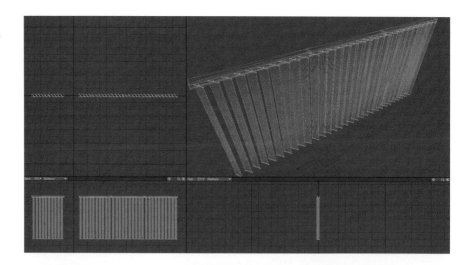

[Figure 10.34] 3D model in flat shade view aligned using foreground plate as positioning reference

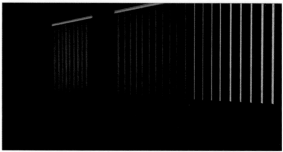

[Figure 10.35] Render of 3D vertical blind element

[Figure 10.36] Composited 3D vertical blind element render

[Figure 10.37] Fake vertical blind shadows added

[Figure 10.38]
Final grain and color
correction pass

For a different type of example, let's look at a completely fabricated 2.5D matte painting scene, extracted from photos and then animated to show how you can build this type of environment piece by piece from the extracted photo source fragments.

This excellent example (provided by one of my very talented former students, Michael Keith) begins with a piece of lightly clouded blue sky (Figure 10.39). To this, Michael added a fake bird (Figure 10.40) to subtly add motion and scale to the composition. He then added a distant building (Figure 10.41), followed by some closer buildings (Figure 10.42), and then nearer tree elements (Figure 10.43). He left holes between the trees to allow cars to be animated (Figure 10.44) behind them, giving the impression of a tree-lined roadway behind these trees. Finally, he filled in the areas behind the cars (Figure 10.45).

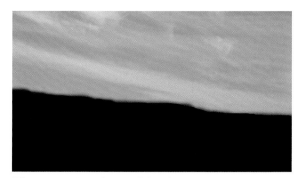

[Figure 10.39] Background sky plate

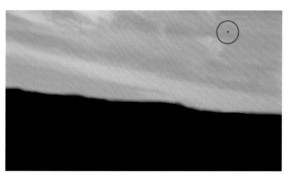

[Figure 10.40] Fake bird added

[Figure 10.41] Background building added to composite

[Figure 10.42] Midground buildings added

[Figure 10.43] Tree elements added

[Figure 10.44] Distant cars added

[Figure 10.45] Areas surrounding cars added back in

[Figure 10.46] Displacement animated lake added

Figure 10.46 shows how Michael proceeded to add an animated lake in the foreground using the water displacement techniques you learned in Chapter 8.

To add more movement and motion (which is critical to bringing a still matte painting to life), he added a swan (seen in Figure 10.47) and its reflection (Figure 10.48) in the foreground, drifting slowly through the water. Next came an animated displacement wake and composited water sparkles (Figure 10.49). In Figure 10.50, Michael goes on to add a large fountain to the lake; he then adds particle system spray to create more motion and to hide the fact that... well... this is a cutout picture of a fountain. In Figure 10.52 you can see the fake reflection of the fountain he has added to the water (again using the fake reflection techniques covered in Chapter 5) as well as foreground grass (Figure 10.53), stone seawall (Figure 10.54), animated drifting wispy cloud (upper right of Figure 10.55), and foreground flower bush (Figure 10.56) elements.

[Figure 10.47] Swan added in foreground

[Figure 10.48] Swan's reflection added

[Figure 10.49] Swan's wake and water sparkle elements added

[Figure 10.50] Fountain element added

[Figure 10.51] Animated fountain water added

[Figure 10.52] Fountain reflection added

[Figure 10.53] Foreground grass element added

[Figure 10.54] Stone seawall element added

[Figure 10.55] Drifting animated wispy cloud added to upper right of frame to give sky slight motion

[Figure 10.56] Foreground flower bush element added

[Figure 10.57] Color desaturation for added realism

With the basic composition completed, Michael desaturated the composition (Figure 10.57) to add a little realism to the previously slightly oversaturated colors. Finally, he then animated all moving camera, water, cloud, swan, fountain, and bird elements (see Figures 10.58 and 10.59), creating an extremely convincing matte painting that appears more like video footage than an animated photo element composite.

Figures 10.60 and 10.61 show these 2.5D elements in 3D space, which allows for natural parallax to occur when the camera trucks across the scene (Figure 10.62). Finally the two car elements are animated (Figure 10.63); they dodge quickly out from, then behind the trees, giving the viewer just enough motion and information to appear completely convincing (Figure 10.64).

[Figure 10.58] Element animation start frame

[Figure 10.59] Element animation end frame

[Figure 10.60]
Scene elements revealed in 2.5D space

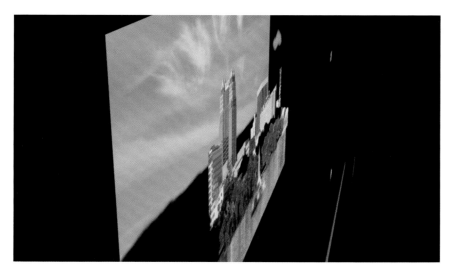

[Figure 10.61]
Layers with no bounding boxes or controls

[Figure 10.62]
When layers have depth variation it allows natural-looking motion parallax between scene elements to be achieved with camera motion.

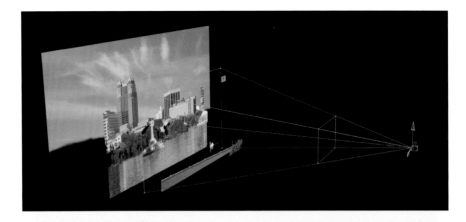

[Figure 10.63]
2D car billboards animated behind trees

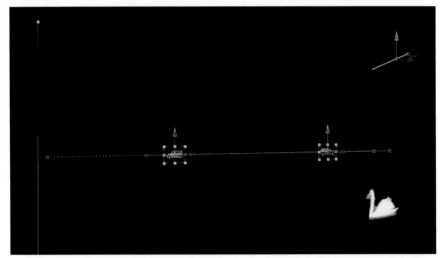

[Figure 10.64]
Finished 2.5D matte painting

Advanced 2.5D Camera Movement

Another clever use of 2.5D VFX is to generate creative, fake camera movements that would otherwise be unlikely (due to enormous technical, financial, or safety challenges) or even impossible under normal circumstances. To illustrate an example of this, let's revisit the shot we looked at for the wire/rig removal in Chapter 9. But in this case, the challenge isn't to remove the bungee harness at all, but to do a Bullet-Time–like camera move while the jumper is falling. In this type of camera move, time appears to slow down but not stop completely as the camera seemingly continues to move around and navigate at will.

As with most VFX, there are many ways to accomplish this effect, including the original bullet-time method used in movies such as *The Matrix*, which required dozens of synchronized cameras and elaborate planning and rigs. This example relies on the more common, "Hey, we shot this footage with no planning at all, can we get this effect?" scenario.

The example uses a variation of the window method covered in Chapter 9. This time, though, we won't roto out the bungee rig but simply roto the whole jumper and rig together as one, as shown in Figure 10.65. After keying the jumper and harness (Figure 10.66), I create the fake super-slow motion movement of the jumper by isolating just that area (Figure 10.67), extracting and creating an alpha (Figure 10.68), and then using a deformation-based animation tool. In this case, I am using the Puppet tool in After Effects, but you can accomplish this technique using almost any application's distort, warp, mesh warp, grid warp, or similar tools.

[Figure 10.65] Jumper and whole bungee rig roto extracted

[Figure 10.66] Sky used as bluescreen to pull key extraction

[Figure 10.67] Jumper element

[Figure 10.68] Keyed jumper element with alpha

[Figure 10.69] The Puppet deformation tool pins placed at character's joints

[Figure 10.71] Original image

[Figure 10.72] Slightly animated (to simulate extreme slow motion) limbs

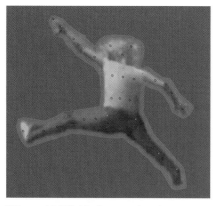

[Figure 10.70] Mesh created and "starched" at rigid limb positions

In the Puppet tool, pins are set to joints of the extracted image, as shown in Figure 10.69. From this, the tool creates a basic mesh that can be *starched* (Figure 10.70), a process that keeps certain areas such as rigid limb sections from bending during the deformation. I keyframe animated very slight motions (as shown in Figures 10.71 and 10.72) to simulate super slow-motion. Figure 10.73 shows the scene setup in 2.5D, and Figure 10.74 shows the virtual camera's view of the scene from this perspective.

[Figure 10.73]
2.5D scene setup

[Figure 10.74]
Camera's view of scene

All that's left to do is animate the virtual camera to follow the jumper (Figures 10.75 and 10.76) and, at the chosen moment, stop the motions of the plates and only animate the camera (Figures 10.77 and 10.78). The camera appears to defy time by moving in and around the scene during this apparent almost frozen moment in time, while the subtle deformation animation of the character suspends disbelief that motion is still happening in the scene.

At the chosen moment (Figure 10.79), you can instantly resume full motion, creating a jarring and excitingly surreal experience for the viewer.

[**Figure 10.75**] Camera following jumper in 2.5D at start of scene

[**Figure 10.77**] Plates freeze and camera pushes in in apparent hyper slow motion.

[**Figure 10.76**] Camera's view of scene

[**Figure 10.78**] Camera's view as character is animated in apparent hyper slow motion by Puppet tool deformation

[**Figure 10.79**]
Character continues full motion plummet

Complex 2.5D Digital Matte Paintings and Camera Projections

Some of the most mind-boggling types of VFX to create and comprehend are complex matte paintings and those using camera projections. Let's begin with an illustration of a complex 2.5D matte painting, run through this process, and explore an example of a simple camera projection, so you can fully wrap your head around this concept.

Complex 2.5D Digital Matte Paintings

For the first example, let's suppose you are approached by a client with the plate shown in Figure 10.80 (a street location, depicting a young actor who will be walking partway down the road). Your job is to create the post-apocalyptic remains of a city far across a canyon, which the foreground road had once crossed to via a bridge.

[**Figure 10.80**] Original jib plate

First place the elements of a canyon wall (Figure 10.81) and futuristic city (Figure 10.82) into position in the comp, then use a spatter brush with the Eraser tool to remove, or destroy, areas of the buildings, as shown in Figure 10.83. Add some additional twisted wreckage, apply a color correction to these elements to match the surrounding elements, and apply an atmosphere layer, as we did in Chapter 8. You can use the same spatter brush to apply black charring to areas to the buildings to further push that burned-out and demolished look (see Figure 10.85).

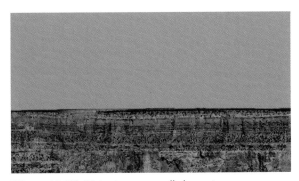

[**Figure 10.81**] Distant canyon wall element

[**Figure 10.82**] Distant futuristic city

[**Figure 10.83**] Spatter brush used with Eraser tool to "destroy" parts of buildings

[**Figure 10.84**] Additional wreckage elements and atmosphere layer added

[**Figure 10.85**] Spatter brush used with black paint to "char" areas of buildings

[**Figure 10.86**] Destroyed bridge on-ramp element added to far canyon wall

In Figure 10.86, I added the far side, disconnected end of the bridge using a color corrected image of an unfinished roadway ramp. I duplicated large piles of road debris, flipped and rotated them for maximum effect, color corrected them to match the scene, and scattered them (Figures 10.87 and 10.88) on both sides of the scene where the road (Figure 10.89) will be composited. Figures 10.90 through 10.92 show damaged road elements composited onto the original road using darken, multiply, and other blend modes to allow them to appear to become part of the original road.

I then extracted the young actor (Figure 10.93) from the original footage using a simple roto matte (Figure 10.94) that isolated and extracted both the boy and his shadow.

[Figure 10.87] Road wreckage added to right foreground

[Figure 10.88] Road wreckage added to left foreground

[Figure 10.89] Original street element roto'd and added to matte painting

[Figure 10.90] End of road element "destroyed" using road wreckage element with blending modes

[Figure 10.91] Right side of road element "destroyed" using road wreckage element with blending modes

[Figure 10.92] Left side of road element "destroyed" using road wreckage element with blending modes

[Figure 10.93] Young actor in original plate

[Figure 10.94] Roto mask used to extract actor and shadow

I brought all these elements into the compositing application. Starting from the back, I added the sky (Figure 10.95), the background canyon and city elements (Figure 10.96), the destroyed bridge connection (Figure 10.97), animated smoke plates as covered in Chapter 8 (Figure 10.98), distant flock of birds (as covered in Chapter 6) for motion and scale (Figure 10.99), another smoke layer over the background buildings and the destroyed foreground road elements (Figure 10.100), and the actor and shadow (Figure 10.101).

Finishing touches included a gradient color grade (as covered in Chapter 9) to darken the sky (Figure 10.102), animated debris and ash elements (Figure 10.103), and one final dark smoke gradient to the upper part of the scene and a grain wash to the entire plate (Figure 10.104).

[**Figure 10.95**] Background sky element loaded into comp

[**Figure 10.96**] Distant canyon wall and city elements added to comp in front of sky element

[**Figure 10.97**] Broken bridge onramp element added to comp

[**Figure 10.98**] Distant smoke elements added

[Figure 10.99] Distant flock of birds added to add motion and scale

[Figure 10.100] Foreground road elements and another layer of smoke in front of city added to comp

[Figure 10.101] Actor added to comp

[Figure 10.102] Dark gradient atmosphere added to sky

[Figure 10.103] Animated debris and aerial ash plates added over entire comp

[Figure 10.104] One final dark smoke gradient added to the upper part of the scene and a grain wash added to entire plate

[Figure 10.105] Original "before" plate

[Figure 10.106] Split view comparison

[Figure 10.107]
Finished "after" composite

Figure 10.105 shows the before plate, Figure 10.106 is a split view comparison, and in Figure 10.107, one final isolated dust layer is added to the city for the completed after shot.

Camera Projections

Camera projections are one of my favorite VFX of all time. Why, you might ask? Because they capture the true magic of VFX and, when done well, create awe-inspiring illusions from seemingly almost nothing. Camera projections reflect the true essence of the VFX artist's "thinking outside the box" mentality.

To see how camera projections work, let's look at a still image of a resort hotel (see Figure 10.108). Assume we need one of those epic, slow-moving establishing crane shots for a movie scene. Creating an actual camera move like that would be expensive and a logistical nightmare.

Whenever I teach a VFX class I always show the class an example like this and ask, "Okay, class, this is the shot you will need to create. If I turn you loose to start creating this shot in 3D right now, what's the first thing you will start doing?" Most of the time, "Begin modeling the building in 3D" is almost always the first answer, but before they get answer number two out of their mouths, I add, "Oh, and I forgot to mention, you only have 45 minutes to complete the entire finished shot." At this point, mouths drop open and I'm met with

[Figure 10.108] Still image of resort hotel

blank stares of complete confusion and bewilderment. You can see from their faces that I have given them what they feel is an impossible task. But we *can* create this shot, very quickly, with nothing more than this still image—using camera projections!

The main concept (and most confusing aspect) of camera projection VFX is that the textures for the entire scene (or just individual elements if preferred) are *projected* from the perspective of a camera (a reference camera) onto geometry in the scene, in effect texturing everything all at once!

Imagine that you take the image of a book, load it into a slide projector, and project it onto a plain white box that is the same shape, size, and in the same position as the book in the picture. The book in the image would perfectly align with the box and so would appear to perfectly texture it. If you had another camera, you could film a moving camera shot of this "book" as long as you didn't stray too far from the projector's location and vantage point, which would break the illusion. This is exactly the concept behind camera projections and explains the concept of the *sweet spot* when doing this type of effect. The sweet spot is the same position and vantage point as the projector. The farther off axis from that vantage point you go, the more the effect stretches and begins to break down. Therefore, before beginning a camera projection shot and planning your camera move (say, a 90-degree arc), it's always better to split the difference of the move, starting off to one side of the sweet spot (perhaps 45 degrees off to one side), moving across the sweet spot, and then 45 degrees off to the other side, rather than beginning or ending the camera move 90 degrees off axis.

In your 3D application, set the image plane or project setting to the size of the image and then load the image you intend to use as your projection into the background. Model basic geometry to encompass each of the main features of your image, as shown in Figure 10.109. Simple cube shapes work perfectly for most buildings, signs, and so on, and simple planes usually work well for ground, sky, and other similar planes.

[Figure 10.109]
Basic geometry cubes modeled to encompass each of the main elements of the image

It is important that objects in the scene sit on the ground plane as they do in reality, do not "float" above the ground, and sit relationally to each other the way they do in reality as well. Building your stand-in geometry to scale (or approximately to scale) can also be very helpful. Where measurements are unknown, deductive reasoning can often help you arrive at a reasonable estimate. For example, counting floors of a building and multiplying that number by a guesstimated floor height of 9 or 10 feet can give you a pretty close estimate as to building height as well as a reasonable guess as to where to place the camera (which should also be as accurate a guesstimate as possible).

After the stand-in geometry is built and put into rough position, it's helpful to immediately move the object's pivot points to the front-most bottom corner. This will allow for quick scaling and rotation fine-tuning about this axis if necessary.

Next position the camera, not the objects, to best approximate the position where the camera was in the original reference photo. Translate and rotate the camera until everything in the scene aligns.

Once all the simple stand-ins have been built and positioned, and the camera is aligned and in place, lock and rename that camera Projection Camera or something similar. Don't move that camera again. Clone or duplicate that first projection camera (Figure 10.110) and rename it Animation Camera or something similar. The animation camera is the camera you will move and animate to record your shot. The Projection Camera will remain in place and be used only as a reference point from which textures will be projected.

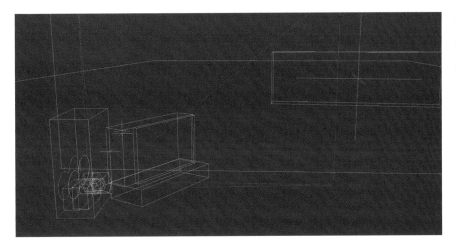

[Figure 10.110]
Projection camera duplicated and then locked. The duplicate Animation Camera is used for filming to create animation.

Each object has a surface. Each surface uses a texture with some sort of projection, whether flat, cylindrical, spherical, UV, or camera referenced. Objects with multiple textured faces may receive multiple, even different, camera projections on each face as long as there is a reference camera for each texture projection. One camera can be used as the reference camera for projecting textures on multiple/different objects from the same vantage point as well. Remember, the camera is only a "reference point" from which its vantage point is used as the basis for the texture's application or projection. The camera itself is not being "occupied" or actually "doing" anything (another major point of confusion).

In Figure 10.111 you can see the rough geometry aligned with the elements in the image (the geometry has been made more complex for this image so it's easier to see).

Any elements that need overlaps clipped (such as the top and railings on the buildings) will need an alpha created and loaded as usual into the opacity/transparency channel of the material to cut away any excess geometry. Create this alpha channel using the same roto or procedural extraction methods I've been covering throughout the book and then load these alpha(s) into the objects' opacity/transparency map channel. Select "camera" or "front" as

[Figure 10.111]
Geometry aligned with all
scene elements

[Figure 10.111]
Geometry aligned with all
scene elements

[note]

The camera is used as the
reference for the object's
texture projection and is
not necessarily "doing" the
projecting. This confuses
many people.

the projection type and the Projection Camera as the reference camera. The color texture will obviously be loaded into the color channel and "camera" or "front" projection set as the projection type (with the Projection Camera selected as the reference camera).

Figure 10.112 shows the texture image being projected from the Projection Camera across the whole scene. Notice the stretching that appears where our viewpoint is too far off axis from the projection camera. Figure 10.113 shows the actual simple geometry with little in the way of complexity.

Now it's time to animate the Animation Camera with the slow-moving crane move. Wherever parts of the image will be revealed behind or around the edges of a piece of geometry, you will need to create/clone a clean plate so there will be something to reveal. That is, as the camera moves closer

[Figure 10.112]
Texture image being
projected from the
Projection Camera across
all of the geometry in the
entire scene at once

[Figure 10.113]
Actual simple geometry with little in the way of complexity

[Figure 10.114] Animation start position

[Figure 10.115] Animation mid position

[Figure 10.116] Animation end position

toward the left side of the building, a clean plate of that area on the background plate will need to be created so different background elements will be revealed. This cleaned background will be loaded as the texture for the background elements but projected from the same Projection Camera. For scenes where multiple depths may be revealed, possibly by more extensive camera movement, multiple clean plate variations may be needed for elements at different depths.

Figures 10.114 through 10.116 show the finished shot and camera movement.

In my live classes I call this the Matrix Moment—when the ramifications of what this technique means can hit you so hard, you may feel as though everything you've ever thought or learned about 2D, 3D, and how to do many VFX is completely meaningless and a complete waste of time… now that you can see the true nature of the matrix.

Let me distill this concept down further. This means that, in effect, you have the ability and choice to be able to work completely backwards! You can complete the finished version and look (digital matte painting) of a complete complex scene *first*—even an entire environment—by just *painting it* in 2D in an application such as Photoshop. After it's exactly the way you want it, you can camera project the entire scene, all at once, onto simple stand-in geometry to arrive at a perfect finished result in 3D that looks exactly like the 2D painting! No intensive modeling, no texturing, nothing! Paint the finished product first, then camera project.

Mind blown!

Digital Environment Applications

Although there are many times when you can get away with a matte painting or camera projection, there are still going to be times when nothing but a full-blown 3D CG scene will do. Luckily, some really great applications are designed just for this purpose. Let's take a look at some of the leaders in this arena.

Vue

In my opinion, the leader by far in this arena is e-on software's Vue (shown in Figures 10.117 and 10.118). Vue has grown over the years into a powerhouse for environmental VFX and has been used on many large-scale blockbuster motion pictures. Its strengths lie in its excellent terrain and atmosphere tools, rendering, and its ability to handle scenes with literally billions of polygons. Although Vue is a very complex program, and its learning curve can be quite steep, Vue xStream (e-on's Vue version that plugs into and works seamlessly with many 3D applications) makes it easy to work with for 3D artists working in their native 3D application as well.

Terragen

Originally a completely free beta product (there's still a free version with limitations and now also an enhanced commercial version) from Planetside Software, Terragen (Figure 10.119) also offers formidable terrains and skies and has been used in many major feature film and television productions as well. It may not be quite as feature rich as Vue, but it's a lot less expensive and continues to have a widespread and loyal user base.

[Figure 10.117]
e-on software's Vue interface showing natural environment creation

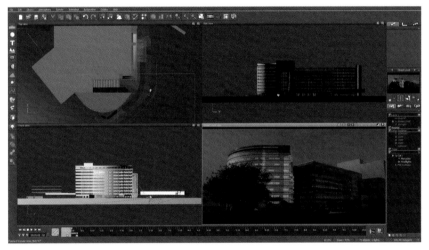

[Figure 10.118]
Vue is equally proficient at manmade environments as well.

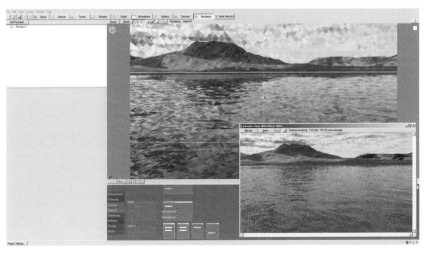

[Figure 10.119]
Planetside Software's Terragen user interface

World Machine

World Machine (Figures 10.120 and 10.121) is a landscape-generation tool that adds an interesting twist to the creation of terrains with its modular node-based creation workflow. Though not an end-to-end solution like Vue and Terragen, World Machine is an excellent and specialized tool for creating amazingly realistic terrains for export to other 3D and rendering applications.

[Figure 10.120]
World Machine's user interface showing node creation tools

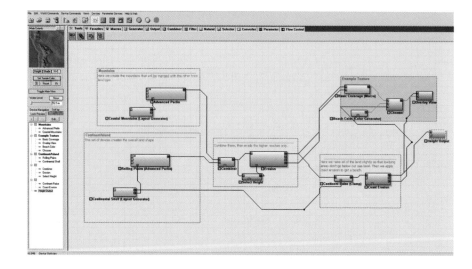

[Figure 10.121]
World Machine's user interface showing 3D terrain view

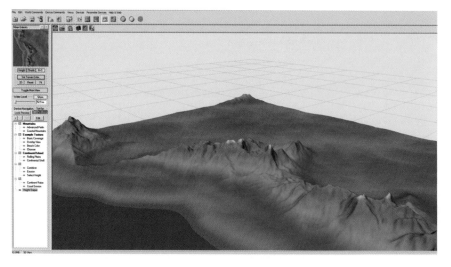

Virtual Sets

Moving to interior environments, the creation of a virtual set involves the same process and workflow as almost any other 3D environment, but with an added emphasis on proper scale and form to assure that sets work with integrated actors, talent, and a production's particular needs. Virtual sets are built (Figure 10.122), lit (Figure 10.123), and rendered like any other 3D set, but special care is taken to assure that set design works for the best production camera angles (Figures 10.124 and 10.125).

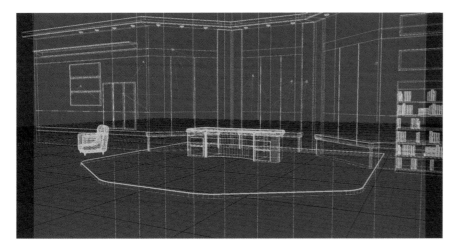

[Figure 10.122]
Wireframe 3D virtual set

[Figure 10.123]
Textured and lit virtual set

[Figure 10.124]
Virtual set rendered from
right camera position

[Figure 10.125]
Virtual set rendered from
left camera position

Virtual Studio

On the new frontier of production is the *virtual studio*, a wide and expansive
landscape with many new, exciting, and promising advancements. Among
them are the virtual camera (Figures 10.126 and 10.127) and virtual cinematography technologies. These allow "filming" of a 3D CG environment in real
time using a *virtual camera*, a piece of technology with a sensor rig that tracks
the camera's motions and streams the data in real time to the 3D application.
This allows you to film within the application in real time, with a hands-on
camera, using and controlling it just as you would in the real world. Figure
10.128 shows, in action, a virtual camera rig I built for pre-viz virtual cinematography within the UDK (Unreal Development Kit) game engine, allowing
for real-time live-action camerawork inside a virtual 3D environment.

[Figure 10.126]
3D virtual camera rig

[Figure 10.127] Close-up of homebuilt 3D virtual camera rig

[Figure 10.128]
Virtual camera rig being used in small office to "film" 3D exterior scene in real time

[Figure 10.129] Calibrating X-Camera prototype

Many 3D applications now support live action virtual set integration (mostly for television and video production), such as LightWave 3D's virtual studio and Maya plugins.

On the bleeding edge of virtual studio technologies are some (such as the prototype shown in Figures 10.129 through 10.131 that I built in a joint effort with technology company pioneer Paracosm) that not only track real-time camera motion data (Figure 10.132) but also acquire depth map data (shown in Figure 10.133, which can be used for the displacement creation of 3D objects, as seen in Figures 10.134 and 10.135), point cloud data (Figures 10.136 and 10.137), and 3D-colored mesh data (Figure 10.138) of the entire environment as well—all in real time!

Used with the advanced lighting techniques you're about to discover in Chapter 11, these technologies are surely the future of 3D motion picture CG VFX!

[Figure 10.130] X-Camera prototype sensor rig mounted on small handheld build of Red Epic camera

[Figure 10.131] Live testing of X-Camera prototype at Paracosm's lab

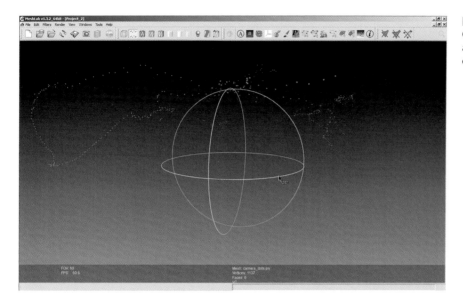

[Figure 10.132]
Camera positional data
acquired (each little dot is a
camera position)

[Figure 10.133]
Depth map acquired in real
time from test

[Figure 10.134]
Depth map data applied to footage as a 3D displacement

[Figure 10.135]
3D model extraction from depth map, which can be used for deep compositing or stereo conversion

[Figure 10.136]
Point cloud acquired
from test

[Figure 10.137]
Opposite side of room point
cloud (notice even people in
the room were captured by
the point cloud)

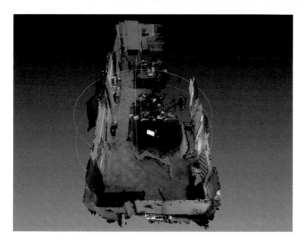

[Figure 10.138]
Textured 3D mesh
auto-acquired from test

CHAPTER ELEVEN

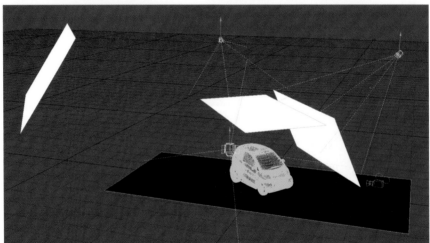

Advanced VFX Techniques II: Beauty and Restoration VFX

VFX is such a cool field because we regularly do "the impossible." We can change the way things actually appeared in an original image, create perfection out of imperfection, and even turn back the hands of time. This chapter shows you how to do all of the above.

Just about anyone who's seen an old black-and-white image has wondered, "What did the actual colors look like in this picture?" And no, the world wasn't in black and white before color photography. This obvious question has led many motion picture companies to colorize famous old black-and-white movies. Colorization raises further questions as viewers try to figure out how it can be done, considering it had no color to begin with and the immense amount of work that it must require to color everything in every frame, 24 frames per second, in a 2-hour movie. The ability to color an image that has no color seems almost magical (especially for those of us who are not professional painters). Let's begin the chapter exploring how to use the VFX wizardry covered so far to conjure up another skill for our bag of tricks.

Film Colorization

To explore colorization, we will use this very old black-and-white image of Frank E. Webner, Pony Express rider, from 1861. I found this photo, shown in Figure 11.1, in the U.S. National Archives. If you want to try this technique out from scratch for yourself, you can find many more great public domain examples on the National Archives site, at www.archives.gov.

Wouldn't it be cool to see what this image might have looked like if it had originally been taken in color? Well, that's what you are about to create.

You will use a combination of rotosplines in this technique, working from the back of the scene forward, to quickly isolate scene components without having to spend excessive time where it isn't necessary.

To begin, create a solid or constant and, with a rotospline, isolate the sky by drawing a large, rough rotoshape around the top of the image and through approximately where you think the sky will be behind elements in the scene (Figure 11.2).

Using your powers of observation, determine what kind of sky appears in the scene and try to find a reference image with a similar sky to determine the color this sky should be. Fill this mask or constant with that sky blue color (Figure 11.3).

As mentioned in previous chapters, because I have the common red-green color deficiency, that I always use reference images (as seen in Figure 11.4) and Photoshop's color picker/info to determine the exact colors to use in

[Figure 11.1] Frank E. Webner, Pony Express rider (1861)

[Figure 11.2] Rotospline to isolate the sky background.

my work. I highly recommend this methodology to even those with perfect color vision because it takes all the guesswork and potential for error out of your color selections. Using your reference image, repeat the process for the ground color (Figure 11.5).

I've used mostly solid colors here, but feel free to use procedurals, gradients, or images for your colors as appropriate. For example, you could give the blanket the man is wrapped in a pattern. Using a mesh or spline warp tool (distortion and displacement tools work for this as well), take an image of the pattern you want to use and then move the control vertices and splines of the warp tool around to simulate the curves and folds in the blanket (Figures 11.6 and 11.7). Use your rotospline masks to cut away any excess image (Figure 11.8).

[**Figure 11.3**] Solid/constant filled with light sky blue color

[**Figure 11.4**] Reference image used to assist with element color selection

[**Figure 11.5**] Solid/constant filled with ground/grass color

[**Figure 11.6**] Mesh warp vertices and splines are adjusted to simulate curves and folds in blanket.

[**Figure 11.7**] Mesh warped pattern

[**Figure 11.8**] Rotospline isolates element shape as well as cuts away any excess texture pattern

Continue this process of creating solids/constants with rotosplines to isolate all the individual scene elements that will require different colors, and fill them with values taken from reference images you feel adequately match the scene you're creating. Here I started with the face of the man in the blanket (Figure 11.9) and then moved on to the rear horse (Figure 11.10), the foreground horse (Figure 11.11), and then the rider's jeans (Figure 11.12), belt (Figure 11.13), shirt (reference research revealed that at one time pony express riders were issued a red shirt, Figure 11.14), bandana (Figure 11.15), face (Figure 11.16), hair (Figure 11.17), and hat (Figure 11.18).

[Figure 11.9] Roto and solid/constant of man in blanket's face color

[Figure 11.10] Roto and solid/constant of rear horse color

[Figure 11.11] Roto and solid/constant of foreground horse color

[Figure 11.12] Roto and solid/constant of rider's jeans color

[Figure 11.13] Roto and solid/constant of rider's belt color

[Figure 11.14] Roto and solid/constant of rider's shirt color

[Figure 11.15] Roto and solid/constant of rider's bandana color

[Figure 11.16] Roto and solid/ constant of rider's face color

[Figure 11.17] Roto and solid/ constant of rider's hair color

[Figure 11.18] Roto and solid/constant of rider's hat color

[Figure 11.19] All roto shapes

[Figure 11.20] All solids/constants

Once all the scene elements are roto'd (Figure 11.19), you should have a fully colored scene that resembles the RGB color pass shown in Chapter 9 (Figure 11.20). Remember to use multiple articulated rotoshapes for motion colorization, as discussed in Chapter 3 and *not* the way they are presented here, for print illustration as single shapes for a still image. By changing the blend mode of each layer using blend modes such as Color, Color Burn, Multiply, and so on, and by using the more foreground rotoshapes as subtract mattes for the broader background shapes (such as sky and ground solids/constants), I achieved the highly colorized but not very realistic image shown in Figure 11.21.

[Figure 11.21] Highly colorized image created using color transfer modes for each solid/constant.

[Figure 11.22] Lowering the opacity of each solid/constant creates the much more realistic-looking effect of an original color photo

For a fantasy movie like *The Wizard of Oz,* a result like Figure 11.21 might be what you're trying to achieve but it's not what you want for a historical photo. For this type of image, you're shooting for a more realistic look. You want it to look as though the photograph were originally taken in color but still shows the same aging and deterioration as the original black-and-white photo. When you lower the opacity of each solid/constant, a much more realistic old color photo (see Figure 11.22) almost magically springs to life.

Digital Beauty

You can use many variations of this technique to both add and remove elements in a scene. Among the most highly secretive invisible VFX work done in the movie industry is that of digital beauty VFX. It's almost never talked about, and in many cases, it's utterly denied, like some UFO conspiracy cover-up. But a simple Google comparison of real-life photos versus movie frames of actors leaves no doubt that digital makeup, blemish removal, and de-aging are not only commonplace, but the de facto standard.

At some point, you *will* be asked to remove a blemish, smooth some wrinkles, or add a little somethin' somethin' to an actor's appearance. Let's take a look at a few very versatile ways to enhance actors' appearances and make them look their best (or worst, if the script requires).

Digital Makeup and Tattoos

This example uses a clip from a scene in *Anunnaki* where we see actors Robin Wilson and Susan Pesel watching a small portable TV (Figure 11.23).

For a simple first task, let's assume that production has asked you to give Susan's character some pink lip gloss. This could be a slightly roto-intensive shot to do, but thanks to Imagineer Systems' Mocha Pro planar tracking, roto, and removal tools (and their excellent integration of these features) this VFX is a snap. Because Mocha Pro is a planar tracker, we will use it to do a tracker-assisted roto of her lips to make this shot much easier and quicker to accomplish.

[Figure 11.23]
Actors Robin Wilson and Susan Pesel
watching a small portable TV

[Figure 11.24] Simple X-Spline used to
planar track the mouth area

[Figure 11.25] X-Spline follows and
deforms to follow pattern movement
and distortion.

[Figure 11.26] Two precise X-Splines
created to outline her lips

First, define a simple X-Spline around her mouth (Figure 11.24), being careful
to avoid her hair, which moves in the wind and can throw off the tracker.
Track this area. Figure 11.25 shows the excellent way Mocha Pro tracks the
area and deforms to follow pattern movement and distortion.

[Figure 11.27] Full motion
roto matte can be exported
for use in other applications

Deactivate the first tracking spline and create two precise X-Splines to
outline her lips (Figure 11.26). Once these are created, link them to the first
spline's track, which takes care of almost all of the work for you; the precise
lip splines follow along nicely and need only fine-tuning adjustments here
and there. When you've finished fine tuning these, you can export a full-
motion roto matte to use in other applications, as shown in Figure 11.27.
Or you can use Mocha Pro's Remove tool (Figure 11.28) with a still clean
plate—or in this case, a still or stills of the scene modified in Photoshop, with
the lips colored using the same method covered in the earlier section "Film
Colorization" (Figure 11.29). Mocha Pro will interpolate this clean plate and
color the rest for you, as shown in Figure 11.30.

[**Figure 11.28**] Mocha Pro's Remove tool

[**Figure 11.29**] Still frame from the scene modified in Photoshop with the lips colored to pink using the same colorization method described earlier

[**Figure 11.30**] Mocha Pro will interpolate this clean plate and color the rest for you.

You can use this same method to add elements as well. To add, say, a tattoo, simply repeat the steps you used to modify the lips. First track the area of the face (Figure 11.31) and create a clean plate with a tattoo added in Photoshop to use with the Remove tool (Figure 11.32). Then let Mocha Pro do the rest, moving and deforming the clean area to the planar-tracked area almost completely automatically (Figure 11.33). In instances where the clean plate starts to distort, you can import additional clean plates to place at intervals as "keyframes," if you will, to help Mocha better affix features.

[Figure 11.31] Tracking the area of the face where the tattoo will appear

[Figure 11.32] Clean plate with a tattoo added in Photoshop and loaded into Mocha Pro to use with the Remove tool

[Figure 11.33] Mocha Pro automatically moves and deforms the Tattoo (clean plate) to the tracked area.

Digital De-Aging

Even more common than the preceding examples is the use of these types of VFX techniques to turn back the hands of time and make aging actors look younger. As mentioned, this is highly secretive and even denied by many studios, but it *is* done... commonly. And why not? If we have the ability to make actors look their best, we should. That is, after all, part of our job—to make the actors look the best they possibly can. That's as true for their looks as it is for their performance and action.

These de-aging techniques can range from drastically reducing wrinkles, age spots, and blemishes to just turning the clock back a few years, as we will do here with this plate of the already youthful actor Steve Roth (Figure 11.34).

Typically, turning back the clock visually means smoothing the skin and easing or removing wrinkles. Usually, you want to keep the skin's original color/tone while removing inconsistencies and texture. Interestingly, that's exactly what blurring does. But you don't want to blur everything, or blur too much. Only blur certain areas, and only enough to reduce the elements you're targeting.

To do this, we will start by creating... yep, you guessed it—rotosplines! This time, I'll show the example in Nuke. Start by creating rotospline mattes of all the smooth skin areas of the face, but avoid any detailed areas you don't want blur applied to, such as the eyes, nose, mouth, ears, or hair (Figure 11.35). Because these mattes are a bit too sharp-edged, apply a blur or feather to them to smooth them out a bit, as shown in Figure 11.36. Figure 11.37 shows an overlay of these mattes onto the plate to show what areas this work will be affecting.

[Figure 11.34] Actor Steve Roth

[Figure 11.35] Rotospline mattes of all the smooth skin areas of the face, avoiding areas that shouldn't be blurred

[Figure 11.36] Blur applied to smooth the matte

[Figure 11.37] Overlaying these mattes onto the plate shows what areas will be affected.

[Figure 11.38] Blur applied to plate

In this example, I applied a slight blur to the entire plate just until the skin was smoothed to the level I was looking for—smooth but not overly blurred, as shown in Figure 11.38. Next, I used the matte I created to limit this blur effect to only the matte areas, as shown in Figure 11.39.

Finally, I added a layer of noise/grain back in, as covered in Chapter 6, over the newly blurred/smoothed layer to replace the original noise or grain that was removed in the blurring process (Figure 11.40). Adding grain helps integrate the slightly blurred areas back into the original and re-introduces the original apparent sharpness. Figure 11.41 shows the before and after comparison of the de-aging process.

[Figure 11.39] Roto matte used to limit the blur effect to only the areas in the roto matte

[Figure 11.40] Layer of noise/grain added back over the blurred/smoothed layer

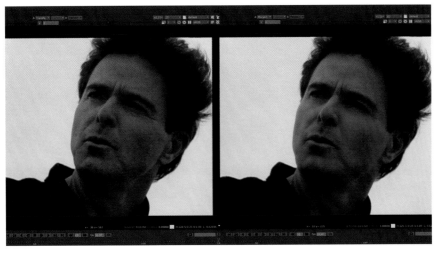

[Figure 11.41]
Before and after comparison

Advanced Lighting and Rendering

It goes without saying that VFX artists are constantly striving for better and more efficient ways to create the best-looking VFX possible. In the realm of 3D CG VFX, much of what we do to attain the best final image is tied to a constant battle with the hardware's calculating and rendering ability. By necessity, you have to have a wide array of skills, tools, and techniques ready to use in any particular situation or circumstance.

Given the opportunity/luxury of being on set, VFX supervisors or artists have to look for the fastest and most efficient ways of getting whatever data or reference they need, while staying out of the production's way as much as possible. Over the years, one of the most valuable tricks I've found—besides great observation, note taking, and set surveying skills—is to always get a complete 360-degree spherical lighting reference of whatever set or location a 3D CG element will be added to. In addition to being a great and complete reference, in a pinch such lighting references can get you some outstanding CG lighting results very quickly and easily as well.

To understand how, you must first know some terminology, technologies, and techniques that I find are widely confused and misunderstood by beginning VFX artists: Global illumination (GI), radiosity, image-based lighting (IBL), high dynamic range images (HDRI), and light probes.

Global Illumination, Radiosity, and Image-Based Lighting

To understand global illumination (GI), it may help to first reconsider the amount of work you need to realistically light a 3D object, as discussed in Chapter 5. To light a car in 3D, for example, you would need to set one light as the sun or key light, and additional lights for sky fill, ground fill, and any additional nearby sources of reflected light. Additionally, aside from the strong sunlight, you wouldn't want all the harsh shadows that multiple lights might cause. You'd want natural, soft shadowing in the areas affected only by bounced light.

What if we could create an illuminated sphere around our car (as seen in Figure 11.42) and color its top sky blue, its bottom the color of the ground, its sides the color of buildings, grass, and so on, and leave a large bright white area where the sun would be? This illuminated sphere would light the entire car all at once, providing *global illumination (GI)*. That's right; global illumination is merely lighting the entire scene all at once by enclosing the scene

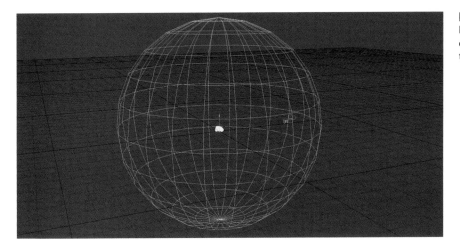

[Figure 11.42]
Illuminated 3D sphere
created around car mesh
to provide GI

[Figure 11.43]
360-degree image wrapped
around 3D sphere to
provide IBL

in an imaginary (or real) illuminated 3D sphere, cube, or other environment that allows the entire scene to be lit all at once.

Let's take this a step further and assume that you could wrap a 360-degree image of a real environment inside this 3D sphere or object, and that you could use it as the source for the illumination's colors and brightness, as shown in Figure 11.43. This would provide more realistic color and light and would be an example of *image-based lighting* (IBL).

But what if this red car sat on a white floor? The white and blue light coming from the sun and sky area of our GI IBL would hit the red car and white floor independently. In the real world, light would be reflected from the red car onto the white floor as well as from the white floor onto the red car. In computer graphics we call the simulation of this phenomenon *radiosity*. Radiosity calculates the diffuse interreflections between surfaces.

For example, imagine that we created a 3D CG bright red ball and placed it on a pure white 3D floor next to a pure white 3D wall (Figure 11.44), turned off all other lights except for one spotlight aimed at the ball from behind the wall (Figure 11.45), and followed one photon of light. We would see that the photon would travel from the spotlight to the surface of the ball (Figure 11.46) and then reflect/bounce and scatter (Figure 11.47) in multiple directions. These scattered rays would be tinted by the surface of the ball and would then hit other surfaces and bounce and scatter again (Figure 11.48), creating the lighting you can see in Figure 11.49. If you look closely at the inside of the wall (Figure 11.50), which received no direct lighting from the spotlight it, you'll notice the realistic tinting of the white wall one would expect to see as a result of being in close proximity to a red ball (Figure 11.51). That is radiosity.

By combining the bounced light and soft shadow effects of radiosity with GI and IBL, you can quickly achieve some powerfully realistic results.

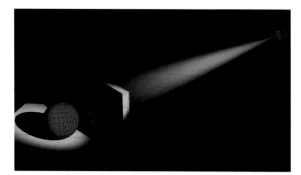

[**Figure 11.44**] 3D CG bright red ball, placed on a pure white 3D floor, next to a pure white 3D wall

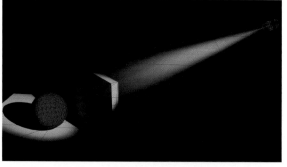

[**Figure 11.45**] All other lights turned off except for one spotlight aimed at the ball from behind the wall

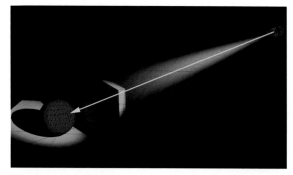

[**Figure 11.46**] Photon's path travelling from the spotlight to the surface of the ball

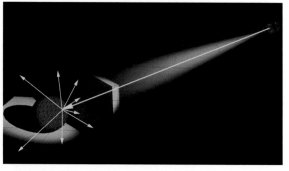

[**Figure 11.47**] Light reflecting/bouncing and scattering

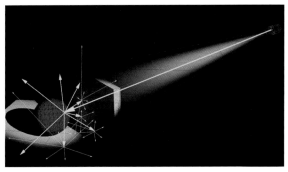

[Figure 11.48] Rays tinted by the surface of the ball bounce/ scatter and then hit other surfaces and bounce/scatter again

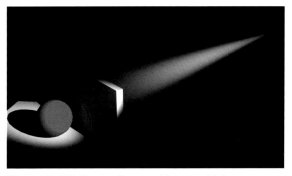

[Figure 11.49] Result of bounced/scattered light

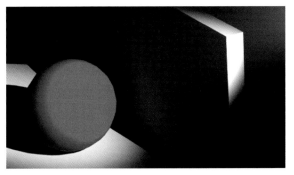

[Figure 11.50] Close-up of inside of wall that received no direct light from spotlight

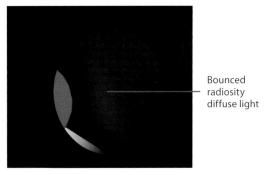

Bounced radiosity diffuse light

[Figure 11.51] Bounced diffuse light using radiosity

High Dynamic Range Images and Light Probes

One limit to the realism achievable with GI IBL is that most common digital images contain only 8 to 14 bits of resolution data, per pixel, per color channel, or 256 to 16,384 levels of intensity per individual RGB channel, as discussed in Chapter 1. But in the real world, the sun can be thousands or millions of times brighter than, say, the light being bounced off of multiple surfaces. This limited range of intensity prompted researchers (most notably, Paul Debevec) to create the high dynamic range image (HDRI) to solve exactly this limitation. The HDRI captures (or can be compiled from a series of bracketed exposure images to contain) a higher dynamic range than the standard 8-bit image, allowing for these wider values.

There is no "one" HDRI standard that equates to a bit depth, which is why the term is abused so much. So theoretically, 2 images bracketed to capture different dynamic exposures can be compiled to create what is, technically, an HDRI, or 20 bracketed images can be compiled to create an HDRI. They

[note]

An 8-bit per channel (bpc) image contains only 256 levels per color channel. You could use a 128-megapixel camera (which refers only to the image "dimension," *not* the color depth) and it still is usually only 8 bit per channel. If you used a 14 bpc RAW camera, your monitor (when viewing it) would *still* likely only show you 8 bpc because that's all most monitors can display. Many of the HDRI modes you see are more or less hacks and not what we would truly consider a usable HDRI.

both are "higher" in dynamic range, but one is much more so than the other. The concept of HDRI can also be headache-inducing because although an HDRI can capture potentially limitless degrees of value, your average monitor can still only display 8 bpc. Which begs the question, "What is the benefit of HDRI at all?"

The value of HDRI lies in what we could call the "unsee-able potential" values it stores in logarithmic format—meaning, in essence, it can subdivide the 0–1 luminance value (or dynamic range) into an infinite potential subdivision of degrees or levels.

The simplest illustration of this concept would be an image of a sunny day used as an IBL to light a 3D scene. In a typical 8-bit image, the darkest blacks would obviously be at a value of 0, and the brightest white (even the center of the sun) at the highest available value of 255. This would light our scene with 256 degrees of brightness, meaning the brightest part of the scene would, at most, be only 255 levels brighter than pure black.

By contrast, in an HDRI the pure white of the sun could easily be 10,000 or more levels brighter than the darkest blacks, rendering the scene's lighting much more realistically distributed. The image on your monitor will likely still be 8 bit but will appear to be lit much more naturally (because that is the way light is in the real world).

Confusion arises when people frequently see HRDI images depicted in 180-degree mirror ball HDRI lighting references called *light probes* (Figure 11.52) and then used in 3D applications as the source for a GI IBL radiosity lighting solution. You can easily see where all this terminology starts getting extremely confusing.

[Figure 11.52] HDRI light probe

So here is an attempt to clarify all this terminology:

- **Global illumination (GI):** The illumination of a 3D scene globally or all at once. GI can be from a flat color, procedural texture, or image (if an image is used, it would be called an IBL global illumination.

- **Image-based lighting (IBL):** Lighting a scene using an image as the projection basis for the lights, colors, and intensities. IBL is usually GI but not necessarily so. An image used as the light source in a scene projected from, say, a card would also be image-based lighting but not globally illuminating.

- **Radiosity:** The computer-generated simulation of calculated diffuse interreflections between surfaces.

- **High dynamic range image (HDRI):** An image containing a captured or compiled range of image exposure wider than that of a common image (if in an omnidirectional format, it would be considered a light probe).

- **Light probe:** An omnidirectional HDRI image that records the incident illumination conditions at a particular point in space.

- **Lighting reference:** Any image-capturing lighting information and data (may be in the same omnidirectional format as an HDRI, but does not contain the high dynamic range of data).

HDRI light probes can be used for GI IBL radiosity lighting solutions, but so can regular spherical images or stitched panoramas… in fact, so can tiny, blurred, common images as seen in Figure 11.53. Because of the limited variations in pixel data, small or blurred images like this sometimes achieve excellent, subtle results and with much less computational overhead and errors in calculating the radiosity.

[Figure 11.53] Tiny, blurred, common image of same scene as in Figure 11.52

Although the creation of HDRI images used to be a somewhat complex and daunting task, today it's as simple as taking a series of bracketed exposure photos (as shown in Figure 11.54) and letting Photoshop's File > Automate > Merge to HDRI Pro do the rest for you automatically.

Getting a light probe or spherical lighting reference of a location can save you a lot of time when you are trying to create realistic lighting. In many cases, with the addition of a simple key or sun light, this method can get you most of the way there with little work or effort.

Figure 11.55 illustrates a simple 3D stone totem model rendered with radiosity and different GI IBL source images. Each of these shows the environment at left, then moving to the right, the spherical lighting reference of that location, the render with the only source of lighting in the scene being the reference image, and at far right, the same setup with only one key/sun light added.

[Figure 11.54] Series of bracketed 180-degree spherical lighting reference images ready to be compiled into an HDRI light probe

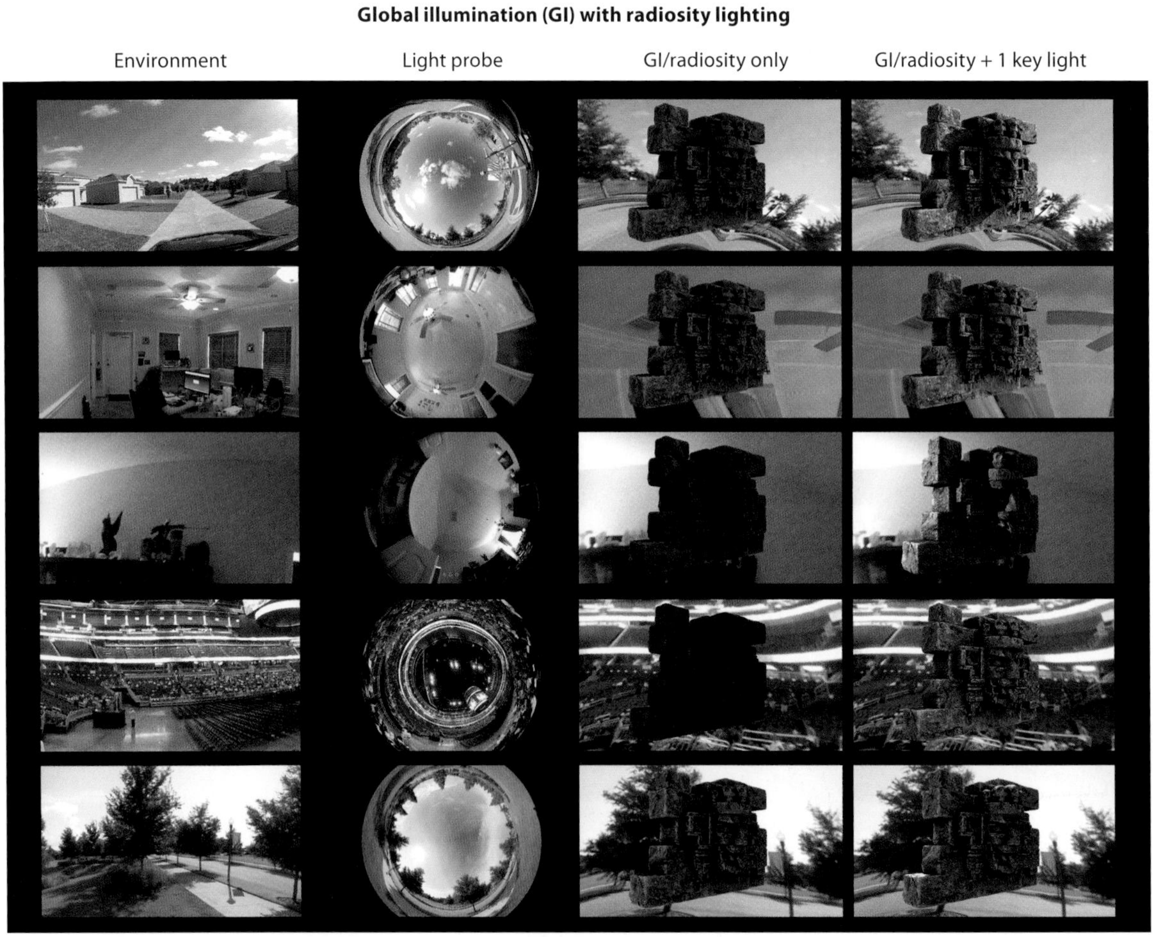

Global illumination (GI) with radiosity lighting

| Environment | Light probe | GI/radiosity only | GI/radiosity + 1 key light |

[**Figure 11.55**] Simple 3D stone totem model rendered with radiosity and different GI IBL source images

Baked sIBL and Spinning Light Rig Solutions

Some inherent problems with radiosity HDRI IBL solutions include long render times, sampling noise, and flickering in animations. *Smart image-based lighting* (sIBL) is software created as one solution to these issues. sIBL software automatically analyzes an HDRI image and creates a super high-resolution panorama as the camera background and a high-resolution HDRI as the specular component for reflections. At the same time it also creates a blurred low-resolution HDRI as the diffuse lighting environment and then creates a sun/key light (matching the color direction and intensity). Finally, the sIBL software converts all of this into one nice little set… all automatically.

Another solution is to use a spinning light rig utility such as Lighting Based on Image Tool Conversion Helper, or Light B.I.T.C.H. (Figure 11.56). This amazing little utility/plugin automatically analyzes an HDRI and sets up (or allows you to manually set up, with a non-HDRI image, as seen in Figure 11.57) and weights (Figure 11.58) a spherical rig of spinning lights (Figure 11.59). These lights spin around an offset axis at many times interframe, creating (with motion blur) a nice soft-shadowed lighting effect that very closely mimics a radiosity render (see Figure 11.60) with no radiosity.

[Figure 11.56]
Light B.I.T.C.H. user interface

[Figure 11.57]
Manual setup of a non-HDRI image-based lighting rig

[Figure 11.58]
Weighting the strength of each light is very intuitive with this graphical representation of the size/influence of each light in the rig.

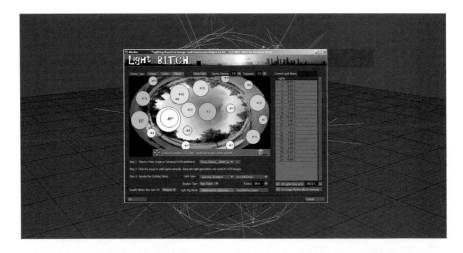

[Figure 11.59]
Spinning light rig

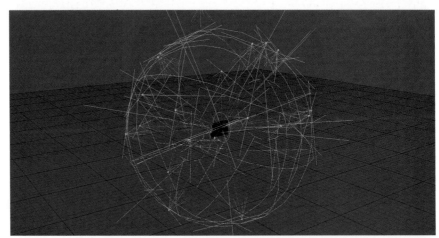

[Figure 11.60]
Spinning light rig creates a nice soft-shadowed lighting effect very closely mimicking a radiosity render… with no radiosity.

Studio No Lighting Radiosity Lighting

The use of radiosity lighting can create some excellent results even when you don't use it in a GI- or IBL-based solution. In a real-world studio, when you film a person, car, or product, in addition to using the lighting techniques covered in Chapter 5, you would regularly use large light boxes or screens illuminated from behind to create the largest light and reflection source possible. Without reflections to show off and highlight the contours of products like cars, wine bottles, and smartphones, these products would appear plain in advertising, to say the least.

You can use the techniques used in a professional studio environment right within your 3D application to achieve similar stunning professional results…

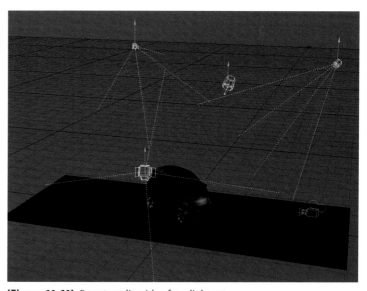

with no lights in the scene at all! To see how you can achieve this, let's start with a basis for comparison. Figure 11.61 shows a 3D smart car model with a four-light setup. The results of this render can be seen in Figure 11.62.

In a real-world studio setup, you would use large light boxes that you would place around the car and fly a large back-lit silk over the top of the car for illumination. In addition, the spaces between the lights—the black areas—are almost as important as the lights themselves because they help break up the reflections and add contour and interest to the subject. You can simulate this lighting setup in 3D by removing all lights in the scene and placing large cards (yes, another card trick) in the scene where you would place light boxes and silks in the real-world studio environment (Figure 11.63). Set these cards' surface properties to fully luminous. Then turn on radiosity in this scene.

[Figure 11.61] Smart car lit with a four-light setup

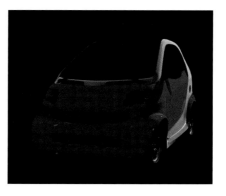

[Figure 11.62]
Render results from the four-light setup

This, in effect, turns the large luminous polys into their real-world equivalent and produces stunning slick results, as seen in Figure 11.64 (all with *no lights*).

In truth, a great deal of this effect is created by the luminous poly's reflections as seen in the reflection-only render in Figure 11.65.

Although this high-end, high-gloss look was very popular a few years back, both in TV commercials as well as print ads, today it's probably more common to find a look mixing the two methods (Figure 11.66 shows the combination of lights and luminous polys) and more closely leaning toward realism than high-polished perfection (see Figure 11.67). These *are* cars, right? And we want to visualize them moving in real life, on the road, in the elements like rain and snow.

Speaking of rain and snow… that's covered next, when we dive into the elements exploring particle systems and dynamics.

[Figure 11.63]
Large cards placed in the scene where you would have light boxes and silks in a real-world studio

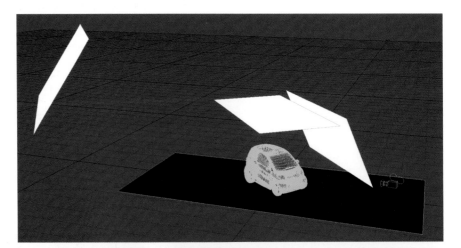

[Figure 11.64] Stunning slick results created with this setup

[Figure 11.65] Reflection-only render

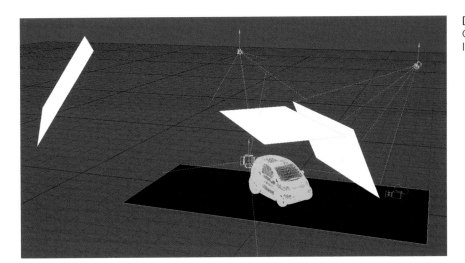

[Figure 11.66]
Combination of lights and luminous polys

[Figure 11.67]
More realistic render result from combination of lights and luminous polys with radiosity render

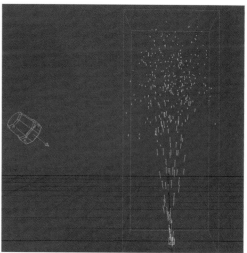

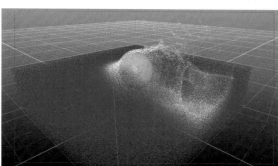

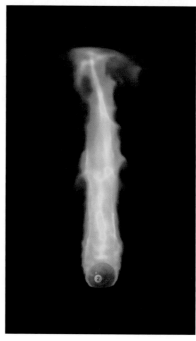

CHAPTER TWELVE

Advanced VFX Techniques III: Particle Systems, Dynamics, and Simulation VFX

Animating one realistic effect at a time can be a challenge, but what happens when you have to animate hundreds or even thousands? When your job is to animate millions of raindrops, snowflakes, or charging warriors, it's time to forget hand animation and start thinking about particle systems, dynamics, and simulations.

To many beginning VFX artists, the mere mention of the terms particle systems, dynamics, or simulations results in an instant look of bewilderment and panic. But broken down into their basics and explained piece by piece (as I'm about to do for you), these concepts, along with how to put them to use creating truly amazing VFX, are quite easy to understand.

The primary advantage of particles, dynamics, and simulations, is that they to allow you to animate a huge number of elements by setting up rules, parameters, or systems that allow the elements to almost animate themselves... all on their own. Animation then becomes more a process of setting up, calculating, testing, tweaking, rinsing, and repeating than animating any individual elements by hand.

Though this might all sound very scientific and complex (which, at its core, I suppose it is), have no fear. I am here to lead the way for you and show you the simple, shortcut path to understanding the limitless possibilities of particle systems, dynamics, and simulation VFX.

Introducing Particle Systems

The first step on the shortest path to enlightenment is to understand particle systems. A *particle system* is a technique used to recreate complex chaotic systems or natural phenomena, using simulations.

Null Objects

Part of the reason many people are so confused by particle systems is that, for the most part, particle systems by themselves usually don't produce anything you can immediately see rendered. The *particles* (or individual elements) contained in these systems are usually nulls. *Null objects*, or *nulls* as they are most commonly known, are non-rendering placeholder or helper objects. These usually have no renderable features of their own but do contain positional, rotational, size, motion, and behavioral data. They usually appear in 3D applications as small dots or three-axis crosses but can appear as any placeholder shape. And that's precisely what nulls are: placeholders for whatever will eventually replace them once the heavy calculations of the particle systems' movement are completed. The power of particle systems is that the intensive computing and calculations to render so many elements doesn't have to be done—only the motions calculations of the hundreds or millions of non-rendering null objects (or particles) that make up the *particle system*.

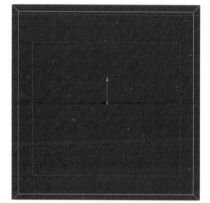

[Figure 12.1] A simple box emitter emitting a few particles

The Components of a Particle System

I have found that understanding particle systems is most easily mastered by breaking down a particle system and explaining each of its components and functions in a simple step-by-step sequence. For these examples, I'll be using Newtek's LightWave (http://lightwave3d.com). Let's start with emitters.

Emitters

Emitters are simply the generators of particles. You can think of a hose or faucet as the emitter of water particles, clouds as the emitters of snow or rain particles, and a rocket engine as the emitter of fire and smoke exhaust. A particle system can have one or many emitters, each emitting the exact same, or completely different, particles.

[Figure 12.2] The same emitter with a spherical nozzle, emitting more particles

Figure 12.1 shows a simple box emitter emitting a few particles within it. These particles don't do anything by themselves except spring to life and appear motionless; they stay there doing just that, nothing, until we set some parameters.

The first parameter usually set is the *birth rate*, also called the *generation rate*. This is the rate at which particles spring to life or appear. The formation that these particles appear in when brought to life is controlled by a nozzle control. A nozzle may emit particles from a primitive shape such as a sphere (shown in Figure 12.2 within the cube-shaped emitter), cube, cone, torus, and so on, or from object vertices, surfaces, or normals. Various Size and Key Effects can control the generated particles' size and keyframe parameters as they leave the nozzle.

In addition, you can also set the Generator (emitter) Size parameter. Figure 12.3 shows a 1m×1m×1m cube-shaped emitter with a spherical nozzle (notice again that the particles emit inside the cube-shaped emitter in the formation of the sphere nozzle). Figure 12.4 shows the same emitter scaled down to 500mm×500mm×500mm.

[note]

If an emitter is set to a 1000-particle limit with a birth rate of 1 particle per frame, the emitter will emit 1 particle per frame, for every frame, until frame 1000, when it will run out of particles and stop emitting (this might be good for something like a machine gun). If this same emitter were set to a birthrate of 1000 particles per frame, on frame 1, it would generate all 1000 particles at once and then stop emitting (this might be good for something like an explosion).

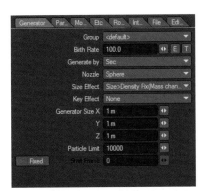

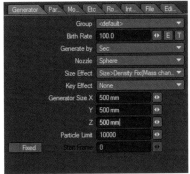

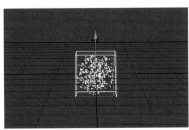

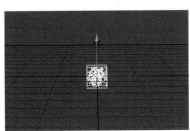

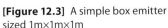

[Figure 12.3] A simple box emitter sized 1m×1m×1m

[Figure 12.4] The same emitter resized to 500mm×500mm×500mm

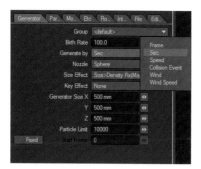

[**Figure 12.5**] Particles "Generated by" seconds being selected in this drop-down menu

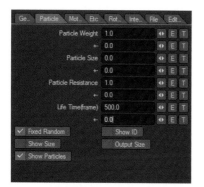

[**Figure 12.6**] Typical Particle parameter menu

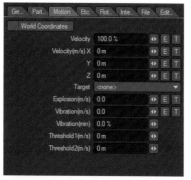

[**Figure 12.7**] Particle Motion parameters

The birth or generation rate is further defined and controlled by a "Generated by" trigger control. Particles can be generated by any kind of *trigger*. This trigger might be "by frame," "by time," (as shown in Figure 12.5), "by keyframe," (good for generating lasers or bullets at exact sporadic times), and even "by collision" events to trigger other particles (bullet particles hitting a wall to trigger spark particles, for instance). Setting a higher value of particles emitted per second quickly increases the number of particles that appear.

Finally, a Particle Limit control determines how many particles will be generated in total.

Particles

Similar to the way emitters have various parameter controls, the particles themselves have their own parameter controls as well, which control the way particles move and behave (shown in Figure 12.6).

You can think of Particle Weight and its corresponding +– variability control as the material or density the particle will represent. Particles such as dust have a much lower weight than solid steel ball bearings, and they move and react to outside forces accordingly.

The Particle Size and corresponding +– variability control the virtual size of the particle.

You can think of Particle Resistance and its corresponding +– variability control as the air or environment resistance to the particle. If the particles are to move through water, this value would be high; if air, much less; and if the particles were to be moving in space, then zero (since space has no resistance so a particle would theoretically float on forever).

The particle's Life Time(frame) and corresponding +– variability control determines how many frames/seconds a particle will live before it ceases to exist and disappears.

Of course, a particle is rarely useful unless it can move. The particle Motion controls (Figure 12.7) determine general particle movement.

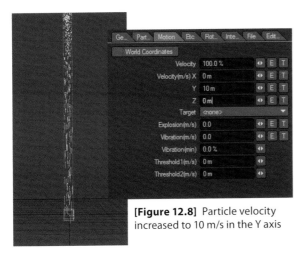

[Figure 12.8] Particle velocity increased to 10 m/s in the Y axis

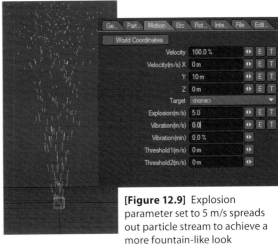

[Figure 12.9] Explosion parameter set to 5 m/s spreads out particle stream to achieve a more fountain-like look

Velocity parameters control the particle's overall velocity, while individual Velocity XYZ parameters control velocity in each individual axis. To create the beginnings of a fountain, Figure 12.8 shows the Y velocity set to 10m/s.

Target controls allow you to aim the particles at a particular object, light, or camera.

In the real world, fountains don't usually go straight up and straight back down. To create a more naturalistic look, increasing the explosivity, or Explosion control (increased to 5 m/s in this case, as shown in Figure 12.9), spreads the upward jet out at the top to arrive at a much more "fountainy" look.

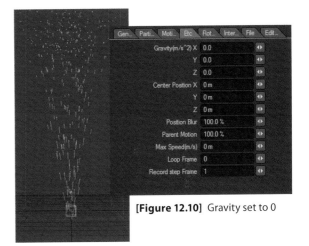

[Figure 12.10] Gravity set to 0

By default, emitters generate particles in a very consistent and uniform pattern. The Vibration and Turbulence parameters allow for the breakup and randomization of the generated particle emission.

Although the Resistance parameter slows the particles in this fountain effect as resistance begins to overcome velocity, the particles just seem to hang there in the air. What's missing? Gravity, of course (as seen in Figure 12.10, set to zero). When you set the Gravity parameter to –5 in the Y axis (as shown in Figure 12.11), you see a more natural fountain effect, as particles

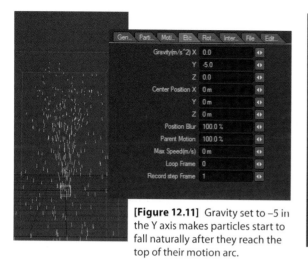

[Figure 12.11] Gravity set to −5 in the Y axis makes particles start to fall naturally after they reach the top of their motion arc.

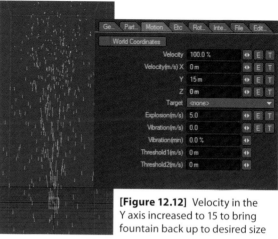

[Figure 12.12] Velocity in the Y axis increased to 15 to bring fountain back up to desired size

that lose velocity begin to return to Earth after reaching the top of their arc (though your fountain has been reduced in size as a result). To bring your fountain back to its original size, you can simply give the Y Velocity a boost (up to 15 in this case, as shown in Figure 12.12) to get the desired look.

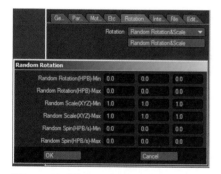

[Figure 12.13] Particle rotation randomization controls

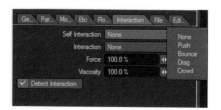

[Figure 12.14] Particle Interaction and Self Interaction controls

In this example, because you are using simple points/particles with no size or depth, the Rotation and Spin parameters (shown in Figure 12.13) won't do very much right now, but you'll see how helpful they are in Chapter 13, when I cover particle-based debris systems.

There are many types of particle systems, classified into dumb and smart/thinking particles. *Dumb* particles are emitted and then just go, or move, in a direction until deflected, without regard for other particles nearby or in their way, whereas *smart/ thinking* particles are capable of *behaviors*, such as pushing, avoiding, bouncing, dragging, and crowding other particles. These parameters are controlled by setting Interaction and Self Interaction controls (Figure 12.14).

Advanced particle systems may even provide artificial intelligence (AI) features that allow for flocking, swarming, and other advanced behaviors. These operate by specifying goal, attract, avoid, deflect, and other objects and behaviors. Particle systems and their motions can also be saved and loaded, cut, copied, and pasted (Figure 12.15) for use and reuse as well as for exporting to other applications.

When working with particle systems, inevitably, one day after working long and hard to achieve a fine-tuned particle effect, you will find that one particle just doesn't seem to want to cooperate. Special particle-editing tools have been designed (as shown in Figure 12.16) for just this situation. They allow you to select any individual particle and move its entire motion path or just delete it if it still won't cooperate.

You can achieve endless looks using particle systems. For example, if you reset the fountain effect's Velocity settings back to the defaults (as shown in Figure 12.17), and also the Resistance and Gravity settings, and set the Explosion parameter to 20 m/s, you get a nice explosion or fireworks effect (Figure 12.18).

[Figure 12.15] Particle system file controls allow you to save, load, copy, and paste particle systems and motions.

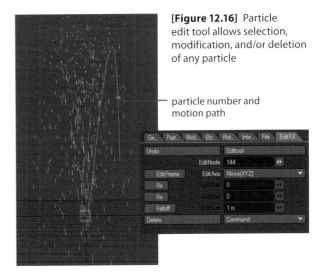

[Figure 12.16] Particle edit tool allows selection, modification, and/or deletion of any particle

particle number and motion path

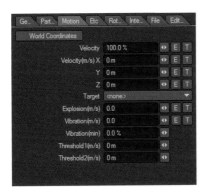

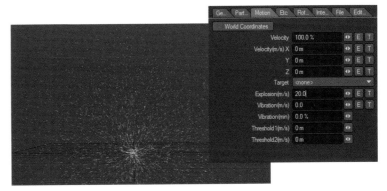

[Figure 12.17] Particle systems Velocity, Resistance, and Gravity parameters reset to default values

[Figure 12.18] Explosion parameter set to 20

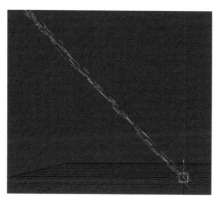

[Figure 12.19] A particle stream emitting at approximately a 45-degree angle

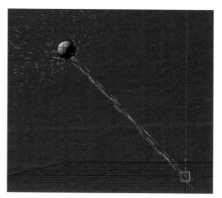

[Figure 12.20] The same particle stream being deflected by a simple sphere collision object

Particle systems not only "spray" in a direction (as shown in Figure 12.19), they can interact with other objects and *force effectors* (tools added to a scene to simulate things such as wind, gravity, vortices, turbulence, and so on). Figure 12.20 shows this particle stream colliding with, and being deflected by, a simple sphere object set to be a collision object.

Particle System Rendering: Partigons and Non-Rendering Nulls

If particle systems could only perform complex motion without being seen, they wouldn't be very useful. Fortunately, you can utilize particle systems in many ways to fully visualize all their amazing possibilities. The visualization of particles requires you to make a decision between two basic types of particle systems: rendering particles, also called *partigons* (for *particles + polygons*), and non-rendering, or null, particles (which require these non-rendering nulls to be replaced with something else that does render).

The first category of rendering particles is partigons, which are basically single-point polygons. They can be textured like any other polygonal surface and are useful for creating effects such as sparks, fireworks, stars, insects, dust, or tiny debris. Figure 12.21 shows a small particle system created with rendering partigons using the same setting we used earlier in the fountain example. Surfaced with a luminous texture and added glow effect, this type of particle system makes for a nice spark or fireworks effect (as shown in Figure 12.22).

You can also use non-rendering particles to create something you will actually see and be able to use in your VFX. It is helpful to think of these particles

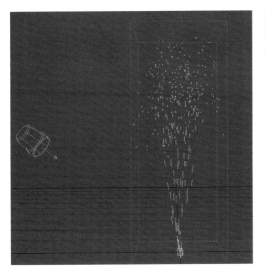

[Figure 12.21] Rendering single-point partigon particle system set up with fountain-like motion parameters

[Figure 12.22] The same particle streams particles surfaced with a luminous glowing texture/material for a firework or spark effect

[Figure 12.23] Two null objects spaced apart

as simple nulls. In fact, you can use actual nulls in this way to illustrate the concept. Figure 12.23 shows two null objects spaced a good distance apart from one another. If you were to try to render this scene at this point, you would be disappointed when absolutely nothing rendered—because nulls are non-rendering objects. You need for these nulls to be replaced with something visible, and preferably something that can provide many different and creative looks. That is precisely what voxels are.

Voxels and Voxel-Based Particle System Rendering

If you were able to tell the computer to "imagine" that each null was the center point of an imaginary sphere or other volume, and to render that imaginary geometry (that doesn't really exist) without that geometry actually being present, you would have a pretty good representation of what a *voxel* is. The word *voxel* is a combination of the words *volume* and *pixel* (*pixel* itself is a

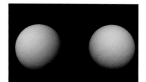

[Figure 12.24] Two null objects rendered with surface voxels applied

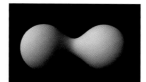

[Figure 12.25] Two null objects designated as additive blending surface voxels and moved closer together start to connect like a liquid.

[Figure 12.26] The same two null objects moved even closer together blend into an almost pill shape.

blend of *picture* and *element*). If you designate these two nulls as voxels (called *hypervoxels* in LightWave) and set the type of voxel to surface voxel, you might see something like Figure 12.24. A *surface voxel* is a voxel that creates an imaginary surface, as opposed to a *volume voxel*, which creates an imaginary volume, or a *sprite voxel*, which either creates slices of a volume (a cheat to simulate a volume with less calculation required) or allows for the substitution of an image or footage (as you will see in the next section).

The cool thing about voxels is that they can behave as if they are actually geometry. For example, if you set the surface voxels of these two nulls to *additive blending* (meaning the imaginary surface they create additively blends together based on an influence or tolerance strength level) and move the

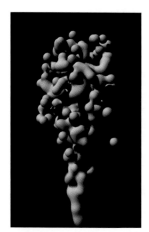

[Figure 12.27] The same fountain particle system setting shown previously, but with surface voxels applied

[Figure 12.28] Directional velocity stretching parameters allow the voxels to stretch more naturally.

nulls a little closer together, the rendered surface appears to connect and blend together like drops of liquid (as shown in Figure 12.25). Moving the nulls even closer together results in even more, and stronger, blending (Figure 12.26).

An obvious use for surface voxels is in creating liquid-like effects, as seen in Figure 12.27—which is the same fountain particle system with surface voxel rendering applied. You can adjust additional parameters to allow for the stretching of these imaginary surfaces based on direction or velocity (as shown in Figure 12.28).

By creating a narrow particle stream (Figure 12.29) and applying the same texture used in Chapter 4 to the mirror ball, you get a result that looks like

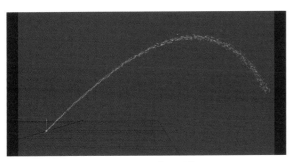

[Figure 12.29] Narrow stream of particles

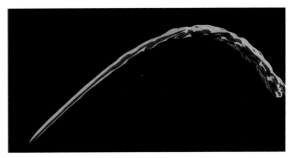

[Figure 12.30] The same narrow stream of particles with mirror ball material applied

a stream of mercury (Figure 12.30). Next, vary the velocity of particles using the +– variables (so that some particles move faster and some move slower) and increase the gravity so that the slower particles start to fall against the gravity earlier than others. If you surface these voxels with a luminous, glowing material, you start to arrive at something resembling a flamethrower (as seen in Figure 12.31).

Although surface voxels are great for things like droplets of liquids, if the effect you're looking for is smoke or fire, you're going to need to turn to volume or sprite voxels.

Volume voxels, like their surface counterparts, also create imaginary geometry, but in the form of 3D volumes rather than surfaces. This allows for the creation of very complex effects such as blood cells, cotton puffballs, popcorn, or billowing smoke (as shown in Figure 12.32) by deforming the virtual surface using procedural functions such as noise, turbulence, and so on and adjusting amplitude, frequency, and other properties. These 3D textures or surfaces are sometimes referred to as *hypertextures*, because they control not only the surface material, but the 3D displacement as well.

[Figure 12.31] The same narrow stream of particles with the velocity of particles varied using the +– variables, the gravity increased, and the voxels surfaced with a luminous, glowing material to get flamethrower effect

[Figure 12.32] The fountain particle system with volume voxels applied to resemble a complex smoke-like surface

Sprite-Based Particle System Rendering

You can achieve additional realism and generate endless creative possibilities by using real image, or footage, sprites (*sprites* are another name for 2D cards or billboards) instead of calculation-intensive volumes. By creating a flipped upside-down version of our fountain particle system (shown in Figure 12.33) and attaching circular (cloud image) sprite voxels to the particles, you can achieve a very convincing rocket exhaust plume (Figure 12.34). Flipped on its side and sent spinning into Z-space, this same emitter (Figure 12.35) appears to be a completely realistic spinning missile trail (Figure 12.36).

Of course, since sprite voxels are merely common images or footage, you can attach practically anything to a particle system as a sprite voxel. In Figure 12.37, I've attached an image of the cover of this book.

[Figure 12.35] The fountain particle system turned on its side and sent spiraling into Z-space

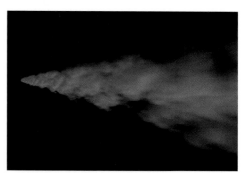

[Figure 12.36] The resulting perspective correct missile trail

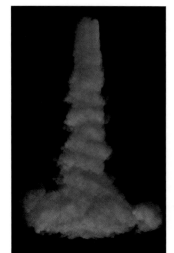

[Figure 12.33] The fountain particle system turned upside down

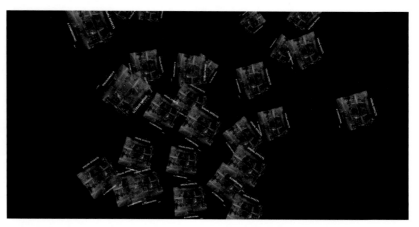

[Figure 12.37] The same fountain particle system with sprite voxels of this book's cover used as the sprite image

[Figure 12.34] The same fountain particle system with small cloud images applied as sprite voxels creates a convincing rocket smoke exhaust effect.

Linked 3D Geometry-Based Particle Systems

For instances when "imaginary" geometry just won't do—for example, flying through spinning objects or debris (remember, although sprites always face the camera, they are still only 2D images)—you can link and replace each particle with actual 3D geometry. Chapter 13 covers this process in detail.

Introducing Dynamics

There will also be times when the effect you're trying to achieve isn't really that of things being "emitted" but of parts of a whole object shattering or blowing up. In these situations, you don't really want debris emanating from a single point or box, but instead, the actual pieces of the geometry reacting to realistic forces affecting them.

For these types of effects, you must go deeper down the VFX rabbit hole and break out the big technological guns: dynamics and simulations.

Dynamics, like particle systems, fall into a few categories, each designed to address a different physically based phenomenon. This section introduces a few of the most common ones.

Rigid Body Dynamics

When you need to knock over thousands of dominos, crash a bowling ball through pins, or blow up a building (as we are about to do), rigid body dynamics are the solution you're looking for.

Rigid body dynamics (also sometimes referred to as *hard body dynamics)* are simulations designed to mimic the way hard objects respond to each other according to the properties of physics. Of course, the VFX artist controls the parameters fed into the simulation, such as the object's size, weight, surface smoothness or roughness, and the world properties such as gravity, resistance, friction, and so on.

In Figure 12.38 you can see the wireframe 3D model of a building that has been fractured. In order to have a simulation explode an object in 3D, you must first break it into the pieces that are then able to react to an explosive force; this is called *fracturing*. You will also need an invisible, non-rendering collision object placed above (in this case) or near the fractured object/mesh to create the force that will destroy the building.

If you keyframe the collision object to slam down onto the fractured building, the rigid body dynamics engine performs intense calculations and tries to compress the building in the direction of the collision object (as shown in Figure 12.39), but like any solid object smashed with excessive force, the building quickly shatters (Figure 12.40) and explodes (Figure 12.41).

With a simple texture applied to the solid rendered model (as shown in Figure 12.42) and motion blur applied to the moving pieces (Figure 12.43), you can see how these can be effectively used to create the main structural wall explosion (Figure 12.44–45) when combined with fire, smoke, debris, and other elements.

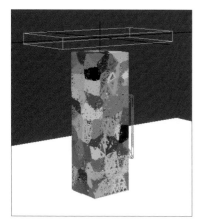
[Figure 12.38] Wireframe of fractured 3D model of a building

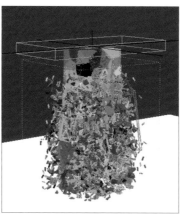
[Figure 12.39] Rigid body dynamics tries to compress the building as collision object slams down onto it.

[Figure 12.40] The wireframe mesh quickly shatters…

[Figure 12.41]
…then explodes.

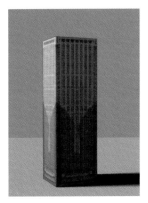

[Figure 12.42] Solid rendered building model (mesh) with simple image texture

[Figure 12.43] Rigid body dynamics tries to compress the solid rendered building as collision object slams down onto it.

[Figure 12.44] The solid rendered model quickly shatters…

[Figure 12.45] …then explodes as the wireframe version did.

Bullet Dynamics

Bullet dynamics is a free and open source physics engine that simulates collision detection and soft and rigid body dynamics. Bullet has been used in many video games and as visual effects for TV and movies, and is one of the most popular and widely used dynamics physics engines.

Soft Body Dynamics

When the objective is not to simulate something solid and rigid, but something soft or pliable, *soft body dynamics* or *cloth simulations* are an amazingly

[Figure 12.46] A simple, flat 3D plane, textured with an image of this book's cover and set as a soft body cloth object, alongside a low-resolution 3D sphere collision object

[Figure 12.47] The collision sphere animated to rush into the soft body plane…

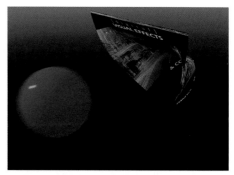

[Figure 12.48] …and then quickly rush back out

useful alternative to hand animating the deformation of a 3D model. Figure 12.46 shows a simple, flat 3D plane, that I've textured with an image of this book's cover and a low resolution 3D sphere alongside it. I set the plane to be a soft body cloth object (except for the very top edge, which I set to rigid to hold the plane up) and the sphere as a collision object.

I animated the collision sphere to quickly run into the plane (as shown in Figure 12.47) and then quickly pull back (Figure 12.48) to show how convincing soft body dynamics can be at simulating cloth and other pliable elements.

Specialized Fluid Simulation and Dynamics Applications and Plugins

Although soft body dynamics are very good at creating rippling surfaces (such as flags or cloth) and soft wobbly objects (such as deflated tires or Jell-O), simulating the extremely complex interactions of particles in a fluid or gas requires the specialized algorithms of a *fluid dynamics simulation*.

RealFlow

One of the pioneering software applications specialized for fluid dynamics is Next Limit Technologies' RealFlow (www.realflow.com). Fluid dynamics applications such as RealFlow work by allowing the creation of huge containers of *smart* or *thinking* particles. These are particles that, in addition to

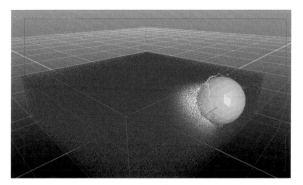

[**Figure 12.49**] Simple sphere collision object is placed in a container of fluid in the RealFlow fluid dynamics simulation application.

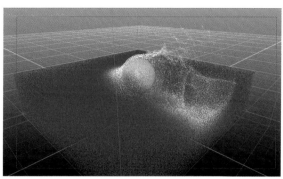

[**Figure 12.50**] The sphere collision object is animated to run through the container of fluid.

reacting to direct collisions or forces, can follow complex rules or physics-based algorithms that allow the particles to interact with animated stand-in geometry and with themselves.

Running a simple sphere collision object (as shown in Figure 12.49) through a container of fluid particles (Figure 12.50) creates all the complex splashes, foam, wake, and ripples one would expect to see in a real fluid (Figure 12.51).

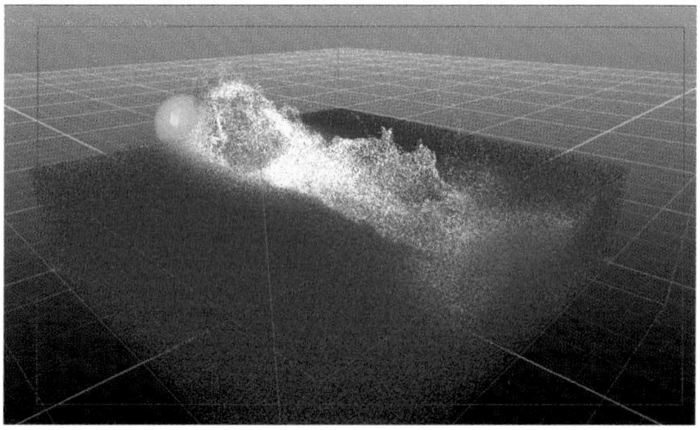

Once these intensive calculations are completed, the particles' motion solution can be converted

[**Figure 12.51**] The fluid dynamics engine calculates all of the complex splashes, foam, wake, and ripples one would expect to see in a real fluid.

into a standard 3D mesh for texturing and rendering or you can export the particles themselves to another application for further 3D interactions or processing.

TurbulenceFD

Fluid dynamics simulations are good for more than just simulating fluids. Gases and fire behave very similarly and can be controlled with great results using fluid dynamics algorithms.

In Figure 12.52, you can see our billiard ball set in a cube-shaped container as an emitter in Jawset Visual Computing's voxel-based fluid dynamics plugin TurbulenceFD (www.jawset.com). By setting the emitter to emit fuel and setting a low temperature for the billiard ball in the simulation (Figure 12.53), you can easily achieve a nice smoke or steam effect (notice the gas realistically pooling and cascading off of the container ceiling as well), whereas increasing the burn temperature ignites the billiard ball (Figure 12.54). As you increase the temperature, or decrease the ignition temperature of the fuel, the fuel begins to ignite past the ball (Figures 12.55 and 12.56) until it erupts in a full flaming burn in Figure 12.57.

[Figure 12.52] Billiard ball set in a cube-shaped container as an emitter using TurbulenceFD

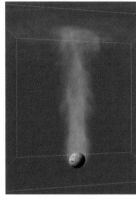

[Figure 12.53] A smoke or steam effect is achieved by setting the emitter to emit fuel and setting a low temperature for the billiard ball in the simulation.

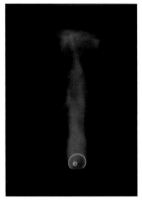

[Figure 12.54] Slightly increasing the temperature of the billiard ball ignites it.

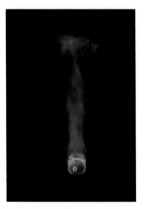

[Figure 12.55] As temperature increases, or the ignition temperature of the fuel decreases, the fuel begins to ignite past the ball.

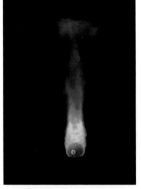

[Figure 12.56] Lowering the fuel ignition temperature further increases the burn…

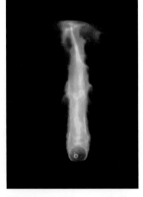

[Figure 12.57] …until all of the fuel erupts into a full flaming burn.

Other Fluid Dynamics Applications

Many fluid dynamics solutions are on the market, ranging from the fluid dynamics built into free applications such as Blender (www.blender.org) to stunning high-end proprietary solutions such as Scanline VFX's Flowline (www.scanlinevfx.com), which are used for more and more complex feature film production fluid dynamics VFX sequences (like those seen in the destruction sequences in *The Day After Tomorrow*, *2012*, and *Pacific Rim*).

In Chapter 13, you will put to use what you learned about particle systems in this chapter and delve into 3D particle-based crowd replication, debris systems, and the art of digital destruction.

CHAPTER THIRTEEN

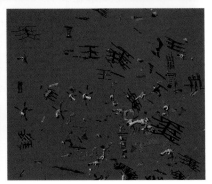

Advanced VFX Techniques IV: Particle, Crowd, and Destruction VFX

As you saw in Chapter 12, particle systems are very versatile and can be used as the basis for many complex VFX. Created as single-point polygons, they can be used for sparks, fireworks, or swarming insects. When they are shaded with voxel shaders, you can use them for liquids, smoke, even popcorn. Attached to sprites, they can even create a fountain of copies of this book.

There is no one right way to do any one thing in VFX. In fact, I regularly have students create an effect in several ways so that they can see how many options there always are. VFX is a *problem-solving* art/job.

I remember having a student who got extremely frustrated, on a regular basis, when he couldn't get an effect to work correctly and would quickly lose his temper. After watching him repeatedly blow up for an entire day (and in the process, stress out everyone around him), I took him aside and told him, to his surprise, that maybe VFX wasn't for him. What he was looking for, I continued, was a *predictable* job. One in which a huge stack of papers arrived on his desk promptly every morning at 8 a.m. and he would have to stamp, log, and file each into its appropriate filing cabinet. He'd always know exactly what to do. Of course, telling an artist something like this is like saying, "Just kill your dreams," but I was making a point. "You can give up all of this frustration and take on a nice predictable job like *that*," I said, "or you can learn to embrace the challenges, enjoy the mystery of not knowing but then learning, and allow yourself to love the whole VFX problem-solving process."

Now you might think that this story ends with the student having an instant epiphany, smiling, and getting back to work. Not quite. He got enormously pissed off at me. He was extremely insulted that I would recommend he quit VFX and get a job pushing papers and he stormed out of the building. I didn't see or hear back from him for three days. On the fourth day I arrived at the VFX lab early to find that this student was the first one there. He looked completely different. His posture and facial expressions were relaxed but intensely focused. The entire day he sat, looking like he was actually enjoying himself. At the end of the class he came over to me and apologized for his previous behavior and for storming out. He explained that he had taken a few days to reflect and had realized what I was trying to teach him. From that day on, he approached VFX with a whole new attitude and ambition and is still working successfully in VFX to this day.

When I'm teaching, I'm frequently asked by VFX artists, "Which is the *best* method to do this VFX?" or, "Is this right?" They are usually a little miffed when my answer is "The way that works best for you" or "Does it look right to you?" I'm not being a smartass when I answer this way (though I am a huge smartass); I'm merely emphasizing this extremely important point in VFX:

"If it looks right, it's right!"

Let's start this chapter by exploring two completely different ways to accomplish a similar-looking complex effect: a moving crowd replication.

2.5D vs. 3D Particle-Based Crowd Replications

Chapter 6 discussed a non-moving crowd replication with layers of pods of people pushed in Z-space to create a crowd effect. But what if you need a moving crowd, a herd/flock/school of animals, or a convoy of military vehicles?

You can approach this effect in many ways, but this section focuses on two very different approaches that arrive at nearly the same effect (with inherent differences in each effect method, of course). First, we'll look at the familiar method discussed in Chapter 6.

2.5D Crowd Replication

To begin, take a short looping run cycle of a person (in my case, I'm using 3D artist Chris O'Connell), apply it to a card in 3D, replicate it three times, and offset these copies from each other, pushing each copy into Z-space as well as offsetting it in time (as shown in Figure 13.1). Next, keyframe animate each card to translate in the X axis to match the running motion.

Place a 3D camera in the scene and align the camera to get the composition that looks best to you (Figure 13.2).

Create the crowd as you did in Chapter 6 by grouping these three, copying them, and then offsetting them (shown in Figure 13.3). Continue grouping, replicating, and offsetting these cards until your desired crowd size is achieved (Figure 13.4).

[tip]

Take special care to make sure the speed of the card motion matches the speed of the run cycle and that the runner's feet stick to the ground and don't slip or slide. Slipping indicates that the animation speed of the card is wrong and needs to be adjusted.

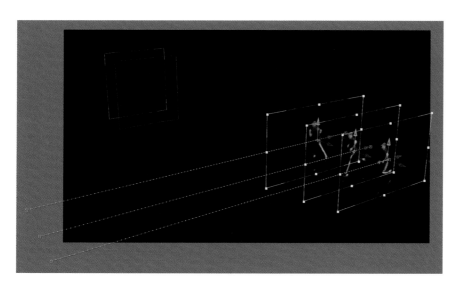

[Figure 13.1]
Looped run cycle of 3D artist Chris O'Connell applied to a card in 3D, replicated three times, and offset in Z-space

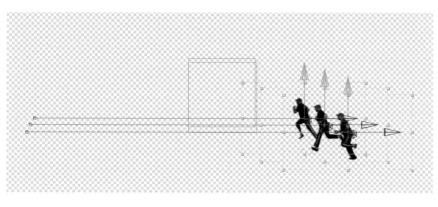

[Figure 13.2]
3D camera placed in scene to achieve desired camera angle and composition

[Figure 13.3]
Continue by grouping,
copying, and then offsetting
these three cards.

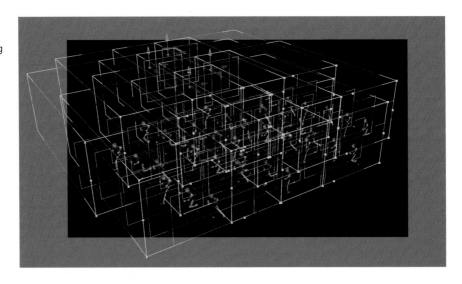

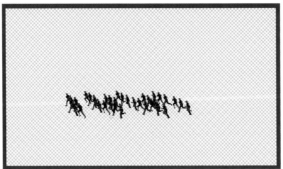

[Figure 13.4]
Copy and offset the groups
until the desired crowd size
is achieved.

Next, let's throw a new, clever little trick into the mix. When creating a background, you could just use a plain 2D image card, but to get an added sense of depth, you can pull another little illusion out of your bag of VFX tricks by creating a simple 3D set using a method I call the *cove method* (taken from the idea of a cyclorama set where the corner, or cove, forms a seamless background when photographed).

[note]

You want the sky and any distant upright features such as mountains on the vertical plane so they don't appear to be lying down.

To create this effect, simply map your chosen background image to a card in 3D space and then duplicate this card. Move the pivot point of this card to the point on the image just under the point at which the sky meets the ground. Next, rotate the entire card on the X axis (as shown in Figure 13.5) until the ground becomes… well… the ground (how much you rotate is completely up to your taste and depends on the camera angle you choose. Remember, if it looks right, it's right!).

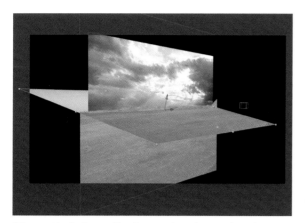

[Figure 13.5] Copy of background card rotated on the X axis to create ground plane and cove

[Figure 13.6] 2D crowd cards placed in 3D on set also made of 2D cards

[Figure 13.7] Camera view of 2.5D crowd scene

[Figure 13.8] Atmospheric gradient dust element added

Your crowd cards are also in 3D space, so you can now place them onto your clever 3D set, as shown in Figure 13.6, for a fully interactive virtual shooting experience (Figure 13.7) complete with proper parallax when you move your camera. Figure 13.8 shows the addition of gradient atmospheric dust.

As an additional benefit to this method, because the cards are actually moving in 3D space horizontally, you can easily add natural, realistic camera motion blur to the crowd by simply increasing the camera shutter angle parameter, as discussed in Chapter 1. Figure 13.9 shows the camera shutter angle increased to 360 degrees, and Figure 13.10 shows the camera shutter angle increased to 720 degrees.

[tip]

Because you are using a 3D virtual camera instead of a real one, you can create exaggerated shutter angles to increase motion blur effects to levels that might not be possible with real-world cameras.

[**Figure 13.9**] Camera motion blur with 360-degree shutter

[**Figure 13.10**] Camera motion blur with 720-degree shutter

3D Particle-Based Crowd Replication

You can also create this type of crowd effect using 3D particles in either a 3D or compositing application. In this example, I've created a simple particle system in eyeon Software's Fusion. I loaded the same run cycle clip of 3D artist Chris O'Connell (Figure 13.11) to use as the input for the sprite-based particles. Next I created a flat rectangular plane emitter lying flat on the ground and emitting particles horizontally in the X axis, as shown in Figure 13.12. I copied this emitter three more times and offset each of the copies' particle emissions' start times (Figures 13.13 and 13.14).

You can use the flexibility of a nodal-based system to create particle-based shadows for this crowd as well. Starting with the same clip, which has been keyed so that it contains an alpha (Figure 13.15), and applying the same fake shadow procedures covered in Chapter 5 (shown in Figure 13.16 and with blur added in Figure 13.17), you can copy the particle system used to create the first crowd and substitute this shadow as the input (shown in Figure 13.18). The only parameter that needs to be changed is the particle emitters' rotation (so they'll be lying down instead of upright). In fact, the entire particle system can just be duplicated and the input can be swapped out with this new shadow source (Figure 13.19).

[**Figure 13.11**] The same run cycle clip of 3D artist Chris O'Connell to use as the input for a true 3D particle system

Compositing/merging the crowd particle system over the crowd shadow particle system gives you a very nice crowd effect (as shown in Figure 13.20) and you can fly around with your camera in 3D to get a wide variety of shots and parallax camera effects (Figures 13.21 through 13.23).

[Figure 13.12]
Flat rectangular plane emitter lying flat on the ground and emitting particles horizontally in the X axis

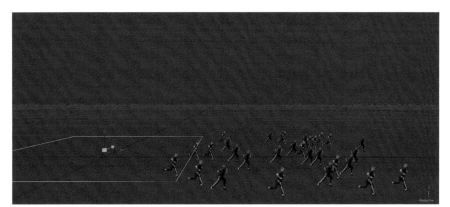

[Figure 13.13]
This emitter was then copied, and the particle emissions' times offset...

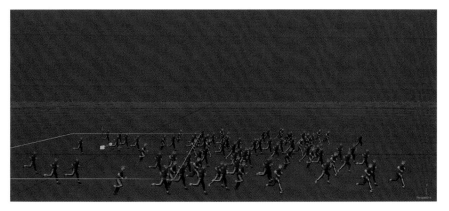

[Figure 13.14] ...and then copied and offset again.

[note]

Notice how similar the particles look and work to those in the 3D application examples in Chapter 12.

[Figure 13.15] The same looped run cycle clip of Chris O'Connell keyed (so containing an alpha)

[Figure 13.16] Fake shadow procedure applied to clip

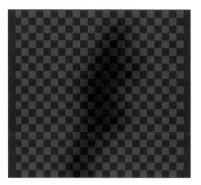

[Figure 13.17] Blur added to shadow effect

[Figure 13.18]
The original emitter copied, the fake shadow particle substituted as the source sprite clip, and the particles rotated 90 degrees on the X plane to get them to appear as if they are lying down on the ground

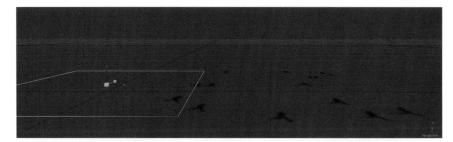

[Figure 13.19]
The other three copies duplicated and the same rotation adjustments made

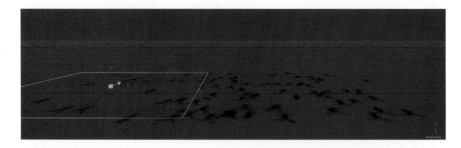

[Figure 13.20]
Compositing/merging the crowd particle system over the crowd shadow particle system provides a very nice crowd effect.

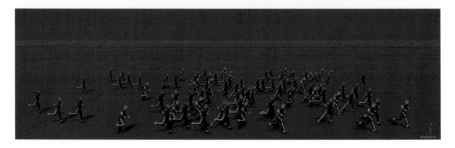

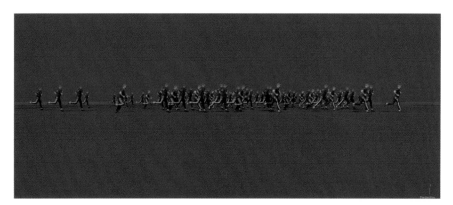

[Figure 13.21]
Flying the 3D camera down to ground level

[Figure 13.22]
Flying in toward the running crowd

[Figure 13.23]
Flying the 3D camera up higher looking down at the crowd

When a circumstance arises that requires the camera to move in such a way that the "flat card sprite" illusion is broken (as discussed in Chapter 7), you need to change your strategy to one that is fully 3D.

3D Particle-Based Debris Systems

Although single-point polygons, voxels, and sprites can get you a long way, there will still be times when only a fully 3D solution will do the job. Digital destruction sequences are particularly common for requiring a fully 3D solution—for example, when an explosion causes debris to spin and fly toward, and even past, the camera. Fortunately, aside from the increase in rendering times, the steps you have to follow are very similar to all the previous particle system procedures. This example has you creating a fully 3D particle-based debris explosion.

To begin, create a simple particle emitter that emits 300 particles per frame and has a particle limit of 300 (meaning that all of the particles will be emitted on the very first frame and then no more will be emitted after that). This is what you want in an explosion, where all of the material is immediately ejected and propelled outward all at once. To create the motion, set Explosivity to 20 m/s to get a violent explosion. Because this example will be a space explosion, turn resistance and gravity both to zero. Figures 13.24 through 13.26 show the particles' motion of this explosion effect. Next, load up a series of broken, bent, and otherwise damaged 3D models. You'll need to create these models to look this way to represent debris that resembles parts of a damaged spacecraft. (In this example, I removed the textures on these models to make them easier to see in print.)

Make sure each model's pivot point is at its approximate center of gravity (COG) and centered at the scene's origin, or XYZ 0, 0, 0. When you import these models into the scene, they will form a clump of debris (as seen in Figure 13.27). Size each of the debris models to the correct proportionate sizes in relation to the scene.

Once all the debris models are sized properly and in position, select them all and, using your 3D application's instancing or linking tool, set the number of copies or instances to be created and link these models to the particle system. Copies or instances of each model will be created and placed at each particle/null location (Figure 13.28) and will inherit all the particles' motion properties.

[tip]

When creating debris for explosions, make sure the models look like something that was originally part of whatever is being destroyed. You wouldn't usually want spaceship parts being blown out of a house, or vice versa. Also, make sure the models' edges and textures look as though they've been through the same type of violent stresses your explosion would create—torn, ripped, burnt, bent, and with twisted edges. A good practice in efficiency is to make various groups of debris models in varying levels of polygonal and textural complexity and detail. Small debris can be low poly, low detail, while large hero debris (debris that will stand out and be seen in close view to the camera) may be high poly and high detail.

[Figure 13.24]
Explosion particle system start frame

[Figure 13.25]
Explosion particle system mid frame

[Figure 13.26]
Explosion particle system end frame

[Figure 13.27]
When imported into the scene, the 3D debris models will form a clump of debris.

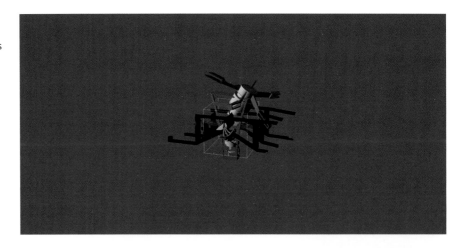

[Figure 13.28]
After being linked to the particle system, copies or instances of each model will be created and placed at each particle/null location.

Figure 13.29 shows the particles' starting position from the camera's POV (point of view) and Figure 13.30 shows the particles/debris at the end frame. Rendered with motion blur, the final rendered debris system (Figure 13.31) is ready to integrate into a digital destruction space sequence.

Digital Destruction

Many students laugh when I describe how to blow something up in VFX as a "finely choreographed ballet of destruction." Aside from the visual mental hook this forever engrains in their minds, the description is actually very accurate. Although in the real world the destruction of something is usually a lightning-fast bang and the resulting oddly scattered mess, in VFX you need to create something that is visually exciting.

[Figure 13.29]
Particles' starting position
from the camera's POV

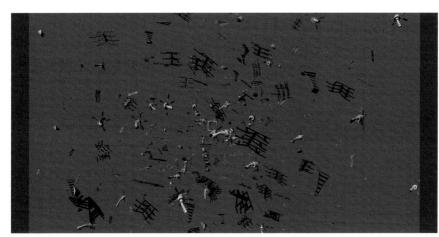

[Figure 13.30]
Particles' ending position
from the camera's POV

[Figure 13.31]
Particle-based debris
system rendered with
motion blur

Beginning VFX artists frequently fail at creating good digital destruction sequences for the same reasons they frequently fail at creating good models or good textures—because they haven't done enough research, comparison, and thinking through of what it is they are actually trying to create. Pasting a clip of an explosion over a 3D model is *not* going to get you a convincing destruction effect.

To understand the components of this "ballet of destruction," it is helpful to first examine the way a destruction sequence is created as a *practical effect* (real, not digital) for movies on a live movie set (using real explosives, miniatures, and so on). You can then determine the parallels and emulate those elements.

Putting It All Together (or Blowing It All Apart)

First, on a real destruction set of, say, a house, they don't build an entire house to destroy—only the outside facade walls and roof are built, which gives the appearance of there being a whole house. Similarly, as a 3D and VFX artist, you wouldn't waste time modeling or rendering elements that won't be seen anyway, so you would do likewise with a 3D model of a house and only build the parts that need to be seen.

[note]

Although higher-end productions can use advanced fluid dynamics/particle systems to generate fire and explosions, lower-end systems tend to look fake and require excessive calculation and rendering times. Therefore, I highly recommend always using real high-quality footage to create the most realistic effects unless you are lucky enough to have these high-end resources.

Obviously, in an explosion, you would expect that the structure of the house (or whatever object you are destroying) would be blown apart and fragmented. You would do the same by cutting apart your object into broken-looking fragments and then reassemble them into their original formation. You would use the whole (uncut) object in the scene until the very last moment before destruction and then—as discussed in Chapter 1 in one of the oldest VFX tricks in the book, the very same simple substitution effect Georges Melies used—you would swap the full model for the cut up, fragmented one, and then animate its pieces flying apart violently. You can do this animation using hard body dynamics (discussed in Chapter 12); by hand, if you want complete control; or more likely, using a combination of both, with the majority of fragments being animated via dynamics and the hero objects being animated by hand.

An explosion wouldn't be an explosion without the fireball and smoke, right? So this example relies on our trusty card tricks to map real explosion footage with alphas onto 2D image planes and carefully place them behind, in between, and in front of fractured model elements to give the illusion of depth.

Next, if a facade like this were the only thing to be seen blowing apart, the audience would quickly suspect that the building was fake, that it was hollow and not enough debris was being ejected from the explosion for it to be real. Therefore, in a movie set explosion, mortars or air cannons are strategically placed to eject debris material out windows and other openings—furniture and wall parts, dust, and other building and content fragments and debris, visually cueing the viewer that these were once the contents of this structure. If you haven't already guessed, this is precisely the function of the particle-based debris systems you are creating. This example will use them in exactly the same way.

In a real-world pyrotechnic destruction, the firing of every element—from the high explosive primacord used to precisely cut away structures, to the mortars and air cannons blasting furniture pieces and debris out the windows, to the release of the giant propane fireball—is precisely choreographed and controlled to perform in perfect sequence, like a ballet. You wouldn't want debris blasting out of visible cannons after the building was already gone.

One thing that would still be missing, though, is that it would be very unlikely that every piece of a structure would be completely blown to bits, disintegrate, and disappear completely. A large-scale VFX production team would actually model all of the destroyed (but remaining) elements. But in a very fast explosion, it's sometimes only necessary to give the "impression" of an object's insides and not necessarily to model and place every little thing (although this is entirely possible and a great detail to add to your work when time permits). Therefore, it is sometimes helpful to pull a couple of quick modeling tricks out of your hat and create some lightning-fast fake substructures. While you're at it, you can create the basis for a cool hull-burn effect (as if the material skinning the ship is slowly burning away). You can also use the same concept for this hull burn effect with the heat and cloaking effects covered in Chapter 8 to create decloaking and/or dematerializing effects.

Let's take a look at how to create both of these and then combine all of these effects into one cool "ballet of destruction."

3D Model Substructures

For this example, I will show you how to destroy the winged disk ship I created for my movie *Anunnaki* (shown in Figure 13.32).

If you look at a 3D model from the outside, up close (Figure 13.33) it will appear to be solid and have a great amount of detail. But pushing in closer

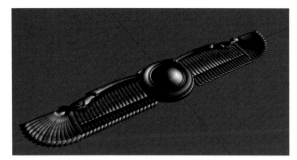

[Figure 13.32] Winged disk ship featured in for *Anunnaki*

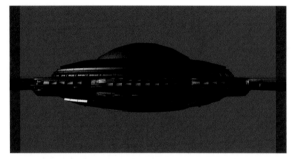

[Figure 13.33] 3D model from the outside, up close

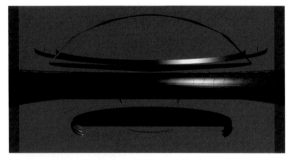

[Figure 13.34] The 3D model is actually the ultimate, infinitely thin-skinned facade.

and closer and eventually *into* the model reveals that a 3D model is actually the ultimate Hollywood facade and infinitely thin-skinned (as shown in Figure 13.34). If you were to blow a hole in this ship's dome, it would instantly reveal the hollow shell, like a chocolate Easter bunny. Because this disc portion of the ship is our hero piece (I'll be breaking off the wings) and will be blown straight into the camera, we will need to see detail inside the burning hull. But because it will be blurred and moving quickly, spending too long modeling huge amounts of internal detail would be a big waste of time, manpower, and rendering resources. All you really need is the suggestion of internal structures, and because most air- and watercraft are built by skinning a ribbed skeleton framework, this will be a piece of cake.

Because I'll also be creating a hull burn effect to reveal this internal substructure, let's get the modeling portion of that effect done first. I begin by making a copy of the disk portion of the ship (Figure 13.35) and setting the material to a highly luminous fire color (Figure 13.36). In fact, label the material and object Fire so that it's easy to remember. Next, resize this object so that it fits snugly, just inside the skin of the original disk (Figure 13.37). That's it for the hull burn geometry. We'll get back to creating that effect in the next section.

For the substructure, I'll make another copy of the original disk (Figure 13.38) and select all the polygons on the top of the dome (Figure 13.39) where I'm going to burn away the ship's skin. With those polygons selected, I'll apply a bevel to them (Figure 13.40) with no inset—and basically just push the faces in while leaving the edges. You can see from the side view (Figure 13.41) this creates nice, corrugated, airframe-like detail on the top of the ship. Next, I'll give this version a dark, splotchy, charcoal gray color, call the texture and object Hull, and resize it to fit inside of the Fire object (Figure 13.42). So to recap, I have the Hull object inside the Fire object inside the original disk object (don't worry, this will all make sense in a few minutes).

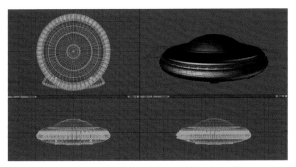

[**Figure 13.35**] A copy of the disk portion of the ship

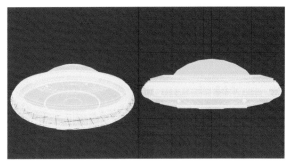

[**Figure 13.36**] Setting the material to a highly luminous fire color

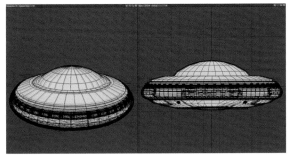

[**Figure 13.37**] Object resized so that it fits just inside the skin of the original disk

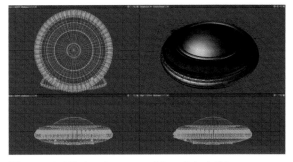

[**Figure 13.38**] Another copy of the original disk

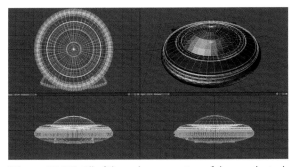

[**Figure 13.39**] All of the polygons on top of dome selected

[**Figure 13.40**] Bevel applied to selected polygons to push them down

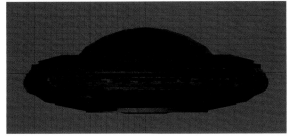

[**Figure 13.41**] Corrugated airframe-like detail created on top of ship

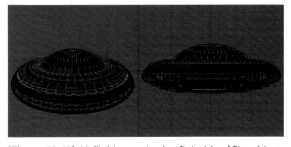

[**Figure 13.42**] Hull object resized to fit inside of Fire object

Hull Burn and Dematerializing VFX

Continuing with this example, to create the hull burn effect, I'll first create a burn map. A *burn map* is simply another form of alpha matte, used in this case for a *clipping map*, which is like a transparency map, but rather than make a surface transparent, it literally clips or cuts it away altogether. To create the burn map in Photoshop, create a 50% gray solid/constant and apply a very tiny bit of noise and then blur to it. This tiny amount of noise allows granular variations in the color values of the map, which will allow it to erode in a natural jagged-edged way. You can use a spatter brush to add areas of lighter spatter to precisely direct how the burn map should erode and burn.

Add and animate a Threshold function over the burn time from 0% to 100%. A Threshold function converts an image to only two colors: pure black and pure white, depending on where on the histogram the threshold is set. Any value darker than the threshold point will be clipped to black, and any value brighter than the threshold point will be clipped to pure white. This results in an animated sequence that starts completely black, begins to erode (Figure 13.43), and continues to erode more and more (Figure 13.44), until it burns away (Figure 13.45) and reaches complete white.

You can use this burn map to tell the 3D application where to keep the model (black) and where to clip or burn away the model (white).

First, I apply this burn map to the original ship model (Figure 13.46), which results in the outer original ship skin being "eaten away" and reveals the Fire object beneath it (shown in Figure 13.47). Finally, I apply this same burn map to the Fire object, but offset it a frame in time so that it lags slightly behind the burn map applied to the original object. After I apply a glow effect to the luminous materials, this results in the slight glowing burning edge, which tightly follows the clipping and reveals the corrugated substructure inside (Figure 13.48).

[Figure 13.43] Animated burn map sequence starts completely black, then begins to erode

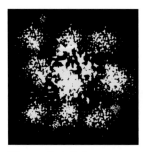

[Figure 13.44] Burn map eroding more

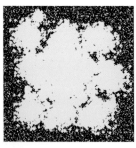

[Figure 13.45] Burn map almost completely eroded near the end of its animation

[Figure 13.46] Dome portion of the original ship model

[**Figure 13.47**] Burn map eats away outer skin to reveal Fire object underneath.

[**Figure 13.48**] Burn map also applied to Fire object (and offset/delayed a frame), and glow effect applied to create glowing burning edges and reveal Hull object underneath

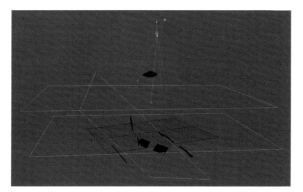

[**Figure 13.49**] Big 2D cards with explosion footage mapped to them placed in between the flying ship parts

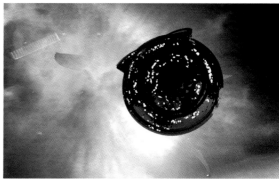

[**Figure 13.50**] Result of adding explosion cards

To wrap this up and put the entire effect together, quickly break apart the wing elements of the ship, animate them to scatter in an exploding motion, and place big 2D cards with explosion footage mapped to them in between the flying ship parts (Figure 13.49). The result already begins to take shape, as you can see in Figure 13.50.

Next add and place the particle-based debris system so that the debris appears to emanate from where the explosion center would be (Figure 13.51) and place a giant sphere of luminous single-point polygons as a star field (Figure 13.52). The result is an even more detailed explosion (shown in Figure 13.53). Adding motion blur helps to add a more natural-motion look to the scene (Figure 13.54). Finally, adding a super-hot lens flare element helps add intensity and makes the whole scene blend together seamlessly into "a finely choreographed ballet of destruction" (Figure 13.55).

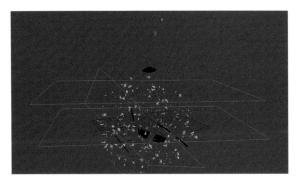

[Figure 13.51] Particle-based debris system added

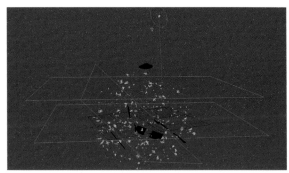

[Figure 13.52] Sphere of single point polygon stars added

[Figure 13.53] Result of added particle debris system and stars

[Figure 13.54] Motion blur added to create more natural motion for debris

[Figure 13.55]
Super-hot lens flare added
to finish shot

No discussion of destruction would be complete without covering gunfire: muzzle flashes, fake interactive lighting, and bullet hits.

Muzzle Flashes and Fake Interactive Lighting

Probably the most important factors in the creation of gunfire are researching the type of muzzle flash that would be appropriate for the weapon being used and the kind of interactive light that would be emitted from such a flash. In this case, because a sci-fi toy gun is the weapon being used, I went over the top a little to make sure the effect was clearly visible in print and used an M-16 muzzle flash.

[Figure 13.56] Background plate of hallway

Start by using the background plate of a hallway, shown in Figure 13.56, and the keyed foreground plate of 3D artist Jeff Yatchum firing a toy sci-fi gun (Figure 13.57). The simple composite and color correction is shown in Figure 13.58. Next size and scale a real footage plate of an M-16 firing (Figure 13.59), align it to the barrel of the weapon, and composite it using an add blend mode to give it a little pop (Figure 13.60).

If this little gun were to actually give off that big of a flash, for that split second, it would light up everything around it. To create fake interactive light, copy the background layer and composite/merge it over the original background. Create two very soft elliptical roto masks to outline the areas where the muzzle flash would light up the wall in front of and behind Jeff. Add an exposure adjustment (a levels adjustment, curves adjustment, or grade will work equally well) and crank up the brightness until those masked areas appear to "light up" the walls (Figure 13.61). Think this through one step

[Figure 13.57] Keyed foreground of VFX artist Jeff Yatchum

[Figure 13.58] Foreground composited over background

[Figure 13.59] M-16 muzzle flash footage aligned into position

[Figure 13.60] Muzzle flash composited using add blend mode

further (and toward getting the plates to talk to each other, as we discussed in Chapter 1); if a light flash were that bright, it would cast a shadow of Jeff on the wall behind him. This can, again, be easily created using the fake shadow method discussed in Chapter 5 (as shown in Figure 13.62).

For the interactive light on Jeff, the technique is almost the same. Duplicate the footage of Jeff shooting and, using soft roto masks, mask off the forward facing areas of Jeff that would be hit by the light from the muzzle flash, such as his face and hat, the front of his arms, the front of his torso, and so on. Again, add an exposure adjustment and crank up the brightness until those masked areas appear to "light up" as well (as shown in Figure 13.63).

[Figure 13.61] Background layer copied and two large, soft-edged, elliptical roto masks created to mask only the areas that will be affected by the exposure adjustment (set to light up the walls)

Keyframe the visibility or opacity of the "lit up" elements to be off (or 100% transparent) until the muzzle flash appears, and then, in the very next frame, make the lit layers fully visible. Keyframe the lit layers back off again as soon as the muzzle flash disappears. Check the results by watching the footage progress from the original plate (Figure 13.64) to muzzle flash (Figure 13.65) and back to original footage again (13.66).

[Figure 13.62] Fake shadow created behind Jeff on the wall

[Figure 13.63] Copy of keyed foreground plate roto masked to show only those areas of Jeff that light from the flash would fall upon (lit up using an exposure adjustment)

[Figure 13.64] "Before" muzzle flash image

[Figure 13.65] Muzzle flash with fake interactive lighting image

[Figure 13.66] "After" muzzle flash image

[tip]

These flashes happen over 1–3 frames (1/24th–1/30th of a second to 3/24ths–1/10th of a second). This is so fast that it is over in the blink of an eye, and so it is very forgiving. As long as the flashing happens in the right areas and you vary it (by changing the matte shapes, expansion/contraction controls, and/or flash strength) with each muzzle flash, the effect should be very effective.

Bullet Hits

The other side of gunfire is, of course, bullet hits. Although bullet hits on walls, floors, or objects can sometimes be a simple matter of animating the visibility of, and color correcting, composited bullet holes, sparks, smoke, and debris elements, bullet hits on people take a little more thought.

To begin, start with the same hallway background plate (Figure 13.67) and the keyed reverse shot of 3D artist Matt Jolly (Figure 13.68) preparing to return fire; composite the two together (Figure 13.69).

In reality, a bullet wound will usually appear vastly different, and much less cinematic, than the ones we are used to seeing in movies. In movies, we are used to seeing cinematic *bullet hits* created by detonating small explosive

[Figure 13.67] Background hallway plate

[Figure 13.68] Keyed foreground plate of VFX artist Matt Jolly

[Figure 13.69] Foreground composited over background

devices (called *squibs*) under fake blood packets and the *pre-scored* (pre-cut) clothing of stunt people or actors. These squibs are dangerous explosives. So dangerous, in fact, that a solid metal or other protective plate must be placed underneath one to prevent serious harm from coming to the person wearing it. One side effect of this is that for, say, a character being shot in the chest, the squib device blows outward in a burst of blood. In real life, a typical bullet entry wound would appear as nothing more than a hole until bleeding began.

Thoughtful special effects supervisors realize that a bullet hit will also often have an associated exit wound (to the dismay of the actor or stunt person—squibs hurt), so the supervisors strap another squib to the respective exit wound location and set it to detonate simultaneously with the entry wound squib. The point here is that, in reality, we might see one thing, whereas in a movie, we are accustomed to seeing something completely different. So, as a digital VFX artist, which are you trying to re-create? For the most part, you're usually trying to create the "appropriate cinematic version." In a family movie, that may mean a mere puff of smoke. In a gory slasher, it could involve fountains of blood. Most commonly, it's somewhere in-between, but leaning more toward the movie squib method than reality.

At the moment Matt reacts as if he is shot in the shoulder, sync up the explosion of a small blood/paint burst footage element (Figure 13.70) and composite it over Matt's shoulder as the entry wound squib (Figure 13.71) using a multiply blend mode.

Similarly, sync, color correct, and composite an elongated paint burst (Figure 13.72) behind Matt's shoulder as the exit wound squib (Figure 13.73), using a roto matte to limit the exit wound burst effect from appearing in front of Matt's shoulder.

[Figure 13.70] Small blood/paint burst footage element, desaturated and darkened

[Figure 13.71] Blood burst element composited over Matt's shoulder as the entry wound squib using a multiply blend mode

[Figure 13.72] Elongated paint burst element

For the final gory detail, tint a still, paint-spray image (using a Tint or Color Correction operation to a blood color) and map it to a 2D card (rotated to align with the approximate perspective of the wall). Composite this using a multiply, darken, or a similar blend mode. The "spraying" motion is created by animating a soft edged matte (or vertical wipe), starting from the bottom of the spray image, and moving up, quickly revealing the entire image over a few frames (Figures 13.74 and 13.75).

The result is a very realistic blood spray (Figures 13.76 and 13.77), completing a very convincing cinematic bullet hit.

The next chapter moves from the amazing to the downright astounding with a discussion of what I call Photoshop and Displacement Modeling Magic.

[Figure 13.73] Elongated paint burst element used as the exit wound

[Figure 13.74] Beginning of spray motion of a still paint-spray image mapped to a 2D card

[Figure 13.75] Soft-edged matte animated over a few frames to create spraying motion

[Figure 13.76] Realistic blood spray effect result—beginning of spray

[Figure 13.77] Blood spray effect result—end of spray

CHAPTER FOURTEEN

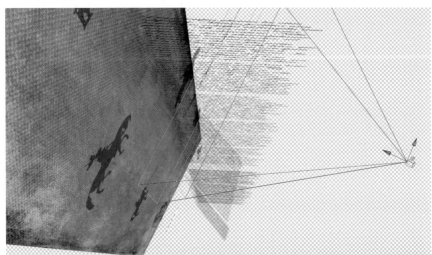

Stereoscopic 3D and 2D to 3D Conversion VFX

Many artists, and even some teachers, guard their chosen art by creating an artificial, seemingly impenetrable air of complexity around it. The worlds of motion pictures, VFX, and particularly stereoscopic 3D seems susceptible to this type of scarcity-mentality obfuscation. I believe that although, indeed, every art or science at its highest level is rife with technical complexity, any concept can be distilled down to its (easily understandable) essence and can be easily communicated to anyone eager to learn.

Because I'm covering stereoscopic 3D, you will need those funny 3D glasses mentioned in the Introduction in order to fully see all of the examples and gain all of the benefits of this chapter.

There are many varieties of 3D glasses, including active, passive, gray LCD shutter, linear and circular polarized, holographic, and anaglyph. *Anaglyph* 3D glasses come in a variety of configurations ranging from red/green, red/blue, green/magenta, amber/dark blue, magenta/cyan, and probably the most common, red/cyan (which we will be creating here in the next section).

Very inexpensive paper 3D glasses (red/cyan) or more durable plastic (even clip-on types for those of us who already wear glasses) can be found online (shown in Figure 14.1) with a simple Google or Amazon search. If you have trouble finding a pair of 3D glasses, I'm happy to help. Just head over to my website at http://jongress.com/vfxbook/3dglasses. If you'll simply to cover the shipping cost, I'll supply you with a pair for free!

[Figure 14.1] Inexpensive paper and more durable plastic and clip-on red/cyan 3D glasses

Guerrilla/Hacker-Style DIY 3D Glasses

For those of you who just can't wait and want to get started right now, I'm going to provide you with the top-secret guerrilla/hacker-style DIY method for creating a pair of 3D glasses in a pinch! Although these aren't perfect, for a couple of dollars spent on common supplies, they will work well enough to give you a full 3D effect and get you working until your real pair arrives.

To begin creating your 3D glasses, you'll need only a few things: a clear plastic CD or DVD case (though any clear plastic, even the clear plastic container top to that salad or sandwich you just had for lunch should do—clean it first, obviously), and red and blue permanent Sharpie markers (shown in Figure 14.2). Another black Sharpie is optional to outline with, but not necessary.

Carefully pop your CD or DVD case apart (you'll only need one half, but save the other in case you want to make another pair). Place a pair of glasses onto the plastic cover (Figure 14.3) as a size guide (or just guesstimate) and draw an outline on the plastic case where your lenses will be placed, being careful not to mark up your glasses with the permanent marker (Figure 14.4). Next, carefully color in the left lens with the red Sharpie. Try to use straight strokes and keep your coverage even and not "scribbly," which tends to cloud the view through them (Figure 14.5). When you're done with the red side, do the same with the blue side (Figure 14.6). Your finished 3D glasses should look something like Figure 14.7.

If you can find wide-tipped Sharpies, use them because they allow you to color the lenses a lot more evenly and provide much better results. Also, if you can find the lighter blue Sharpie (Figure 14.8), use that instead of the more common darker one since it is closer to the cyan you typically want and will also provide much better viewing results. You want your red to be darker and your blue to be lighter to more closely resemble the tones in typical red/cyan 3D glasses (Figure 14.9).

That's it! You're all set and ready to start creating your own stereoscopic 3D!

History, Background, and Core Concepts

Although many would have you believe that stereoscopic 3D is the latest in technology (and, of course, there are many new technical advancements and refinements), the art and science of stereoscopic 3D is, in fact, even older than motion pictures. The first known stereograph was created by Sir Charles Wheatstone in 1833, whereas motion pictures didn't appear until the 1850s.

[Figure 14.2] All you need is a clear CD or DVD case and red and blue Sharpies (a black one for outlining is optional).

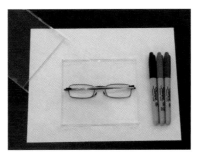

[Figure 14.3] Place a pair of glasses on half of the case as reference (or just guesstimate).

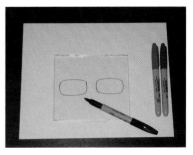

[Figure 14.4] Outline where the "lenses" will go.

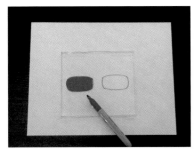

[Figure 14.5] Color the left one red…

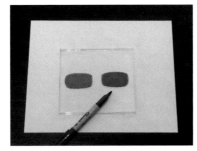

[Figure 14.6] …and the right one blue.

[Figure 14.7] Your finished 3D glasses (technically red/blue, not red/cyan, but close enough)

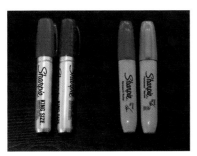

[Figure 14.8] If you can find the really large Sharpies, use those. And if you can find the lighter blue Sharpie (on the right), use that instead of the darker blue one.

Darker red   Lighter blue (closer to cyan)

[Figure 14.9] Ideally you want an evenly distributed and well-covered darker red and lighter blue.

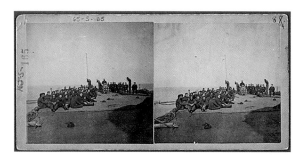

[**Figure 14.10**] Religious services on the deck of the USS *Passaic* (1864)

This 150 plus year-old stereoscopic 3D image (or side-by-side *stereograph*) I found in the National Archive (www.archives.gov/research/search/, shown in Figure 14.10) shows religious services being performed on the deck of the monitor USS *Passaic* in 1864!

Stereoscopic 3D is, at its core, a very simple principle that is inherently familiar and second nature to almost all humans.

Hold a finger up very close to your nose and look at it. Open and close each eye independently and notice that your finger appears to jump back and forth from side to side. Slowly move your finger farther and farther away from your face while you continue to open and close each eye independently. Notice that your finger jumps side to side less and less the farther away it gets from your face. Each of your eyes sees a slightly different view, angle, and perspective of your finger. This apparent movement (your finger isn't actually moving) is the phenomenon we call *parallax* and is the effect of stereoscopic 3D vision.

If you continue to open and close each eye and watch your finger jump from side to side, but suddenly you open both eyes, for a split second, you will likely see two fingers (which quickly merge into one as your eyes move quickly and adjust the focus to your finger). We call this merging phenomenon *convergence* (the focal point at which your angles of vision converge). This is, perhaps, one of the two most important concepts in the creation of stereoscopic 3D.

The other important concept is the separation of what each eye sees. Although there are countless devices, methods, and techniques for creating stereoscopic 3D, the principle I want you to ingrain into your memory is this one simple concept:

All you need is two separate, slightly horizontally offset images of a scene.

In order to view these as one stereoscopic 3D image, each image is then simply viewed separately by its respective eye.

The only thing that makes this confusing to people is how (the method being used) to separate them. There are hundreds of simple and super-complex ways to separate these views so that only the left eye sees the left view and only the right eye sees the right view. These can be as sophisticated as using polarized light, electronic LCD shutters, micro-barriers, and lenticular lenses, or as simple as a children's toy—the View-Master—a cardboard barrier, paper filter glasses, or simply crossing one's eyes.

Creating Stereoscopic 3D

The most straightforward way to create a 3D stereoscopic image is, of course, to mimic the way we see and capture images in our minds—by using cameras in the same way we use our two slightly horizontally offset eyes.

Stereoscopic Cameras and Camera Rigs

There are many solutions for capturing stereographic 3D movies and images, including high-end (and high-cost) multiple camera and mirror rigs as well as inexpensive multiple camera setups (such as 3D GoPro rigs and inexpensive HD cameras mounted side by side). There are also many great self-contained stereoscopic 3D solutions such as the Aiptek 3D, the LG Thrill smartphone, and the Fuji FinePix REAL 3D W3 (shown in Figure 14.11).

Creation of Stereoscopic 3D

To keep the concept of stereoscopic 3D creation crystal clear in your mind, always remember that all you are doing is creating two slightly horizontally offset images and combining them. In cases in which you are converting a 2D image to 3D, simply think of this 2D image as "one of the eyes" (say, the left eye). All you have to do then is create the other eye's view. By extracting elements of the scene (patching the holes they might leave when extracted using the cloning techniques covered in

[Figure 14.11] (Rear) Inexpensive HD camera side-by-side stereo setup; (Front, from left to right) LG Thrill 3D smartphone, Aiptek 3D camera, Fuji FinePix REAL 3D W3 camera

Chapter 2, to fill in those holes, creating a clean plate) and offsetting them, you can simulate the way the other eye's view would appear. Then, by combining the original image with the made-up/created other-eye's-view image, you can achieve surprisingly realistic stereoscopic 3D effects.

To best demonstrate the creation of stereoscopic 3D it's helpful to examine a simple 3D scene, its components, and effects. In Figure 14.12, you can see an overhead view of two eyes looking at the new, improved 3D model of William Vaughan (thanks for the v2.0, Will!). Viewed with a single camera, or in *monocular* (one-eyed) view, the model of William looks like this (Figure 14.13). But if you set up two cameras, and offset them slightly from each other to get a *binocular* (or stereoscopic, two-eyed) view of the model, the left eye view would appear like Figure 14.14 (with William appearing to shift slightly to the right) and the right eye view would appear like Figure 14.15 (with William appearing to shift slightly to the left). Since each eye is looking straight forward, we call this *parallel* viewing and this gives us an excellent stereoscopic 3D result when these two images are combined (we'll get to that part in just a minute).

In reality, however, your eyes angle in, depending on how close a subject is to you, in order to focus on a subject (to see this effect for yourself, focus on your finger and continue to bring it closer and closer to your nose). You'll notice your eyes are crossing. We call this *toeing in*. This also is an effective technique for creating stereoscopic 3D (and some say it is more natural and easier on your eyes). If you toe in the cameras to focus on William, the left eye's view would appear like Figure 14.16, while the right eye's view would appear like Figure 14.17.

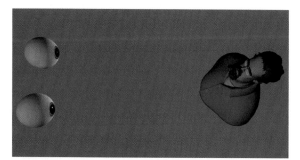

[Figure 14.12] Two eyes looking at the new and improved 3D model of William Vaughan

[Figure 14.13] Monocular view of 3D William model

[Figure 14.14] Left eye's view of 3D William model (as seen from a parallel binocular camera pair)

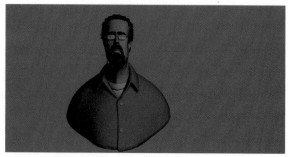

[Figure 14.15] Right eye's view of 3D William model (as seen from a parallel binocular camera pair)

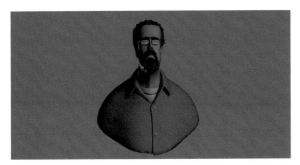

[Figure 14.16] Left eye's view of 3D William model (as seen from a toed-in binocular camera pair)

[Figure 14.17] Right eye's view of 3D William model (as seen from a toed-in binocular camera pair)

The key to creating stereoscopic 3D is to independently record two, slightly horizontally offset image views and then view those separated images *independently* with each eye. That's it. You can separate the images using a simple barrier (as shown in Figure 14.18), which when you are viewing a parallel stereo pair, results in the your left eye seeing something similar to Figure 14.19 and your right eye seeing something that resembles Figure 14.20. When you view a toed-in stereo pair, your left eye sees something similar to Figure 14.21 and the right eye sees something resembling Figure 14.22. Figure 14.23 shows an overhead view of what a parallel stereo viewing would look like, whereas Figure 14.24 illustrates toed-in viewing.

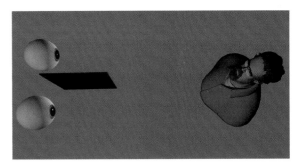

[Figure 14.18] A simple barrier separating the left and right eyes' views

[Figure 14.19] Left eye's view of 3D William model (as seen from a parallel binocular camera pair), with barrier

[Figure 14.20] Right eye's view of 3D William model (as seen from a parallel binocular camera pair), with barrier

[Figure 14.21] Left eye's view of 3D William model (as seen from a toed-in binocular camera pair), with barrier

[Figure 14.22] Right eye's view of 3D William model (as seen from a toed-in binocular camera pair), with barrier

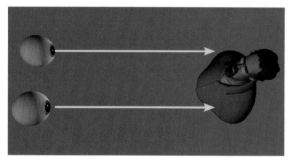

[Figure 14.23] Overhead perspective of a parallel binocular view

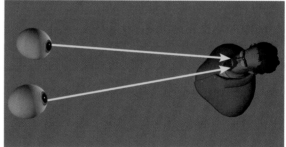

[Figure 14.24] Overhead perspective of a toed-in binocular view

The main difference between the two is in the type of parallax they create. This is most apparent when you view elements that are staged in depth. Therefore, of course, I've staged three Williams! Figure 14.25 shows the left eye's view of a parallel setup and Figure 14.26 shows the right eye's view. By contrast, in a toed-in setup, Figure 14.27 shows the left eye's view whereas Figure 14.28 shows the right eye's view.

You have a lot of control over how things will ultimately appear to the viewer in 3D. The point at which the two separate images line up (the convergence point) determines where the viewer will perceive the *screen depth* (or *stereo window*) to be. This is the perceived relationship between objects in the scene and the physical screen the image is viewed on. As you will see, you can adjust this for dramatically different effects.

If you position the left and right images so that they align at the most distant William model, the viewer will perceive that that is the depth at which the physical screen is, and all elements in the scene in front of this will appear to *pop out* at the viewer (as shown in Figure 14.29).

[**Figure 14.25**] Left eye's view (as seen from a parallel binocular camera pair), with characters staged in-depth

[**Figure 14.26**] Right eye's view (as seen from a parallel binocular camera pair), with characters staged in-depth

[**Figure 14.27**] Left eye's view (as seen from a toed-in binocular camera pair), with characters staged in-depth

[**Figure 14.28**] Right eye's view (as seen from a toed-in binocular camera pair), with characters staged in-depth

[**Figure 14.29**] Optical convergence point aligned at rearmost character

[**Figure 14.30**] Optical convergence point aligned at frontmost character

If you position the left and right images so that they align at the frontmost William model, the viewer will perceive that that is the depth at which the physical screen is, and all other elements in the scene behind this will appear to push deep into the frame as if the screen becomes a window the viewer looks into (as shown in Figure 14.30).

[tip]

Always properly align stereoscopic images vertically and rotationally; even the slightest vertical misalignments or torsional disparities will cause viewer discomfort or distress.

Screen

[Figure 14.31] Optical convergence point aligned at center character

The most natural and comfortable viewing for audiences occurs from a balance of these two approaches. If you position the left and right images so that they align at the middle William model, the viewer will perceive that this central depth is the depth at which the physical screen is. All elements in the scene behind this William will appear to push deep into the frame and all elements in front of this William will appear to pop out at the viewer (as shown in Figure 14.31).

Now it is time to use your 3D glasses! Figure 14.32 shows parallel left and right views combined but not properly aligned. You can see how this causes stress on your eyes (don't stare at this image for too long). Figure 14.33 shows these two views brought into alignment.

[Figure 14.32] Parallel left and right views combined but not properly aligned

[Figure 14.33] Parallel left and right views combined and brought into alignment

[Figure 14.34] Toed-in left and right views combined but not properly aligned

[Figure 14.35] Toed-in left and right views combined and brought into alignment

[Figure 14.36] Full-color stereoscopic 3D image

[Figure 14.37] Left and right images desaturated and then combined (but not yet properly aligned)

[Figure 14.38] Uncolored 3D anaglyph with optical convergence point aligned to frontmost character

[Figure 14.39] Uncolored 3D anaglyph with optical convergence point aligned to rearmost character

Figure 14.34 shows toed-in left and right views combined but not properly aligned and Figure 14.35 shows these two views brought into alignment.

Sometimes it can become difficult to see the 3D effects being created because of distracting colors in a scene. You can remove the color of a full-color stereoscopic 3D image (such as Figure14.36) and create a black and white anaglyph version to better view and analyze a 3D effect. Figure 14.37 shows the combined (but not yet aligned) gray-scale left and right eye views. Figure 14.38 shows the convergence point on the frontmost William, Figure 14.39 shows the convergence point on the rearmost William, and Figure 14.40 shows the convergence point on the William in the middle.

[Figure 14.40] Uncolored 3D anaglyph with optical convergence point aligned to center character

3D Animation

Creating stereoscopic 3D in a 3D modeling and animation application is easy, because all that is really required (in its simplest form) is to set up two cameras (Figure 14.41), offset them slightly horizontally (Figure 14.42 and Figure 14.43), render each "eye" separately (Figures 14.44 and 14.45), and then combine them for viewing using whatever convergence point works best (Figure 14.46–Figure 14.48), in whichever viewing method you choose.

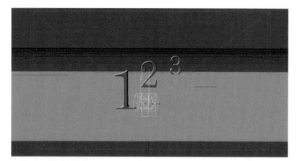

[Figure 14.41] Two cameras, viewing a simple scene, set up as a binocular pair

Anaglyph (the colored red/cyan type) is one of the simplest and most straightforward to create.

The distance you place the cameras apart is referred to as the interocular distance. The average interocular distance in humans is about 63mm or roughly 2.5 inches. Please note that the stereo 3D effect is proportional to the interocular distance. This means that with an average interocular distance of 63mm, things close up will exhibit a much more pronounced 3D effect and things very

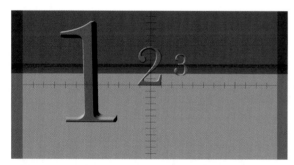

[Figure 14.42] The first camera is offset slightly to the left.

[Figure 14.43] The second camera is offset slightly to the right.

[Figure 14.44] The rendered left eye's view

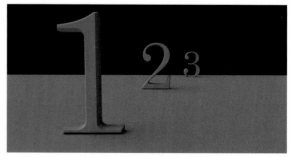

[Figure 14.45] The rendered right eye's view

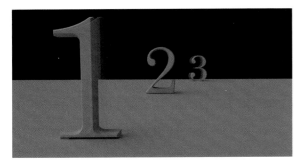

[Figure 14.46] 3D anaglyph with convergence point moved to number 2

[Figure 14.47] 3D anaglyph with convergence point moved to number 1

far away will typically lose much of the 3D effect and appear more as flattened planes. These 3D effects, however, can be unnaturally exaggerated by changing the interocular distance to very small or very large to achieve distinct effects (such as miniaturization).

Creating Color Anaglyph Stereoscopic 3D

[Figure 14.48] 3D anaglyph with convergence point moved to number 3

The term *anaglyph* refers to motion (or still) images in which, usually, the red color channel of the left eye's view replaces the red color channel of the right eye's view. The combination forms the RGB as usual, but using the left eye's view red channel and the right eye's view green and blue (cyan) color channels. This produces a three-dimensional effect when viewed through correspondingly colored (red/cyan) filtered spectacles.

[Figure 14.49] The green and blue color channels turned off in the left eye's view and the red color channel turned off in the right eye's view. The results are a stereoscopic 3D anaglyph image—convergence point is on the number 2 in this image.

To achieve this in Photoshop, load both the left and right views into layers of the same document and name these layers appropriately *left eye* and *right eye*. Double-click the thumbnail image of the left eye's view and under the Advanced Blending selections, uncheck both the G (green) and B (blue) checkboxes, and then click OK. Next double-click the right eye's view and uncheck only the R (red) checkbox and, again, click OK. Congratulations! You have just created your first stereoscopic 3D image (Figure 14.49).

[Figure 14.50] The convergence point set to the number 1

[Figure 14.51] The convergence point set to the number 3

To adjust the convergence, select the left eye's view layer and then the Move tool (the very top tool on the Photoshop toolbar on the left). While pressing the Shift key (to constrain the motion to only one direction), slide the left/red image until it aligns the way you want it to and gets the depth effect you are trying to achieve. Figure 14.50 shows a deep-screen effect with the convergence point set at the image of the number 1. Figure 14.51 shows the opposite popping-out-of-the-screen effect with the convergence point set at the image of the number 3. Remember to make sure that your images/channels are aligned vertically.

You can create these same kind of stereoscopic images with an ordinary camera (even your cell phone) by simply taking two photos slightly offset horizontally (2.5 inches is a good starting point, but feel free to experiment). You can correct for some slight vertical disparities or misalignments by adjusting the position of the layer in Photoshop as well. You can use the arrow keys while the Move tool is selected to nudge the position of images more accurately.

Creating Black and White Anaglyph Stereoscopic 3D

Creating a black and white (or uncolored) stereoscopic 3D anaglyph image is as easy as removing the color from each of the left and right channels individually. You can do this by applying a Hue/Saturation and desaturating each image layer or by using any other method you choose (such as the Black & White tool). I highly recommend that you apply these desaturations using Adjustment Layers so you can easily remove them to bring back your full color images.

Channel Shift and 2D Layer Extraction Offset

You can create a cheat, of sorts, to create 3D-like effects (using simple flat images) by simulating the effect that 3D achieves.

In Figure 14.52 you can see the ground plane from a previous example rendered by itself as a flat 2D image. Figures 14.53–14.55 show the 1, 2, and 3 images, respectively, also rendered into flat 2D images. By assembling these images in layers (Figures 14.56 and 14.57) and duplicating each of the 1, 2, and 3 images into identical pairs, you can apply the same channel settings technique (shown in the previous examples) and simply reposition the red channel of each element manually to "simulate" depth. To create fake depth, align the convergence point (which will align perfectly) and move the ghosted red channel to the left in objects that you want to go deep into the screen window and to the right for objects that you want to pop out of the screen window.

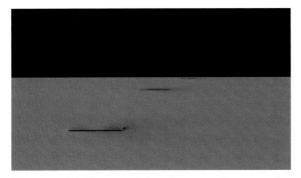

[Figure 14.52] The ground plane from a previous example, by itself as a flat 2D image

[Figure 14.53] The number 1 rendered into flat 2D image

[Figure 14.54] The number 2 rendered into flat 2D image

[Figure 14.55] The number 3 rendered into flat 2D image

[Figure 14.56] The flat 2D elements reassembled into a composite (remember, all of these elements are flat and 2D with no depth in the scene at all)

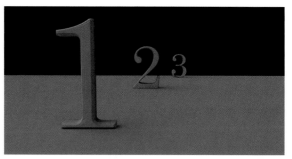

[Figure 14.57] The flat 2D number images 1, 2, and 3 duplicated into identical pairs; and, using the same exact channel settings technique (shown in the previous examples), the Red channel of each number element is manually repositioned to simulate depth.

Although this results in what appear to be flat planes moved in 3D space, you can sometimes use this technique quite creatively for stylized 3D effects (such as making flat 2D animations appear as if they are inhabiting 3D space).

2.5D Layer Offset

I always enjoy the creative use of 2.5D VFX and, in the case of stereoscopic 3D, this is no exception. You can use many of the same 2.5D VFX techniques we have covered throughout this book to create amazing stereoscopic 3D VFX as well. To demonstrate this, I've created a stereoscopic 3D motion graphics (or *mograph*) title or credits shot (like you might see rolling as the credits at the end of a 3D movie) using some very basic 2.5D VFX card tricks (covered in Chapter 6).

Figure 14.59 shows some simple 2D cards I've arranged in 3D space. I created one long card with an old worn parchment texture to appear as a scrolling background for the sequence, some semi-transparent cards textured with medieval-themed silhouette cut-outs, and two large transparent cards (arranged in a V shape, extending outward toward the camera) with the text that will appear to be floating in 3D. All of these flat 2D cards are arranged, staged in 3D depth, and animated to slowly scroll downward.

Once I set up and animated the scene, I created and offset two virtual cameras to record left and right eye views. I then combined these two views exactly the same way as in the Photoshop method described in the previous sections.

The stereoscopic 3D effect is truly eye-popping, as you can see from two screenshots of the sequence (Figures 14.60 and 14.61).

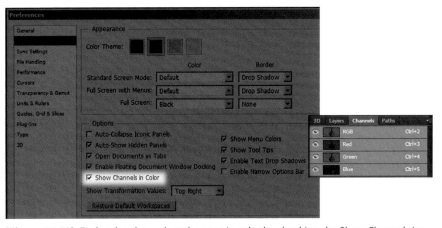

[Figure 14.58] Each color channel can be seen in color by checking the Show Channels In Color checkbox from the Photoshop Edit menu > Preferences window.

Although I recommend leaving this setting off/ unchecked (because color/ luminance perception and information can be so deceiving to the eye), you can temporarily see what each color channel looks like (in color by checking the Show Channels In Color checkbox from the Photoshop Edit menu > Preferences window, as shown in Figure 14.58).

[Figure 14.59] Simple textured 2D cards arranged in 3D space using 2.5D card tricks create a stereoscopic 3D mograph title sequence.

[Figure 14.60] The eye-popping results of this simple card trick

[Figure 14.61] View of the stereoscopic 3D title sequence at a later frame.

Photoshop 3D Tools

Figure 14.62 shows the comparison of some stereoscopic 3D examples in both side-by-side and red/cyan anaglyph presentation formats. When you shoot with a stereoscopic camera that records in the stereoscopic-native .mpo (multi-picture object) file format (Figure 14.63), you can open these files in new versions of Photoshop (these automatically open the 3D Camera tool shown in Figure 14.64), which allows you to make adjustments to the anaglyph image.

[Figure 14.62] Comparison of some stereoscopic 3D examples in both side-by-side and red/cyan anaglyph formats

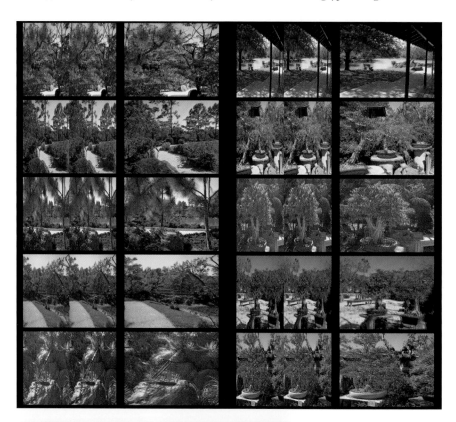

[Figure 14.63] Stereoscopic-native .mpo file format

[Figure 14.64] New versions of Photoshop will automatically open the 3D Camera tool when an .mpo formatted file is opened, which allows adjustments to be made to the anaglyph image's presentation.

Pulfrich Effect

One extremely effective and almost completely automatic method of creating motion stereoscopic 3D is using the *Pulfrich effect*. First described by German physicist Carl Pulfrich in 1922, the concept for this somewhat complicated effect (as it applies to our creation of stereoscopic 3D effects) can be distilled down to this very basic over-simplification: If a stereoscopic 3D image is simply two slightly horizontally offset views/images of the same scene, then if a camera (say, in a car) is moving horizontally, duplicating the footage, offsetting it in time by a frame or so and recombining the two (slightly horizontally offset views) as "left" and "right" eye/views should yield a stereoscopic 3D result. And indeed it does. Figure 14.65 shows three frames from footage of an old pier taken from a moving car. If you copy this footage, offset it a frame, and recombine it using the same anaglyph creation processes I previously described, it yields truly amazing stereoscopic 3D results (as seen in Figure 14.66).

[Figure 14.65] Three frames of footage taken from a moving car of on old pier

[Figure 14.66]
Duplicating this footage, offsetting it in time by a frame, and then combining the two copies into anaglyph footage creates an amazing stereoscopic 3D effect… compliments of the Pulfrich effect.

2D to 3D Stereoscopic Conversions

Many people are surprised to learn that 2D images can be converted into 3D images. I have shown you a few ways to do this—by extracting elements and offsetting them horizontally to mimic parallax, or by repositioning elements in 2.5D to re-create the other eye (or view).

Methods of 2D-to-3D Stereoscopic Conversions

People who are surprised that 2D images can be converted to 3D might be even more shocked to learn that many live-action blockbuster 3D movies they go to see weren't 3D at all to begin with; instead, they were common 2D movies that underwent a 2D-to-3D conversion process. Although 2D to 3D conversion sounds like some kind of automated process, nothing could be further from the truth. In fact, huge teams of artists endure burdensome amounts of roto, depth, and background occlusion fill (filling in the gaps created by extracting elements to create "the other eye") and paint work to create these amazing, moving works of 3D art. Just watch the end credits to your favorite live action 3D movie to see how many hundreds and hundreds of people are required to pull off this giant magic trick.

Technology and Implementation

Many technologies (many proprietary) are used to create 2D to 3D stereoscopic conversions, and they all rely on versions of some commonly used methodologies. The heart of 2D to 3D conversion is the *depth map*. Yes, the same depth map we have talked about in many chapters of this book and, in fact, just a version of the same fake Z-depth method we covered in Chapter 8, only very refined and taken to a whole new level. Most of these conversion methods rely on these depth maps to create some kind of displacement to create "the other eye" (or view).

Let's take a look at one example, running through the entire process from start (2D) to finish (3D), this time using Nuke.

Figure 14.67 shows a bluesceeen shot of actor Allen Reidel. Using the keying techniques shown in Chapter 2, I performed an initial key extraction to remove the blue background (Figure 14.68). Notice all the blue spill? I add a quick Hue Correct tool to isolate and remove this spill (Figure 14.69). I then use the alpha created by the keyer (Figure 14.70) to extract Al from the original pristine footage.

[Figure 14.67] Original plate of actor Allen Reidel, shot on bluescreen

[Figure 14.68] Key applied to image to extract bluescreen—notice the blue spill.

[Figure 14.69] Hue correction applied to reduce blue spill

[Figure 14.70] Alpha created by keyer (and used to extract the subject from the original pristine footage)

Depth Maps—Roto

If the heart of the 2D to 3D conversion process is depth mapping, the soul (to many artists' dismay) would have to be roto. And again, yes, the same roto I covered in Chapter 2. By using the original image of Al as a guide to roto, I create layers of gradients pretty much the same way we did with fake Z-depth maps in Chapter 8 (using rotosplines and gradient fills), only in full motion… and of every element… in every scene!

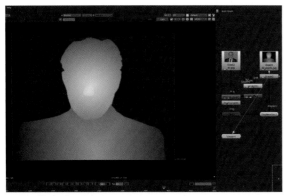

[Figure 14.71] Depth map created using layered rotosplines filled with gradients

Figure 14.71 shows the depth map of Al. The darker grays represent positions farther back in the scene, whereas the lighter grays represent feature positions that are closer.

Depth Maps—Procedural and Complex

There are new tools that can create procedural depth maps for you to some degree (and in some scene conditions). In Chapter 15, I also show you some promising new cutting-edge technologies. But, although there are some useful methods for extracting depth, by far the most common method for creating depth maps is still using roto.

As with all other VFX, methods of depth map creation are not just one tool, or one click, solutions and require you to use whatever method works the best for the particular task at hand. This can mean roto, procedural extraction, depth sensor, or any combination of tools and methods available.

Depth Maps—2D Displacement

As you saw in Chapter 2, which discussed how to create photorealistic surfaces, you can use a grayscale image as a 2D displacement to move (or push) pixels in 2D. By applying a depth map as a 2D displacement to a copy of an image and using that 2D displaced image as "the other eye" or view, you can create a degree of stereoscopic 3D with some success (and great success in some proprietary systems), but using depth maps for true 3D displacement can allow you to produce some truly astonishing results.

Depth Maps—3D Rubber Sheet Method Displacement

To create a 3D displacement conversion (also sometimes referred to as the *rubber sheet method*), you start by applying the original image to a flat subdivided plane/card (or sheet) as shown in Figure 14.72. When you apply the depth map to this sheet as a 3D displacement (as we will cover in even more detail in Chapter 15) the values in the depth map begin to extrude the image in 3D (as seen in Figure 14.73).

You can add Levels, Curves, Grade, and other adjustments to increase, decrease, and otherwise shape and modify the way the plane displaces (as shown in Figure 14.74). This displacement creates enough 3D depth (Figure 14.75) that setting up a virtual two-camera (or stereo) rig (as seen in Figure 14.76) creates just enough difference between the left camera/eye (Figure 14.77) and the right camera/eye (Figure 14.78) to produce a great, natural-looking stereoscopic 3D effect. Figure 14.79 shows the result in uncolored anaglyph and Figure 14.80 shows the result in full-color anaglyph.

[**Figure 14.72**] The extracted image applied to a subdivided flat card

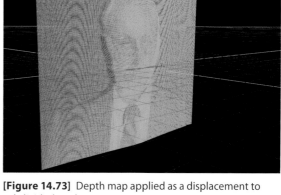

[**Figure 14.73**] Depth map applied as a displacement to subdivided card

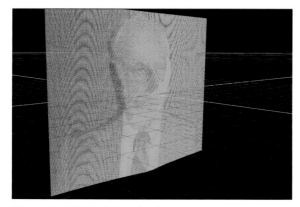

[**Figure 14.74**] Grade/Levels adjustments can increase, decrease, and otherwise shape and modify the way the plane displaces.

[**Figure 14.75**] Full-color view of displaced "rubber sheet" plane

[Figure 14.76]
Two slightly horizontally offset cameras created to "film" the left and right eye views

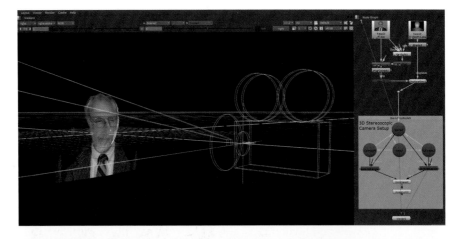

[Figure 14.77]
Left camera/eye view

[Figure 14.78]
Right camera/eye view

[Figure 14.79] Uncolored anaglyph stereoscopic 3D result

[Figure 14.80] Full-colored anaglyph stereoscopic 3D result

Leveraging and pushing forward the concepts and techniques used in this chapter to create complexity with 3D displacements, Chapter 15 explores advanced displacement modeling, photogrammetry extractions, and amazing new cutting-edge technologies.

CHAPTER FIFTEEN

Advanced VFX Techniques VI: Cutting-Edge 3D VFX

As I've shown throughout this book, VFX is all about creating "effects"—meaning, creating things that either don't really exist or re-creating things that do exist but that wouldn't be practical, cost effective, or safe to film in real life. I've also explained how the goal of a VFX artist is to always keep an eye on creating the absolute best possible effects using the most efficient and economical means possible. If you project these values forward to the future, you can easily see how beneficial it would be to, say, not have to model and light an entire set or environment but to automatically (or semi-automatically) "capture" or "extract" it in 3D somehow, using inexpensive and common tools. What if you could take a photo of an office hallway and somehow just make it 3D so you could simply place your 3D dinosaur into the actual environment, or create an entire 3D mountain range or city to scale in an instant? What if you could walk around with a simple device that could not only film the scene but create a 3D camera track, 3D point cloud, 3D mesh, 3D depth map—automatically… all at once… in real time … while you were filming?

That's what this chapter covers: cutting-edge 3D VFX, beginning with some cool existing technology and ending with the latest in experimental cutting-edge tech that will be coming down the pike. I begin with a section about what I call *Photoshop magic*.

Advanced 3D and Photoshop Magic

Photoshop version CS2 introduced a clever new tool that, surprisingly, very few people have fully experimented with or even know about. It's called the Vanishing Point tool/filter.

[Figure 15.1] Photo of long office hallway loaded into Photoshop

[Figure 15.2] Vanishing Point tool/filter with four points of grid selected to align with perspective lines in floor tile

[Figure 15.3] Blue grid showing valid plane

The Vanishing Point tool/filter has many uses, from perspective cloning (as shown in Chapter 2, in the parking lot example) to the more advanced and little-known re-creation of entire sets for use in full 3D environments.

Vanishing Point Photogrammetry

Using photogrammetry (discussed in Chapter 4) it is possible to extract 3D point clouds and models from images. The Vanishing Point tool/filter uses a simplified manual creation version of this concept by creating a series of flat adjustable planes in 3D space. By drawing out planes that are all connected/oriented to one another and then projecting the image itself from the camera's vantage point, a surprisingly realistic and 3D environment can be created.

Let's create one of these from scratch. Load the photo of the long office hallway into Photoshop, shown in Figure 15.1 (see the Introduction for instructions on downloading files for use with this book). Select the Vanishing Point tool/filter by clicking Filter menu > Vanishing Point.

It's important to establish a reliable starting grid when doing a complex model like this, so it might take a few tries. I like to start with any reliable perspective lines in a scene. The edges of walls, baseboards, railings, windows, ceilings, or floor tiles are all usually good starting points. In this case, the floor tiles are easy to follow, so let's start there. Select the Create Plane tool (the second from the top button on the Vanishing Point toolbar on the left) and place four points along well-defined perspective lines in the tile, as shown in Figure 15.2. After you place these points, the interface will give you visible, real-time feedback as to how well the plane is being drawn. A blue grid (such as the one shown in Figure 15.3) indicates a well-formed plane,

[Figure 15.4] Floor plane edges extended to completely match and cover entire floor area

[Figure 15.5] Right edge of floor "torn off" at 90-degree angle by holding Ctrl/Cmd and pulling the center edge point upward, creates a new wall

whereas a red outline indicates that adjustments are required. You can make edits using the Edit Plane tool (the top button on the toolbar).

Once the last of the four points is placed and the grid is formed, you can extend it in any edge direction by simply grabbing the point in the middle on any edge and dragging it outward. Extend this floor plane outward until it completely fills the area of the office floor in the image as shown in Figure 15.4. If any edges don't line up, you can use the Edit Plane tool to adjust them now. Be as accurate as you can, because as you add planes, adjustments become more difficult and eventually even impossible.

Edges can be "broken off" at 90-degree angles by holding the Ctrl/Cmd key while dragging a middle edge point (versions of Photoshop later than CS2 allow the breaking off at any angle by holding the Alt/Option while dragging a middle edge point). In this case, while holding Ctrl/Cmd, pull up a 90-degree wall plane from the right edge of the floor until it meets the ceiling overhang, and then adjust the depth of the wall until it covers only one wall section, as shown in Figure 15.5. Creating this wall section will allow you to create the doorways in 3D as well.

[note]

All these planes can be made as simple or as complex as you'd like. In this case, the wall sections were created as small sections to demonstrate the creation of 3D doorways and alcoves and the ability to relight the hallway, but they could just as easily have been created as simple singular floor, wall, and ceiling planes (though if you'd done this, they wouldn't have the ability to react to light as realistically).

Once again, while holding Ctrl/Cmd, pull a middle point on the small wall section's edge to the right to create one of the doorway insets. Pull it in until it is well inside the doorway. Repeat this process of tearing off perpendicular edges, back and forth, until the entire wall is created (as shown in Figure 15.6). Creating interior doorway and alcove spaces like this might take a little practice, but visually aligning the "pulled in" sections horizontally, with wall/doorway corners, can help you rapidly acquire the skill of quickly estimating where to break the next section by eye.

Repeat the same process on the other side, tearing off the other edge of the floor into the opposite wall plane (Figure 15.7). Resize the wall section and create the center alcove the same way you created the doorways, extending the wall until it reaches the end of the floor plane (as shown in Figure 15.8).

Tear off the end floor edge upward using this same technique to create the rear wall (shown in Figure 15.9). Finish the ceiling and recessed areas the same way by tearing off and resizing the edges of the walls (Figure 15.10) and then repeating the process to create the recessed lighting area (as shown in Figure 15.11).

[**Figure 15.6**] Pull a middle point on the small wall section's edge to the right to create the first wall of one of the doorway insets and repeat this process (creating perpendicular walls), back and forth, until the entire section is created.

[**Figure 15.7**] Repeat the same process on the opposite side to create the left wall section. Again, resize to just the part of the wall before the alcove.

[**Figure 15.8**] Repeat the process of tearing off perpendicular grid segments to form the alcove and the rest of the wall.

When completed, your grid should look something like Figure 15.12. These planes might appear simply as outlines unless each plane is selected, and that's perfectly fine—I Shift+selected them all here for illustration purposes, so you can see them.

[Figure 15.9] Create the back wall by tearing off a grid from the center point of the far floor edge and pulling up while holding Ctrl/Cmd.

[Figure 15.10] Tear off one of the top wall edges to create the ceiling overhang section. Then resize it to cover the entire section.

[Figure 15.11] Continue tearing off perpendicular grid planes and resizing them to form the lighting recess and ceiling contours.

[Figure 15.12] The completed grid plane environment

[note]

Every plane in these extractions should be torn from a previously existing plane. This allows all the planes to maintain their relative orientation to one another and allows the scene to easily stay together, with everything aligned properly. Although it's entirely possible to draw completely detached planes, they will have no orientation with respect to one another, and so they will likely wind up in a giant mess when exported to 3D.

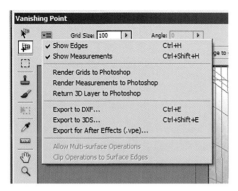

[**Figure 15.13**] Export the finished scene in 3D using the small drop-down menu located at the top left of the Vanishing Point interface.

3D Extractions

With all the grids created to match the scene, the magic of the 3D extraction is as simple as clicking the dropdown menu at the top left of the interface and exporting the scene as a .dfx, .3ds, or .vpe (Figure 15.13).

Loading the exported scene into your 3D application of choice will reveal something similar to Figure 15.14. Notice that the walls seem invisible or "inside-out." This is because, by default, the texture being mapped is to the inside of the model, so, technically, like a Hollywood facade, nothing exists on the outside. By enabling the two-sided material feature (this feature's name may vary from program to program) in your 3D application, you can fix this unimportant anomaly for ease of viewing, as shown in Figure 15.15. Looking down the hallway in the 3D application, you can see the original scene re-created in full 3D (shown in Figure 15.16).

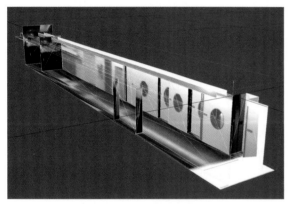

[**Figure 15.14**] Exported scene loaded into 3D application. Notice the invisible or "inside-out" looking walls.

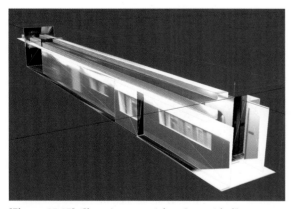

[**Figure 15.15**] Changing materials to "two-sided" corrects this visible anomaly.

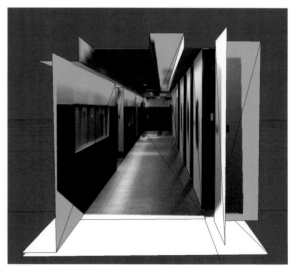

[**Figure 15.16**] The original scene now in full 3D

3D Re-Lighting

Set up a 3D camera to look down the hallway and place a point light somewhere in the middle of your new 3D virtual hallway (as shown in Figures 15.17 and 15.18). Figure 15.19 shows the result from the camera's point of view (POV)—a completely different, re-lit scene. Because this scene is truly 3D, you can also move or animate that light to, say, move down the hallway, as shown in Figure 15.20.

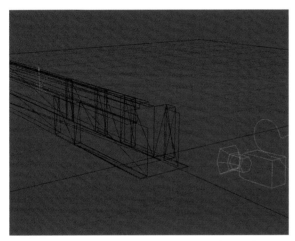

[**Figure 15.17**] Point light placed in middle of 3D hallway

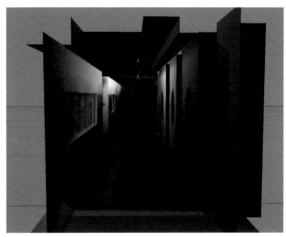

[**Figure 15.18**] Point light viewed from the end of the model

[**Figure 15.19**] Rendered view of one point light in scene

[**Figure 15.20**] Rendered view of point light animated to move closer to the camera, re-lighting the scene

Placing two more point lights in the scene (Figure 15.21) starts to emulate a more realistically lit scene (Figure 15.22), with lighting that can be adjusted or even dramatically changed (Figure 15.23). But you can see that the lighting doesn't really match the physical fixtures in the scene, namely the recessed lighting. For this, you can delete those lights and replace them with two long linear lights, as shown in Figure 15.24. These lights (Figure 15.25) start to more accurately emulate the lights in the original scene.

With the extracted scene lit, place your 3D dinosaur in the hallway, Enabling radiosity, as covered in Chapter 11, to allow the light to more accurately bounce around the scene, produces a great-looking VFX scene, shown in Figure 15.26. And all of this is originally from one still image!

[Figure 15.21]
Three point light positioned at increments down the hallway

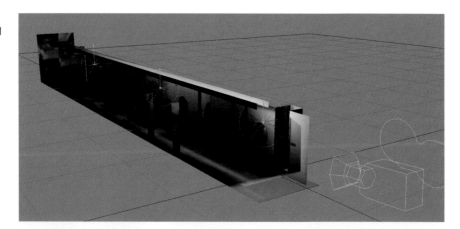

[Figure 15.22] 3D virtual hallway lit by three point lights

[Figure 15.23] Lights' color changed to red completely re-lights scene.

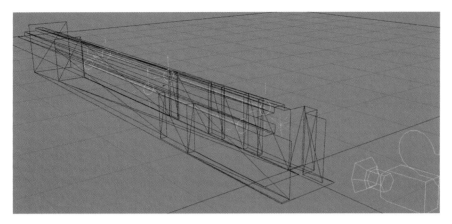

[Figure 15.24]
Point lights replaced with two linear lights (more closely resembling the original lighting conditions in the scene)

[Figure 15.25] Results of changing point lights to linear lights

[Figure 15.26]
The completed scene with 3D dinosaur added and radiosity enabled

Displacement Modeling

Another creative way to use Photoshop is for procedurally creating maps with matching textures for what I call *displacement modeling*. These are eye-popping ways to get you out of a pinch. They're almost magical creations that work amazingly well when you don't have to get too close to a model in a VFX shot.

Some of these creations start off, seemingly, so simple yet evolve into results you might never have thought you were capable of accomplishing. Let's begin by creating a complex futuristic or space habitat design.

Procedural Futuristic or Space Complex Design

In this example, start with a new, plain, square, solid black document in Photoshop (1000 × 1000 pixels should do just fine, but you can make it larger or smaller depending on the resolution you require). I don't know about you, but I am *not* an architectural designer. But when we envision futuristic or space complexes, we tend to think of streamlined, complex, curved features. These are very difficult to design… except when you use this little trick.

Begin creating simple white rectangular shapes on another layer above the black background, as if you were designing the overhead map for a college campus or office park, like in Figure 15.27. It's okay to overlap shapes to get larger, more complex-looking "building footprints" (shown in Figure 15.28). Using a Hue/Saturation, Levels, or other adjustment, darken this layer down to a mid gray.

On yet another layer, create little details (hatches, panels, rooftop entries, and so on) as smaller simple shapes in near-white, as shown in Figure 15.29. This will be your displacement map.

You also want a texture to use that will match your displacement. In this case, I've used some old metal texture with welds, holes, and solders, but feel free to use whatever you'd like. I loaded the rectangular "building" outlines into a selection using the same technique covered in Chapter 2 for loading grunge maps as selections. Then I simply deleted the rest of the metal texture outside the building edges, as shown in Figure 15.30. In a real production, I would accurately create and "fit" the texture exactly to the building pattern, but I want you to see how forgiving this technique is. So, for demonstration purposes, I'm not taking any particular care with the texture.

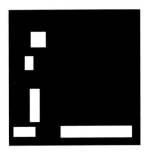

[Figure 15.27] Begin by creating simple white rectangular shapes on a layer above the black background.

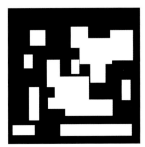

[Figure 15.28] You can overlap shapes to get more complex "building footprints."

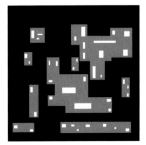

[Figure 15.29] On another layer, create little details as smaller simple shapes in near-white.

[Figure 15.30] Metal texture trimmed to only the areas in the white rectangular-shaped layout areas

[Figure 15.31] The displacement map with Polar Coordinate distortion applied

[Figure 15.32] The completed alpha map

[Figure 15.33] The same Polar Coordinate distortion applied to the metal texture

Turn off your texture layer and, with only the displacement layers visible, Select All (or Ctrl/Cmd+A), do a Copy Merged (or Shift+Ctrl/Cmd+C), and then paste the merged copy into a new layer (Ctrl/Cmd+V).

Now for the magic. Select the layer with the merged copy and then click Filter menu > Distort > Polar Coordinates. There are only two options in this tool, and the one you want is Rectangular To Polar (as you might've guessed, the other option does the opposite and is handy for converting spherical images to rectangular). The result should be an awesome space-age layout similar to Figure 15.31. Save this out as Space_Station_Displace or some equally descriptive filename.

Filling all the non-black areas with pure white gives you a lightning-fast alpha channel (shown in Figure 15.32), and repeating the Polar Coordinates tool with the image layer gives you a matching texture, shown in Figure 15.33. Save these out as Space_Station_Alpha and Space_Station_Texture, respectively.

[tip]

A great place to start your search for free textures, if you don't already have your own, is CG Textures at www.cgtextures.com.

To quickly create an alien surface to place your space station on (and for a simple example of the technique I cover next), I've downloaded a NASA moon map (Figure 15.34) and bump map from (http://pdsmaps.wr.usgs.gov/ maps.html), which I will use for the ground texture map and subtle displacement map (Figure 15.35). Again, I've named and saved these out with easily identifiable names.

To create the space station, create a square, flat, single polygon *sub-d* (or subdivision surface) plane in your 3D application of choice (as shown in Figure 15.36). I've used a sub-d surface here, which automatically smoothes and rounds itself as much as possible during render time. The outline of the square is the actual geometry, whereas the circle is the subdivided and smoothed rendered version preview. With the subdivision level set low, applying the space station displacement map as a displacement starts to push the geometry up a little but looks more like an '80s video game icon than a space station (Figure 15.37). Increasing the subdivision level to a very high degree starts to give you the form of the space station, as if it were stamped into the plane (Figure 15.38). By greatly increasing the displacement value, the space station is effectively extruded from the ground plane, as shown in Figure 15.39. Applying the texture map gives us a decent looking space station (Figure 15.40).

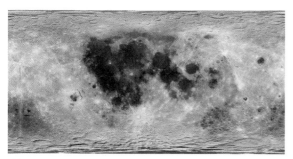

[Figure 15.34] NASA moon map

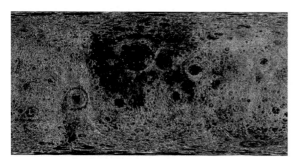

[Figure 15.35] NASA moon bump map.

[Figure 15.36] Flat single polygon sub-d surface plane

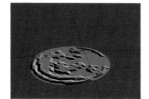

[Figure 15.37] Applying the space station displacement map as a displacement (with the subdivision level set low) starts to push the geometry up a little

[Figure 15.38] Increasing the subdivision level appears to extrude the form of the space station

[Figure 15.39] The space station is effectively extruded from the ground plane.

Repeating the process with a large plane to serve as the alien terrain (Figure 15.41) and placing it under the space station results in a nice subtle texture to the ground (Figure 15.42) and finally a pretty cool crater-marked surface (Figure 15.43).

Placing one light in the scene and a star field background gives us a pretty amazing space station scene, as shown in Figure 15.44—especially considering there are actually only two flat planes in the scene… the ultimate card trick.

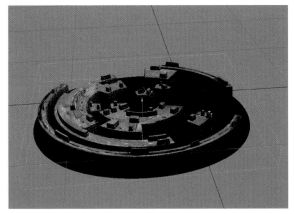

[Figure 15.40] Space station displacement model with texture applied

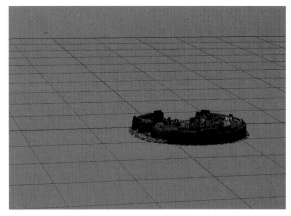

[Figure 15.41] Repeat the process with a large plane to serve as alien terrain.

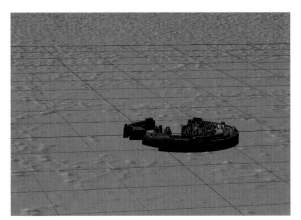

[Figure 15.42] Moon bump map applied as a displacement gives a nice subtle variation to the ground.

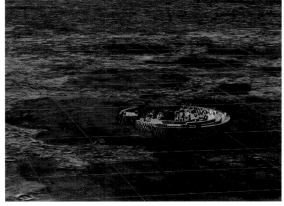

[Figure 15.43] Moon texture map applied

[Figure 15.44]
Scene rendered with star
field background and single
sun light added

Creating Complex Terrains Using DEM and SRTM Data

You can use the same technique covered in the last section to create
extremely accurate and complicated terrains. Nature is almost infinite in its
complexity. Why should you spend endless hours trying to model that when
you can just download it?

A digital elevation model (or DEM) is an ASCII or binary file that contains
only spatial elevation data in a regular gridded pattern in raster (pixel/image)
format, where each pixel stores a number that represents the value of the
average altitude of the area represented by that pixel.

There are many DEM sources and formats. The most common DEMs come
from the United States Geological Survey (USGS). They usually are found in
ASCII formats .dem and .ddf, but in more recent years, the newer National
Elevation Dataset (.ned) format has also been established. There are many
other resources, such as NASA's Space Shuttle Radar Topography Mission
(SRTM), which provides DEMs in the heightfield file format (.hgt), GTOPO
30, ASTER, and more, which provide DEMs in many other formats, such
as GeoTiff (.tif) and binary formats such as .dem and .txt as well. These file
formats come in both colored and grayscale versions.

DEMs come in many resolutions as well. The resolution determines how far
apart each elevation was sampled and, hence like an image, the higher the
resolution, the higher the detail and "smoothness" of your final result.

The most common resolutions are as follows:

- 1/3 arc-second, referred to as 10m (which is really 10.3m or 33.79ft)

- 1 arc-second, referred to as 30m (30.86m or 101.2ft)

- 3 arc-seconds, referred to as 90m (92.6m or 303.6ft)

- 30 arc-seconds, referred to as approximately 1km (926m or 3038.6ft)

The highest resolutions are 5 meters and 1 meter.

SRTM, since it is derived from radar, represents the elevation of "first reflected surface"—quite often treetops, buildings, and so forth, so the data is not necessarily representative of the ground surface, but rather the top of whatever is first encountered by the radar. But in most cases, this works just fine for VFX work.

Some sources for DEMs include the following:

- GTOPO30 (30 arc-second or approximately 1km)

- Advanced Spaceborne Thermal Emission and Reflection Radiometer (ASTER) (30m)

- Space Shuttle Radar Topography Mission (SRTM) (US 30m, rest of world 3 arc-seconds or approx. 90m)

- Submarine Elevation (bathymetry)

- SRTM30Plus dataset

- RADARSAT-2

- TerraSAR-X

- TanDEM-X

- Mars DEM's Mission Experiment Gridded Record (MEGDR), Mars Global Surveyor's Mars Orbiter Laser Altimeter (MOLA), and NASA's Mars Digital Terrain Model (DTM)

And here are a few good sources for DEM downloads:

- http://data.geocomm.com/dem/demdownload.html

- http://data.geocomm.com/catalog/

- http://eros.usgs.gov/elevation-products

- http://www.usgs.gov/pubprod/

- http://eros.usgs.gov/find-data

- http://ngdc.noaa.gov/mgg/dem/

In addition, you can create DEMs using applications such as Terragen (http://planetside.co.uk) and World Machine (www.world-machine.com).

When opened, many DEMs appear like Figure 15.45—a featureless black image. Not to fear. Your image isn't broken. It just needs a little adjusting.

First, to minimize banding as much as possible, convert your DEM to the highest bit depth possible in Photoshop by clicking Image menu > Mode > 32 Bits/Channel (as shown in Figure 15.46).

[Figure 15.45] When opened, many DEMs will appear like a featureless black image.

Apply your old friend the Levels adjustment (shown in Figure 15.47). Notice from the histogram that all the data in the DEM is in the very darkest range of values. Carefully bringing the white and gamma levels all the way to the darks reveals all the intricate data in the DEM (in this case—Figure 15.48—a mountain range with peaks at the lightest values and valleys at the darkest values). Once enough detail is visible, save out this gamma-corrected DEM. (Depending on your 3D application, you may have to reconvert the DEM image back to a lower bit depth, such as 8 Bits/Channel, if the application doesn't support higher bit depths.)

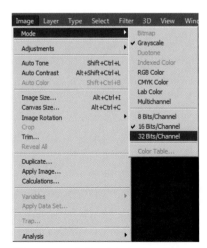

[Figure 15.46] To minimize banding as much as possible, convert your DEM to the highest bit depth possible.

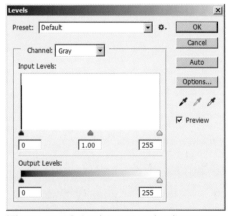

[Figure 15.47] Applying a Levels adjustment reveals that all the data in the DEM is in the very darkest range of values.

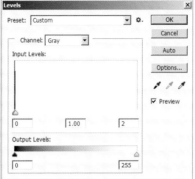

[Figure 15.48] Bringing the white and gamma levels up to the darks shows mountain ranges with peaks at the lightest values and valleys at the darkest values.

Create another sub-d plane, as shown in Figure 15.49. This time, slice the edges so that they stay fixed and don't collapse into a circle (referred to as *hold edges* or *support edges* in the world of sub-d modeling), and increase the subdivision amount a little, shown in Figure 15.50. Next, as with the previous example, load in the DEM as a displacement map and increase the displacement value, shown in Figure 15.51. Increasing the displacement value further (Figure 15.52) begins to reveal some mountains, albeit very unrealistic ones. Changing from a wireframe to a shaded surface view (as shown in Figure 15.53) reveals how lo-res and jaggy these appear at this still low subdivision level. Finally, carefully increasing the subdivision level to a very high value allows for the maximum amount of detail to be seen, as shown in Figure 15.54. You can then map a matching aerial or satellite photo onto this model as a texture.

[caution]

Be extremely careful when increasing subdivision levels using this technique. Test your increases little by little, because increasing way too much could bring your computer's processor to its knees, resulting in a definitive lockup and crash.

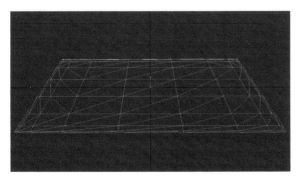

[Figure 15.49] Creating another sub-d plane, this time with the edges sliced so that they stay fixed and don't collapse into a circle

[Figure 15.50] The subdivision amount increased just a little.

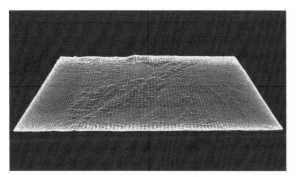

[Figure 15.51] DEM is loaded in as a displacement map and the displacement value is increased, revealing some mountains.

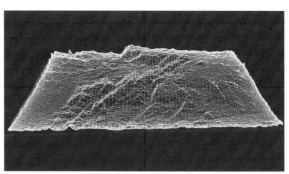

[Figure 15.52] Increasing the displacement value further defines the mountains, albeit very unrealistic ones.

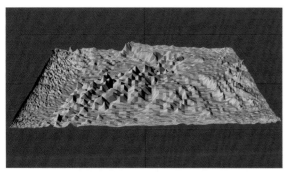

[Figure 15.53] Changing from a wireframe to a shaded surface view reveals how lo-res and jaggy these appear at this still low subdivision level.

[Figure 15.54] Carefully increasing the subdivision level to a very high value allows for the maximum amount of detail to be seen.

Quick and Dirty Procedural City Extractions Using Displacements

"I need a completely accurate 3D aerial shot of a square mile of Washington, D.C.… every street… every building," your VFX supervisor says. No problem, you think, you'll get right on it; you look up some references and start modeling the buildings stat. "Oh, and I need it completed in an hour!" your supervisor adds while heading out the door. Normally, this kind of request would send a VFX artist into an all-out panic. But not you. Because I'm going to give you the secret that will allow you to calmly reply, "No problem!" without batting an eyelash, while other artists around you fall off their chairs with their mouths open.

I developed this technique while in exactly such a circumstance. Necessity became not only the mother of invention, but of outside-the-box thinking as well. As I promised at the beginning of this book, because each chapter builds on the next, you're going to tackle this exact request and accomplish it using a combination of techniques you've learned all throughout this book—from the procedural extractions covered in Chapter 2, to the atmosphere concepts covered in Chapter 8, to the displacement modeling effects covered here in Chapter 15.

First you'll need a good aerial or satellite image that covers the area you're interested in creating. NASA's Visible Earth (http://visibleearth.nasa.gov) and the USGS (www.usgs.gov) are great places to start; they are where I found the aerial of Washington, D.C. shown in Figure 15.55. Ideally, you want to find an image with some good contrast between the streets and buildings and with low-contrast, nondescript sun lighting. In this case, one out of two will have to do. (There is quite a lot of green everywhere that's not buildings, which will allow for a calculations-based extraction, but there is very harsh directional lighting. In such a case, you just have to work with it and try to use it to your advantage somehow.)

[Figure 15.55] Satellite aerial of Washington, D.C.

Using the same techniques for procedural extraction you used in Chapter 2, you first need to somehow increase the contrast between the buildings and non-buildings. Calculations or the Black & White filter can darken the streets and lighten the buildings somewhat, getting you part of the way there, as shown in Figure 15.56. One immediate problem jumps out. The huge trees in the center of the city circle went black because the greens were pushed to black to separate them from the buildings. In the displacement model, you know that light values will be raised and dark values lowered. These trees are very old and huge and need to stand out, so they will need to be isolated independently.

Creating another copy of the original image and doing another Calculations, work to bring out the values in the circle of trees. When you've finished, isolate them and paint everything else back to black, as shown in Figure 15.57. Combine this tree layer with the first extraction using a Lighten or Add blend mode to arrive at something similar to Figure 15.58.

[Figure 15.56] Streets procedurally darkened using Calculations or Black & White filter to create displacement map

[Figure 15.57] Trees in city circle isolated and made white on their own layer

[Figure 15.58] Tree layer combined with displacement layer using Lighten or Add blend mode

[Figure 15.59] Levels adjustment added to increase contrast further

[Figure 15.60] Flat sub-d plane

[Figure 15.61] Displacement map applied to sub-d plane and subdivision increased a little

[Figure 15.62] The subdivision amount increased a little at a time—bumps begin to form.

[tip]

Many iteration and procedural operations can be added, subtracted, multiplied, divided, and so on to isolate and extract or exclude anything you want or need. Think outside the box with your strategy. Be creative.

[tip]

You will sometimes need to add a slight blur to this map if the results look too jagged and grainy, but always try it without blur first to retain as much detail as possible.

Using a Levels adjustment, carefully crush the values to make the buildings as bright as possible and the streets as dark as possible (without killing all the detail, of course). You should have something that looks like Figure 15.59. Save this map out and name it—you will use this as your displacement map and the original as your matching color map.

As in the previous section, create a flat sub-d plane, as shown in Figure 15.60, and apply the displacement map. Slowly and carefully increase the subdivision level slightly (Figure 15.61). When you increase it more, little by little, you should start to see bumps forming, as in Figures 15.62 and 15.63; hints of the road formations begin to appear the higher the subdivision level is increased (Figure 15.64. Once an adequate level of detail is achieved by increasing the subdivision level (Figure 15.65), create a camera and frame up your shot (Figure 15.66).

Now you can apply the original full-color map as the color channel for the texture. The results should look something like Figure 15.67. Match the lighting using the shadows in the scene as cues for how to place the sun light. Because the shadows are long in the image, it would appear to be nearing sunset, so a lower color temperature (covered in Chapter 1) would seem appropriate (Figure 15.68).

[Figure 15.63] The subdivision amount increased more

[Figure 15.64] Carefully increasing the subdivision amount even more begins to reveal the outline of city streets.

[Figure 15.65] The subdivision amount increased until an adequate amount of detail is achieved

[Figure 15.66] 3D camera added to scene and shot framed up

[Figure 15.67] The original full color map is applied to the surface as the color channel for the texture.

[Figure 15.68] Lighting the scene using the shadows in the original image as cues for how to place the sun light

[Figure 15.69] 3D fog for atmosphere and volumetric clouds added to the scene

This is supposed to be an aerial, so there would be considerable atmospheric build-up between your vantage point as a plane and the ground. You can apply this atmosphere as light volumetric 3D fog, 2.5D atmosphere planes, or even 2D color correction after the fact—it's completely up to you. In this case, to mix things up a little, I've used a very light 3D fog as the atmosphere and added volumetric clouds, as shown in Figure 15.69. Again, you could create these clouds with voxels, sprites, extracted images, and so on. As I say in Chapter 1, always be thinking, "There are always a hundred ways to do every effect."

[Figure 15.70] Bluish color correction layer added to "cool" the scene a little

[Figure 15.71] A final desaturation finishes the scene and helps add a polish of realism.

The scene seems overly warm, so I added a bluish color correction layer to "cool" the scene a bit (Figure 15.70). Finally, as discussed in Chapter 2, decreasing the saturation in a CG image often helps add realism. That's definitely the case here, as you can see in Figure 15.71, which, when motion blur is added, should easily pass for a real aerial flyover.

Congratulations! Not bad for an hour's work, creating an entire, accurate square mile of a city in 3D with every street and building.

New Technologies

No book on VFX would be complete without exploring at least a few cutting-edge technologies that are, or will be, available to you. Although many amazing technologies are being developed in cutting-edge research or for the high-end studios, most of these (at least for now) are out of the reach of the masses. Therefore, I will focus these few recommendations on a handful of new (and not very well known), easily accessible tech gems that I have tried, tested and found to be amazingly useful for the individual artist and studio pro alike.

Ricoh Theta

It is truly amazing how fast technological advances can radically change, speed up, and streamline your workflow. This is definitely the case with the new Ricoh Theta (https://theta360.com), shown in Figure 15.72. Up until now, creating spherical images to use for IBL solutions has been a time-consuming chore. Having to set up and shoot mirror balls—or worse, manual spherical panoramas, which later had to be stitched in software—is now a thing of the past.

This amazing, tiny little device captures full 360-degree images in a split second! That's it. No catch, no extra steps. It even creates its own Wi-Fi hotspot so you can download the 360-degree spherical images directly to your smartphone to instantly view and review.

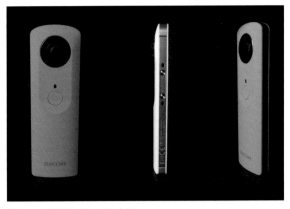

[Figure 15.72] The Ricoh Theta

The 360-degree images can then be rotated around any way you like, using a very simple and intuitive interface, which has almost no controls—just roll around the 360-degree image using your fingers or zoom in and out using common smartphone finger-pinching gestures. Having all 360 degrees available to you allows you to create and use any angle you choose for your radiosity IBL setup or export as flat .jpg files as well (Figure 15.73). The Ricoh Theta sells for about $400.

[Figure 15.73] Examples of Ricoh Theta 360-degree images as flat .jpg and multiple spherical views

Reallusion iClone, 3DXchange, and Mocap Plugin

Sometimes innovation catches you off-guard. One day, you suddenly realize that you've been turning more and more to a solution that you never originally expected to be so useful or important to you. That's what happened to me with Reallusion's incredibly useful software tools.

I first came across Reallusion's software while teaching a course on pre-viz for movies. To refresh, *pre-viz*, *post-viz*, and *pitch-viz* (covered in Chapter 1) are all terms for *pre-visualizations* done at different stages of a motion picture's development. They are extraordinarily useful in the efficient production of a movie. Pitch-viz is done to pre-visualize VFX shots before a movie is in production to "pitch" or sell the movie. Pre-viz is done before a movie is filmed to plan how to shoot complex VFX sequences most efficiently. And post-viz is done after the initial filming of scenes to most efficiently complete the VFX shots using the footage that was actually shot.

Creating digital doubles for characters was always the realm of character modelers, who required great amounts of time to model, rig, and animate the likenesses of an actor or character. Looking for a way to speed up this process for my own crew, I came across Reallusion's iClone Pro (www.reallusion.com). With iClone Pro, you don't have to be a character modeler to get a decent-looking likeness of your actor. In fact, you don't really need to know how to model at all, or rig, or perhaps even animate.

[Figure 15.74] You start in iClone Pro with a premade character.

To create a digital double, start in iClone Pro with a premade character, as shown in Figure 15.74. Import a photo of the actor or character you want to create (in this case, myself) into the face modification interface (Figure 15.75). You can then set the boundaries of the facial region, as shown in Figure 15.76, and use various tools to move, scale, and rotate the head's perspective (Figure 15.77). You can see the progress of your character in the 3D Preview window on the left as you continue to adjust facial features (Figure 15.78). You have the ability to zoom in to adjust individual facial features in great detail, as shown in Figure 15.79. After adjusting a comprehensive set of positon, scaling, rotation, and proportion settings, a likeness is surprisingly easy to achieve (Figure 15.80).

How to get this model into any other 3D application was my next concern. Again, to my surprise, Reallusion confidently stepped up to the plate with another amazing tool: 3DXchange (Figure 15.81). 3DXchange allows you to take models and animations and convert them to formats usable by almost

[**Figure 15.75**] Import an image of the character or actor you want to create.

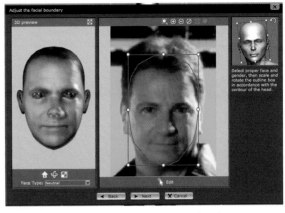

[**Figure 15.76**] Set the boundaries of the facial region.

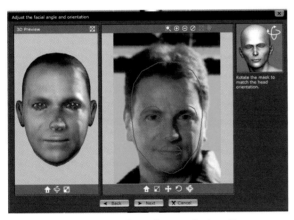

[**Figure 15.77**] Move, scale, and rotate the head's perspective.

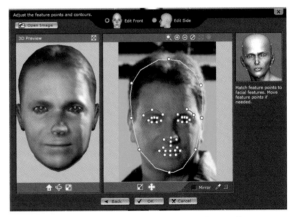

[**Figure 15.78**] You can see the progress of your character in the 3D Preview window.

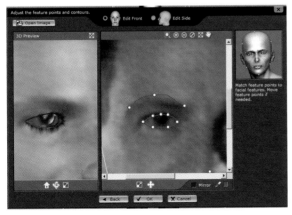

[**Figure 15.79**] Zoom in to adjust individual facial features with high precision.

[**Figure 15.80**] After adjusting positon, scaling, rotation, and proportion settings, you can easily create a likeness.

[Figure 15.81]
The 3DXchange interface

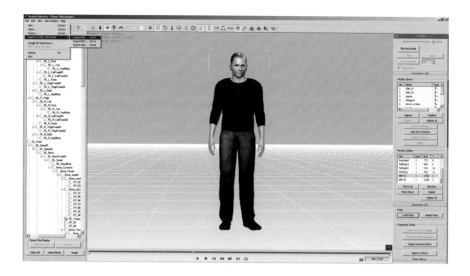

any 3D application or game engine. In fact, for a course on game development I found myself turning to 3DXchange as my main tool for "one-button-click model conversions" to use in game engines. Prior to finding 3DXchange, getting animated characters into some game engines was a giant hassle (and that's putting it kindly).

Speaking of rigging and animation, Reallusion knocks it out of the park again with its amazing Mocap (short for motion capture) plugin for iClone. Unlike many huge, expensive, complicated even convoluted motion capture systems, iClone's Mocap plugin allows you to do your motion capture yourself, in your own home or office, using nothing more than a Microsoft Kinect, which you can probably find used at a local gaming store for under $50. Rather than being covered with optical tracking markers with a huge array of cameras, or being wired up with a set of wireless motion sensors, you simply stand in front of the Kinect and perform your motions (as shown in Figure 15.82). This motion is automatically applied to your (already fully rigged) character for instant playback (Figure 15.83), editing, or, if you want, layered animation refinement.

Although this Mocap solution has a few limitations, such as distance, lighting conditions, and exacting movements, I've found it excellent for many common applications. Once your animation is refined, simply go back to 3DXchange to effortlessly export both character and animation to your 3D application or game engine of choice.

[Figure 15.82]
A complete Mocap session right in my office (note the character is following along with my actions on-screen).

[Figure 15.83]
Recorded Mocap animation automatically applied to character with no rigging or retargeting of the character's skeleton necessary.

123D Catch

But what about, sets, locations, and props? Surely there has to be an easier way than modeling everything to get it into a 3D environment for your VFX. Well, out on the horizon… there it is! And one of the first to implement it is Autodesk (www.autodesk.com) with 123D Catch (www.123dapp.com/catch).

123D Catch is one of the first in the industry to use cloud computing and computer vision technology to allow advanced 3D photogrammetry right from your smartphone. When you capture multiple images of a person, place,

[Figure 15.84] Fly around of 3D model captured with 123D Catch initial view

[Figure 15.85] Right side view

[Figure 15.86] Overhead view

[Figure 15.87] Closer view

or thing into the free 123D Catch app, a 3D mesh is created using advanced photogrammetry algorithms and cloud computing. Taking the photos and uploading takes only minutes. Depending on your technique and the subject matter, the resulting 3D models are surprisingly good and can be edited, exported to a 3D application, or even 3D printed using their simple interface. The extremely complex 3D model shown in Figures 15.84 through 15.87 was created in minutes (taking the photos and uploading) using 123d Catch and only took about a half hour to calculate to download-ready status. Although this technology is still in its early stages, and inconsistencies like holes in the meshes still have to be edited and fixed manually, the outlook for this type of portable photogrammetry is very promising.

X-cam and Paracosm

A little farther out onto the technological horizon are cutting edge experimental projects. One of them—my own, done in cooperation with the amazing technology innovation company Paracosm—is still in developmental

[Figure 15.88] X-cam rig mounted on my RED Epic handheld build

[Figure 15.89] Calibrating the X-cam using a grid chart

[Figure 15.90] X-cam rig with depth camera and Windows tablet to record data

[Figure 15.91] Filming handheld test with the X-cam prototype

stages, and as of yet has no official name. I call it the *X-cam* (see Figures 15.88 and 15.89). The X-cam is a Frankenstein of sorts, piecing together multiple technologies to create an amazing, single, unified technological production solution. It combines features used in depth sensor cameras with Paracosm's dense mapping algorithms and some VFX wizardry to create a solution that films at feature motion-picture quality, in real time. It also acquires a 3D camera track, depth map, and high-resolution, full-color point cloud, and can create a 3D model of everything the camera sees!

Figures 15.90 and 15.91 show the first prototype calibration and tests using this system. Figures 15.92 through 15.94 show the resulting high-resolution, full-color, dense-mapped point cloud that was created by the system and captured in real time. Every little object (and even people) are captured in full high-res 3D models, completely automatically!

[Figure 15.92]
Dense mapped point cloud created from the test

[Figure 15.93]
The unbelievable amount of detail/data captured in one pass with this prototype

[Figure 15.94]
Zooming out from the color point cloud reveals just how dense the point cloud is (it almost looks like a solid mesh).

This technology is still in its infancy, but Paracosm will soon be releasing a version of its "secret sauce" in an app form for consumer-level depth cameras such as the Microsoft Kinect (www.microsoft.com/en-us/kinectforwindows/), Google Project Tango, (www.google.com/atap/projecttango/#project), and Occipital Structure Sensor (http://structure.io). Keep an eye out!

This was just a small sampling of some of the amazing technology that is out there now and on the horizon. As a VFX artist, it is vital that you continue to stay in touch with developments like these so that you always learn and grow.

A Final Note to You

If I can leave you with a few last words to remember, it would be these: Keep looking for new innovations. Keep honing your skills, pushing your boundaries, moving out of your comfort zone, and learning new concepts and techniques. Stay healthy. Eat right, try to sleep right (I know, easier said than done), and exercise. Make yourself get up and move every once in a while. Balance your work with a life. And above all, follow your dreams, love what you do, and keep the passion for what you love blazing every moment of every day of your life!

Please feel free to write me with your questions or comments, or just let me know how you liked the book and how you're doing with your VFX work. Email me at jongressvfx@gmail.com and visit my website at http://jongress.com.

I wish you the best of luck always!

Best regards,
Jon

[APPENDIX]

The VFX Compositor's Checklist and Other Resources

Working in the movie and VFX industry the majority of my life, I have witnessed many trends, dug hard for golden nuggets of secret information, had insightful "a-ha!" moments, and even stumbled across the occasional jewel of wisdom or two. In-depth discussions over the years with legends such as Ron Thornton, Glenn Campbell, and William Vaughan uncovered many universal truths and truisms. So years ago, I began making a habit of writing down and collecting all these nuggets of wisdom into one document that I could share with colleagues and students. To my surprise, many of my friends had done the same. Ron, Glenn, William, and others shared their insights and lists freely with me, and vice versa. This chapter is the culmination and consolidation of decades of knowledge and wisdom—the things you need to do to be an excellent VFX artist and successful in your career—and even in life. Distilled down to its purest form, this chapter is the most potent "nitroglycerine" of VFX knowledge! Read with care.

The VFX Compositor's Checklist

Black, white, and gamma densities: Check all elements to be sure these densities match in your foreground and background elements. No element should be brighter that the brightest white or darker than the darkest black of your background plate.

Alpha channel: After pulling a key, immediately check your alpha channel to be sure your matte foreground and background are clean.

Garbage matte, edge matte, core matte: Don't try to key an entire image at once, like rotoscoping; address parts of the matte individually by first eliminating garbage, next preserving edge detail, and then core matting any holes in the alpha.

Matte edges: Always work to preserve the detail in the matte's edges.

Color temperature: All elements must live in the same color space. The best way to ensure this is to try and shoot your background plates first. This allows you to set the lighting tone for your scene.

Color match: Always check and level individual color channels to ensure a color match.

Plates talk to one another: Always be sure plates/elements talk to one another, meaning elements of the foreground plate reflect attributes of the background and vice-versa. These attributes can include shadows, reflections, interactive lighting, and so on.

Lighting match: Foreground and background are both lit from the same direction, with the same intensity, same color, and same quality.

Perspective: Foreground and background should have the same vanishing point so that during any scaling, the foreground and background scale in the same perspective. To help, shoot foreground and background elements with the same camera lens.

Interactive lighting: Show interactive (or secondary) lighting to help make composite look more realistic.

Shadows and reflections: Don't forget to add proper shadows to your scene. They help to make your elements "live" in the shot.

Roto strategy 1: When rotoscoping, always use multiple rotosplines to break shapes into their respective parts. *Do not* try to roto complex objects using just one complex spline.

Roto strategy II: When animating rotosplines, always try to translate/rotate/scale the entire shape first if you can; if not, work on the largest groups of points possible and only work on individual points if absolutely necessary.

Blur: Film, video, and high definition (HD) are not sharp, so be sure to add slight soft blurs to your composites to match the levels of softness that appear in the actual live action plate.

Motion blur: Film, video, and HD each have motion blur characteristics; be sure to match the type and level of motion blur that appear in the actual live action plate.

Grain: Film has grain, and video has noise. Be sure to add these to your final comp.

Key Phrases to Live By as a VFX Artist

Cheat! This is one occupation where cheating (simplifying or shortcutting to save valuable production time, cost, and energy) is a *good* thing. If there's a way to get a shot completed better, cheaper, and faster, *do it!*

If it looks right, it's right. See above. It doesn't really matter *how* you get the shot done, only that you get it done and that it looks great. If it looks right, it's right.

If you can't bare it, flare it. Lens flares are your friends; they can help blend a scene.

If you can't solve it, dissolve it. Adjust opacity or exposure of an element to help blend scene objects.

If you can't abide it, hide it. If you can't fix an element in a shot, hide it by putting something in front of it.

Crop it, flop it, or drop it. If none of these techniques helps make your element work in your scene, then drop it from your scene altogether.

VFX Artist Quick Reference Lists

These quick reference lists are your "one-stop cheat sheet" of all of the most important VFX concepts, techniques, strategies, reminders, and data reference information. All in one place.

VFX Lighting Cues

1. Location/direction
2. Quantity—intensity
3. Color
4. Quality—hardness/softness
5. Movement
6. Distribution (throw)

Finished Lighting

1. Black (shadow), white (highlight), gray (gamma) density match
2. Brightness and contrast match
3. Color match
4. Light direction match
5. Light quantity/intensity
6. Light quality match
7. Interactive lighting
8. Shadow match
9. Atmospheric haze

VFX Camera Cues

1. Format
2. Aspect ratio
3. Height
4. Angle
5. Focus
6. Movement
7. Motion blur
8. Film stock/video source (grain/noise)

Finished Camera Lens Matching

1. Focus
2. Depth of field
3. Lens flare
4. Light fog glare
5. Lens distortion

Comparison of Theatrical Screen Sizes

Figure A.1 shows a comparison of screen sizes.

Common Screen Aspect Ratios

Figure A.2 shows a comparison of screen aspect rations.

Standard PC (4:3)
Standard PC—Vertical (3:4)
Photo (36:24)
Square (1:1)
16mm (18:13)
IMAX (10:7)
Television HDTV (16:9)

70mm (46:21)
Panavision (47:20)
Cinemascope (8:3)
65mm (11:4)
UltraPanavision 70mm (69:25)
U.S. Letter (279:216)
A4 (297:210)

3D Object Inspection

1. What is the object?
2. What are the base colors?
3. How was the object made?
4. What is the object made of?
5. Where was the object made?
6. When was the object made?
7. Who made the object?
8. What is the object's history?
9. How was the object used?
10. What kind of wear would this use cause to this object?
11. How has the weather affected it?
12. What does it feel like?

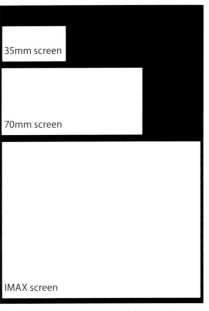

[Figure A.1] Comparison of theatrical screen sizes

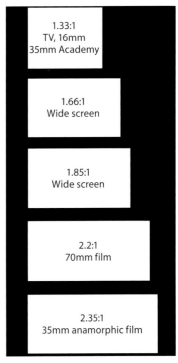

[Figure A.2] A few of the most common screen aspect ratios

13. How does light affect the object?
14. How has the environment affected the object?
15. What kind of damage and dirt buildup should the object show and where?

Photography for 3D Textures

1. Even lighting, no harsh directional shadows (overcast days)
2. Orthographic (step far back and zoom in to reduce parallax distortion)
3. Resolution (highest possible)

On-Set VFX Camera Data and Scene Reference

1. Camera make and model
2. Film back, CCD, or CMOS sensor size
3. Camera mount
4. Film stock or video acquisition format
5. Lens information (make, model, focal length, zoom, and so on)
6. Aperture/F-stop
7. Shutter speed
8. Depth of field
9. Camera height
10. Camera distance to subject/focal distance
11. Camera angle or tilt
12. Camera settings (iris, filters, zoom, and so on)
13. After shoot (shoot reference and registration photos using a reference object of known dimensions, camera lens distortion correction grid, lighting reference/probes, and take set and prop measurements)

Color Terminology

Hue: Categorical name of a color.

Value: Lightness or darkness of a color (Low = closer to black; High = closer to white).

Intensity: Power, brightness, purity, and strength of a color (decreases when gray, black, or white are added).

Saturation: Intensity of color.

Tint: Light value of a hue, created by adding white.

Shade: Dark value of a color, created by adding black.

Tone: Grayed value of a hue.

Color temperature: The color of light based on the Kelvin light temperature scale. This is slightly counterintuitive because the Kelvin temperature is inversely related to what we consider the aesthetic color. We consider cooler Kelvin color temperatures (in the 3200 degree range) warm aesthetic colors: yellow, orange, red. We consider higher Kelvin color temperatures (in the 5600–10,000 degree range) cooler aesthetic colors: blues and violets.

Chroma: Strength of a color. Weak chroma colors tend to be more gray. Strong chroma colors are more pure. (Other names for chroma include saturation, purity, brilliance, and intensity.)

Key: Dominant value or related values in a composition (high key composition = lighter values are dominant; low key composition = darker values are dominant).

Luminosity: Light given off by an object.

Primaries: Three colors that cannot be derived from other colors but from which other colors can be created. In light, these colors are red, green, and blue. In pigment colors, these are red, yellow, and blue.

Secondaries: Three colors that are created by mixing equal portions of two primaries (red + blue = purple; red + yellow = orange; blue + yellow = green).

Intermediates: Colors created by combining a primary color with its neighboring secondary color (orange + red = yellow orange; green + yellow = spring green; red + purple = violet).

Complementaries: Colors directly opposite each other on the color wheel, which neutralize each other when mixed (yellow across from purple; blue across from orange).

Neutral: Two complements mixed together form a neutral color (when white is added to a neutral, it becomes almost gray).

Monochromatic: Color schemes using variations of just one color.

Matte Painting Tips

- Closer objects should be darker; frame/border should be darker.
- Use variation in your colors; don't be monochromatic.
- Block in and rough out quickly and don't get caught up in details until the end.
- Your light source should be, or highlight, your point of interest.
- Flip your canvas often to check composition and perspective.

- Work from back (farthest Z-depth) to front (nearest Z-depth). Background > Midground > Foreground
- Use reference!

VFX Shot Framing

A good thing to remember when creating your VFX is to keep your framing varied and interesting.

Try using the framings in Figure A.3 and allow the action to happen in the highlighted areas; don't focus too much on the center of the frame.

[Figure A.3]
Shot framing examples

Important Movies in the History of VFX (in Chronological Order)

1. *Le Voyage dans la Lune (A Trip to the Moon)* (1902, Fr.)
2. *The Great Train Robbery* (1903)
3. *Deux cent milles sous les mers ou le cauchemar du pêcheur (Under the Seas)* (1907, Fr.)
4. *The Lost World* (1925)
5. *Metropolis* (1927, Ger.)
6. *King Kong* (1933)
7. *The Shape of Things to Come* (1933)
8. *The Wizard of Oz* (1939)
9. *The Thief of Bagdad* (1940, UK)
10. *Citizen Kane* (1941)
11. *When Worlds Collide* (1951)
12. *The War of the Worlds* (1953)
13. *20,000 Leagues Under the Sea* (1954)
14. *Forbidden Planet* (1956)
15. *The Ten Commandments* (1956)
16. *Darby O'Gill and the Little People* (1959)
17. *The Time Machine* (1960)
18. *Mary Poppins* (1964)
19. *Fantastic Voyage* (1966)
20. *2001: A Space Odyssey* (1968)
21. *Close Encounters of the Third Kind* (1977)
22. *Star Wars Series* (1977–2015)
23. *Star Trek: The Motion Picture* (1979)
24. *Alien* (1979)
25. *An American Werewolf in London* (1981)
26. *Raiders of the Lost Ark* (1981)
27. *The Thing* (1982)

28. *Poltergeist* (1982)
29. *Blade Runner* (1982)
30. *Star Trek II: The Wrath of Khan* (1982)
31. *Tron* (1982)
32. *Brainstorm* (1983)
33. *Koyaaniqatsi* (1983, Fr.)
34. *The Terminator* (1984)
35. *The Last Starfighter* (1984)
36. *Young Sherlock Holmes* (1985)
37. *Return to Oz* (1985)
38. *Back to the Future* (1985)
39. *Aliens* (1986)
40. *Legend* (1986)
41. *Who Framed Roger Rabbit* (1988)
42. *The Abyss* (1989)
43. *Back to the Future Part II* (1989)
44. *Indiana Jones and the Last Crusade* (1989)
45. *Total Recall* (1990)
46. *Jacob's Ladder* (1990)
47. *Terminator 2: Judgment Day* (1991)
48. *Jurassic Park* (1993)
49. *The Crow* (1994)
50. *Forrest Gump* (1994)
51. *Contact* (1997)
52. *The Fifth Element* (1997)
53. *Starship Troopers* (1997)
54. *Titanic* (1997)
55. *What Dreams May Come* (1998)
56. *Dark City* (1998)
57. *Fight Club* (1999)
58. *The Matrix* (1999)
59. *Gladiator* (2000)
60. *O Brother, Where Art Thou?* (2000)
61. *The Lord of the Rings* Series (2001–2003)
62. *Harry Potter* Series (2001–11)
63. *Spider-Man* Series (2002–14)
64. *Pirates of the Caribbean* Trilogy (2003–16)
65. *King Kong* (2005)
66. *Children of Men* (2006)
67. *300* (2007)
68. *Transformers* Series (2007–14)
69. *The Golden Compass* (2007)
70. *The Curious Case of Benjamin Button* (2008)
71. *The Dark Knight* (2008)
72. *Avatar* (2009)
73. *Inception* (2010)
74. *Hugo* (2011)
75. *Life of Pi* (2012)
76. *Gravity* (2013)

"Laws" Pertinent to the VFX Artist

Sergei Eisenstein's Law: When two (or more) elements are adjacent and in conflict, their collision sparks a new meaning of higher order (two separate scenes cut adjacent to one another in time may infer to the viewer a third, new meaning).

Moore's Law: Computing power doubles every 18 months.

Brook's Law: The complexity and communication costs of a project rise with the square of the number of developers, whereas the work done rises only linearly, at best.

Linus's Law: Given enough eyeballs, all bugs are shallow.

Murphy's (Sod's) Laws:
1. Nothing is as easy as it looks.
2. Everything takes longer than you think.
3. Anything that can go wrong will go wrong, usually in the worst way.
4. If there is a possibility of several things going wrong, the one that will cause the most damage will be the one to go wrong. Corollary: If there is a worst time for something to go wrong, it will happen then.
5. If anything simply cannot go wrong, it will anyway.
6. If you perceive that there are four possible ways in which a procedure can go wrong and circumvent these, then a fifth way, unprepared for, will promptly develop.
7. Left to themselves, things tend to go from bad to worse.
8. If everything seems to be going well, you have obviously overlooked something.
9. Nature always sides with the hidden flaw.
10. Mother Nature is a bitch.
11. It is impossible to make anything foolproof because fools are so ingenious.
12. Whenever you set out to do something, something else must be done first.
13. Every solution breeds new problems.

Grabel's Law: Two is not equal to three—not even for very large values of two.

Best's Law: If data resides in two places, it will be inconsistent.

Gutterson's Laws: Any programming project that begins well ends badly. Any programming project that begins badly ends worse.

Farvour's Law: There is always one more bug.

Pournelle's Law: Cables do matter. When something doesn't work, always check the cables and their connectors first.

Lansam's Law: Everything depends. Nothing is always. Everything is sometimes.

Glasgow's 3rd Law: Quality is not free, but it is cheaper than the alternatives.

Glasgow's 4th Law: If you can't describe it in writing, you can't build it. If you haven't described it in writing, don't try to build it. If it's so small it doesn't need documentation, then it doesn't do anything worthwhile.

VFX Truism

You will likely be able to get 95% of a shot done very quickly, but it is always the last 5% that takes the majority of the time and effort and that becomes the crucial difference which determines whether your shot ends up looking absolutely real.

Starting Your VFX Career

Top Visual Effects Job Titles

Producer	Graphic Artist	Renderer
Director	FX Artist	Matchmover
Creative Director	Texture Artist	Rotoscoper
CG Supervisor	Effects Animator	Software Engineer
Post-Production Supervisor	Character Animator	Computer Programmer
Video Editor	Modeler	Engineer
Technical Director	Digital Matte Artist	Audio Engineer
Videographer	Digital Effects Artist	
	Compositor	

14 Market Categories for VFX Jobs

1. Production companies
2. Broadcast/cable studios
3. Corporate film and video companies
4. Visual effects/animation studios
5. Postproduction facilities
6. Video recording/editing studios
7. Game companies
8. Simulation companies (includes military)
9. Web/interactive media
10. Advertising agencies/design firms
11. Architectural firms
12. Independent filmmakers
13. Religious facilities
14. Audio recording/mixing studios

Your Demo Reel

- A reel submission should usually have five components:
    1. The reel
    2. The cover letter
    3. The resume
    4. The reel table of contents
    5. The reel submission form (downloadable PDF document located on our website)
- Your reel should be no more than three to four minutes.
- Nobody cares about music/soundtrack, so keep it classy and subtle.

- The preferred medium is now an updated online demo reel via (working) web link.
- Update your reel periodically (quarterly or annually).
- Put your best work first and finish strong.
- Include only your best work; don't try to fill space; better shorter and excellent than long and mediocre.
- Use title cards, breakdowns, and a table of contents.
- Include a title card at the beginning and end with your name, address, phone, and email.
- Show work that proves that you know what you did.
- Take the time to polish.
- Show it to other people. Have other people critique it.
- If you really don't have stuff to put on a reel, don't send one.

19 Tips for Show Reel Success

1. Neat, clean, professional, simple packaging.
2. Be clear about what position you're applying for.
3. Focus on what you want to do, and spend your time working on that.
4. Play the reel first (in front of other people; you'd be amazed how you will immediately see it differently this way, especially its flaws).
5. You do not have to tell a story. Although a story can be good, there is a very good chance that you won't have the time to finish it.
6. Create a "Trailer Style" demo reel. Instead of telling a story, include all the good parts of several different animations.
7. Include only your best work.
8. Put your very best material first.
9. Do not use canned content that comes with the program.
10. During an interview, do *not* point out flaws (but if asked about them, be prepared to explain how you would fix them).
11. Make it consistent.
12. Keep it short.
13. By all means, try anything innovative.
14. Do not start your reel with space footage or space ships unless you're ILM.
15. Sound is nice but should not carry the reel.
16. Choose non-offensive music if you include music at all.
17. Be honest.
18. No glowing orbs.
19. In fact, no flying spaceships (unless that's the specific job you are applying for).

Landing a Job in VFX in 15 Steps

1. Know your skills.
2. Be the absolute best you can be.
3. Network and promote yourself.
4. Have a clear job objective.
5. Target specific companies.
6. Research those companies and the kinds of work they do.
7. Target your reel to those companies.
8. Improve your interviewing skills.
9. Learn to spell.
10. Keep your show reel short and simple.
11. Show original work.
12. Don't bluff or puff on your resume.
13. Don't over-decorate your demo reel, resume, or website.
14. Interview, submit reels, and follow up on all contacts.
15. Get your foot in the door.

Media Kit (for Promoting Yourself)

1. Photographs (5×7 or 8×10 black and white portrait photo and 5×7 or 8×10 black and white informal photo)
2. Biography (short bio and narrative biography)
3. Information sheet (contact info and reference information)
4. Materials (business cards, brochures, and so on)
5. Statements/recommendations/reviews
6. Family information (optional)

Avoid Wasting Your Time Doing Unnecessary Proposals

1. Beware of browsers who are only looking for multiple bids.
2. Don't be used as leverage in a pricing battle with the prospect's present supplier.
3. Don't fall for the "horse and carrot" trick, or doing the job for less now hoping to get the next one at a higher rate (in other words, the horse never gets the carrot).
4. Don't undervalue yourself (figure out your hourly rate and then double that number for starters—projects will always take longer than you expect).
5. Don't be a fountain of free education.
6. Don't mistake mild interest as a proposal request.

Planning Phone Negotiations

For many contractors, myself included, the phone is always an invaluable tool for finding new clients, negotiating deals, and communicating throughout the design and development process. The best way to handle any type of phone conversation is to be prepared. Here are a few tips for your next important phone call:

1. Prepare a checklist of points to cover during the call.
2. Dry run the phone call in your mind and with friends.
3. Attempt to anticipate the tactics and questions of the other party.
4. If there is something you don't have an answer to, tell the other party you will send them the information after your call, therefore giving yourself time to research the topic further.
5. Try to have all the relevant facts and figures on hand when you make the phone call.
6. Concentrate and avoid distractions. Give the phone call your undivided attention.
7. At the end, summarize what was agreed upon and define the responsibility for follow-up action.
8. Follow up the phone call with a gracious letter to remind the other party that you have spoken and are ready for the job.
9. Get all agreements, and changes to those agreements, *in writing*.

Effective Goal Setting

1. Define your goals clearly in writing (increases your chances of success by 80%).
2. Develop an action plan, set deadlines, and act.
3. Establish priorities.
4. Make a public commitment.
5. Be realistic.
6. Attaining an ambitious goal is like climbing a mountain—don't look down (to see how far you might fall) or up (to see how far you still have to go) only look to the next rock (the next step immediately in front of you)—before you know it, you'll be at the top.
7. Keep learning new skills and practice them.
8. Allow your goals to be flexible and adaptable.

15 Rules for Success

1. Get and stay out of your comfort zone.
2. Never give up.
3. When you are ready to quit, you are closer than you think.
4. Accept and quantify what the worst thing could be.
5. Focus on what you want to have happen.
6. Take things a step, and a day, at a time.
7. Always move forward.
8. Be decisive.
9. Anything that is not managed will deteriorate.
10. Pay attention to your work and what you are doing; be aware of, but don't fixate on, others' work.
11. Never let anybody push you around.
12. Never expect life to be fair.
13. Solve your own problems.
14. Do not take yourself too seriously.
15. Do what you love and be passionate about it.

Index

Image Credits

The following images are in the public domain: Figures 1.35 and 36, Figure 1.39 1–5, Figure 1.43 1–6, Figure 1.46 1–5, Figure 1.47 1–2, Figure 1.52, Figure 1.62 1–4, Figures 11.1 and 11.2, Figures 11.4–11.19, Figures 11.21 and 22, Figure 14.10, Figures 15.34 and 15.35, and Figure 15.48 (provided by U.S. Geological Survey, Department of the Interior/USGS).

The following images are used by permission of Footage Firm, Inc.: Figure 5.23, Figures 9.1–9.20, Figures 9.34 and 9.35, Figures 9.43–53, Figure 9.57, Figures 9.61 and 9.62, Figures 9.70–9.74, Figure 9.83, Figure 9.96, Figures 9.101–9.116, Figures 10.65–68, Figures 10.70–79, and Figure 11.3-4.